The Financial Times Guide to Understanding Finance

The Financial Times Guide to Understanding Finance

A no-nonsense companion to financial tools and techniques

Second edition

Javier Estrada

Financial Times
Prentice Hall
is an imprint of

Harlow, England • London • New York • Boston • San Francisco • Toronto • Sydney • Singapore • Hong Kong
Tokyo • Seoul • Taipei • New Delhi • Cape Town • Madrid • Mexico City • Amsterdam • Munich • Paris • Milan

PEARSON EDUCATION LIMITED

Edinburgh Gate
Harlow CM20 2JE
Tel: +44 (0)1279 623623
Fax: +44 (0)1279 431059
Website: www.pearsoned.co.uk

First published in Great Britain in 2005 as *Finance in a Nutshell: A no-nonsense companion to the tools and techniques of finance*
Second edition published 2011

© Pearson Education Limited 2005, 2011

The right of Javier Estrada to be identified as author of this work has been asserted by him in accordance with the Copyright, Designs and Patents Act 1988.

Pearson Education is not responsible for the content of third party internet sites.

ISBN: 978-0-273-73802-2

British Library Cataloguing in Publication Data
A catalogue record for this book is available from the British Library

Library of Congress Cataloging-in-Publication Data
Estrada, Javier, 1964-
  The Financial Times guide to understanding finance : a no-nonsense companion to financial tools and techniques / Javier Estrada. -- 2nd ed.
      p. cm.
  Previously published under title: Finance in a nutshell.
  Includes bibliographical references and index.
  ISBN 978-0-273-73802-2 (pbk. : alk. paper) 1. Business enterprises--Finance--Handbooks, manuals, etc. 2. Corporations--Finance--Handbooks, manuals, etc. I. Title. II. Title: Guide to understanding finance.
  HG4027.3.E88 2011
  658.15--dc22
                                        2011005720

10 9 8 7 6 5 4 3 2 1
15 14 13 12 11

Typeset in 9.5/14pt ITC Stone Serif by 30
Printed and bound in Great Britain by Ashford Colour Press, Gosport, Hampshire.

Contents

part 3 # Other important topics

part 4 # Statistical background

Excel examples

The Excel files to accompany this book can be downloaded from:

www.pearsoned.co.uk/estrada

Publisher's acknowledgments

We are grateful to the following for permission to reproduce copyright material:

Tables 7.1 and 12.1 adapted from DIMSON, ELROY; TRIUMPH OF THE OPTIMISTS, © 2002 Elroy Dimson, Paul Marsh, and Mike Staunton. Published by Princeton University Press. Reprinted by permission of Princeton University Press; Table 19.1 from 'Standard & Poor's Ratings Definitions', © August 2010, published by Standard & Poor's. Reproduced with permission of Standard & Poor's Financial Services LLC; Table 19.2 adapted from 'Defaults and Returns in the High-Yield Bond Market: The Year 2007 in Review and Outlook', Working Paper (Altman, E. and Karlin, B. 2008). Reproduced with permission of E. Altman.

In some instances we have been unable to trace the owners of copyright material, and we would appreciate any information that would enable us to do so.

Preface to the second edition

I had mixed feelings when I received the request to write a second edition of *Finance in a Nutshell*. On the one hand it made me happy. I thought that publishers ask authors to write a new edition of a book only when they make a positive evaluation of the previous edition and are bullish about the prospects of a follow-up. I also thought it was a good chance to clarify explanations, update the data, correct typos, and ultimately take a fresh look at all the material discussed in the first edition and improve it.

But on the other hand I was not so happy. Writing a book is fun, or at least it was to me; but rewriting it is not, or at least not nearly as much. I also had many more time constraints than I had when I wrote the first edition. So I did think long and hard about it, at times leaning one way and at other times leaning the other way.

It was a hard decision but in the end I accepted, as evidenced by the book you're holding in your hands. And I'm glad I did, because this edition retains all the positive characteristics of the first but also improves upon it in more than one way. If you liked *Finance in a Nutshell*, I have no doubt you'll like *The FT Guide to Understanding Finance* even more.

Why do I say this? Two reasons. First, I did not try to fix what was not broken. I received a lot of positive feedback about both the coverage and the style of the first edition. Readers found that the topics discussed properly reflected those they considered most relevant, and liked the conversational style in which those topics were discussed. Retaining both the topic selection and the style, then, was a no-brainer. Second, I tried to repair what was damaged. Very often when working on this second edition, I found things that I could have explained better. So, whatever readers thought was well done in the first edition, I'm sure it's better done in this one.

Which brings me to the following recommendation to whoever is considering buying this book. If you liked *Finance in a Nutshell*, you'll find *The FT Guide to Understanding Finance* to be an improved and updated version of the original. If you never read *Finance in a Nutshell* but heard a good thing or two about it, see for yourself why the original was well received. And if you never even heard about *Finance in a Nutshell*, well, give a chance to this book which at least is not nearly as expensive or heavy as the typical 900-page textbook!

This second edition is divided into the same 4 parts and 30 chapters as the first edition was. The first part consists of 12 chapters and tackles issues related to risk and return. It covers a wide range of topics such as different ways of calculating returns and mean returns; ways of assessing risk; diversification; the CAPM, the three factor-model, required returns, and the cost of capital; risk-adjusted returns; and portfolio optimization.

The second part consists of eight chapters and focuses on the valuation of stocks and bonds. It covers different models for stock valuation including four versions of the discounted cash flow model, reverse valuation, and multiples. It also discusses bonds, their valuation, their return, and the factors that affect their risk.

The third part consists of six chapters that, unlike those in the other three parts of the book, are not closely related to each other. These are topics that, in my view, no book of essential tools could afford not to cover, which include project evaluation through NPV, IRR, and real options; corporate value creation; derivatives such as options, futures, and forwards; and currencies.

Finally, the last part provides some statistical background. It covers some widely-used statistical terms, such as the mean, median, variance, standard deviation, covariance, and correlation; two widely-used distributions, the normal and the lognormal; and regression analysis.

Readers of *Finance in a Nutshell* will find that *The FT Guide to Understanding Finance* retains the same 30 topics (chapters) of the first edition. As already mentioned, I received positive feedback on the topic selection, which gave me no reason to fix what was not broken. But beyond that, my fresh look at the whole book did not bring to mind any topic that I considered essential and was missing.

Having said that, I did receive some requests from *Finance in a Nutshell* readers to include this or that topic in subsequent editions of the book. Some of those topics included market efficiency, capital structure, and dividend policy, to name but a few. But, however important or interesting those topics are, this is *not* a corporate finance textbook. Such a book typically contains several topics not discussed here, but also omits several topics discussed in this book. In other words, they are very different books.

One of the reasons I strongly resist considering this book a textbook is because such books tend to have 900 pages, weigh 5 pounds, and have unbearably long chapters. *This book is a reaction to that!* I tried to make it short, light, and with chapters short enough that they can be read in one sitting, without falling asleep.

Yes, this book discusses many issues typically covered in a corporate finance textbook. But it also discusses many issues typically covered in an investments textbook. In fact, I think this book is much closer to the latter than to the former. But again, this is no textbook. Hold this book in your hand and curl your arm 10 times, or put it in your purse and walk around a few blocks; you probably can't do either with a textbook, but you can with this book!

Wide coverage, short chapters, conversational style, intuitive explanations, and real-world examples are the trademarks of this book. And that's why, as was the case with *Finance in a Nutshell*, I think *The FT Guide to Understanding Finance* will appeal to a wide range of current and future finance practitio-ners, as well as to all those who always wanted to know a bit more about finance but found it intimidating to begin with.

As was also the case with the first edition, this second edition shows how to implement in Microsoft Excel all the tools discussed. Which brings me to a couple of points you should keep in mind. First, I have used and described everything for the US version Excel 2007. Most of the commands discussed in this book are virtually identical across different versions of Excel, but if yours is not the 2007 version and you have trouble implementing something, keep this point in mind.

Second, if you want to reproduce precisely all the calculations discussed in this book, it's important that you use the data in the accompanying Excel file (on the book's website, **www.pearsoned.co.uk/estrada**). I have performed all calculations in spreadsheets, which remember many more decimal places than would be wise to report in a book. If you try to reproduce the calcula-tions discussed in the following chapters, with the figures discussed in those chapters, you may find that your results are close but not exactly equal to those reported. If you use the Excel file that contains the data I used instead, you should have no problem with rounding errors. Note also that dates are presented in the US style: month, day, year.

I wrote every word and crunched every number in this book, but that doesn't mean I didn't receive any help. First and foremost, I would like to thank students and executives in countless programs without whose encouragement this book would never have existed. I would also like to thank readers of *Finance in a Nutshell* for their comments, suggestions, feedback, and ideas; had I felt that the first edition of this book was ignored, I wouldn't have had the enthusiasm to write this second edition.

Last, but certainly not least, I would like to deeply thank my research assistant, Gabriela Giannattasio. Her *extremely* detailed comments on each and every chapter were of invaluable help. And because I know her attention to detail is such that she'd find any mistake I could have made, I had the peace of mind I needed to write this book. Needless to say, I'm the only one to blame for any mistakes that may remain in the following chapters.

Regardless of how many more books I write, *Finance in a Nutshell* will always be the first one. But as much as I'll always hold dear that first little guy, I have to admit that *The FT Guide to Understanding Finance* you hold in your hands is better.

Barcelona, November 2010

Preface to the first edition

I always thought I'd write a book but never quite knew when or on what topic. I never felt the need of doing it and, to be honest, I never set it as a goal for myself. But eventually I got to a point when I decided to surrender to the evidence: Too many people were asking for the same thing, and the market, in my opinion, had not delivered. So I thought I'd deliver it myself.

A brief history of this book

It happened many times. During the course of an executive education program, I'd come in to give a few sessions on finance topics. After finishing those sessions, someone would come to me and say something like, 'Listen, this was very interesting and, though my job is only marginally related to finance, I'd like to know more about it. What would you advise me to read?' Or something like, 'Hey, I work in finance but my job is so specialized that I feel I need to refresh my knowledge of the basics. Can you recommend some book that covers a wide range of essential topics?'

Depending on the topic I had discussed in the program and what the participant had asked, I usually did one (or both) of the following: Recommend a few short books that, when put together, would cover a wide range of topics; or recommend a textbook, which as you are well aware usually contains between 600 and 900 pages and chapters no less than 20 pages long. Often, I would show the recommended references to the inquiring participant.

And that's when I started getting the two standard replies. If I recommended the few short books, the reply would be something like, 'Well, all these books look very interesting, but isn't there *one* book that tackles all these topics?' If I recommended the textbook, the reaction would be something like, 'Listen, I'm sure this book is very good, but I really have no time to read so many pages, or even half of them. Plus, you don't expect me to carry this book around with me, do you? They'd charge me for excess luggage at the airport!' (OK, I'm dramatizing a bit.) I can't really tell how many times I went through similar exchanges, but I do know that eventually there was a straw that broke the camel's back.

But wait, it wasn't then that I decided to write this book. In fact, it was then that I decided to do something that would take a lot less of my time: I decided to look for a book I could recommend to all these people. I made a mental list of the characteristics that were in high demand and started my search. And, to my surprise, such a book didn't exist. Or maybe I didn't find it. Either way, it was then, and only then, that I thought I had to write this book.

Distinctive features

The stylized story above happened many times, give or take a few details, in many executive programs. It also happened many times while teaching in MBA and executive MBA programs. And it happened often while talking with former students who needed to refresh or broaden their knowledge of finance. After failing in my search for a book to recommend, and starting to think that maybe I should write the book myself, I thought long and hard about the characteristics of the book the market had, in my opinion, failed to deliver. This was, more or less, my list:

- *The book needs to be comprehensive.* It doesn't have to address a few issues in depth; rather, it should cover a wide variety of topics, concepts, and tools that professionals forget, find hard to understand, and need or would like to know more about.

- *The book needs to be easy to read.* Professionals are put off by academic books written in academic style. There is a need for a book written in a way that sounds pretty much like having an instructor talking right in front of them.

- *The book needs to be relatively short.* Not an 800-page, 5-pound book, but one that could be easily taken around from the office to home, and from the hotel to the airport. Something that could be always at hand, like a desktop companion.

- *The book needs to have relatively short chapters.* Most professionals dislike starting a chapter and not being able to finish it after two or three sittings. There is a need for a book with short chapters that can be read in one sitting. Short chapters would also make it easy for readers to quickly grasp the essentials of a concept or tool.

■ *The book needs to contain some elementary theory and many real-world examples.* It's a lot easier to understand and remember concepts and tools when an elementary conceptual framework and its application are discussed together. And if the application is not hypothetical but about an actual situation the reader can quickly identify with, even better.

■ *The book needs to explain how to implement things in Microsoft® Excel.* Spreadsheets have become an inseparable tool for finance, and the book needs to show how to implement in Excel all the concepts and tools discussed.

■ *The book needs to have a few short problems at the end of each chapter.* Many books have them, to be sure, but this book would have just two or three that go to the heart of the issues discussed in the chapter.

■ *The book needs to be self-contained.* Other than some elementary math, no other previous knowledge should be required.

Well, that's a long list! But I promised myself that I wouldn't start writing a book before making sure I could deliver one that had *all* of the characteristics above. I trust the book you have in your hands does. So, if I had to define this book in one paragraph, it would be this:

> *Many professionals have long forgotten some key financial concepts or tools; others never learned them properly; some need to broaden the scope of their financial knowledge; others need a desktop companion for quick reference; and most of them have neither the time nor the motivation to dig into either several books or an 800-page textbook. This book solves all these problems in 30 short, easy-to-read, very practical chapters full of real-world examples and applications in Excel.*

Target audience and intended use

Let me tell you first what this book is *not*. First, it is not a textbook; I didn't write it as a required reference for a specific course. Second, it is not a specialized book; it's not for those who want to acquire a deep knowledge of one or two topics. And third, it is not a cookbook; I didn't write it for those who want to blindly follow a few steps to solve a problem without understanding what's going on. If you're looking for a book to satisfy any of these needs, you've picked the wrong one.

The distinctive features of this book outlined above should give you an idea of who this book is for. Again, it was born as an answer to the demand of professionals who wanted to broaden their knowledge of finance; refresh their memory of some topics; learn other topics from scratch; or simply have a light desktop companion covering a wide range of essential topics in finance. And all that subject to the constraints of limited time and lack of patience to read an academic textbook.

I firmly believe that executives, professionals, and practitioners in different areas unrelated to finance will find this book useful. Their need to understand financial concepts and tools at the user level was constantly in my mind as I wrote this book. I also firmly believe that finance professionals such as investment bankers, portfolio managers, brokers and security analysts will find this book valuable. Their need for a reference book to quickly get up to speed on many different issues was also in my mind. In this regard, participants of executive education programs, MBA and executive MBA students, and former students, all of them in both finance and non-finance jobs, provided invaluable feedback.

I also trust the individual investor will find this book valuable. It provides the tools to value assets, assess risk, diversify and optimize portfolios, evaluate performance, and invest for retirement, to name just a few issues interesting to investors and covered in the book. And it discusses these and many other issues from scratch, showing how to implement everything in Excel.

Finally, I think that academics in finance and economics will find this book useful. It could be used as a complementary or recommended reference in many general courses such as corporate finance or investments; or in more specific courses dealing with asset pricing, stocks, bonds, and portfolio analysis, among other topics. I also think academics themselves will find the book useful as a personal desktop companion, a reference book to consult on a wide range of finance topics.

Organization of the book

The book is divided into four parts. The first, entitled 'Risk and return,' covers a wide range of issues that deal with different definitions of returns, different ways of assessing risk, different ways to put risk and return together, and the optimization of portfolios.

The second part, entitled 'Valuation,' focuses on stocks and bonds. It covers different models of stock valuation, including several versions of the DCF model, reverse valuation, and relative valuation. It also covers issues related to fixed-income securities, including pricing, sources of risk, duration, and convexity.

The third part, entitled 'Other important topics,' puts together several issues that no book of finance essentials could ignore. These include project evaluation through NPV, IRR, and real options, as well as derivatives such as options, futures, and forwards.

Finally, the fourth part, entitled 'Statistical background,' contains a refresher of essential statistical topics for practitioners, including summary statistics, the calculation of probabilities with the normal and lognormal distributions, and regression analysis. The discussion includes the implementation of all these concepts and tools in Excel.

How to read this book

I wrote the book thinking of professionals who needed to jump in for a specific issue. As a result, I wrote the chapters as independent of each other as possible. This means that this is not a book that you need to start reading at Chapter 1 and finish at Chapter 30. Some readers will not need to read the statistical background and others will find it essential reading. Some readers will be interested in stocks and others in bonds. Others may want to focus on issues related to investing or corporate finance.

Every chapter concludes with an Excel section and a Challenge section. The Excel sections aim to show how to implement in Excel the concepts and tools discussed in the chapter. These sections range from discussing some elementary functions, such as logs and exponentials, to more complex implementations, such as multiple regression analysis and portfolio optimization programs. If you're not fully familiar with Excel, I think you will find these sections essential. And if you are familiar with Excel, these sections will probably take you a few steps further.

The Challenge sections aim to test the essential concepts and tools discussed in each chapter. The problems are few, short, and go straight to the key points. Most of them are based on data from well-known companies so that you can not only test what you've learned but also learn a bit about the companies too. Some people may find these sections useful and others will probably ignore them. It's your choice.

Finally, if you want to reproduce precisely all the calculations discussed in the book, it is important that you use the data in the accompanying Excel file (see **www.pearsoned.co.uk/estrada**). I have performed all calculations in Excel, which 'remembers' many more decimals than would be wise to report in a book. That's why you may find 'rounding errors,' particularly in calculations based on previous calculations. Similarly, if you go over the problems in the Challenge sections, you may want to use the data in the accompanying Excel file rather than that provided in the tables and exhibits.

Take a good look at the index and a quick look at the rest of the book. I trust you will find the scope comprehensive, the chapters short, the style engaging, the approach practical, and the discussions easy to follow. You will also find loads of information on many companies that are household names, which are used throughout to keep your feet firmly on the ground.

Acknowledgments

My deepest gratitude goes to the long list of participants in executive education programs, MBA students, executive MBA students, and former students who directly or indirectly encouraged me to write this book. Most of them did not actually ask me to write a book, but their search for a book that the market had not provided was the main reason for writing this one.

I'm also indebted to my research assistant, Alfred Prada, who read every chapter, checked every formula, double checked every table, and triple checked every calculation. He put up with all my demands, which were not few, and delivered every time he had to. Needless to say, he is in no way responsible for any errors that may remain in this book. Those are, of course, my sole responsibility.

Finally, I want to dedicate this book to my dad, who was alive when I started writing it but did not live to see me finish it. I know he would have been even prouder than I am for having written this, my first book. I'm sure he would have read it just because I wrote it, and I'm sure he would have told me that *even he* could understand what I was writing about. And of course, I also dedicate this book to my mom, who will most likely not read it, but will proudly and insistently show it to every single person that passes by within a mile of her house.

A final word

Time will tell whether I have delivered the book that so many people seem to have been looking for. I certainly hope so. And yet I'm also sure it can be improved. For this reason, if you have any comments or suggestions, feel absolutely free to send me an email at *jestrada@iese.edu*. I would be more than glad to know your opinion.

This concludes what for me has been a long journey. And as much as I wanted to finish, I now realize that I'll miss working on this book. It was, above all, a whole lot of fun. I certainly hope you enjoy reading it as much as I enjoyed writing it.

Barcelona, March 2005

Risk and return

1

Returns I: Basic concepts

- Simple returns
- Continuously compounded returns
- Multiperiod returns
- The big picture
- Excel section

W e'll start easy, with a few concepts, definitions, and notation that we'll use throughout the book. In this first chapter we'll discuss simple returns, continuously compounded returns, and multi-period returns, along with a few other things. We're just going to warm-up.

Simple returns

Table 1.1 shows the year-end stock price (p) of Coca-Cola between 2000 and 2009, and the annual dividend per share (D) paid by the company in each of those years. Suppose we had bought a share of Coca-Cola at the end of 2008 and sold it at the end of 2009; what would have been our one-year return?

table 1.1

Year	p ($)	D ($)	R (%)	r (%)	C ($)
2000	60.94	0.72			100.0
2001	47.15	0.72	−21.4	−24.1	78.6
2002	43.84	0.80	−5.3	−5.5	74.4
2003	50.75	0.88	17.8	16.4	87.6
2004	41.64	1.00	−16.0	−17.4	73.6
2005	40.31	1.12	−0.5	−0.5	73.2
2006	48.25	1.24	22.8	20.5	89.9
2007	61.37	1.36	30.0	26.2	116.9
2008	45.27	1.52	−23.8	−27.1	89.1
2009	57.00	1.64	29.5	25.9	115.4

That's easy. We bought at $45.27, sold at $57.00, and received a dividend of $1.64 along the way. Hence, our return would have been

$$\frac{(\$57.00 - \$45.27) + \$1.64}{\$45.27} = 29.5\%$$

More generally, a **simple return (R)** is defined as

$$R = \frac{(p_E - p_B) + D}{p_B} \qquad (1.1)$$

where p_B and p_E denote the stock price at the beginning and at the end of the period, and D the dividend per share received during the period. The column of Table 1.1 headed R shows the annual returns for Coca-Cola between 2001 and 2009 calculated this way.

Note that simple returns have two components. The first is the **capital gain or loss** and is given by the change in price during the period, relative to the price at the beginning of the period; that is, $(p_E - p_B)/p_B$. The second is the **dividend yield** and is given by the dividend per share received during the period, relative to the price at the beginning of the period; that is, D/p_B. The sum of these two components is the simple return. As you could easily calculate yourself, during 2009 Coca-Cola delivered a capital gain of 25.9% and a dividend yield of 3.6%; the sum of these two components adds up to the 29.5% return we already calculated.

Note, also, that this definition of return can be applied to any asset, not just to stocks. If, for example, we buy a bond and hold it for one period, instead of a dividend we'll receive an interest payment. But we can still calculate a simple return as the sum of the change in the price of the bond (between the beginning and the end of the period) and the interest payment received, both relative to the price at the beginning of the period. In short, a simple return for any asset over any given period can be calculated by simply adding the capital gain or loss from the change in price and the cash flow we put into our pocket, and expressing that sum relative to the price at the beginning of the period.

Note, finally, that simple returns can go by other names such as **arithmetic returns** or **holding-period returns**. All these are names for the same concept and we'll use them interchangeably throughout the book.

Continuously compounded returns

If someone asked me what is the distance between Miami and Chicago, my answer would depend on who's asking. If an American was asking, I'd say the distance was roughly 1,200 miles; if a European was asking, I'd say that the distance was roughly 1,900 kilometers. The distance is the same; I'm simply expressing it in different units, in each case so that the person asking can understand what I mean.

Same with returns. We can express our gain from holding Coca-Cola stock during the year 2009 as we just did and say that we obtained a 29.5% simple return. Alternatively, we could calculate the **continuously compounded return (r)**, which is defined as

$$r = \ln(1 + R) \tag{1.2}$$

where 'ln' denotes a natural logarithm. So, if we had bought a share of Coca-Cola at the end of 2008 and sold it at the end of 2009, our continuously compounded return would have been $r = \ln(1+0.295) = 25.9\%$. (Just in case your eyes fooled you, note that the simple return and the continuously compounded return look similar but are different; the former is 29.5% and the latter is 25.9%.) The column of Table 1.1 headed r shows the annual returns for Coca-Cola between 2001 and 2009 calculated this way.

Just as expression (1.2) shows how to calculate a continuously compounded return as a function of a simple return, we can also go the other way around and calculate a simple return as a function of a continuously compounded return; that is

$$R = e^r - 1 \tag{1.3}$$

where e = 2.71828. So, just as a moment ago we calculated Coca-Cola's 25.9% continuously compounded return during the year 2009 starting from its 29.5% simple return, we can alternatively start from the 25.9% continuously compounded return and calculate the simple return as $R = e^{0.259} - 1 = 29.5\%$.

Think of continuously compounded returns simply as another way to express our periodic gain or loss. We can express the distance between Miami and Chicago in miles or in kilometers; similarly, we can express our periodic gain or loss in an asset with simple returns or with continuously compounded returns. The distance between Miami and Chicago is, roughly, 1,200 miles or 1,900 kilometers; similarly, our gain by holding Coca-Cola during the year 2009 was a 29.5% simple return or a 25.9% continuously compounded return.

Now, you may think that simple returns are enough for most investors' purposes, and there's no denying that. Investors do care about the amount of money they start with and the amount of money they end up with, and that is straightforwardly measured by the simple return. Continuously compounded returns, however, are also important and widely used in finance, and as you can see there's nothing difficult about their calculation, so you might as well know about them. In any case, we'll return to them later in the book.

For the time being, let's highlight three more things. First, note that the smaller a simple return is, the smaller is the difference between the simple and the continuously compounded return. You may know that for any small x it is the case that $\ln(1+x) \approx x$; and you surely know by now that $r = \ln(1+R)$. Then, when R is small, it is the case that $r = \ln(1 + R) \approx R$; that is, $r \approx R$. In words, when simple returns are small it does not make much of a difference whether we calculate simple or continuously compounded returns. As you can see in Table 1.1, in some years these two types of returns are very close to each other; in some other years, however, the difference between them is substantial.

Second, continuously compounded returns also go by the name of **logarithmic returns** or **log returns**; all three are different names for the same concept and we will use them interchangeably throughout the book. And third, note that whenever in the rest of the book we refer to 'returns' without specifying whether they are simple or continuously compounded, we'll be referring to *simple* returns.

Multiperiod returns

One more thing and we'll finish this warm-up. Often we want to calculate the return of an investment not just over one period but over several periods. In that case it is important to keep in mind that simple returns are multiplicative, but continuously compounded returns are additive. Let's see what this means.

Suppose we bought a share of Coca-Cola at the end of 2000, held it to the end of 2009, and reinvested all the dividends received; what would have been our return over this whole nine-year period? There are at least two ways of answering this question, so let's first focus on simple returns. A *T*-year simple return, *R(T)*, is calculated as

$$R(T) = (1 + R_1)\cdot(1 + R_2)\cdot \ ... \ \cdot(1 + R_T) - 1 \tag{1.4}$$

which shows why we mentioned before that simple returns are multiplicative. So, back to Coca-Cola, the nine-year simple return from holding this stock between 2001 and 2009 was

$$R(9) = (1-0.214)\cdot(1-0.053)\cdot \ ... \ \cdot(1+0.295) - 1 = 15.4\%$$

Alternatively, we can define the *T*-year continuously compounded return, *r(T)*, as

$$r(T) = r_1 + r_2 + ... + r_T \tag{1.5}$$

which shows why we mentioned before that continuously compounded returns are additive. So, back to Coca-Cola again, the nine-year continuously compounded return from holding this stock between 2001 and 2009 was

$$r(9) = -0.241 - 0.055 + ... + 0.259 = 14.3\%$$

As was the case before with one-period returns, we can also go back and forth between simple and continuously compounded *multiperiod* returns, that is

$$r(9) = \ln[1+R(9)] = \ln(1+0.154) = 14.3\%$$

and

$$R(9) = e^{r(9)} - 1 = e^{0.143}-1 = 15.4\%$$

Finally, suppose we invested $100 in Coca-Cola stock at the end of 2000, held it throughout 2009, and reinvested all the dividends received; what would have been the capital accumulated by the end of 2009? The last column of Table 1.1 shows how our capital (*C*) would have evolved over time, and as you can see in the last row of the same column, $100 would have turned into $115.4.

There are at least two ways to arrive at this number, one going through simple returns and the other through continuously compounded returns. Using simple returns we arrive at $115.4 by calculating

$$\$100 \cdot (1-0.214) \cdot (1-0.053) \cdot \ldots \cdot (1+0.295) = \$100 \cdot (1+0.154) = \$115.4$$

Alternatively, using continuously compounded returns we arrive at $115.4 by calculating

$$\$100 \cdot e^{(-0.241 - 0.055 + \ldots + 0.259)} = \$100 \cdot e^{(0.143)} = \$115.4$$

The difference with the previous calculation is that instead of just multiplying $100 by the multiperiod (simple) return, now we need to raise 'e' to the multiperiod (continuously compounded) return and then multiply that by $100.

In general, then, if we start with a capital C_0 and invest it over T periods, we can calculate our terminal capital (C_T) in two ways, namely

$$C_T = C_0 \cdot (1 + R_1) \cdot (1 + R_2) \cdot \ldots \cdot (1 + R_T) = C_0 \cdot \{1 + R(T)\} \qquad (1.6)$$

or

$$C_T = C_0 \cdot e^{(r_1 + r_2 + \ldots + r_T)} = C_0 \cdot e^{r(T)} \qquad (1.7)$$

As the calculations above show, in both cases we'll arrive at exactly the same figure.

The big picture

Just in case the distinction between simple returns and continuously compounded returns sounds confusing, let's stress once again a couple of things we mentioned before. First, think of simple returns and continuously compounded returns simply as different definitions of return. Second, investors are largely interested in simple returns. And third, continuously compounded returns play an important role in the background of many financial calculations, at least one of which we'll discuss later in the book.

We can calculate simple and continuously compounded returns over one or more periods. Multiperiod returns enable us to calculate the capital accumulated over two or more periods. And we can arrive at this terminal capital by using simple or continuously compounded multiperiod returns.

In short, for investment purposes stick to simple returns, but remember that there is another definition of returns that plays an important role in the background of many financial calculations.

Excel section

There is little work to be done with Excel at this point. The magnitudes discussed in this chapter can easily be calculated in Excel simply by applying their definitions. For example, you can compute simple and continuously compounded returns by using expressions (1.1), (1.2), and (1.3). Note that:

■ To get the 'e' number in Excel you use the 'exp' function. For example, if you type

=exp(1)

and press the Enter key, you will get 2.71828, which is the value of 'e.' Similarly, by typing

=exp(x)

and hitting Enter you can find the value of 'e' raised to any number x.

■ To get a natural logarithm in Excel you use the 'ln' function. For example, if you type

=ln(1)

and hit Enter, you will get 0. Similarly, by typing

=ln(x)

and hitting Enter you can find the natural log of any number x.

2

Returns II: Mean returns

I n the previous chapter we discussed how to compute periodic returns. In this chapter we'll focus on how we can summarize some of the information provided by those returns. We'll look at two ways to assess the return performance of an asset and the relationship between them. We'll also discuss how to assess the performance of an investor in an asset, and why it may differ from the performance of the asset itself.

The arithmetic mean return

Take a look at Table 2.1, which shows the (simple) annual returns of the Russian market and the Swiss market between 2000 and 2009. In both cases the returns are based on MSCI indices, in dollars, and accounting for both capital gains and dividends. Let's focus on the Russian market first.

table 2.1

Year	Russia (%)	Switzerland (%)
2000	−30.0	6.4
2001	55.9	−21.1
2002	15.7	−10.0
2003	75.9	35.0
2004	5.7	15.6
2005	73.8	17.1
2006	55.9	28.2
2007	24.8	6.1
2008	−73.8	−29.9
2009	104.9	26.6
AM	**30.9**	**7.4**
GM	**15.6**	**5.3**

As you can see in the table, the Russian market fluctuated widely (or wildly!) during this 10-year period, with gains of over 100% in 2009 and loses of almost 75% in 2008. Can we somehow aggregate all these returns into one number that summarizes the return performance of the Russian market over the 2000–09 period? You bet.

A straightforward way to summarize return performance is to simply average the relevant returns; that is, to add them all up and then to divide the sum by the number of returns. This is the good-old average we all learned in school. More formally, the **arithmetic mean return (AM)** of a series of returns is given by

$$AM = \frac{R_1 + R_2 + \ldots + R_T}{T} \tag{2.1}$$

where R_t denotes the (simple) return in period t and T the number of returns. Using this expression we can easily calculate the arithmetic mean annual return of the Russian market between 2000 and 2009, which was

$$\frac{-0.300 + 0.559 + \ldots + 1.049}{10} = 30.9\%$$

Although some issues related to the interpretation of this figure are a bit tricky, this much we can safely say. First, we can think about the 30.9% mean annual return in the same straightforward way we usually think about any other average; that is, some annual returns were high, some low, some positive, some negative, and on average they were 30.9%.

Second, under some conditions, this arithmetic mean return is the return most likely to occur in the next period. This does not mean that this is the best way, or even a good way, to predict returns. But if the underlying distribution of returns is reasonably symmetric, and there are no clear patterns in the data that we can use to improve our forecast, it is indeed the case that the arithmetic mean yields the next period's most likely return.

Third, and very important, the arithmetic mean return does *not* properly describe the rate at which an invested capital evolved over time. To see this, assume that we invest $100 for two years in an asset that returns –50% in the first year and 50% in the second year. The arithmetic mean return over this two-year period is (–0.50+0.50)/2 = 0%. But do we have after two years the same $100 we started with as the 0% mean return seems to indicate?

Not really. After losing 50% in the first year, our $100 were reduced to $50; and after gaining 50% in the second year, our $50 turned into $75. So by investing in this asset with an arithmetic mean return of 0% we lost 25% of our money! What is going on? Simply that, as just mentioned, the arithmetic mean return does not properly describe the rate at which an invested capital evolved over time.

A bit confused? That's fine, just read on.

Russia, 1995–98

Let's focus on the Russian market again, but let's go back a bit further in time and focus now on the 1995–98 period. Table 2.2 shows the returns of the Russian market, again based on the MSCI index, in dollars, and accounting for both capital gains and dividends. Needless to say, it was a pretty wild ride!

table 2.2

Year	Russia (%)
1995	−27.1
1996	152.9
1997	112.1
1998	−83.0

Suppose that Vladimir, who manages a fund that invests in Russian stocks, writes an article in the financial press and argues that 'between 1995 and 1998 the Russian stock market delivered a 38.7% mean annual return.' The reader of the article could hardly be blamed for thinking that, had he invested $100 at the beginning of 1995, he would have accumulated $370.5 by the end of 1998; that is, $100 \cdot (1+0.387)^4 = \$370.5$. If asked to defend his statement, Vladimir could readily provide the four annual returns for the years 1995–98 and the calculation of the mean return. He didn't lie.

Now suppose that in another article in the financial press I argue that 'between 1995 and 1998 the Russian stock market delivered a *negative* 9.7% mean annual return.' A reader of this article could not be blamed for thinking that, had he invested $100 at the beginning of 1995, he would have ended up with $66.5 by the end of 1998; that is, $100·(1−0.097)^4 = $66.5. If asked to defend my statement, I could readily provide the four annual returns for the years 1995–98 and the calculation of the mean return, just like Vladimir did. I didn't lie, either.

So what's going on here? How can Vladimir and I both *truthfully* argue that between the years 1995 and 1998 the Russian stock market delivered a positive 38.7% and a negative 9.7% mean annual return? Very simple: Vladimir's figure is the *arithmetic* mean return, and my figure is the *geometric* mean return. Both are mean returns, but their calculation, interpretation, and use are different.

Vladimir's figure, the arithmetic mean return, we know by now how to calculate: add up the four annual returns and divide the sum by 4. If you do that you will obtain the 38.7% mean annual return mentioned above. Does that number properly describe the rate at which an investment in the Russian market evolved between 1995 and 1998? Not at all.

By way of proof, consider an initial investment of $100 at the beginning of 1995 and the four annual returns in Table 2.2, and compute the accumulated capital by the end of 1998. If you remember how to calculate multi-period returns, which we discussed in the previous chapter, you should have no problem calculating that the initial $100 were reduced to $66.5 four years down the road; that is, $100·(1−0.271)·(1+1.529)·(1+1.121)·(1−0.830) = $66.5. That is a far cry from the $370.5 that the 38.7% arithmetic mean return over this period seems to imply. In other words, as already mentioned, the arithmetic mean return does *not* properly describe the rate at which an invested capital evolved over time.

The geometric mean return

This is a good time to introduce a different way of computing mean returns. The **geometric mean return (GM)** of a series of returns, often also referred to as the **mean compound return**, is given by

$$GM = \{(1 + R_1)\cdot(1 + R_2)\cdot \ldots \cdot (1 + R_T)\}^{1/T} - 1 \qquad (2.2)$$

How do we interpret this magnitude? Let's start by going back to our hypothetical asset that returned −50% in the first period and 50% in the second period. Recall that, although the arithmetic mean return of this asset over these two periods was 0%, we actually lost 25% of the $100 we initially invested and ended the two-year period with $75. Let's calculate the geometric mean return of this asset. According to expression (2.2) it is

$$GM = \{(1-0.50)\cdot(1+0.50)\}^{1/2} - 1 = -13.4\%$$

One way of interpreting this figure is as follows. If we had invested $100 in this asset over the two years considered, we would have lost our capital at the *compound* annual rate of 13.4%. That is just a fancy way of saying that we would have lost, on average, 13.4% *on top of* 13.4%; that is, $100\cdot(1-0.134)^2 = $75. In other words, the geometric mean return does appropriately describe what happened to the capital we invested over the two-year period considered: We started with $100, lost money at a mean annual (compound) rate of 13.4%, and ended up with $75.

Just to drive this point home let's go back to the Russian market over the 1995–98 period. Using the four returns in Table 2.2 we can easily calculate that the geometric mean return over this four-year period was

$$\{(1 - 0.271)\cdot(1 + 1.529)\cdot(1 + 1.121)\cdot(1 - 0.830)\}^{1/4} - 1 = -9.7\%$$

In other words, had we invested our money in the Russian market over the 1995–98 period, we would have lost it at the mean annual (compound) rate of 9.7%. And had that been the case, our initial $100 would have turned into $100\cdot(1-0.097)^4 = $66.5 four years down the road, which is the same figure we calculated using multiperiod returns.

The relationship between *AM* and *GM*

Table 2.1 shows that the difference between the arithmetic and the geometric mean return is far larger in the Russian market (over 15 percentage points) than in the Swiss market (just over 2 percentage points). Why is this so? It all comes down to one word, which we haven't quite defined yet: Volatility. Everything else being equal, the higher the **volatility** of an asset, the higher is the difference between its arithmetic and its geometric mean return.

We will formally define volatility in the next chapter, but for the moment think of it as variability or uncertainty in returns. Take another look at Table 2.1 and your eyes won't fool you; the returns of the Russian market fluctuated far more widely than those of the Swiss market. Hence, the difference between the arithmetic and the geometric mean return is much larger for the former than for the latter.

Here's an important conclusion you should draw from this discussion and keep in mind at all times: When assessing the performance of very volatile assets, such as internet stocks, emerging markets, or hedge funds, to name but a few, it is virtually meaningless to discuss 'mean returns.' The difference between arithmetic and geometric mean returns can be very large, and only the latter properly describes the evolution of an invested capital over time. Remember, Vladimir and I both truthfully reported the 'mean return' of the Russian market for 1995–98. Without lying, he might have led you to believe that your money in the Russian market would have increased at a 38.7% annual rate. But now you know better; you actually *lost* money at the annual rate of almost 10%. Therefore, when discussing the performance of an asset, particularly if it is a very volatile one, *never* be afraid to ask what type of 'mean return' the other person is talking about!

One final thing: Note that in the three examples we discussed so far the arithmetic mean return is larger than the geometric mean return. This is no coincidence; it is always the case. To be more precise, the arithmetic mean is always larger than or equal to the geometric mean. In fact, only in the hypothetical case in which returns do not fluctuate at all (that is, when all returns are the same, which is an obviously uninteresting case when considering financial assets) these two magnitudes are equal to each other; in all other cases, the arithmetic mean return is larger than the geometric mean return.

The dollar-weighted mean return

Now that you're hopefully at ease with the fact that there are two ways to calculate mean returns, let's introduce a *third* one! Yes, another one, and here's why: One thing is the return of *an asset* and another is the return of *an investor* in that asset. These two returns may be different from each other, and this is the issue we'll briefly discuss in this section. (To understand what follows, you need to be familiar with the concepts of present value and internal rate of return; if you're not, you may want to take a look at these concepts in Chapter 21.)

By now we know two ways to assess the mean return of an asset. We also know that if we want to assess the rate at which an invested capital evolved over time, we need to focus on the asset's geometric mean return. Importantly, this magnitude also properly captures the performance of a passive (buy-and-hold) investor in the asset; that is, an investor that bought the asset at the beginning of an evaluation period, sold it at the end of such period, and did nothing in between (other than reinvesting in the asset the cash flows received, if any). In other words, an asset's geometric mean return properly captures a passive investor's mean compound return.

Having said that, it is obvious that not everybody is a passive investor. Some people believe, despite plenty of evidence to the contrary, that they can find the right times to buy and sell. And depending on whether they actually trade at the right times or at the wrong times, the mean compound return obtained by these active investors may be higher or lower than the asset's geometric mean return. Let's illustrate this with a simple example.

Take a look at the figures in Table 2.3, which show a hypothetical stock's price (p) at the end of three consecutive years ($5, $10, and $5); the stock's returns (R) over the first and the second year (100% and −50%); and the stock's arithmetic (AM) and geometric (GM) mean returns over this two-year period (25% and 0%).

table 2.3

			Passive strategy			Active strategy		
Year	p ($)	R (%)	Shares	CF ($)	C ($)	Shares	CF ($)	C ($)
0	5		+100	−500	500	+100	−500	500
1	10	100.0		0	1,000	+100	−1,000	2,000
2	5	−50.0	−100	500	500	−200	1,000	1,000
AM (%)		25.0						
GM (%)		0.0						
DWM (%)				0.0			−26.8	

Let's first consider an investor following a passive strategy. In our case this means an investor buying, say, 100 shares of our hypothetical stock at the beginning of our two-year evaluation period; selling the 100 shares at the end of such period; and doing nothing in between. To buy 100 shares this investor needs to take $500 out of his pocket, thus experiencing a cash flow (CF) of −$500; after this purchase he has a capital (C) of $500 invested in the stock. Two years down the road when our investor sells his shares he will pocket $500, which becomes his capital (now in cash) at the time. The internal rate of return (IRR) of this investor's cash flows, then, is given by

$$-\$500 + \frac{\$0}{(1+\text{IRR})} + \frac{\$500}{(1+\text{IRR})^2} = 0$$

and solving for the IRR we get 0%. Unsurprisingly, the IRR of the investor is the same as the geometric mean return of the stock. This is the case simply because he bought 100 shares of the stock at the beginning of our evaluation period, held them passively, and cashed out at the end of such period. In cases like this, the return of an asset and the return of an investor in the asset always coincide.

Let's introduce a definition and formalize this result a bit. The **dollar-weighted mean return (DWM)** is the discount rate that sets the present value of a series of cash flows equal to 0; that is

$$CF_0 + \frac{CF_1}{(1+DWM)} + \frac{CF_2}{(1+DWM)^2} + \dots + \frac{CF_T}{(1+DWM)^T} = 0 \qquad (2.3)$$

where CF_t denotes the cash flow in period t, and T is the number of periods over which we're evaluating performance. Note that, by definition, *the dollar-weighted mean return is the investor's internal rate of return.* And paraphrasing what we already mentioned, the dollar-weighted mean return of a passive investor is always equal to the geometric mean return of the asset in which he invests.

If everybody invested passively, there would be no need to introduce the concept of dollar-weighted mean return; the geometric mean return of an asset would appropriately describe the mean compound return obtained by investors. But not everybody is a passive investor, and therefore the concept of dollar-weighted mean return becomes important. To see this, consider the last three columns of Table 2.3.

This investor pursues an active strategy, by which we mean that he makes at least one transaction during our two-year evaluation period. More precisely, he buys 100 shares at the beginning of our evaluation period, just like our previous investor did; then buys another 100 shares at the end of the first year, at which time he'll have a negative cash flow of $1,000 and a capital of $2,000 invested in the stock; and finally sells the 200 shares and pockets $1,000 at the end of the second year. The geometric mean return of the stock has obviously not changed; it remains at 0%. But what about *the investor's* return in this stock?

Well, we can calculate his dollar-weighted mean return just as before, the only difference being that this investor's cash flows are different from those of our previous investor. In this case, the dollar-weighted mean return solves from the expression

$$-\$500 - \frac{\$1,000}{(1+DWM)} + \frac{\$1,000}{(1+DWM)^2} = 0$$

and is equal to –26.8%. That's quite a difference from 0%! But it is this dollar-weighted mean return, not the asset's geometric mean return, that appropriately captures the mean compound return obtained by this second investor. Note that the critical difference with respect to the passive investor is that the active investor buys the 100 additional shares at a 'bad' time; that is, at the end of the first year when the stock price is 50% higher than it is at the time when he finally sells the stock.

Just to make sure you're on top of this important concept, let's go over one more example, but not a hypothetical one. Let's make it more fun! Table 2.4 shows the closing price (p) of Google at the end of the years 2004 through 2009. During this time, Google did not pay any dividends and therefore its annual return (R) was equal to the capital gain or loss produced by the stock. As shown in the table, Google's arithmetic and geometric mean annual returns during this five-year period were 44.5% and 26.3%, a very large difference because Google is a very volatile stock.

table 2.4

Year	p ($)	R (%)	Passive strategy			Active strategy		
			Shares	CF ($)	C ($)	Shares	CF ($)	C ($)
2004	192.8		+1	−192.8	192.8	+1	−192.8	192.8
2005	414.9	115.2		0.0	414.9		0.0	414.9
2006	460.5	11.0		0.0	460.5		0.0	460.5
2007	691.5	50.2		0.0	691.5	+1	−691.5	1,383.0
2008	307.7	−55.5		0.0	307.7		0.0	615.3
2009	620.0	101.5	−1	620.0	620.0	−2	1,240.0	1,240.0
AM (%)		44.5						
GM (%)		26.3						
DWM (%)				26.3			13.1	

Let's first consider an investor following a passive strategy. In our case that means buying one share of Google at the end of 2004 (at $192.8), selling it at the end of 2009 (at $620.0), and doing nothing in between. Had an investor followed such a passive strategy, his mean annual compound return would have been the same as Google's geometric mean annual return; that is, a healthy 26.3%.

Let's consider now an investor following an active strategy. After buying one share of Google at the end of 2004 (at $192.8), just like our previous investor did, this investor buys an additional share at the end of 2007 (at $691.5), and finally sells his two shares at the end of 2009 (at $620.0), pocketing $1,240. Before running any calculation, note that the purchase at the end of 2007 was made at a 'bad' time; that is, at a time when the price was much higher than when the investor finally sold the shares. If you calculate this investor's dollar-weighted mean return (you should know by now how to do it!), you'll find that it is 13.1%. So, just by making one badly timed decision, our active investor reduced his mean annual compound return to almost exactly *one half* of Google's geometric mean annual return.

To be sure, it is not always the case that the dollar-weighted mean return of an active investor will be lower than the geometric mean return of the asset in which he invests. It may be the case that an investor actively trades at 'good' times (buying at times of relatively low prices and selling at times of relatively high prices) and therefore his dollar-weighted mean return may be higher than the asset's geometric mean return. Therefore, in general, an investor's dollar-weighted mean return may be higher than, equal to, or lower than the geometric mean return of the asset in which he invests.

The big picture

The discussion in this chapter suggests that many times it makes little sense to talk about 'mean returns' without specifying whether we are referring to an arithmetic or a geometric mean. This becomes particularly important when considering very volatile assets, such as internet stocks, emerging markets, or hedge funds, because it is in these cases that the difference between arithmetic and geometric mean returns can be very large. The 'mean' performance of the Russian market between 1995 and 1998 hopefully drove this point home.

Until we get back to this issue in the next chapter, keep in mind the following. First, for any given series of returns, the arithmetic mean return is always larger than the geometric mean return. And second, everything else being equal, the higher the volatility of returns, the larger is the difference between these two magnitudes.

It is also important to keep in mind that the return of an asset may be different from the return of an investor in the asset. When an investor follows a passive strategy, his performance and that of the asset in which he invests are the same, and both are properly described by the asset's geometric mean return. However, when an investor pursues an active strategy, his return is properly described by his dollar-weighted mean return, which may be higher than, equal to, or lower than the asset's geometric mean return.

Excel section

Calculating arithmetic and geometric mean returns in Excel is fairly simple and can be done in more than one way; here we'll address the easiest way. Suppose you have a series of 10 returns in cells A1 through A10; then, you do the following:

▦ To calculate the *arithmetic mean return*, type

=average(A1:A10)

in cell A11 and then hit Enter.

▦ To calculate the *geometric mean return*, type

=geomean(1+A1:A10)–1

in cell A12. But note two important things. First, the 'geomean' command as just stated yields 1 plus the geometric mean return; hence, you do need to subtract 1 as shown above. Second, the 'geomean' is what Excel calls an 'array,' which means that instead of typing an expression and hitting Enter, you type the expression and then press Ctrl+Shift+Enter *simultaneously*. (If you just hit Enter you will obtain an error message.)

Excel also easily calculates internal rates of return and therefore dollar-weighted mean returns. This calculation, as well as that of present values and net present values, are discussed in Chapter 21.

3

Risk I: Total risk

n the previous chapter we discussed three ways to summarize return performance, but so much for the 'good' stuff; here comes the 'bad' stuff. In this chapter we'll focus on one way to summarize risk. Keep this in mind, though: Risk can be defined in more than one way and we'll explore other definitions later in the book.

What is risk?

Silly question, huh? Well, not really. The fact is that, simple as it may sound, academics and practitioners in finance have been wrestling with this definition for a very long time. And it gets worse. Nobody seems to have provided a definition that everybody else agrees with. In fact, it may well be the case that risk, like beauty, is in the eyes of the beholder.

Now, don't throw your arms up in despair just yet. The fact that there is no universally accepted definition of risk doesn't mean that risk cannot be quantified in a variety of more or less plausible ways. But before we get into definitions and formulas, take a look at Figure 3.1, which shows the annual returns of Intel and ExxonMobil in 2000–09.

Now, the concept of risk may be hard to pin down, but your eyes probably won't fool you: Compared with ExxonMobil, Intel's steep rises and falls have given investors quite a ride. At the same time that ExxonMobil's returns fluctuated within a range of –15% to 40% (no small range, to be sure), Intel delivered losses in excess of 50% and gains larger than 100%. Just by looking at the graph, most people would agree that Intel appears to be a lot riskier (that is, more volatile or unpredictable) than ExxonMobil.

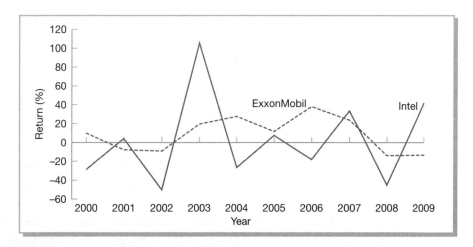

figure 3.1   Returns on Intel and ExxonMobil

So here's one informal way to think about risk: The more returns fluctuate over time, the greater the uncertainty about the prices and returns we'll observe in the future; and the greater that uncertainty, the greater the risk. Makes sense? Well, if it does, then read on so we can formalize this idea a bit.

The standard deviation of returns

One way to formally capture the uncertainty we just mentioned is to compute the **standard deviation of returns (SD)**, which is (hold on to your seat) the square root of the average quadratic deviation with respect to the arithmetic mean return. Read that again. Does it still sound like Sylvester Stallone speaking Chinese? If so, then stop reading this chapter and go to the stats review in Chapter 27. Otherwise, keep reading for more insight into this measure of risk.

The standard deviation of a series of returns, often referred to simply as **volatility**, is formally defined by the expression

$$SD = \sqrt{(1/T) \cdot \sum_{t=1}^{T}(R_t - AM)^2}$$

(3.1)

where R_t denotes returns in period t; AM the (arithmetic) mean return of the series of returns; and T the number of observations. Note that sometimes the standard deviation is calculated by dividing the sum of quadratic deviations by *T*–1 instead of by *T*. For practical purposes, you don't really have to worry about this distinction, but if you want to know a bit more about it, take a look at the (very) brief discussion on this issue in Chapter 27.

Just to make sure you understand the idea behind the calculation of this magnitude, let's go over a step-by-step calculation of the standard deviation of Intel's returns. Table 3.1 shows the returns of Intel (*R*) between 2000 and 2009; the arithmetic mean annual return (*AM*) during this period was 3.3%. The column (*R*–*AM*) shows the difference between each annual return and the mean annual return. And the last column shows the figures in the (*R*–*AM*) column, squared. The average of the numbers in the fourth column is the *variance of returns* (0.2059), but this is not widely used as a measure of risk largely because it is expressed in per cent squared. The number in the intersection between the last row and the last column, the square root of the variance, or the square root of the average quadratic deviation with respect to the mean, is the standard deviation of returns, which in the case of Intel is 45.4%. Although not shown in the table, over the same period the standard deviation of ExxonMobil's returns was just 17.9%.

table 3.1

Year	R (%)	R–AM (%)	(R–AM)²
2000	−26.9	−30.2	0.0912
2001	4.9	1.6	0.0002
2002	−50.3	−53.6	0.2878
2003	106.6	103.3	1.0667
2004	−26.6	−29.9	0.0894
2005	8.1	4.8	0.0023
2006	−17.2	−20.5	0.0421
2007	34.2	30.9	0.0954
2008	−43.5	−46.8	0.2191
2009	43.9	40.6	0.1646
Average	**3.3%**		**0.2059**
Square root			**45.4%**

Of course, you don't have to go through all these calculations to estimate a standard deviation; Excel calculates this magnitude in the blink of an eye and in just one cell. But the table helps you to see where the number that Excel calculates come from, and hopefully to understand what we're really calculating too.

Interpretation of the standard deviation

Let's think a bit about the interpretation of the standard deviation as a measure of risk. Here's an easy way to think about it: The larger this number, the riskier the asset. Not too difficult, huh?! Well, the best part of it is that, when assessing the risk of individual assets (that is, assets taken one at a time rather than combined in a portfolio), this is a perfectly correct way to interpret this magnitude. For informal confirmation, take another look at Figure 3.1, and recall that the standard deviation of returns of Intel and ExxonMobil are 45.4% and 17.9%. Doesn't a comparison of these two figures confirm what your eyes tell you about the relative risk of these two stocks? There you have it.

Now let's push it a bit further. Basically, a small standard deviation indicates that returns fluctuate closely around the mean return, and a large standard deviation indicates the opposite. In other words, the larger the standard deviation, the more that returns tend to depart from the mean return (both above and below), and therefore the higher is the uncertainty about the returns we'll obtain in the future.

Here's another (complementary) way to think about it. You may (or may not!) recall that, if the distribution of returns considered is normal, then approximately 68.3%, 95.4%, and 99.7% of the returns are clustered one, two, and three standard deviations around the (arithmetic) mean. Keeping this in mind, consider two hypothetical assets with a mean return of 20% and standard deviations of 5% (asset A) and 30% (asset B).

Note that there is roughly a 95% probability that the returns of asset A will fluctuate between 10% and 30%; that is, two standard deviations around the mean return. However, in the case of asset B, there is roughly 95% probability that returns will fluctuate between –40% and 80%, a range so large as to be useless. We could drive a train sideways between these two numbers!

This simple example illustrates another way to see why the standard deviation is a measure of risk: We can use it to estimate the interval within which returns will fluctuate with any chosen probability; the larger the interval, the larger the uncertainty, and therefore the riskier the asset. In fact, if you run a similar calculation for Intel and ExxonMobil (you should, it's easy!), you'll find that there's roughly a 95% probability that the returns of Intel will fluctuate between –87.4% and 94.1%, and those of ExxonMobil between –26.6% and 45.0%. So, given that the range between the low end and the high end of the interval is far larger in the case of Intel (181.5%) than in the case of ExxonMobil (71.5%), we have another way to see that Intel is far riskier.

Having said that, do keep in mind the following: The calculations we just ran are *exclusively* valid when the returns considered are normally distributed. This assumption, widely used and abused, may be plausible in some cases and implausible in some others. So, as long as you can safely determine that the returns of the asset you're considering are normally distributed, the intervals calculated as just discussed are plausible. If you don't know the type of distribution those returns follow, or do know that it is not normal, then stay away from running this type of calculation.

Mean returns and the standard deviation

We intuitively know that risk is 'bad,' and the discussion in the previous section attempts to explain why the standard deviation may be a plausible measure of how 'bad' an asset may be. Essentially, the standard deviation is a measure of variability and uncertainty, both of which most investors would agree are 'bad.'

Now we'll take another, usually less explored, look at why volatility is bad for investors. Consider the six hypothetical assets in Table 3.2, all of which have an arithmetic mean return (*AM*) of 10% but different volatility (*SD*). Note that as we move from asset A to asset F volatility increases; that is, as we move from left to right the assets become riskier.

table 3.2

Year	A (%)	B (%)	C (%)	D (%)	E (%)	F (%)
1	10.0	12.0	15.0	20.0	25.0	40.0
2	10.0	8.0	5.0	0.0	−5.0	−20.0
3	10.0	12.0	15.0	20.0	25.0	40.0
4	10.0	8.0	5.0	0.0	−5.0	−20.0
5	10.0	12.0	15.0	20.0	25.0	40.0
6	10.0	8.0	5.0	0.0	−5.0	−20.0
7	10.0	12.0	15.0	20.0	25.0	40.0
8	10.0	8.0	5.0	0.0	−5.0	−20.0
9	10.0	12.0	15.0	20.0	25.0	40.0
10	10.0	8.0	5.0	0.0	−5.0	−20.0
AM (%)	**10.00**	**10.00**	**10.00**	**10.00**	**10.00**	**10.00**
SD (%)	**0.00**	**2.00**	**5.00**	**10.00**	**15.00**	**30.00**
GM (%)	**10.00**	**9.98**	**9.89**	**9.54**	**8.97**	**5.83**
GM-2 (%)	**10.00**	**9.98**	**9.89**	**9.55**	**8.98**	**5.98**
GM-3 (%)	**10.00**	**9.98**	**9.87**	**9.50**	**8.88**	**5.50**
TC ($)	**25,937**	**25,895**	**25,671**	**24,883**	**23,614**	**17,623**

Now take a look at the geometric mean returns (*GM*). As we move from left to right, the arithmetic mean return remains constant, volatility increases, *and the geometric mean return decreases.* This is sometimes referred to as the 'variance drag,' which is just a fancy way of saying that volatility reduces mean compound returns.

As you hopefully remember from our discussion in the previous chapter, an investment does not compound over time at its arithmetic mean return but at its geometric mean return. So here we have another way to rationalize why volatility is bad: Because it lowers the compound return of an investment, thus reducing its terminal value.

The last row of the table shows the terminal capital (*TC*) that results from a $10,000 investment in each of the six assets in the table at the beginning of the 10-year period considered. The six assets, remember, have the same arithmetic mean return of 10%. However, because as we move from asset A to asset F volatility increases, the geometric mean return decreases and so does the rate at which each asset compounds our money. Put differently, our terminal capital is negatively related to the volatility of the assets.

Formally, the relationship between the arithmetic mean, the geometric mean, and volatility is given by this expression

$$GM \approx \exp \left\{ \ln(1 + AM) - \frac{(1/2) \cdot SD^2}{(1 + AM)^2} \right\} - 1 \tag{3.2}$$

which holds well as an approximation for returns not much larger than ±30%. The row labeled 'GM-2' in Table 3.2 shows the geometric mean return of the six assets considered calculated with this expression. If you compare these figures with those from the row above (the *exact* geometric mean returns), you can see that the approximation is in fact very good. You can also see that, as the size of the returns increases, the approximation becomes worse.

If you find the expression above intimidating, here comes the good news: There's a simpler approximation that works almost as well

$$GM \approx AM - (1/2) \cdot SD^2 \tag{3.3}$$

The row labeled 'GM-3' in Table 3.2 shows the geometric mean return of the six assets considered calculated with this expression. And once again, if you compare these figures with those of the exact geometric means you'll find that this approximation, though a bit worse than the previous one, is also pretty accurate.

The big picture

Risk is probably the most elusive concept in finance. One of the most widely accepted ways to assess it, however, is with the standard deviation of returns, usually also referred to as the volatility of an asset. This volatility can be thought of as uncertainty about future prices or returns, or as dispersion around the asset's arithmetic mean return.

Importantly, volatility is 'bad' not only because we use it as synonymous with risk. It is also 'bad' because it causes a drag on mean compound return, thus decreasing an asset's ability to compound our money over time.

Excel section

Just as in the Excel sections of the previous two chapters, the stuff in this section is straightforward.

■ To calculate a square root in Excel you need to use the 'sqrt' function. Calculating the square root of any number x is as simple as typing

=sqrt(x)

and hitting Enter.

Calculating a standard deviation in Excel is also simple. Suppose you have ten returns in cells A1 through A10; then, you do the following:

■ To calculate a standard deviation that divides the average of squared deviations from the mean by T, you type

=stdevp(A1:A10)

in cell A11 and hit Enter.

■ To calculate a standard deviation that divides the average of squared deviations from the mean by $T-1$, type

=stdev(A1:A10)

in cell A11 and hit Enter.

4

Risk and return I: Portfolios

ost investors don't put all their money in just one asset but in a
portfolio of assets. This begs the question of how to estimate the
risk and return of a portfolio, as opposed to those of an individual
security, which is the issue we'll discuss in this chapter. We'll also discuss a
few related concepts, such as feasible sets, efficient sets, and the minimum
variance portfolio.

Two assets: Risk and return

table 4.1

	Panel A				Panel B		
Year	AT&T (%)	BofA (%)		x_1 (%)	x_2 (%)	Return (%)	Risk (%)
2000	0.1	−4.5		100.0	0.0	1.2	22.6
2001	−16.1	42.7		90.0	10.0	1.5	21.2
2002	−28.3	14.5		80.0	20.0	1.8	20.1
2003	1.7	20.1		70.0	30.0	2.1	19.5
2004	3.7	21.5		60.0	40.0	2.4	19.4
2005	0.2	2.4		50.0	50.0	2.7	19.8
2006	53.2	20.7		40.0	60.0	3.1	20.6
2007	20.6	−18.9		30.0	70.0	3.4	21.9
2008	−28.0	−63.1		20.0	80.0	3.7	23.5
2009	4.8	7.5		10.0	90.0	4.0	25.4
AM	1.2	4.3		0.0	100.0	4.3	27.5
SD	22.6	27.5					

Let's kick off this discussion by considering the annual returns of AT&T and Bank of America (BofA) between 2000 and 2009, shown in panel A of Table 4.1. As the table shows, over this period BofA delivered a higher arithmetic mean return (*AM*) than AT&T, and it did so with higher volatility (*SD*). By the way, if the 1.2% and 4.3% mean *annual* returns look tiny, remember, the first decade of the 2000s was an awful period for equities in general. (For perspective, in this period the mean annual compound return of the S&P 500 was –0.9%.)

Let's first consider the calculation of the return of a portfolio containing these two stocks in a given year, which will obviously depend on how much we invest in each stock. Let's denote with x_i the proportion of capital invested in stock i (that is, the amount of money invested in stock i relative to the amount of money invested in the portfolio) and with R_i the return of stock i. Then, the **return of the portfolio (R_p)** in any given year is given by

$$R_p = x_1 \cdot R_1 + x_2 \cdot R_2 \qquad\qquad (4.1)$$

where $x_1 + x_2 = 1$. Note that regardless of the number of assets in the portfolio, we'll always assume that the sum of the weights is equal to 1. This assumption implies that we are concerned with the *proportion* of capital invested in each asset. In other words, it doesn't matter whether we have $100 or $100 million; what matters is how much we invest in each asset relative to the total investment in our portfolio.

To illustrate the use of expression (4.1), consider the figures in Table 4.1, the year 2009, and weightings of 60% for AT&T and 40% for BofA. It is then straightforward to determine that such a portfolio would have had a (0.60) (0.048) + (0.40)(0.075) = 5.9% return in that year. Simple enough.

We can run a similar calculation not just for an annual return but also for the *mean* annual return of the portfolio over any desired period. To do so, we replace in expression (4.1) the observed returns of the two assets in any given year by their mean annual returns over the desired period. For example, the mean annual return of a portfolio invested 60% in AT&T and 40% in BofA over the 2000–09 period, rebalanced at the end of each year to keep the 60–40 proportions constant, would have been (0.60)(0.012) + (0.40) (0.043) = 2.4%. Again, very simple.

There is no mystery about how to calculate the return of a two-asset portfolio. It is straightforward to do it both for any given year or on average over any given period. Similarly, to calculate the *expected* return of a portfolio, we simply replace in (4.1) the observed returns of the two assets in any given year by their expected returns. And don't be fooled by the word 'simply.' It only means that *if* we have the expected returns for the two assets, the rest of the calculation is trivial. But as we'll briefly discuss in Chapters 11 and 12, there's nothing trivial about the actual estimation of those expected returns.

Now, what about the risk of a portfolio? That's a bit more complicated, but still rather simple in the two-asset case. The **standard deviation of a portfolio** (SD_p), also referred to as the volatility of the portfolio, is given by

$$SD_p = \{(x_1)^2 \cdot (SD_1)^2 + (x_2)^2 \cdot (SD_2)^2 + 2x_1 \cdot x_2 \cdot SD_1 \cdot SD_2 \cdot Corr_{12}\}^{1/2} \tag{4.2}$$

where SD_1 and SD_2 denote the standard deviation of assets 1 and 2, and $Corr_{12}$ is the correlation between assets 1 and 2 (AT&T and BofA, in our case). Note that because, by definition, the covariance between two assets 1 and 2 (Cov_{12}) is given by $Cov_{12} = SD_1 \cdot SD_2 \cdot Corr_{12}$, then you may occasionally find the third term of the right-hand side of (4.2) written as $2x_1 \cdot x_2 \cdot Cov_{12}$. (If your knowledge of covariances and correlations is rusty, you may want to take a look at Chapter 27.)

Back to the 60–40 portfolio we considered before, note that at this point we know all the magnitudes in expression (4.2) except for one, the correlation between AT&T and BofA, which over the 2000–09 period was a rather low 0.24. (You could calculate this figure yourself from the data in Table 4.1.) With this correlation, the 60–40 weights, the standard deviations in Table 4.1, and expression (4.2), we can easily calculate that the volatility of the 60–40 portfolio over the 2000–09 period would have been

$$\begin{aligned} SD_p &= \{(0.60)^2(0.226)^2 + (0.40)^2(0.275)^2 + 2(0.60)(0.40)(0.226)(0.275)(0.24)\}^{1/2} \\ &= 19.4\% \end{aligned}$$

In short, calculating the risk and return of a two-asset portfolio is simple and can even be done with a handheld calculator. However, as we'll discuss shortly, the computational burden increases exponentially with the number of assets, which means that for portfolios larger than three or four assets, spreadsheets become essential. Before we discuss portfolios of more than two assets, however, let's take a look at a few useful definitions in the two-asset case.

Two assets: Other concepts

Now that we know how to compute the risk and return of a two-asset portfolio, let's take a look at panel B of Table 4.1. Using expressions (4.1) and (4.2), the mean returns and standard deviations of AT&T and BofA over the 2000–09 period (in panel A), and the correlation between these two stocks mentioned before (0.24), you should have no difficulty replicating the figures in this panel, which show the return and risk that several portfolios of AT&T and BofA would have delivered in 2000–09.

Note that if we invest all of our money in either stock, the portfolio reflects the risk and return of that stock. Note, also, that although the numbers in the 'Return' column are equal to the weighted average of the returns of AT&T and BofA, the numbers in the 'Risk' column are *not* equal to the weighted average of the risks of these two stocks. (This is due to diversification, an issue we'll discuss in the next chapter.)

The relationship between risk and return summarized in the last two columns of Table 4.1 is depicted in Figure 4.1. This line is called the **feasible set** and shows the return and risk that different portfolios of AT&T and BofA would have delivered over the whole 2000–09 period. The points labeled AT&T and BofA indicate a 100% investment in each of these stocks, and all the (infinite) points in between indicate other combinations of these two stocks. Point A, for example, indicates a portfolio invested 80% in AT&T and 20% in BofA, and point B indicates a portfolio invested 10% in AT&T and 90% in BofA.

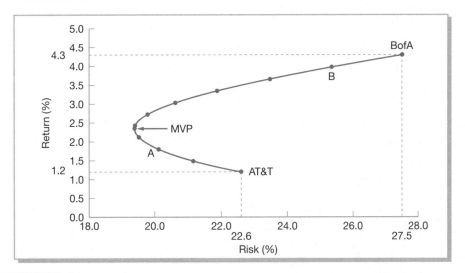

figure 4.1   Feasible set for AT&T and Bank of America (BofA)

Note that the feasible set could extend beyond the points marked AT&T and BofA in the presence of short-selling; that is, when an investor borrows one asset, sells it, and invests the proceeds in the other asset. In this case, the investor will end up with a negative position in the borrowed asset and more than 100% of his capital invested in the other asset.

Finally, and importantly, note that the points along the feasible set can be thought of as the return and risk that different portfolios of AT&T and BofA would have delivered over the 2000–09 period. Or, if we believe that the 2000–09 period is representative of what we can expect in the future, then the points along the feasible set can be thought of as the return and risk *expected* from different portfolios of AT&T and BofA. (In this particular case, given that the first decade of the 2000s was a very unusual period, this feasible set is probably not a good representation of what we can expect from these two companies in the future.)

For all the obvious reasons, the point of the feasible set farthest to the left is called the **minimum variance portfolio (MVP)**. Of all the possible combinations between AT&T and BofA, this is the one that minimizes our risk. In the two-asset case, in fact, the expression to determine how much we should invest in one asset to minimize the risk of the portfolio is not too difficult and is given by

$$x_1 = \frac{(SD_2)^2 - Cov_{12}}{(SD_1)^2 + (SD_2)^2 - 2 \cdot Cov_{12}} \tag{4.3}$$

And because $x_1 + x_2 = 1$, then it follows that $x_2 = 1 - x_1$.

Note that in our case $Cov_{12} = SD_1 \cdot SD_2 \cdot Corr_{12} = (0.226)(0.275)(0.24) = 0.0148$. Then, plugging this figure and those for the standard deviations of the two assets into expression (4.3), we find that the proportion of capital to be invested in AT&T (x_1) to minimize the risk of the portfolio is equal to 62.6%; the rest of the capital (37.4%) should be invested in BofA. At this point you should have no problem calculating that this portfolio would have had a return of 2.4% and a volatility of 19.4%. (Actually, the volatility is 19.39%, just slightly lower than the 19.41% volatility of the 60–40 portfolio.)

Finally, the **efficient set** is the upper half of the feasible set, beginning at the MVP. Take another look at Figure 4.1. Would you choose a portfolio in the lower branch of the feasible set (that is, the branch that goes down and to the right from the MVP)? Of course not. For each portfolio in the lower branch, you could choose another portfolio with the same level of risk but higher return in the upper branch. That's why it's called the *efficient* set: It's the set of portfolios that, for any chosen level of risk, offers the highest possible return.

Three assets

Before considering the general *n*-asset case, let's take a quick look at a three-asset portfolio. The return of this portfolio is straightforward; it is, again, the weighted average of the returns of all the assets in the portfolio; that is

$$R_p = x_1 \cdot R_1 + x_2 \cdot R_2 + x_3 \cdot R_3 \tag{4.4}$$

And, similar to the two-asset case, $x_1 + x_2 + x_3 = 1$.

Now for the bad news. The inclusion of just one more asset complicates the calculation of the risk of the portfolio quite a bit. It's not difficult, just messy. Let's start with the expression, which is given by

$$SD_p = \{(x_1)^2 (SD_1)^2 + (x_2)^2 (SD_2)^2 + (x_3)^2 (SD_3)^2 + \\ + 2 \cdot x_1 \cdot x_2 \cdot Cov_{12} + 2 \cdot x_1 \cdot x_3 \cdot Cov_{13} + 2 \cdot x_2 \cdot x_3 \cdot Cov_{23}\}^{1/2} \tag{4.5}$$

It looks scary but there's really nothing to it. Let's compare this expression to (4.2) and think a bit about both.

Note, first, that expression (4.2) has four terms (the third term is multiplied by 2, so it's actually two identical terms) and expression (4.5) has nine terms (again, the last three terms are multiplied by 2 so each is made up of two identical terms). Can you see the pattern? The expression for the risk of a portfolio has as many terms as the square of the number of assets in the portfolio; that is, $2^2 = 4$ in the two-asset case and $3^2 = 9$ in the three-asset case.

Note, also, that for each asset in the portfolio we'll have a 'variance term' that consists of a weight multiplied by a standard deviation, both squared; these are the $(x_i)^2 (SD_i)^2$ terms. To determine the number of 'covariance terms' $(x_i \cdot x_j \cdot Cov_{ij})$, we just count all the different combinations of assets and multiply this number by 2. In the two-asset portfolio, we find only one combination (1-2), so there should be two covariance terms $(2 \cdot x_1 \cdot x_2 \cdot Cov_{12})$. In the three-asset portfolio, we find three combinations (1-2, 1-3, and 2-3), so there should be six covariance terms $(2 \cdot x_1 \cdot x_2 \cdot Cov_{12}, 2 \cdot x_1 \cdot x_3 \cdot Cov_{13},$ and $2 \cdot x_2 \cdot x_3 \cdot Cov_{23})$.

Importantly, note that in the three-asset case the feasible set is no longer a line as it is in the two-asset case. In fact, as shown in Figure 4.2, the feasible set becomes a bullet-shaped *surface*, which is the case for all portfolios with more than two assets. The MVP still is the point farthest to the left of this feasible set, and the efficient set still is the upper border of the feasible set, beginning at the MVP.

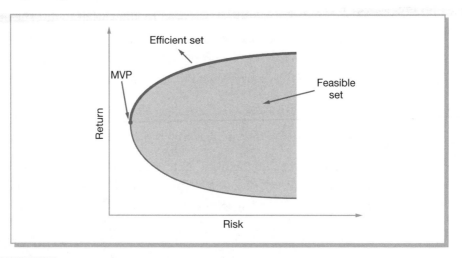

Feasible set, efficient set, and MVP: The three-asset case

n assets

Now for the general case. As mentioned before, regardless of the number of assets, the return of a portfolio is always equal to the weighted average of returns of all the assets in the portfolio; that is

$$R_p = x_1 \cdot R_1 + x_2 \cdot R_2 + \ldots + x_n \cdot R_n \tag{4.6}$$

with $x_1 + x_2 + \ldots + x_n = 1$. No trouble here.

The risk of an *n*-asset portfolio, however, is much more cumbersome to estimate, particularly when the number of assets is large. As we've seen, even for a very small portfolio of three assets the expression to estimate its risk is not simple. Formally, the standard deviation of an *n*-asset portfolio can be written as

$$SD_p = \left\{ \sum_{i=1}^{n} \sum_{j=1}^{n} x_i \cdot x_j \cdot Cov_{ij} \right\}^{1/2} \tag{4.7}$$

It doesn't look that scary, but that may be simply because the two sum signs are hiding the burden. In a relatively small portfolio of 20 assets, expression (4.7) implies that we have to come up with 400 terms. For all practical purposes, we may as well forget this expression, which is just another way of saying that, when calculating the standard deviation of a portfolio, we'd better have a spreadsheet at hand.

However, even with a spreadsheet, we need to know what to do. The optimization tool we'll build for Excel in Chapter 11 provides a simple way to estimate both the risk and return of a portfolio for any number of assets. In any case, when calculating the standard deviation of a portfolio, it's important to keep in mind the following. First, we need as many 'variance terms,' $(x_i)^2(SD_i)^2$, as assets we have in the portfolio. Second, we need to determine every possible combination of assets (1-2, 1-3, ..., 1-n, 2-3, 2-4, ..., 2-n, ...) and write down two 'covariance terms' for each; that is, $2 \cdot x_1 \cdot x_2 \cdot Cov_{12}$, ..., $2 \cdot x_1 \cdot x_n \cdot Cov_{1n}$, ..., $2 \cdot x_2 \cdot x_3 \cdot Cov_{23}$, ..., $2 \cdot x_2 \cdot x_n \cdot Cov_{2n}$, ... Third, we need to add up all the terms. And fourth, we need to take the square root of the sum.

Sometimes it may help to visualize the variance–covariance matrix, including all the relevant weights. In the general, n-asset case, this matrix looks like the one displayed in Table 4.2.

table 4.2

	1	2	3	...	n
1	$(x_1)^2(SD_1)^2$	$x_1 \cdot x_2 \cdot Cov_{12}$	$x_1 \cdot x_3 \cdot Cov_{13}$	...	$x_1 \cdot x_n \cdot Cov_{1n}$
2	$x_2 \cdot x_1 \cdot Cov_{21}$	$(x_2)^2(SD_2)^2$	$x_2 \cdot x_3 \cdot Cov_{23}$	...	$x_2 \cdot x_n \cdot Cov_{2n}$
...	...	...	...	...	...
n	$x_n \cdot x_1 \cdot Cov_{n1}$	$x_n \cdot x_2 \cdot Cov_{n2}$	$x_n \cdot x_3 \cdot Cov_{n3}$	...	$(x_n)^2(SD_n)^2$

Note that, at the end of the day and regardless of the number of assets, *the variance of a portfolio is given by the sum of all the elements in this matrix*, and the standard deviation of the portfolio by the square root of this variance. Think about this matrix a bit and relate it to our previous discussion for portfolios of two and three assets. If you were able to follow that discussion, you should have no trouble writing down this matrix for any number of assets.

Finally, note that the feasible set, efficient set, and MVP of an n-asset portfolio, when n is larger than 2, look just like those in Figure 4.2. In other words, the feasible set is a bullet-shaped surface; the MVP is the point farthest to the left of the feasible set; and the efficient set is the upper border of the feasible set beginning at the MVP.

The big picture

Calculating the risk and return of a portfolio may be time consuming without a spreadsheet or some other specialized software. However, the intuition behind the calculations is relatively simple. The same applies to some portfolios in which investors may be particularly interested, such as those in the efficient set or the minimum variance portfolio. In Chapter 11 we'll build an optimizer in Excel that quickly and easily estimates all the portfolios discussed in this chapter.

Importantly, note that this chapter is mostly about mechanics; that is, about *how to calculate* the risk and return of different portfolios. But we still haven't discussed *why* investors may want to build portfolios. That is precisely the issue we'll discuss in the next chapter.

Excel section

There are two new concepts in this chapter to implement in Excel, covariance and correlation. Both are very easy to deal with. Suppose you have two series of ten returns each, the first in cells A1–A10 and the second in cells B1–B10. Then you do the following:

■ To calculate the *covariance* between the assets, type

=covar(A1:A10, B1:B10)

in cell A11 and then hit Enter.

■ To calculate the *correlation coefficient* between the assets, type

=correl(A1:A10, B1:B10)

in cell A12 and then hit Enter.

You may also find it useful to know that in Excel you can sum numbers not only along a row or a column but also over a whole matrix, such as the variance–covariance matrix discussed in this chapter. Suppose you have a 3×3 variance–covariance matrix in the range A1:C3.

■ To sum all the elements in the matrix, type

=sum(A1:C3)

in cell D4 and hit Enter.

5

Risk II: Diversification

T he idea that the risk of an asset can be thought of as the volatility of its returns measured by the standard deviation seems plausible, doesn't it? Well, the problem is that it doesn't extend well to portfolios of assets. And diversification, the issue discussed in this chapter, is the main culprit. You have probably heard the expression 'Don't put all your eggs in one basket.' At the end of the day, this chapter explores the financial side of that time-tested truth.

Three hypothetical assets

Let's start by considering the returns of the three hypothetical assets in Table 5.1. We know by now how to calculate their arithmetic mean return (AM) and standard deviation (SD), which are also reported in the table. And given those volatilities, we can agree that asset 1 ($SD = 10.0\%$) is riskier than asset 3 ($SD = 5.0\%$), which in turn is riskier than asset 2 ($SD = 1.5\%$).

Now, instead of thinking of each of these assets individually, let's think of combinations of them. Let's combine, for example, assets 1 and 2. Suppose that at the beginning of year 1 we invest $1,000, 13% in asset 1 and 87% in asset 2. We know by now how to calculate the return of this portfolio in any given year; in the first year, for example, the return is $(0.13)(0.250) + (0.87)(0.213) = 21.7\%$. And if we calculate in the same way the return of the portfolio in all subsequent years we find … surprise! The return of the portfolio *each and every year* is the exact same 21.7%!

Year	Asset 1 (%)	Asset 2 (%)	Asset 3 (%)
1	25.0	21.3	32.5
2	5.0	24.3	22.5
3	22.5	21.6	31.3
4	6.0	24.1	23.0
5	17.5	22.4	28.8
6	4.0	24.4	22.0
7	31.0	20.4	35.5
8	5.5	24.2	22.8
9	24.0	21.4	32.0
10	4.0	24.4	22.0
AM	**14.5**	**22.8**	**27.2**
SD	**10.0**	**1.5**	**5.0**

Nope, not kidding. Take a look at Figure 5.1, which plots the returns of assets 1 and 2, as well as the return of the 13–87 portfolio. Although assets 1 and 2 fluctuate over time, the return of the portfolio remains constant at a 21.7% return. Magic? Not really. But before we discuss what's going on, let's consider another combination of these hypothetical assets.

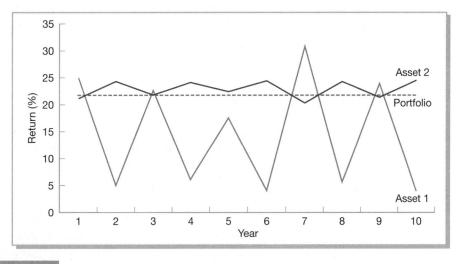

figure 5.1   **Maximum diversification**

Suppose now that at the beginning of the first year, we split our $1,000 evenly between assets 1 and 3. Figure 5.2 plots the returns of these two assets as well as the returns of the equally-weighted (50–50) portfolio. Pretty different picture, huh?

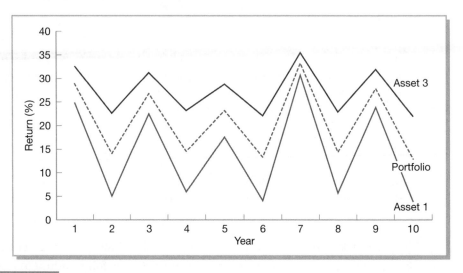

figure 5.2   **No diversification**

If we compare the two-asset portfolios in Figures 5.1 and 5.2, it is obvious that they are different; the first has no volatility, although it results from the combination of two volatile assets, whereas the second is pretty much as volatile as the two assets it contains. If you're wondering what is the main driver of this result, you're asking the right question.

The correlation coefficient

So what is the main driver? If we combine two assets, what is the factor that determines that in one case we end up with a portfolio that yields a constant return, while in the other we end up with a very volatile portfolio? It all comes down to one parameter: The correlation coefficient.

This coefficient, which is also discussed in Chapter 27, measures the strength of the (linear) relationship between two variables. Such a relationship can be positive or negative, weak or strong. When two variables tend to move in the same direction this coefficient is positive, and when they tend to move in opposite directions this coefficient is negative. It can take a minimum value of

–1 and a maximum value of 1, with these two extremes indicating a perfect (linear) relationship. The closer a correlation is to –1 or 1, the stronger is the relationship between the underlying variables; the closer a correlation is to 0, the weaker is the relationship between the variables.

Importantly, although the theoretical extremes of this parameter are –1 and 1, for reasonably long periods of time it is nearly impossible to find a negative correlation between two stocks within a market, or between two equity markets. We'll explore why in the next chapter, but for now keep in mind that the *empirical* values of the correlation coefficient are within a much narrower band than the theoretical [–1, 1] range.

Back to the two portfolios we've been discussing, what's going on between assets 1 and 2? Simply that they are perfectly negatively correlated; that is, their correlation is –1. In such situations, we can always find a specific combination of the two assets that would enable us to lock a fixed return and therefore have a 0-volatility portfolio. Unfortunately, however interesting or appealing this may sound, it has little practical importance; assets with a very strong negative correlation, let alone with a correlation of –1, are almost impossible to find.

What's going on, in turn, between assets 1 and 3? Pretty much the opposite. They are perfectly positively correlated (that is, their correlation is 1), and in such situations the volatility of a portfolio is always equal to the (weighted) average volatility of the two assets in the portfolio. In other words, in terms of risk reduction, there is nothing to gain by combining these two assets.

In fact, the *only* case in which the volatility of a two-asset portfolio is equal to the weighted-average volatility of the assets in the portfolio is when the correlation between the assets is 1. In every other case, the risk of the portfolio is *lower* than the weighted average of the individual risks. Formally, then, we could say that

$$SD_p \leq x_1 \cdot SD_1 + x_2 \cdot SD_2 \tag{5.1}$$

where SD_p is the volatility of the portfolio; SD_i is the volatility of asset i; and x_i is the proportion of the portfolio invested in asset i. If the correlation between assets 1 and 2 is 1, then the equality holds; if this correlation is lower than 1, then the left-hand side (the volatility of the portfolio) is lower than the right-hand side (the weighted-average volatility); and the lower this correlation is, the lower is the volatility of the portfolio relative to the weighted-average volatility. If the goal is to reduce risk, then, we should look for assets with low correlations to each other; the lower, the better.

Importantly, don't think of the correlation coefficient as a statistical magnitude with little practical importance. We simply cannot build a proper portfolio if we disregard the correlations between assets. These correlations are the main determinant of the extent to which risk can be reduced by combining assets. When you think of the risk of a portfolio, don't just think about the volatility of each individual asset; make sure you also think about how the assets move relative to each other.

An example may help to drive this point home. Emerging markets taken individually are very volatile, but the correlations between them are rather low. Therefore, when we combine emerging markets into a portfolio, we find that the volatility of the portfolio is substantially lower than the volatility of the average emerging market. To illustrate, over the 1988–2009 period, the annualized volatility of the MSCI Emerging Markets Index was around 24%; however, the average volatility of the components of this index was around 37%. It is precisely the low correlations between these markets that largely determines this result. We could go over countless other examples, but hopefully you've already got the point: Don't underestimate the *practical* importance of the correlation coefficient.

Three views on diversification

So, what is diversification? The popular way to think about it is as the combination of assets into a portfolio with the goal of reducing risk. Nothing wrong with that, but there's more to diversification than risk reduction. As we'll discuss in a minute, diversification can be thought of in other ways, and its ultimate goal is more comprehensive than just reducing risk.

Now, many people do diversify to avoid having all their money invested in an individual asset that unexpectedly tanks and takes their whole portfolio with it. Think about Enron. Many employees had over 90% of their pension money invested in Enron stock when the company went bankrupt. That's a lesson in diversification learned the hard way!

Having said that, it is important to keep in mind that diversification can be thought of in at least three other ways, all of them very useful though often less explored. Take a look at panel A of Table 5.2, which shows the returns of Boeing and IBM between the years 2000 and 2009. As the figures in this panel show, during this period Boeing delivered a higher return than IBM, and it did so with higher volatility. The correlation between these two stocks (not reported in the table) is a very low 0.04, which points to potentially-high diversification benefits.

table 5.2

	Panel A				Panel B		
Year	Boeing (%)	IBM (%)	x_1 (%)	x_2 (%)	Return (%)	Risk (%)	RAR
2000	61.3	−20.8	100.0	0.0	11.1	34.1	0.324
2001	−40.4	43.0	90.0	10.0	10.6	30.9	0.344
2002	−13.4	−35.5	80.0	20.0	10.2	28.1	0.364
2003	30.4	20.5	70.0	30.0	9.8	25.7	0.382
2004	24.9	7.2	60.0	40.0	9.4	23.8	0.394
2005	37.9	−15.8	50.0	50.0	9.0	22.7	0.396
2006	28.4	19.8	40.0	60.0	8.6	22.3	0.383
2007	−0.1	12.8	30.0	70.0	8.1	22.8	0.357
2008	−50.0	−20.8	20.0	80.0	7.7	24.2	0.320
2009	31.7	58.6	10.0	90.0	7.3	26.1	0.280
AM	11.1	6.9	0.0	100.0	6.9	28.7	0.241
SD	34.1	28.7					

Panel B of Table 5.2 shows different portfolios of Boeing and IBM. The first two columns of this panel show the weights of Boeing (x_1) and IBM (x_2) in the portfolios; the next two columns the mean annual return and risk of the portfolios considered, based on the performance of these two companies over the whole 2000–09 period; and we'll get to the last column in a minute. The 'Return' and 'Risk' columns can be used to plot the feasible set, which is shown in Figure 5.3.

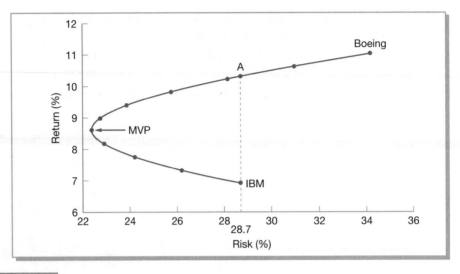

figure 5.3   **Feasible set for Boeing and IBM**

Let's first consider the minimum variance portfolio (MVP); that is, the combination of Boeing and IBM that yields the lowest possible risk. As we discussed in the previous chapter, this portfolio is very easy to determine in the two-asset case. If you crunch the numbers, you will find that investing 41% in Boeing and 59% in IBM yields a portfolio with a standard deviation of 22.3% (and a return of 8.6%), which is as low as it gets when combining these two stocks. In fact, the volatility of this portfolio is 22.33%, just a tiny bit lower than the 22.34% volatility of the 40–60 portfolio shown in panel B of Table 5.2.

Now, if you think about it, this portfolio highlights a slightly different reason for diversifying: If we're happy holding IBM, we should be even happier to hold the MVP. This is so because the MVP, relative to holding IBM by itself, has *both* a lower volatility (22.3% versus 28.7%) *and* a higher return (8.6% versus 6.9%). In other words, *diversification may enable investors to lower risk and at the same time increase returns*.

Let's also consider a slightly different perspective. It is possible that we're comfortable with (or used to) bearing the volatility of any given asset, like IBM in our example. Fine. But what if someone offered us an asset with the same volatility but a higher return? Wouldn't we want it? Of course we would, and that is just what we can obtain through diversification.

Take a look at the portfolio labeled A in Figure 5.3. Given the choice between putting your money in IBM or in portfolio A, what would you choose? Exactly. Portfolio A has an 82.1% allocation to Boeing and a 17.9% allocation to IBM, and by construction has the same volatility as IBM (28.7%). However, this portfolio has a 10.3% mean annual return, which is 3.4 percentage points higher than the mean annual return of IBM (6.9%). That is as close to a free lunch as we can get in financial markets! Why would you ever hold IBM by itself when you can hold a portfolio with the same level of risk but a higher return? This brings us to another way of thinking about diversification: *It may enable investors to increase returns given a target level of risk.*

Now, it seems that convincing someone who's happy holding IBM to diversify would be an easy task; both the MVP and portfolio A would make any investor better off. But here's a challenge: How would you convince someone who's happy holding *Boeing* to diversify? We obviously can't give this investor the same reasons we discussed before. We cannot offer him a portfolio with lower risk *and* a higher return, or one with the same risk but a higher return; we can only offer him less risk *if* he's willing to sacrifice some return. Is it, then, that diversification is not beneficial for someone who's happy holding a high-return, high-risk asset such as Boeing? Does it work only for holders of low-return, low-risk assets such as IBM?

The ultimate benefit of diversification

Not really. Investors do not just care about returns; they also care about risk. In fact, what investors really care about are *risk-adjusted returns*. There are different ways of defining this concept (which we'll explore in Chapter 10), but for the time being let's simply think about it as return divided by risk; that is, the return obtained per unit of risk borne. This is exactly what the last column of Table 5.2 shows: The **risk-adjusted return (RAR)** defined as the 'Return' column divided by the 'Risk' column.

Can you see now why, even if we're happy holding all our money in Boeing, it would be beneficial for us to diversify? Because we can increase the risk-adjusted return of our portfolio. In our case, the 'best' portfolio of those shown in Table 5.2 is a 50–50 split between Boeing and IBM, simply because it is the portfolio with the highest RAR (0.396).

Having said that, of all the (infinite) possible combinations between Boeing and IBM, the portfolio with the highest RAR is not shown in the table. It consists of an investment of 53.6% in Boeing and 46.4% in IBM, and it would have a RAR of 0.397, just slightly higher than that of the 50–50 portfolio. The portfolio-optimization tool discussed in Chapter 11 can find this optimal combination in the blink of an eye.

Importantly, unless the correlation between two assets is exactly equal to 1 (largely an empirical impossibility), it will never be the case that the highest RAR is delivered by a portfolio fully invested in one asset. In other words, the portfolio with the highest RAR has a positive allocation in both assets and is therefore diversified. Which brings us to the best way to think about why diversification is beneficial: *It enables investors to enhance, and ultimately to maximize, risk-adjusted returns.* And, don't forget, that's the most we could ever ask for of any investment strategy. In short, when grandma told us not to put all our eggs in one basket, she was, as usual, wiser than we probably gave her credit for.

The role of funds

At this point you hopefully have little or no doubts about the benefits of diversification. But in case you're still doubtful, just look around you. The number of mutual funds, index funds, and ETFs (exchange-traded funds) has been growing at a staggering rate throughout the world. And a lot of that explosive growth has to do with the fact that these financial instruments provide investors with broad and low-cost diversification.

Think about the obstacles that an individual investor faces when trying to diversify his portfolio broadly. First, he would have to consider thousands of assets and choose wisely from that huge pool. Then he would have to decide how much to invest in each of the selected assets. And after investing a great deal of his time to determine the composition of his portfolio, he would still have to go through the worst part: Paying the substantial brokerage fees to buy, one by one, the chosen assets. Those fees are certainly going to be much higher than those paid by the big boys in Wall Street.

Compare all that with buying shares in a financial instrument that aims to track (index funds and ETFs) or outperform (mutual funds) a benchmark chosen by the investor. By buying shares in a fund, he solves the problems of determining which assets to buy, how much money to put in each, and importantly, the high cost of building a broadly-diversified portfolio. Just one share in a fund may represent ownership in hundreds of companies. There's no question about it, when considering how to diversify properly, it doesn't get any better than investing through funds.

The big picture

Most investors diversify their holdings and they do so for a good reason: To lower the risk of their portfolios. But diversification is not about just risk reduction; it is about enhancing and ultimately maximizing risk-adjusted returns.

A critical part of the process of building a diversified portfolio is the correlation coefficient. Far from being a 'statistical thing' with little practical importance, this magnitude plays a central role in the selection of assets to be included in portfolios.

If you're still not convinced that diversification is essential, there are two things you can do. First, just think about the explosive growth of funds that offer broad diversification at a low cost. And second, read the next chapter, where we elaborate on the benefits of diversification.

Excel section

There is no new Excel material in this chapter. The calculation of the portfolio that maximizes risk-adjusted returns is not trivial and we need more advanced tools to handle it. The optimization tool we'll discuss in Chapter 11 will enable us to do that and more.

6

Risk III: Systematic risk

B y now we know that when assessing the risk of a portfolio there is more to it than the volatility of each individual asset. In this chapter we'll explore why this is the case, and while we're at it, we'll end up refining the way we assess risk. We'll also explore the role of correlations in portfolios and briefly discuss the benefits of international diversification.

Total risk and systematic risk

When we started our discussion of risk in Chapter 3 we stressed that unlike the concept of return, which is straightforward, the concept of risk is slippery. That's one of the reasons why more than one chapter of this book is allocated to discuss it from different points of view. Having said that, we've been arguing that a possible way to think about risk is as volatility, or the standard deviation of an asset's returns.

In fact, under some conditions, that is the most widely-accepted way to think about risk. What are the conditions? Basically that we consider an asset in isolation, as opposed to being part of a portfolio. Yes, risk does depend on the context on which we evaluate it and that should come as no surprise. Giving darts to a monkey and setting him loose on the street may be dangerous, but giving him the darts in a crystal cage may be less so.

Let's think about volatility for a minute. We see stock prices fluctuating all the time. Have you ever wondered why? Of course we can think of a million reasons, but let's try to fit all possible reasons into two boxes. Let's put in one box all the factors that are specific to the companies behind the stocks. You know, a new chief executive, the introduction of a new product, the departure of a well-known executive, a competitor's release of a better technology, good and bad corporate decisions ... you get the picture. These and many others are all idiosyncratic factors that originate in a company (or perhaps in the industry) and affect the company's stock price (and perhaps that of its competitors).

Now, there are also many factors that affect a company's stock price that are unrelated to the company. Think about, for example, macroeconomic events, such as changes in interest rates, in expected inflation, or in the expected growth of the economy, to name but a few. Or think about political events, such as elections. Or think, more generally, about any event that affects the economy as a whole. These economy-wide factors influence the stock price of all companies, at the same time, and largely in the same direction (though not necessarily to the same extent). That's our second box.

Let's give names to these two boxes before we go on. The idiosyncratic events that originate in the company or the industry are usually referred to as *unsystematic factors*; the economy-wide events exogenous to the company are usually called *systematic factors*. Most of the time we should have little trouble placing most of the events that affect stock prices into one of these two boxes, which is another way to say that volatility is determined by systematic and unsystematic factors. Or, put differently, *total risk is the sum of systematic (or market) risk plus unsystematic (or idiosyncratic) risk.*

Diversification again

In the previous chapter we discussed more than one way to think about the benefits from diversification; now we'll discuss where those benefits come from. Suppose we (unwisely) invest all our money in one stock. In that case, the risk of our (one-asset) portfolio is given by the total risk of this stock; that is, by the standard deviation of its returns.

Now suppose we decide to add another stock to our portfolio. As we discussed in the previous chapter, as long as this second stock is not perfectly correlated to the one we already have, then we will obtain some diversification benefits. Note that in a two-stock portfolio, events that affect the returns of either one stock or the other *only partially* will affect our portfolio. Also, it now becomes possible that if one stock is hit by bad news, good news on the other stock may partially or fully offset the losses in our portfolio.

What happens as we add more and more stocks to our portfolio? The same thing over and over again: The more stocks we have, the lower is the impact of bad (and good) news about one stock on the whole portfolio; and the more that the many idiosyncratic factors that affect the price of the stocks in our portfolio will cancel each other out. In a fully-diversified portfolio, the whole impact of unsystematic events vanishes and we're left bearing only systematic risk. In other words, diversification is a way of reducing, and in the limit eliminating, *unsystematic* risk.

Figure 6.1 displays a graphical representation of the preceding arguments. The graph assumes that we start with one stock that has a volatility of 30%; in that case, that's also the risk of our (one-stock) portfolio. We then add a second stock that has the same 30% volatility, a correlation of 0.5 with the first stock, and we form an equally-weighted portfolio. And then we keep doing the same thing over and over; that is, adding stocks with a volatility of 30%, a correlation of 0.5 to the stocks already in the portfolio, and forming equally-weighted portfolios. Your eyes will tell you most of what you need to know.

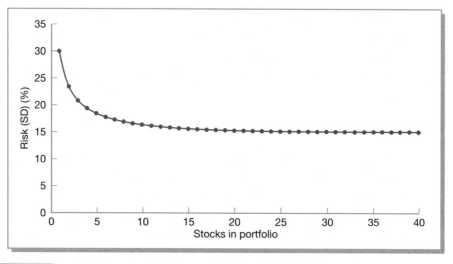

figure 6.1   Limits to diversification

First and obvious, note that each additional stock decreases the volatility of the overall portfolio. Second, note that as we add more stocks the risk of the portfolio falls at a decreasing rate; that is, each additional stock reduces risk a bit less than the previous one. Eventually, adding more assets to the portfolio reduces risk by a negligible amount, at which point we have achieved a fully-diversified portfolio. In that situation, all the unsystematic risk has been diversified away and we're left bearing only the systematic risk. It should come as no surprise, then, that unsystematic risk is sometimes referred to as *diversifiable* risk, and systematic risk as *undiversifiable* risk.

The reason why we can't diversify away the systematic risk is hopefully clear by now. As we discussed before, these are economy-wide factors that affect all companies, at the same time, and largely in the same direction, and therefore there's no escaping from these events. (Well, that's not entirely true, but more on this later.)

It should also become clear now why finding stocks with a negative correlation is almost impossible in practice. Although unsystematic factors may push different stocks in different directions, the systematic factor pushes all of them in the same direction. This induces a positive correlation among all stocks in the market, from which the limit on the benefits from diversification follows.

All this explains why diversification enables us to reduce risk but never to eliminate it completely. How much risk we can diversify away, however, is an empirical question with a different answer across markets and over time. And much the same could be said about the number of stocks we need to achieve a fully-diversified portfolio; estimates vary widely across markets and over time. In short, it is pointless to discuss these two issues without a specific market and point in time in mind.

Now, how do we assess an asset's risk if instead of being considered in isolation we consider it within a diversified portfolio? The calculations are less than trivial and the intuition less than great, but the bottom line is this: The risk of a stock that is part of a diversified portfolio is measured *by the contribution of the stock to the risk of the portfolio*. This contribution can be assessed in absolute or in relative terms; the absolute contribution is measured by the covariance between the stock and the portfolio, and the relative contribution by the beta of the stock relative to the portfolio.

Feel like you just heard Sylvester Stallone speaking Chinese again? Fear not, an example's coming right up.

An example

Table 6.1 shows the annual returns of three companies, Apple, Hewlett Packard (HP), and Microsoft, as well as an equally-weighted portfolio of these three companies, between 2000 and 2009. It also shows, for 2000–09, the arithmetic mean return (*AM*) and volatility (*SD*) of each stock, the covariance between each stock and the equally-weighted portfolio, and the beta of each stock relative to the same portfolio. (Note that, by definition, the covariance between the portfolio and itself is the portfolio's variance, and the beta of the portfolio relative to itself is 1.)

table 6.1

Year	Apple (%)	HP (%)	Microsoft (%)	Portfolio (%)
2000	−71.1	−28.6	−62.8	−54.2
2001	47.2	−34.0	52.7	22.0
2002	−34.6	−13.9	−22.0	−23.5
2003	49.1	34.5	6.8	30.1
2004	201.4	−7.3	8.9	67.7
2005	123.3	38.3	−0.9	53.5
2006	18.0	45.2	15.8	26.4
2007	133.5	23.4	20.8	59.2
2008	−56.9	−27.6	−44.4	−43.0
2009	146.9	43.2	60.5	83.5
AM (%)	**55.7**	**7.3**	**3.5**	**22.2**
SD (%)	**88.6**	**30.9**	**36.8**	**45.2**
Covariance	**0.3815**	**0.0947**	**0.1366**	**0.2043**
Beta	**1.868**	**0.464**	**0.669**	**1.000**

We know that the mean return of the equally-weighted portfolio is given by the weighted average of mean returns, which in this case is $(1/3)(0.557+0.073+0.035) = 22.2\%$. But right now we're more interested in the risk of this portfolio, for which we need all variances and covariances, which are shown in panel A of Table 6.2.

table 6.2

Panel A	Apple	HP	Microsoft
Apple	0.7858	0.1363	0.2223
HP	0.1363	0.0956	0.0523
Microsoft	0.2223	0.0523	0.1353
Panel B	Apple	HP	Microsoft
Apple	0.0873	0.0151	0.0247
HP	0.0151	0.0106	0.0058
Microsoft	0.0247	0.0058	0.0150
Panel C	Apple	HP	Microsoft
Sum	0.1272	0.0316	0.0455
Proportion	0.623	0.155	0.223

We know that the risk of any portfolio is given by the sum of all the elements in the variance–covariance matrix, which contains all the relevant variances, covariances, *and weights*. (If this is not clear to you, take a look at Chapter 4.) That is precisely what is shown in panel B of Table 6.2. The 0.0873, for example, is calculated as (1/3)(1/3)(0.7858); the 0.0151 is calculated as (1/3)(1/3)(0.1363); and so on. The sum of these nine elements yields the variance of the equally-weighted portfolio (0.2043); and the square root of this number yields its standard deviation (45.2%).

Note that the 45.2% volatility of the portfolio is lower than the weighted average of the individual volatilities, which is (1/3)(0.886+0.309+0.368) = 52.1%. The difference between these two figures is the result of diversification. In other words, when we put these three stocks together in a portfolio, part of their unsystematic risk vanishes and the risk of the portfolio is lower than the weighted average of the individual risks.

Let's focus now on panel C of Table 6.2. The row labeled 'Sum' is the vertical sum of the rows in panel B; for example, 0.0873+0.0151+0.0247 = 0.1272. Each of these 'Sum' figures is equal to the *covariance* between a stock and the portfolio, multiplied by the weight of the stock in the portfolio; for example, 0.1272 = (1/3)(0.3815), with 0.3815 being the covariance between Apple stock and the equally-weighted portfolio (as shown in Table 6.1). Each of these 'Sum' figures represents the *absolute contribution* of each stock to the risk of the portfolio, so that if we add them up we obtain the risk of the portfolio as measured by its variance; that is, 0.1272+0.0316+0.0455 = 0.2043.

In the same panel, the figures in the row labeled 'Proportion' are calculated as the figures in the 'Sum' row divided by the variance of the portfolio; for example, 0.1272/0.2043 = 0.623. Each of these 'Proportion' figures is equal to the *beta* of a stock relative to the portfolio, multiplied by the weight of the stock in the portfolio; for example, 0.623 = (1/3)(1.868), with 1.868 being the *beta* of Apple stock relative to the equally-weighted portfolio (as shown in Table 6.1). Each of these 'Proportion' figures represents the *relative contribution* of the stock to the risk of the portfolio, so that if we add them up we obtain 1; that is, 0.623+0.155+0.223 = 1. These figures suggest that Apple, HP, and Microsoft contribute 62.3%, 15.5%, and 22.3% of the risk of the equally-weighted portfolio.

In short, then, the risk of an individual stock that is part of a portfolio is measured by its contribution to the risk of the portfolio. The absolute contribution is measured by the covariance between a stock and the portfolio, and the relative contribution by the beta of a stock relative to the portfolio. We'll formally define and discuss betas in the next chapter but for the time being note that, as we just discussed, they are calculated as the covariance between the returns of a stock and those of the portfolio divided by the variance of the portfolio returns.

A brief digression on covariances

It is hopefully clear by now that the risk of an asset depends on the context in which it is evaluated. If we consider an asset in isolation, its risk is measured by the standard deviation of its returns; if we consider the same asset within a diversified portfolio, its risk is measured by its beta. In the first case, we bear the asset's total risk; in the second case we bear only its systematic risk. The larger the number of assets in a portfolio, the less relevant is the total risk of each asset and the more relevant is the asset's contribution to the risk of the portfolio.

We can reinforce this idea by considering two additional perspectives. First, note that as the number of assets in a portfolio grows, the number of covariances grows much faster than the number of variances. In a 2-asset portfolio, we have 2 variances and 2 covariances; in a 20-asset portfolio we have 20 variances and 380 covariances; in a 100-asset portfolio we have 100 variances and 9,900 covariances. Which do you think will have more impact on the risk of the portfolio, those few variances or those very many covariances?

Second, let's make a couple of assumptions that are not really necessary to get to the final conclusion but we'll make them just to get the point across more easily. Assume, first, that all the n assets in a portfolio have the same variance (let's call it V); second, that the covariance between any two assets in the portfolio is the same (let's call it C); and third, that we invest an equal amount in each of the n assets (which makes all weights equal to $1/n$). Then, the risk of this portfolio, measured by its variance (Var_p), is given by

$$Var_p = n \cdot \left(\frac{1}{n}\right)^2 \cdot V + (n^2 - n) \cdot \left(\frac{1}{n}\right)^2 \cdot C = \left(\frac{1}{n}\right) \cdot V + \left(1 - \frac{1}{n}\right) \cdot C \tag{6.1}$$

Just in case this expression looks complicated, let's think about it a bit. We have n assets, n variances, n^2-n covariances, the weight of each asset is $1/n$, all the variances are the same (V), and all the covariances are the same (C). Got that? OK then, now think what happens as we increase the number of assets in the portfolio. As n grows, $(1/n) \cdot V$ tends to 0, $(1-1/n) \cdot C$ tends to C, and therefore Var_p tends to C. In words, as the number of assets grows, the risk of the portfolio becomes largely determined by covariances and largely independent of variances.

Finally, and importantly, note that everything we said about covariances also applies to correlations. More precisely, it is indeed the case that the larger the number of assets in the portfolio, the less relevant is the risk (volatility) of each individual asset and the more relevant are the correlations between the assets. As we argued in the previous chapter, then, correlations are essential to assess the risk of a portfolio properly.

A brief digression on international diversification

So far we have been implicitly thinking of portfolios of stocks within a given market. That's why, after obtaining a fully-diversified portfolio that eliminates all the unsystematic risk, we are left bearing the (undiversifiable) systematic risk of any given market. But think about it: Why end there?

Suppose we have a fully-diversified portfolio of US stocks and we're therefore subject to the systematic risk of the US market. Now, there's no reason to think that the factors that affect Japanese stocks should be perfectly correlated to those that affect US stocks. In fact, there are good reasons to think otherwise; think of events in the US that would be irrelevant to Japanese stocks, and events in Japan that would be irrelevant to US stocks. Which means that if we add Japanese stocks to our portfolio, its risk should fall. That's good; but again, why end there?

What about European stocks? Same story. As long as the factors that affect European stocks are not perfectly correlated to those that affect American and Japanese stocks, and of course they never are, European stocks should provide diversification benefits. In other words, the risk of our portfolio should fall again.

Can you see where we're going? In the same way that within a market we add stocks to our portfolio until we are fully diversified in that market, we can also add international stocks (or markets) to our portfolio until we are fully diversified internationally. And, needless to say, the volatility of a fully-diversified portfolio of international stocks is lower than that of a fully-diversified portfolio of stocks in any single country.

Now for the bad news, which you probably expected anyway. No matter how many stocks from how many countries we include in our portfolio, we will never be able to eliminate risk; we'll only be able to reduce it. In other words, even the world market is subject to systematic factors (international crises, conflicts, oil prices, and so on) that will prevent us from eliminating the risk of our portfolio. As before, proper diversification will enable us to eliminate all the unsystematic risk but only to reduce the total risk. Although it is lower in a portfolio diversified across international markets than in one diversified only within a local market, there's really no escaping from systematic risk.

But wait. Note that our discussion focused on diversifying across stocks within a market and across international *equity* markets. However, a proper diversification should not restrict the scope only to stocks; diversification *across asset classes* is essential. A properly-diversified portfolio should contain not just stocks but also bonds, commodities, real estate, and more. In other words, put your eggs in different baskets, and make sure that the baskets have many colors and sizes.

The big picture

However volatile an asset might be, we don't have to bear all its risk; that's one of the reasons why we diversify. But diversification does not eliminate risk; it merely reduces it. How much we can reduce risk and how many stocks make up a fully-diversified portfolio are empirical questions that depend on the time and place we ask the question. In both cases, the estimates vary widely across countries and over time.

Unlike an asset in isolation, whose risk is measured by its volatility, the risk of an asset within a diversified portfolio is measured by the *contribution* of the asset to the risk of the portfolio. This contribution can be assessed in absolute terms by the covariance between the asset and the portfolio, or in relative terms by the asset's beta. And this relative contribution to portfolio risk is, as we'll discuss in the next chapter, the measure of risk in the CAPM, the most widely used asset pricing model.

7

Risk and return II: CAPM and the cost of capital

I t is obvious that investors expect to be compensated with a higher return the higher the risk they are exposed to. The question is, how much more? That is precisely what one of the most widely-used models in finance, the CAPM, is designed to answer. The required return on equity the CAPM enables us to estimate, in turn, is a critical component of the cost of capital, an essential magnitude for every company. These are the issues we'll discuss in this chapter.

Required returns

Question: What is the *minimum* return we should require from a *risk-free* investment before parting with our money for one year? Let's see. If we take $100 from our pocket to put in a risk-free investment opportunity for one year, it looks like the least we should require is not to lose purchasing power. In other words, we would require that, one year down the road, we're still able to buy the same amount of goods and services that we can buy today with $100. Actually, maybe we should demand a bit more than that; otherwise, why bother reaching for our wallet? But not much more; after all, we're not really bearing any risk.

So it looks like we should require a small compensation over and above the expected loss of purchasing power. And that is, roughly, the return we would get if we deposited our money in the bank for one year. It is also, roughly, the rate we would get if we bought a one-year Treasury bill. Both rates track very closely the expected (and ultimately the observed) rate of inflation. In fact, over the 1900–2000 period, the mean annual rate of inflation in the US was 3.3% and the mean annual return of US Treasury bills was 4.1%.

Now, what if instead of risk-free the investment were risky, in the sense that we would be uncertain about the amount of money to be received one year down the road? Obviously, in this case we would require a higher return. How much higher? That depends on the risk or uncertainty of the investment; the higher the risk we perceive, the higher the return we'd require.

Let's formalize this discussion a bit by stating that the required return on any asset is the sum of two components, a risk-free rate and a risk premium. The risk-free rate is the compensation for the expected loss of purchasing power, and the risk premium is the compensation for bearing the risk of the asset. More formally, the **required or expected return on asset *i*** is given by

$$E(R_i) = R_f + RP_i \tag{7.1}$$

where R_f denotes the risk-free rate and RP_i the risk premium of asset *i*.

It is important to notice the subscript *i* on $E(R_i)$ and RP_i but not on R_f. Intuitively, this means that *regardless* of the asset in which we invest, we always require the same compensation for the expected loss of purchasing power. However, *depending* on the asset in which we invest, we require an additional compensation for bearing the risk of *that* asset. In other words, when estimating the required return on two different assets, in both cases we would start from the *same risk-free rate*, then add *different risk premiums* for each asset, and obtain a *different required return*.

CAPM: Overview

The capital asset pricing model (CAPM) is one of the most widely-used models in finance. And that is for the very simple reason that it yields an essential result: The return investors should require from an asset given the asset's risk. Surprising as it may seem, until the CAPM was developed in the mid-1960s, no model provided investors with such a critical number. Sure, academics and practitioners agreed that given two assets with different risk, investors should require a higher return from the riskier asset. But no model enabled investors to estimate *how much more* they should require.

Take another look at expression (7.1). To calculate the required return on an asset we need a risk-free rate and a risk premium; the former is the same for all assets and the latter is specific to each asset. The CAPM defines a measure of risk and makes an asset's risk premium a function of that magnitude. Essentially, then, the CAPM is a model that provides investors with a formal way to estimate the risk premium, and therefore the required return, of an asset. Here, in a nutshell, is how.

The CAPM follows from a framework in which an investor aims to maximize his utility, which depends on the risk and return of his portfolio. In equilibrium, this investor ends up splitting his money between two assets: Part of his money is invested in a fully-diversified basket of risky assets called the *market portfolio* (*M*) and part of his money is invested at a risk-free rate. The market portfolio is the optimal combination of *risky* assets in the sense that it maximizes risk-adjusted returns. It contains no unsystematic risk (which has been diversified away), and therefore the risk of each individual asset is measured by the contribution of the asset to the risk of this portfolio. That contribution, as discussed in the previous chapter, is measured by beta, and that is, precisely, the CAPM's definition of risk.

Although the CAPM can in principle be used to estimate the required return on any asset, more often than not it is used to estimate the required return on *equity*. For that reason, from now on we'll focus our discussion on stocks. As suggested in the previous chapter, then, the beta of a stock is defined as the covariance between an asset and the portfolio of which it is part. Our only refinement to that definition now is to consider a specific portfolio, which is the market portfolio as just defined. Formally, then, the **beta of stock *i*** (β_i) is defined as

$$\beta_i = \frac{Cov_{iM}}{Var_M} \tag{7.2}$$

where Cov_{iM} denotes the covariance between stock *i* and the market portfolio, and Var_M denotes the variance of the market portfolio.

Although in the CAPM this beta is the appropriate measure of risk, there is more to the risk *premium* than beta. In fact, the CAPM defines the risk premium of stock *i* as

$$RP_i = \{E(R_M)-R_f\}\cdot\beta_i = MRP\cdot\beta_i \tag{7.3}$$

where $E(R_M)$ is the required return on the market portfolio and *MRP* denotes the *market* risk premium defined as $E(R_M)-R_f$. Combining (7.1) and (7.3) we get that, according to the CAPM, the **required or expected return on stock *i*** follows from the expression

$$E(R_i) = R_f + \{E(R_M)-R_f\}\cdot\beta_i = R_f + MRP\cdot\beta_i \tag{7.4}$$

This expression is one of the most widely used by finance academics and practitioners and its importance can hardly be overstated. For this reason, let's think a bit about it.

CAPM: Interpretation

Let's start with the left-hand side of expression (7.4), which we defined before as the required or expected return on stock i. Although we will not get into theoretical issues here, it is important to understand that in the equilibrium the CAPM follows from, what we expect from a stock and what we require from it must be the same. It is easy to see why this is the case.

Suppose that investors require a 10% annual return from a stock but they expect it to yield 15%; then they would rush to buy this stock, driving its price up and its expected return down. Conversely, if investors expected this stock to yield only 5%, then they would rush to sell it, driving its price down and its expected return up. In both cases, the adjustments will continue until the required and the expected return are the same. For this reason, $E(R_i)$ denotes *both* the required and the expected return from stock i and we'll use both expressions interchangeably.

On to the right-hand side now where we have two terms, the risk-free rate and the risk premium. The interpretation of the first is straightforward and, as we discussed, it is the compensation required for the expected loss of purchasing power. The other term, the risk premium, we have discussed in general; it is the compensation required for bearing the risk of a given stock. Let's now see how the CAPM proposes to estimate this risk premium.

According to the CAPM, the risk premium of a stock is given by the product of two terms, the market risk premium and the stock's beta. It is important to note that there is no i in the market risk premium. This means that, just like the risk-free rate, this magnitude is the same regardless of the stock we consider. Intuitively, the market risk premium is the compensation required by investors for investing in (risky) stocks rather than in a risk-free alternative. It then follows that this magnitude should be positive, $MRP = E(R_M)–R_f > 0$, and therefore there is a positive relationship between risk (measured by beta) and return.

Let's think a bit about beta now. Note, first, that beta is an unbounded number. Recall that $\beta_i = Cov_{iM}/Var_M$. Well, because a variance is a non-negative number and a covariance can be positive, negative, or 0, then so can be beta. But that's just in theory. Empirically, as we discussed in the previous chapter, it is nearly impossible to find a stock with a negative correlation to another or to the market, which means that in practice we deal almost exclusively with positive betas.

There are two other ways to think about beta and both are useful. First, we can think of it as the sensitivity of the returns of stock i to changes in the returns of the market. If $\beta_i > 1$, the stock amplifies the fluctuations of the market; and if $\beta_i < 1$ the stock mitigates the fluctuations of the market. For example, a stock with a beta of 2 indicates that, as the market goes up and down 1%, this stock will (on average) go up and down 2%. A stock with a beta of 0.5, on the other hand, indicates that as the market goes up and down 1%, this stock will (on average) go up and down 0.5%. This is why beta is sometimes called a measure of *relative* volatility, as opposed to the standard deviation which is a measure of *total* volatility: Because it measures the volatility of a stock *relative to that of the market.*

Alternatively, replacing Cov_{iM} in expression (7.2) by $SD_i{\cdot}SD_M{\cdot}Corr_{iM}$, we can express the beta of stock i as

$$\beta_i = \left(\frac{SD_i}{SD_M}\right){\cdot}Corr_{iM} \qquad\qquad (7.5)$$

where SD_i and SD_M denote the standard deviation of returns of stock i and the market, and $Corr_{iM}$ denotes the correlation between the returns of stock i and those of the market. This expression highlights why a very volatile asset is not necessarily very risky from a portfolio perspective: Because if its correlation to the market is very low then it may add very little risk to the portfolio.

In sum, the CAPM provides investors with a simple and intuitive way to estimate the required or expected return of a stock. It argues that investors should require compensation for the expected loss of purchasing power (R_f) and for bearing risk (RP_i). And it specifies that the compensation for risk should be measured by the risk premium required for investing in risky stocks rather than in safe bonds (MRP), corrected by a factor specific to each stock, the latter assessing how much more or less risky that stock is relative to the market (β_i). All very simple and intuitive, and yet, as usual, the devil is in the detail.

CAPM: Two issues

Before discussing each of the three inputs the CAPM requires, let's briefly address two important issues. First, it's important to note that the required or expected return of a stock is a *forward*-looking factor. This implies that we need forward-looking estimates of the risk-free rate, the market risk premium, and beta. Although this poses no problem with respect to the risk-free rate (we'll shortly discuss why), forward-looking estimates of the market risk premium and beta are not trivial to obtain. In fact, in practice, these estimates are almost always based on historical data. Whether or not this is the best we can do is controversial, but at least keep in mind that, ideally, we need to estimate *expected* market risk premiums and betas.

Second, it is important to highlight that, however simple it may look, the CAPM is not trivial to implement. This is because the CAPM is silent about the exact definition of the three elements we need for its implementation. As we'll discuss shortly, the exact definitions of a risk-free rate, a market risk premium, and beta are far from obvious. This implies that rather than being able to defend a particular choice of inputs on theoretical grounds, more often than not we'll find ourselves defending it simply as being the consensus of, or the most common choice made by, practitioners.

CAPM: Estimating the risk-free rate

It seems that all we'd need to do to put a specific number on R_f is to open a financial newspaper or go to a website and just look for it. But what exactly do we look for? The CAPM is actually silent about what exactly is a risk-free rate. Even if we agreed that it can be thought of as the yield on a government bond, is that rate over one year? Ten years? Thirty years? The CAPM leaves that hole for us to fill.

Some argue that the CAPM is a one-period model and that we usually discount annual cash flows, so we should use the yield on a one-year bill. Those who defend this view may also argue that only the one-year yield is really risk-free; that is, yields on longer-term government bonds are free from default risk but not from interest-rate risk. (These two sources of risk are discussed in Chapter 19.)

Now for the drawbacks. First, using one-year yields would force us to estimate the one-year yields that will prevail two, three, and more years down the road. Needless to say, it is far from clear that we have any ability to do that. Second, even if we could forecast future yields accurately, that would leave us with a time-varying discount rate (if R_f changed from period to period so would the required return on equity), which makes discounted cash flow calculations messier. Last but not least, practitioners do not use one-year yields very often.

What about the yield on a 30-year Treasury bond? It's not free from problems, either. Many companies that tend to invest in short-term or medium-term projects find this yield too high, particularly when the yield curve is steep. Having said that, practitioners do seem to have a preference for relatively long yields, although perhaps not as long as 30 years. This brings us to the two options that seem to be most widely accepted by practitioners.

One is to use the yield on a government bond with a maturity similar to that of the average maturity of a company's projects. In this case, toy makers would tend to use short-term yields, and airplane manufacturers would tend to use long-term yields. The other (increasingly popular) option is to use the yield on 10-year notes. The plausibility of this is at least partly explained by the fact that the 10-year yield has become widely accepted as the benchmark rate. Open a financial newspaper or go to a website to look for a brief summary of government bond yields and you'll find the yield on 10-year notes.

Two more things to conclude: First, note that the size of the difference across the yields we've been discussing depends on the slope of the yield curve; the steeper this curve, the higher the difference between short yields and long yields, and the more relevant is the specific choice of R_f. And last, but certainly not least, something that just about everybody (finally!) agrees upon: The risk-free rate is the *current* value of the chosen yield, not a historical average of those yields.

CAPM: Estimating the market risk premium

As we discussed before, the market risk premium aims to measure the additional return required by investors for investing in risky assets as opposed to investing in risk-free assets. More often than not, this market risk premium is estimated as the average historical difference between the return of the stock market and the return of a risk-free rate. But again the CAPM leaves holes for practitioners to fill. What 'market' should we consider? What risk-free rate? How many years should we include in the historical average? Should we calculate an arithmetic average or a geometric average? The CAPM doesn't really say, theory doesn't really help, and we're left again evaluating alternatives and paying attention to what practitioners often do.

In theory, the market portfolio should contain *all* risky assets, not just stocks. In practice, however, the market portfolio almost always is a broadly-diversified portfolio of stocks. In fact, in most countries there is a benchmark index used to describe the behavior of the overall stock market, and that is the practitioners' standard choice for the market portfolio. To illustrate, in the US the usual choice for the market portfolio is the S&P 500.

We discussed choices for the risk-free rate, and the same issue of having to choose a maturity for the yield of a government bond applies to the calculation of the market risk premium. In this case, calculating the risk premium with respect to the yield of long-term bonds (maturities of 10 years or longer) seems to be the more standard choice.

Unfortunately, our problems don't end there. Even if we agreed on the benchmark for the stock market and the maturity of the government bond yield, we'd still need to decide how many years we should include in the calculation of the historical average. Most people agree that the average should be taken over a 'long' period of time, but then again 'long' is an ambiguous term. (More on this in a minute.)

Last but not least, even if we agreed on all of the above, and after having calculated the annual risk premiums over a 'long' period of time, what average should we calculate, arithmetic or geometric? Again, theory does not really guide us. Some argue that the arithmetic mean is the more appropriate choice because it captures the risk premium *expected* in the coming period; but others disagree and recommend using the geometric mean instead. A middle road is to rely more heavily on the arithmetic average the shorter is the period for which the estimate of the market risk premium is needed, and more on the geometric average for relatively longer periods.

Table 7.1 shows the market risk premium for several countries over the 1900–2000 period based on both bonds and bills, and calculated with arithmetic and geometric averages. These figures are useful on two counts. First, they show that different countries have different market risk premiums, and that this magnitude may vary widely from one country to the next. Second, a very common choice for the market risk premium in the US is a number in the 5–6% range, which the table shows to be consistent with the geometric historical average based on medium-term bonds (that is, somewhere between the market risk premium based on short-term and on long-term bonds).

table 7.1

Country	With respect to bills		With respect to bonds	
	Geometric (%)	Arithmetic (%)	Geometric (%)	Arithmetic (%)
Australia	7.1	8.5	6.3	8.0
Belgium	2.9	5.1	2.9	4.8
Canada	4.6	5.9	4.5	6.0
Denmark	1.8	3.4	2.0	3.3
France	7.4	9.8	4.9	7.0
Germany	4.9	10.3	6.7	9.9
Ireland	3.5	5.4	3.2	4.6
Italy	7.0	11.0	5.0	8.4
Japan	6.7	9.9	6.2	10.3
Netherlands	5.1	7.1	4.7	6.7
South Africa	6.0	8.1	5.4	7.1
Spain	3.2	5.3	2.3	4.2
Sweden	5.5	7.7	5.2	7.4
Switzerland	4.3	6.1	2.7	4.2
UK	4.8	6.5	4.4	5.6
US	5.8	7.7	5.0	7.0
World	4.9	6.2	4.6	5.6

Source: Adapted from *Triumph of the Optimists: 101 years of global investment returns* by Elroy Dimson, Paul Marsh, and Mike Staunton. Princeton University Press, New Jersey, 2002. Reprinted by permission of Princeton University Press.

In short, when estimating the market risk premium practitioners seem to have converged around whatever is the widely-used benchmark for the stock market in each country as a proxy for the market portfolio; the yield on medium-term or long-term bonds as proxy for the risk-free rate; returns for the stock market and the risk-free rate for as long a period as available; and though there is no clear consensus on whether to use an arithmetic or a geometric average, the longer the period for which the estimate is needed, the more plausible the geometric average becomes.

CAPM: Estimating beta

Just like the other two inputs of the CAPM, estimating betas may appear to be trivial but, as usual, the devil is in the details. Let's start with the uncontroversial part. Estimating the beta of stock i requires running a time-series regression between the risk premium of stock i and the market risk premium; that is

$$R_{it} - R_{ft} = \alpha + \beta \cdot (R_{Mt} - R_{ft}) + u_t \tag{7.6}$$

where R_i and R_M denote the returns of stock i and those of the market; R_f the risk-free rate; α and β are two coefficients to be estimated; u is an error term; and the subscript t indexes time. The slope of this regression is the beta we want to estimate. (As a shortcut, you may find betas estimated from a regression that omits the risk-free rate; that is, $R_{it} = \alpha + \beta \cdot R_{Mt} + u_t$. More often than not, the betas estimated from these two regressions are very similar.)

Now for the tricky issues, aside from the choice of the market portfolio and the risk-free rate, which we discussed. First, should we collect daily, weekly, monthly, or annual returns? Second, should we estimate betas over a year, 5 years, 10 years, or more? Again, theory does not really help, so we'll look at what practitioners frequently do.

Regarding the frequency of the data, weekly and monthly returns are the most widely used, with monthly returns being the more typical choice. Daily returns are too noisy (they capture a lot of volatility that is useless for the purposes of estimating the required return on equity) and annual returns usually yield too few observations. Monthly returns are the way to go.

Regarding the time period over which betas should be estimated, three to five years seems to be a widely-accepted range, with five years being the more typical choice. If we estimate beta over a very short period of time, like one year, we run the risk of capturing an unusually good or bad period for the company, and it would not be wise to extrapolate it too far into the future. With very long periods of time, on the other hand, we run the risk of using data that no longer accurately characterizes a company. Think of European telecommunication companies, most of which in the early 1990s went from being monopolies offering one service to compete at home and abroad over a range of services. Obviously, estimating a beta for these companies based on, say, 40 years of data would capture a lot of information that is useless in properly assessing the systematic risk of these companies.

Obviously, there is no way to formally defend an estimation period of five years, or asserting that it is much better than four years or six years. It is typically just thought of as a compromise between not going too many years back, on the one hand, and not focusing only on the very recent past, on the other hand.

In short, this discussion suggests that a plausible way to estimate betas is by using some five years of monthly data; that is, with 60 or so observations. Consistent with this, Table 7.2 in the next section shows the beta of the 30 components in the Dow Jones Industrial Average (the Dow) estimated on the basis of monthly returns over the January 2005–December 2009 period.

CAPM: Application

Let's finally put all the pieces together and use the CAPM to estimate the required return on equity for the 30 stocks of the Dow at the beginning of 2010. Expression (7.4) requires the current value of a risk-free rate and an estimate of the long-term market risk premium (both common to all companies), as well as an estimate of beta (specific to each company).

Consistent with our previous discussion, we'll use the yield on 10-year US Treasury notes as our estimate for the risk-free rate, which at the beginning of 2010 was 3.9%. For the market risk premium we'll use 5.5%, which is the mid-point of the widely used 5–6% range for the US market. Using these two figures we can rewrite expression (7.4) as

$$E(R_i) = 0.039 + 0.055 \cdot \beta_i \qquad (7.7)$$

Finally, we'll estimate the beta for the 30 stocks of the Dow using expression (7.6), 5 years of monthly returns (January 2005–December 2009), the S&P 500 as a proxy for the stock market, and the yield on 10-year notes (expressed monthly) as a proxy for the risk-free rate. Table 7.2 shows these betas and the required returns on these companies based on expression (7.7).

As the table shows, Wal-Mart has the lowest beta (0.25) and therefore the lowest required return on equity (5.3%). On the other hand, Bank of America has the highest beta (2.42) and therefore the highest required return on equity (17.2%). Across all 30 companies, the average beta is just over 1 (1.02) and the average required return on equity is 9.5%.

| table 7.2 | | | | | |

Company	β_i	$E(R_i)$ (%)	Company	β_i	$E(R_i)$ (%)
3M	0.78	8.2	IBM	0.80	8.3
Alcoa	2.09	15.4	Intel	1.17	10.3
American Express	2.14	15.7	Johnson & Johnson	0.55	6.9
AT&T	0.68	7.7	JPMorgan Chase	1.10	10.0
Bank of America	2.42	17.2	Kraft Foods	0.59	7.1
Boeing	1.29	11.0	McDonald's	0.64	7.4
Caterpillar	1.82	13.9	Merck	0.92	9.0
Chevron	0.65	7.5	Microsoft	0.96	9.2
Cisco Systems	1.21	10.6	Pfizer	0.77	8.1
Coca-Cola	0.60	7.2	Procter & Gamble	0.60	7.2
DuPont	1.40	11.6	Travelers	0.68	7.6
ExxonMobil	0.45	6.4	United Tech	0.97	9.2
General Electric	1.55	12.4	Verizon	0.62	7.3
Hewlett-Packard	1.03	9.6	Wal-Mart	0.25	5.3
Home Depot	0.70	7.7	Walt Disney	1.10	10.0

The cost of capital

Few variables are as critical for a company as its cost of capital, a figure they need to evaluate projects, value potential targets, and optimize their capital structure, to name but a few of its uses. Ultimately, the cost of capital yields the minimum return that should be required on a company given its risk; and the required return on equity derived from the CAPM that we just discussed is one of its components.

Let's assume for now that a company finances its projects only with debt (D) and equity (E). Investors obviously require a compensation for bearing the risk of holding these two instruments, so let's call R_D the required return on debt (or the cost of debt) and R_E the required return on equity (or the cost of equity). Then, a company's **weighted-average cost of capital (R_{WACC})** is given by

$$R_{WACC} = (1-t_c) \cdot x_D \cdot R_D + x_E \cdot R_E \qquad (7.8)$$

where t_c is the corporate tax rate; $x_D = D/(D+E)$ and $x_E = E/(D+E)$ are the proportions of debt and equity; and $x_D+x_E = 1$.

If we ignore for a minute the corporate tax rate, expression (7.8) basically says that a company's cost of capital is the average return required on the financial instruments (debt and equity) issued by a company, weighted by the proportion in which the company uses each instrument. The corporate tax rate simply indicates that interest payments on debt are tax deductible, which means that the company's effective cost of debt is lower than R_D. Put differently, the *after-tax* cost of debt, which is the cost the company actually bears, is $(1-t_c){\cdot}R_D$.

The required return on debt is usually captured by the *yield* on the bonds issued by the company, *not* by their interest rate. (If this distinction is not clear, take a look at Chapter 18.) Also, x_D should be measured at *market value*, *not* at book value; obviously, the same goes for x_E. Note that there is wide agreement about both of these statements, and neither academics nor practitioners would find them controversial. If a company does not have any bonds traded in the market, then R_D can in principle be assessed by the rate at which the company could borrow funds from a bank. Finally, the type of debt considered in the estimation of the cost of capital is only the interest-bearing (usually long-term) debt; non-interest-bearing (usually short-term) debt typically does not enter into the calculation.

The required return on equity is usually estimated with the CAPM, although as we'll discuss in the next chapter there are other models for this purpose. Importantly, note a fundamental difference between the cost of debt and the cost of equity. The former is *objective* in the sense that it is given by either a bond's yield or the rate charged by a bank, both of which can be directly *observed*. The cost of equity, however, is nowhere to be observed and therefore must be estimated; that's why we need a model, and that's where the CAPM comes in. But because of the ambiguity on the exact definition of R_f, MRP, and β we already discussed, or because of the existence of models other than the CAPM, the cost of equity is a rather subjective estimate. Do keep that in mind in case you ever have to negotiate about the value of a company!

Although (notation notwithstanding) you will typically see the expression for the cost of capital written as in expression (7.8), it does not really have to have two terms. It can have only one, when the company is fully financed by equity, or more than two, when the company is financed with more than just debt and equity. In fact, the cost of capital can have as many terms as different financial instruments a company uses to finance its projects. To illustrate, if a company issues debt, equity, and preferred equity (P), then its cost of capital would be expressed as

$$R_{WACC} = (1-t_c) \cdot x_D \cdot R_D + x_E \cdot R_E + x_P \cdot R_P \qquad (7.9)$$

where $x_P = P/(D+E+P)$ is the proportion of preferred equity; R_P the required return on the preferred equity; and $x_D+x_E+x_P = 1$, with $x_D = D/(D+E+P)$ and $x_E = E/(D+E+P)$.

One of the critical uses for the cost of capital is as a hurdle rate; that is, as the minimum return required on a company's projects. Both the NPV and the IRR, two widely-used tools for project evaluation (both discussed in Chapter 21), use the cost of capital as an input to assess the viability of a project. The cost of capital is also the discount rate in the WACC version of the discounted cash flow model, the most widely-used method to value companies. When we discuss this model in Chapter 14 we'll go over a step-by-step estimation of the cost of capital of Starbucks.

The big picture

There is no question that the CAPM is one of the most widely-used models in finance, in part because it provides a simple answer to a critical question: What compensation should investors require from a company given the company's risk? Simple as the CAPM appears to be, however, the three inputs the model requires may be interpreted in a variety of ways, and lacking theoretical guidance about the most appropriate choice for each input, we're left following the consensus of practitioners.

The required return on equity the CAPM enables us to estimate is a component of the cost of capital, a critical magnitude for every company and an essential input in the evaluation of projects and the valuation of companies. But the CAPM is not the only model devised to estimate required returns on equity; in the next chapter we'll discuss its main contender, the three-factor model.

Excel section

Running regressions such as those in expression (7.6) is fairly simple in Excel. However, because we discuss regressions in Chapter 30, there is no need to do it here. Having said that, let's consider here a shortcut to estimate the slope of a linear regression, which is what we need to estimate the beta of a company. Suppose you have a series of 10 observations on a dependent variable in cells A1:A10, and a series of 10 observations on an independent variable in cells B1:B10. Then,

- to estimate the slope of the linear regression, type

  =linest(A1:A10, B1:B10)

  in cell A11 and hit Enter.

If you think of the dependent variable as the returns on stock i and the independent variable as the returns on the market, then the result of using the 'linest' command as indicated above will be the beta of stock i.

8

Risk and return III: The three-factor model

T he CAPM we discussed in the previous chapter states that the *only* variable that matters when estimating a company's required return on equity is systematic risk measured by beta. That's a very strong statement, particularly when the empirical evidence points to other variables that seem to be clearly correlated to returns. Two of these variables are market capitalization and the book-to-market ratio, which can be articulated, together with beta, into the increasingly-popular three-factor model.

A quick review of the CAPM

In a popularity contest the CAPM beats the competition hands down; 70–80% of practitioners claim to use the CAPM when calculating a company's required return on equity. Does that make it the 'best' model for that purpose? Not necessarily. It is by far the most popular, though which one is the best, whatever that means anyway, remains an open question.

The difference across the models used to estimate required returns on equity largely comes down to the way each proposes to estimate a stock's risk premium. As we discussed in the previous chapter, the CAPM states that the risk premium of stock i (RP_i) can be estimated as the product of the market risk premium (MRP) and the stock's beta (β_i); that is, $RP_i = MRP \cdot \beta_i = [E(R_M)-R_f] \cdot \beta_i$, where $E(R_M)$ is the required return on the stock market and R_f is the risk-free rate. Therefore, the required return on stock i, $E(R_i)$, can be estimated with the expression

$$E(R_i) = R_f + [E(R_M)-R_f] \cdot \beta_i = R_f + MRP \cdot \beta_i \qquad (8.1)$$

where beta captures systematic risk, the *only* relevant source of risk according to the CAPM.

Now, *that* is a strong statement! Think about it. Total risk (volatility), default risk, liquidity risk, currency risk, and as many other sources of risk as you can imagine … they don't matter. They provide no information about the required or expected return on stocks. If this sounds strange, it's simply because it is.

And yet, a die-hard supporter of the CAPM would justify the model's strong statement in at least two ways. The first line of defense would be theoretical. He would claim that, unlike the vast majority of its contenders, the CAPM is solidly grounded in theory. In fact, he would argue that in a model in which investors behave optimally, beta *must* be the only relevant source of risk. In other words, this 'strange' statement of the CAPM is not an assumption but the *result* of a model of optimal behavior.

Very little can be argued against this line of reasoning. It is indeed true that the CAPM is supported by a solid theoretical background and that it results from a model of optimal behavior. And it is also true that the vast majority of its competitors are models in which the variables that determine the required return on equity come from plausible stories, or guesses, or worse, from the result of trying variable after variable until something correlates with returns.

The second line of defense would be empirical, but this is a tricky one. We could fill a room with studies that test the validity of the CAPM, in different countries, over different time periods, and with different methodologies. The problem is that there is a huge amount of evidence on *both* sides of the fence. Both those who defend the CAPM and those who defend alternative models could point to a vast amount of evidence that supports their position. As a result, evidence doesn't go a long way toward embracing or rejecting the CAPM.

The size and value premiums

And yet, at least *some* empirical evidence is surprisingly consistent. Data for different countries and over different time periods show a consistent *negative* relationship between market capitalization and returns; that is, in the long term, small companies tend to deliver higher returns than large companies. This empirical regularity is usually known as the *size premium*.

Similarly, data for different countries and over different time periods show a consistent *positive* relationship between book-to-market ratios (BtM) and returns; that is, in the long term, companies with high BtM tend to deliver higher returns than those with low BtM. This ratio, recall, is a measure of cheapness in the sense that high and low BtM indicate cheap and expensive stocks relative to book value. Then, the evidence shows that in the long term cheap (also called *value*) stocks tend to outperform expensive (also called *growth*) stocks. This empirical regularity is usually known as the *value premium*.

Now, however clear the evidence may be, the theoretical reasons for the existence of the size and value premiums are far less clear. In other words, no model of optimal behavior leads to a result in which stock returns depend on market cap and BtM. Some people may not consider this a problem; they would claim that as long as we can isolate the variables that explain differences in returns, we should use them to determine required or expected returns. Yet others would argue that there is no point using models that do not follow from a robust underlying theory. You can pick your side in this debate.

If you think about it, though, at first glance these two risk premiums seem to make sense. Small companies are probably less diversified and less able to withstand negative shocks than large companies. As for cheap companies, well, there must be a reason why they're cheap! When buying cheap or value stocks investors are betting on a rebound rather than on a falling knife. In short, it's not very difficult to come up with plausible stories to explain why small stocks and cheap stocks are riskier than large stocks and expensive stocks, and, therefore, why they should deliver higher returns.

But those are just stories. A better way may be to link empirically size and value to obvious sources of risk. The evidence on this seems to point to the fact that small companies and value companies are less profitable (they have lower earnings or cash flow relative to book value) than large companies and growth companies. In other words, small companies and value companies may be distressed because of their poor profitability, and are therefore perceived as riskier by investors.

The CAPM argues that stocks with high systematic (or market) risk should outperform those with low systematic risk. In addition, the evidence clearly shows that small stocks outperform large stocks, and that cheap (value) stocks outperform expensive (growth) stocks. Put all this together and we get that stock returns are determined by a *market* premium, a *size* premium, and a *value* premium. And that is, precisely, the idea underlying the three-factor model, which from this point on we'll refer to simply as the 3FM.

One last thing before we discuss this model. Although the evidence on the existence of the size and value premiums is largely undisputed, there's a heated controversy about whether or not the excess returns of small and value stocks (relative to large and growth stocks) are the result of their higher risk. Some argue that this is not the case; that is, small and value stocks are not riskier than large and growth stocks, and therefore the additional returns they provide are a free lunch courtesy of an inefficient market. Yet others argue exactly the opposite; that is, small and value stocks offer higher returns than large and growth stocks simply because they are riskier, which is exactly what would be expected in an efficient market.

Again, you can pick your side but, importantly, note that whenever we estimate required returns with the 3FM we are implicitly siding with the second view. This is because, as we'll see in a minute, this model states that the higher the exposure of a company to the size and value premiums, the higher should be the required return on that company. In other words, the higher the risk (as defined by the 3FM), the higher should be the required return.

Three-factor model: Overview

Estimating required returns from the 3FM is only a tiny bit more difficult than doing it with the CAPM. That is simply because we need some additional data and we have to estimate two additional betas. Other than that, the model poses no real challenge to any practitioner who wants to implement it.

According to the 3FM, the **required return on stock *i*** follows from the expression

$$E(R_i) = R_f + MRP{\cdot}\beta_i + SMB{\cdot}\beta_i^S + HML{\cdot}\beta_i^V \tag{8.2}$$

where *SMB* (small minus big, referring to market cap) and *HML* (high minus low, referring to BtM) denote the size premium and the value premium, and β_i^S and β_i^V denote the sensitivities (betas) of stock *i* with respect to these premiums. Let's think a bit about this expression.

Recall that *MRP*, the market risk premium, seeks to capture the additional compensation required by investors for investing in riskier stocks as opposed to in safer bonds. Recall, also, that it is measured by the average historical difference between the return of a widely-diversified portfolio of stocks and the return of government bonds. And recall, finally, that β_i measures the sensitivity of the returns of stock *i* to changes in the market (or, more precisely, the sensitivity of the risk premium of stock i to fluctuations in the market risk premium).

Similarly, *SMB*, the size premium, seeks to capture the additional compensation required by investors for investing in riskier small companies as opposed to investing in safer large companies. It is measured as the average historical difference between the returns of a portfolio of small stocks and those of a portfolio of large stocks. And the beta associated with this factor, usually called the size beta (β_i^S), measures the sensitivity of the returns of stock i (or, more precisely, the risk premium of stock i) to fluctuations in the size premium.

Finally, *HML*, the value premium, seeks to capture the additional compensation required by investors for investing in riskier value stocks as opposed to investing in safer growth stocks. It is measured as the average historical difference between the returns of a portfolio of high-BtM stocks and those of a portfolio of low-BtM stocks. And the beta associated with this factor, usually called the value beta (β_i^V), measures the sensitivity of the returns of stock i (or, more precisely, the risk premium of stock i) to fluctuations in the value premium.

Note that, just as we stressed in the previous chapter about *MRP*, neither *SMB* nor *HML* in expression (8.2) has a subscript i. This means that the average size and value premiums, as well as R_f and *MRP*, are independent from the specific stock we're considering and therefore are the same for all stocks. Note, on the other hand, that the size beta and the value beta, as well as the market beta, all do have a subscript i, and therefore are specific to the company we're considering.

Three-factor model: Implementation

The 3FM, just like the CAPM, is silent about several practical issues that we inevitably encounter when implementing the model. What is a portfolio of small stocks? And one of large stocks? What is a portfolio of value stocks? And one of growth stocks? Should we estimate betas using daily, weekly, monthly, or annual data? And how long a period should we use to estimate those betas? Again, theory offers no clear answers and we'll find ourselves looking at the convergence of practitioners for guidance.

A quick comment before we get to specifics. The 3FM was proposed by Eugene Fama and Kenneth French in a series of articles published in the 1990s (which is why you may occasionally find this model referred to as the Fama–French 3FM). In the 'data library' of Ken French's web page (**http://mba.tuck.dartmouth.edu/pages/faculty/ken.french/data_library.html**), you will find plenty of information on this model, as well as the data necessary to implement it (in the 'historical benchmark returns' section of the page). For that reason, we'll focus here on the essentials; if you want to get into the details of the 3FM, do visit Ken French's web page.

So, let's start with what we know from the previous chapter regarding the estimation of the CAPM. We need a risk-free rate, which we can approximate with the yield on 10-year Treasury notes. We need a market portfolio, which we can approximate with a widely-used benchmark of stocks, such as the S&P 500 in the US or the Nikkei in Japan. And we need a market risk premium, which we can estimate as the (arithmetic or geometric) average historical difference between the returns on the chosen benchmark of stocks and those of medium-term or long-term government bonds, calculated over a 'long' period of time. (We also need a company's market beta, but we'll get to betas in a minute.)

Note that the *MRP* returns available from Ken French's web page are calculated differently from the way we discussed them in the previous chapter (and from standard practice), but this is nothing you should worry about from a practical point of view. Table 8.1 displays the annual returns of the *MRP* portfolio as calculated by Fama and French for 2000–09. The last two rows of the table show the arithmetic (*AM*) and geometric (*GM*) average over the much longer 1927–2009 period. Note that between 1927 and 2009 stocks beat bonds by over 8 percentage points a year (based on the arithmetic average).

To estimate *SMB* we need to calculate the average historical difference between the returns of a portfolio of small stocks and those of a portfolio of large stocks. The formation and rebalancing of these two portfolios is tricky but you don't have to worry about that; on Ken French's web page you'll find annual returns for the *SMB* portfolio from 1927 on. The *SMB* column of Table 8.1 displays these returns for 2000–09. The next-to-last row of the table shows that between 1927 and 2009 small stocks outperformed large stocks by almost 4 percentage points a year (based on the arithmetic average).

Year	MRP (%)	SMB (%)	HML (%)
2000	−16.7	−5.7	21.4
2001	−14.8	28.4	27.2
2002	−22.9	4.4	3.7
2003	30.7	28.1	15.1
2004	10.7	6.3	13.2
2005	3.2	−2.7	3.7
2006	10.6	1.0	11.9
2007	0.8	−7.0	−21.6
2008	−38.4	0.2	−9.1
2009	29.1	17.7	23.7
AM (1927–2009)	**8.1**	**3.8**	**4.4**
GM (1927–2009)	**5.9**	**2.9**	**3.3**

The estimation of *HML* is similar. We need to calculate the average historical difference between the returns of a portfolio of high-BtM stocks and those of a portfolio of low-BtM stocks. Again, the formation and rebalancing of these two portfolios is tricky, but again you don't have to worry about that; in Ken French's web page you'll find annual returns for the *HML* portfolio from 1927 on. The final column of Table 8.1 displays these returns for 2000–09. The next-to-last row of the table shows that between 1927 and 2009 value stocks outperformed growth stocks by almost 4.5 percentage points a year (based on the arithmetic average).

Importantly, the three betas we need to implement the 3FM must be estimated *jointly* by running a time-series regression between the risk premium of stock i, $RP_i = R_i - R_f$, and the three portfolios that capture the market, size, and value premiums (*MRP*, *SMB*, and *HML*), that is

$$R_{it} - R_{ft} = \alpha + \beta_1 \cdot MRP_t + \beta_2 \cdot SMB_t + \beta_3 \cdot HML_t + u_t \tag{8.3}$$

where R_i and R_f denote the returns of stock i and a risk-free rate; α, β_1, β_2, and β_3 are coefficients to be estimated; u is an error term; and t indexes time. Note that β_1 is the usual (market) beta, β_2 is the size beta (β_i^S), and β_3 is the value beta (β_i^V). As is the case with the CAPM, this regression is typically estimated with monthly data over a five-year period. Monthly returns for the *MRP*, *SMB*, and *HML* portfolios for this purpose are available from Ken French's web page.

Three-factor model: Application

Let's now put everything together and estimate required returns on equity with the 3FM. And let's do it, as in the previous chapter, for the 30 stocks of the Dow at the beginning of 2010 so we can compare the required returns estimated with this model with those we estimated with the CAPM.

For the risk-free rate we'll use, also as in the previous chapter, the yield on the 10-year US Treasury note, which at the beginning of 2010 was 3.9%. To estimate the long-term *MRP*, we'll depart slightly from the last chapter. Instead of using a market risk premium of 5.5% as we did before, we'll now use 5.9%, which is the (geometric) average *MRP* since 1927 as calculated by Fama and French (see the last line of Table 8.1). To estimate the long-term *SMB* and *HML* we'll also use the portfolios calculated by Fama and French; and as the last line of Table 8.1 shows, from 1927 on the (geometric) average *SMB* and *HML* are 2.9% and 3.3%.

Given these figures, then, we'll estimate the required return on the 30 stocks of the Dow at the beginning of 2010 with the expression

$$E(R_i) = 0.039 + 0.059 \cdot \beta_i + 0.029 \cdot \beta_i^S + 0.033 \cdot \beta_i^V \qquad (8.4)$$

Note that this expression is the same as (8.2) but with specific values for R_f, *MRP*, *SMB*, and *HML*. All we need now to estimate required returns with this model are the beta, size beta, and value beta of the Dow companies.

We'll estimate these three betas using expression (8.3), five years of monthly returns (January 2005–December 2009), and data on the *MRP*, *SMB*, and *HML* portfolios downloaded from Ken French's web page. The estimated betas are shown in the second, third, and fourth columns of Table 8.2. The required returns on each of the 30 companies of the Dow that follow from these betas and expression (8.4) are shown in the fifth column (3FM). The sixth and seventh columns show the beta and required return on these companies estimated with the CAPM, taken from Table 7.2 in the previous chapter. The last column of Table 8.2 shows the difference between the required returns estimated with the 3FM and those estimated with the CAPM.

table 8.2

Company	β_i	β_i^S	β_i^V	3FM (%)	β_i	CAPM (%)	Diff. (%)
3M	0.66	0.05	0.18	8.5	0.78	8.2	0.4
Alcoa	2.11	0.69	−0.38	17.1	2.09	15.4	1.7
American Express	1.15	0.38	1.79	17.7	2.14	15.7	2.0
AT&T	0.82	−0.23	−0.23	7.3	0.68	7.7	−0.3
Bank of America	1.55	−1.15	2.20	17.1	2.42	17.2	−0.1
Boeing	1.21	−0.64	0.44	10.7	1.29	11.0	−0.3
Caterpillar	1.67	0.00	0.25	14.6	1.82	13.9	0.7
Chevron	0.96	−0.58	−0.44	6.5	0.65	7.5	−1.0
Cisco Systems	1.20	0.67	−0.31	11.8	1.21	10.6	1.3
Coca-Cola	0.75	−0.72	−0.01	6.2	0.60	7.2	−1.0
DuPont	1.10	−0.18	0.67	12.1	1.40	11.6	0.5
ExxonMobil	0.72	−0.70	−0.30	5.2	0.45	6.4	−1.2
General Electric	1.21	−0.36	0.79	12.6	1.55	12.4	0.2
Hewlett-Packard	1.03	0.48	−0.26	10.5	1.03	9.6	0.9
Home Depot	0.38	0.55	0.41	9.1	0.70	7.7	1.3
IBM	0.81	0.36	−0.18	9.1	0.80	8.3	0.8
Intel	1.45	−0.09	−0.58	10.3	1.17	10.3	0.0
Johnson & Johnson	0.60	−0.51	0.09	6.3	0.55	6.9	−0.7
JPMorgan Chase	0.45	−0.50	1.51	10.2	1.10	10.0	0.2
Kraft Foods	0.46	−0.17	0.29	7.1	0.59	7.1	0.0
McDonald's	0.86	−0.58	−0.25	6.5	0.64	7.4	−0.9
Merck	1.36	−0.89	−0.55	7.5	0.92	9.0	−1.4
Microsoft	1.09	−0.04	−0.30	9.2	0.96	9.2	0.0
Pfizer	0.71	−0.68	0.38	7.4	0.77	8.1	−0.7
Procter & Gamble	0.61	−0.27	0.04	6.9	0.60	7.2	−0.3
Travelers	0.71	−0.51	0.12	7.0	0.68	7.6	−0.6
United Tech	0.87	−0.32	0.32	9.2	0.97	9.2	−0.1
Verizon	0.87	−0.30	−0.43	6.8	0.62	7.3	−0.5
Wal-Mart	0.30	−0.41	0.09	4.8	0.25	5.3	−0.5
Walt Disney	0.89	0.12	0.35	10.7	1.10	10.0	0.7
Minimum	**0.30**	**−1.15**	**−0.58**	**4.8**	**0.25**	**5.3**	**−1.4**
Maximum	**2.11**	**0.69**	**2.20**	**17.7**	**2.42**	**17.2**	**2.0**
Average	**0.95**	**−0.22**	**0.19**	**9.5**	**1.02**	**9.5**	**0.0**

Note, first, that the market betas estimated with the 3FM are in most cases very similar to those estimated with the CAPM. This is the case despite the fact that the betas we estimated in the previous chapter were the only variable explaining returns and were calculated with respect to a different *MRP* portfolio. To be sure, there are substantial differences in a few cases (Bank of America, Home Depot), but they seem to be the exception rather than the rule. As the last line of Table 8.2 shows, on average, the market betas estimated with the 3FM (0.95) and the CAPM (1.02) are very similar.

Importantly, note that although it is nearly impossible to find negative market betas, it is far from unusual to find negative size betas and value betas, as Table 8.2 shows. In fact, this is exactly what we would expect to find in the case of large companies and growth companies. This is so because a negative size beta indicates a company that is negatively affected by an increase in the outperformance of small stocks relative to large stocks. Similarly, a negative value beta indicates a company that is negatively affected by an increase in the outperformance of value stocks relative to growth stocks.

This is an important insight of the 3FM so let's put it in a different way to make sure the concept is clear. A positive exposure to the size premium (a positive size beta) indicates a company whose returns tends to increase when the outperformance of small stocks (relative to large stocks) increases; and because the 3FM assumes that small stocks are riskier than large stocks, then the required return on the company increases. Conversely, a negative exposure to the size premium (a negative size beta) indicates a company whose returns tend to fall when the outperformance of small stocks (relative to large stocks) increases; and because the 3FM assumes that large stocks are less risky than small stocks, then the required return on the company decreases. (If you understood the preceding lines, you should be able to make a similar argument for positive and negative value betas. Try!)

Finally, compare company by company the required returns in the fifth column of Table 8.2 (estimated with the 3FM) with those in the seventh column (estimated with the CAPM). As you can see, in most cases the differences are not substantial. Sure, there are cases in which the difference is considerable (Alcoa, American Express, and Merck), but on average across all 30 companies the required return from both models is the same 9.5%.

Could this explain, at least partially, the popularity of the CAPM? Note that the CAPM is widely taught in business schools, is easy to understand, and is easy to implement. Most other models, including the 3FM, are often not taught in business schools, are more demanding in terms of data collection, are more difficult to implement, and their intuition is not always clear. Is the more costly implementation of the 3FM relative to the CAPM worth a practitioner's time? That is hard to say, but at least one thing is clear: The differences between the required returns calculated from these two models often are well within the differences we'd find between a short and a long risk-free rate, or an arithmetic or geometric average market risk premium when implementing the CAPM.

An alternative use of the model

One last word on the 3FM before we conclude this chapter. Note that after introducing the size and value premiums, understanding the intuition of the 3FM, and discussing the implementation of this model, our application focused on the estimation of the required return on several *companies*. That can be thought of as a typical corporate finance application, where the required return or cost of equity becomes an input in the cost of capital, which in turn is an input in the valuation of target companies, the evaluation of investment projects, and so forth.

But, importantly, the 3FM is perhaps more widely used as a tool to evaluate the performance of active portfolio managers (those that aim to outperform, rather than just track their benchmark) and more generally to estimate the required return on *funds*. We'll get back to this issue in Chapter 10 when we discuss risk-adjusted returns, but for now let's say that it follows from our discussion in this chapter that when a fund is, relative to the market, skewed toward small stocks or value stocks, its risk is higher, and so should be the return required by investors. In other words, the 3FM is widely used to estimate the return that investors should require from funds, taking into account not just market risk but also the risk of exposure to the size and value premiums.

The big picture

The CAPM makes the strong statement that the only variable that should influence the required or expected return on equity is beta. However, evidence from both the US and other markets clearly shows that size and value do matter; that is, small stocks tend to outperform large stocks, and value stocks tend to outperform growth stocks. Under the assumption that size and value are risk factors, the 3FM articulates the market risk premium, the size premium, and the value premium into a model that yields required returns.

Although its popularity has been steadily increasing over time, the jury is still out on whether the 3FM is a 'better' model than the CAPM in the sense of estimating more accurate required returns. We will obviously not attempt to offer the last word on this matter here. But we will go as far as saying that you should definitely consider the 3FM as an important tool in any practitioner's toolkit.

Excel section

As mentioned in the Excel section of the previous chapter, Chapter 30 discusses how to run regressions in Excel and there is no need to do it here again. However, in the same way that in the previous chapter we discussed a shortcut to estimate the slope of a regression with one explanatory variable using the 'linest' command, we discuss here a similar shortcut to estimate the slopes of a regression with several explanatory variables.

Suppose you have a series of 10 observations on a dependent variable in cells A1:A10. Suppose, also, that you have two series of 10 observations, each on one independent variable, in cells B1:B10 and C1:C10. Then, to estimate the two slope coefficients, one for each of the two independent variables, select the cells B11:C11, type

=linest(A1:A10, B1:C10)

and then press Ctrl+Shift+Enter *simultaneously*.

Now, it's very important that you note the following: Excel will display the beta coefficients *in reverse order*! Instead of displaying the slope coefficients in the same order as that of the independent variables, which would imply that each beta is displayed below the last observation of its respective variable, the coefficients are displayed the other way around. Don't ask ... Just make sure that when you read the coefficients you remember that instead of finding β_1 in cell B11 and β_2 in cell C11, you will find β_1 in C11 and β_2 in B11. More generally, if you have n independent variables and follow a procedure similar to the one described above, you will *not* find the slope coefficients listed (left to right) as $\beta_1, \beta_2, ..., \beta_n$ but as $\beta_n, ..., \beta_2, \beta_1$.

9

Risk IV: Downside risk

As much as we can very quickly agree on how to assess the return performance of an asset, we may have far more trouble agreeing on how to assess its risk. There are many ways to do it and which one is best, whatever that means anyway, is arguable. And yet at least one thing we can safely say: Although investors tend to associate risk with negative outcomes, the two factors most widely used to assess it, standard deviation and beta, do not. In this chapter we'll discuss a relatively new but increasingly popular framework that focuses on the downside, just as investors do when they think of risk.

Did we ask what is risk?

We sure did. Twice in fact. First we argued that when we consider an asset in isolation we bear its total risk, which we can quantify with the standard deviation of the asset's returns. Then we argued that when we hold an asset within a diversified portfolio we bear only its systematic risk, which we can quantify with beta. In this second case, diversification eliminates the unsystematic risk and the systematic risk that remains is the asset's contribution to the risk of the portfolio.

Now, if you really think about it, there's something inherently implausible with the standard deviation as a measure of risk: It treats an $x\%$ return above and below the mean in the same way; that is, in both cases this measure of risk increases by the same amount. But investors obviously don't feel the same way about these two fluctuations. They are obviously happy when the asset generates returns above the mean, and unhappy when the opposite happens. Shouldn't then a plausible measure of risk capture this asymmetry? Plus, why measure deviations with respect to the mean? Most investors have more meaningful benchmarks in mind, such as the risk-free rate, 0, or a target return, to name but a few.

There are several measures of risk that isolate and assess the downside. In this chapter we'll focus on two: One is the semideviation, which is the counterpart of the standard deviation in a downside risk framework; and the other is VaR, which is a measure of the 'worst' expected outcome under some specified conditions. Before we discuss these two, though, let's think a bit harder about the limitations of the standard deviation, perhaps the most widely used measure of risk.

Problems with the standard deviation

Take a look at Table 9.1, which in the R column displays the annual returns of Oracle between 1995 and 2009. As the next-to-last row shows, the mean annual return during this period was a healthy 32.6%. And as your eyes can tell you without resorting to any formal measure of risk, Oracle treated its shareholders to a rocky ride.

table 9.1

Year	R (%)	R–AM (%)	$(R$–$AM)^2$	Min(R–AM, 0) (%)	$[Min(R$–$AM, 0)]^2$
1995	44.0	11.4	0.0130	0.0	0.0000
1996	47.8	15.1	0.0229	0.0	0.0000
1997	−19.8	−52.5	0.2754	−52.5	0.2754
1998	93.3	60.6	0.3676	0.0	0.0000
1999	289.8	257.1	6.6109	0.0	0.0000
2000	3.7	−28.9	0.0836	−28.9	0.0836
2001	−52.5	−85.1	0.7247	−85.1	0.7247
2002	−21.8	−54.4	0.2964	−54.4	0.2964
2003	22.5	−10.1	0.0103	−10.1	0.0103
2004	3.7	−28.9	0.0838	−28.9	0.0838
2005	−11.0	−43.7	0.1906	−43.7	0.1906
2006	40.4	7.7	0.0060	0.0	0.0000
2007	31.7	−0.9	0.0001	−0.9	0.0001
2008	−21.5	−54.1	0.2930	−54.1	0.2930
2009	39.4	6.7	0.0045	0.0	0.0000
Average	**32.6**		**0.5988**		**0.1305**
Sqr root			**77.4%**		**36.1%**

We know how to calculate a standard deviation of returns easily in Excel, but let's take the long road here. The third column of Table 9.1 ($R - AM$) shows the difference between each annual return and the arithmetic mean annual return (AM); to illustrate, for 1995, 11.4% = 44.0%–32.6%. The fourth column displays the square of the numbers in the third column; to illustrate, for 1995, $0.0130 = 0.114^2$. The average of these squared deviations from the mean is the variance (0.5988). And the square root of the variance is the standard deviation of returns, which in this case is 77.4%.

Take a look now at the figures in the fourth column. All those figures are positive, which means that every one of these observations adds to the standard deviation. In other words, every annual return, regardless of sign or magnitude, increases this measure of risk. In fact, note that the largest number in this fourth column (6.6109), *the one that contributes to increasing the standard deviation the most*, is that for 1999 when Oracle delivered a return of almost 290%. Now, if you had held Oracle during that year, would you have been happy or unhappy?! Would you have counted that performance *against* Oracle as the standard deviation does?

One step in the right direction

Tweaking the standard deviation so that it accounts only for fluctuations below the mean return is not difficult. The next-to-last column of Table 9.1 shows the lower of each annual return minus the mean return or 0, which we can informally refer to as 'conditional returns' because each figure is the result of an if-then question. More precisely, if a return is higher than the mean (R–$AM > 0$), then the column shows a 0; if the return is lower than the mean (R–$AM < 0$), then the column shows the difference between the two (R–AM).

To illustrate, in 1995, Oracle delivered a 44% return, which is higher than the mean return of 32.6%; therefore the column shows a 0. In 2000, however, Oracle delivered a 3.7% return, which is lower than the mean return of 32.6%; therefore, the fifth column shows the difference between these two figures, 3.7%–32.6% = –28.9%. If you compare the third and the fifth columns you will notice that when the number in the third column is positive (a return higher than the mean), the associated figure in the fifth column is 0; when the number in the third column is negative (a return lower than the mean), the associated figure in the fifth column is the same as that in the third column.

The last column of Table 9.1 shows the square of the numbers in the fifth column. As the next-to-last row shows, the average of these numbers is 0.1305; and, as the last row shows, the square root of this number is 36.1%. What does this number indicate? It has a simple and intuitive interpretation: It measures volatility *below* the mean return of 32.6%.

This obviously looks like a step in the right direction. Measuring risk this way would imply 'punishing' Oracle only when it delivers returns below the mean but not when it does it above the mean. Now, is there anything special about the mean return? Isn't it possible that some investors would be interested in measuring volatility below the risk-free rate? Or below 0? Or, more generally, below *any* given number that they may consider relevant?

The semideviation

As Sherlock Holmes would say, it is more than possible; it is likely. And, we could add, it is plausible too. In fact, that is precisely what one of the two measures of risk we'll discuss in this chapter aims to measure. Formally, the **semideviation of returns with respect to B (SSD$_B$)** is defined as

$$SSD_B = \sqrt{(1/T) \cdot \sum_{t=1}^{T}[\text{Min}(R_t - B, 0)]^2} \qquad (9.1)$$

where B is *any* benchmark return chosen by an investor; T is the number of observations; and t indexes time.

Let's think a bit about expression (9.1), which is not as complicated as it may seem. The expression suggests that we take the following steps:

1 Calculate the difference between each return and the benchmark return B;

2 Take the lower of each return minus B or 0;

3 Square each number in the previous step;

4 Take the average of all the numbers in the previous step;

5 Take the square root of the number in the previous step.

Take a look at Table 9.2, which gives the returns (R) for Oracle for 1995–2009, as well as three benchmarks: the mean return, and a risk-free rate (R$_f$) of 5% and 0%. Each figure in the third column is the result of performing the first three steps of the five above. The figure in the intersection between the third column and the next-to-last row is the fourth step;

and the figure in the intersection between the third column and the last row is the fifth step, or the semideviation with respect to the mean return of 32.6%. (Note that the figures in this third column are identical to those in the last column of Table 9.1.)

table 9.2

Year	R (%)	$[Min(R–AM, 0)]^2$	$[Min(R–R_f, 0)]^2$	$[Min(R–0, 0)]^2$
1995	44.0	0.0000	0.0000	0.0000
1996	47.8	0.0000	0.0000	0.0000
1997	−19.8	0.2754	0.0617	0.0393
1998	93.3	0.0000	0.0000	0.0000
1999	289.8	0.0000	0.0000	0.0000
2000	3.7	0.0836	0.0002	0.0000
2001	−52.5	0.7247	0.3304	0.2754
2002	−21.8	0.2964	0.0718	0.0475
2003	22.5	0.0103	0.0000	0.0000
2004	3.7	0.0838	0.0002	0.0000
2005	−11.0	0.1906	0.0256	0.0121
2006	40.4	0.0000	0.0000	0.0000
2007	31.7	0.0001	0.0000	0.0000
2008	−21.5	0.2930	0.0701	0.0461
2009	39.4	0.0000	0.0000	0.0000
Average	**32.6**	**0.1305**	**0.0373**	**0.0280**
Sqr root		**36.1%**	**19.3%**	**16.7%**

The fourth column of Table 9.2 shows similar calculations with respect to a different benchmark, in this case a risk-free rate of 5%. And the last column once again shows similar calculations but in this case with respect to a benchmark of 0%. The last row shows the semideviations with respect to all three benchmarks, namely, 36.1% with respect to the mean return, 19.3% with respect to the risk-free rate, and 16.7% with respect to 0%. So, how should we interpret these figures?

Each semideviation measures volatility below, but not above, its respective benchmark. Note that because the risk-free rate of 5% is below Oracle's mean return of 32.6%, we would expect, and do find, less volatility below the risk-free rate than below the mean return. For the same reason, we would expect and do find even less volatility below 0%.

To add even more intuition to the interpretation of the semideviation, note that this measure of risk is best used in two ways: One is in relation to the standard deviation and the other is in relation to the semideviation of other assets. To illustrate this, take a look at Table 9.3, which shows the semi-deviations with respect to the arithmetic mean (SSD_{AM}), with respect to a risk-free rate of 5% (SSD_{Rf}), and with respect to 0% (SSD_0) for both Oracle and Microsoft for 1995–2009. It also shows the arithmetic mean return (AM) for both companies over the same period. The semideviations for Oracle are obviously the same as those calculated in Table 9.2.

table 9.3

Company	AM (%)	SD (%)	SSD_{AM} (%)	SSD_{Rf} (%)	SSD_0 (%)
Oracle	32.6	77.4	36.1	19.3	16.7
Microsoft	27.1	47.1	34.0	22.8	20.7

Note that although Oracle is far riskier than Microsoft when we assess risk with the standard deviation, the semideviations tell a different story. First, note that although the volatility of Oracle below its mean is less than half of its volatility (0.361/0.774 = 46.7%), the same ratio for Microsoft is over 70% (0.340/0.471 = 72.1%). In other words, given the volatility of each stock, much more of that volatility is below the mean in the case of Microsoft than in the case of Oracle.

Of course, it is still the case that Oracle's semideviation with respect to the mean is larger than Microsoft's. But recall that the mean return of Oracle (32.6%) is higher than that of Microsoft (27.1%), so we're measuring volatility below two different benchmarks. In fact, the most revealing way of assessing the risk of different assets with the semideviation is to use the same benchmark for all assets. If we measure, for example, volatility below a risk-free rate of 5%, Table 9.3 shows that Microsoft (SSD_{Rf} = 22.8%) is riskier than Oracle (SSD_{Rf} = 19.3%). And if we do a similar comparison with respect to a benchmark of 0%, we again find that Microsoft (SSD_0 = 20.7%) is riskier than Oracle (SSD_0 = 16.7%).

In short, Table 9.3 highlights an important point: When assessing risk it is essential to clearly define and agree upon a specific way to measure it. Note that if we think that the standard deviation is the proper measure of risk, then Oracle is riskier than Microsoft. On the contrary, if we think that the semideviation is the proper measure of risk, and we assess that risk with respect to the same benchmark for both companies, then Microsoft is riskier than Oracle.

A brief digression on the semideviation

It is hopefully clear from our discussion that a critical aspect of the semideviation is that it isolates the downside volatility that investors view as harmful. Importantly, note that in a downside risk framework volatility is no longer necessarily bad; volatility below the benchmark is bad and undesirable, but volatility above the benchmark is good and desirable. Doesn't this make sense?

The semideviation also has the advantage of having a flexible benchmark. Rather than measuring deviations with respect to the mean return, the semideviation accommodates any benchmark an investor may find particularly useful. This implies that, given the asset, different investors may perceive it as more or less risky depending on the benchmark they use to evaluate it. And, of course, it is perfectly plausible that different investors have different benchmarks; after all, not all of them invest for the same reasons, have the same goals, and hold their portfolios the same period of time. Again, doesn't this make sense?

Last but not least, note that although expression (9.1) may look complicated, calculating a semideviation in Excel is only a bit more difficult than calculating a standard deviation. As we'll see at the end of the chapter, the semideviation can be calculated in Excel in just one cell.

VaR

It is often important for investors and companies to have an idea of how bad adverse outcomes can really be. To answer this question, in 1994 JP Morgan introduced value at risk (VaR), which measures the 'worst' expected outcome over a given time horizon at a given confidence level. Don't panic, we'll clarify what this means.

To calculate a VaR, two parameters need to be chosen in advance. The first parameter is a time interval, which can be any that is relevant for an investor or company. A bank, for example, may want to know its 'worst' expected outcome each day to set aside appropriate reserves; a long-term investor, on the other hand, may be interested in the 'worst' expected outcome over 5 or 10 years. The second parameter is a confidence level (c); the most typical choices in this case are $c = 95\%$ and $c = 99\%$.

Formally, the **value at risk (VaR)** measure is defined as

$$\text{VaR}_c = x \quad \text{such that} \quad P(X \le x) = 1{-}c \tag{9.2}$$

In words, this expression says that VaR is a number x such that the probability that the variable X takes a value lower than or equal to x is equal to $1{-}c$, where c is the chosen confidence level. If this does not sound intuitive, it's because it's not. Here comes the thinking behind this expression.

Take a look at Figure 9.1, which shows the probability distribution of a variable X, which we could think of as returns, revenues, profits, or any other variable of interest. Let's assume that the variable is measured every day (the time interval), and let's choose a 95% confidence level ($c = 95\%$). There are two ways of thinking about VaR in this context. We could define it as the 'worst' expected outcome, over one day, at a 95% confidence level. Or, perhaps more telling, we could say that *a daily outcome worse than the calculated VaR will occur with a probability of 5%.*

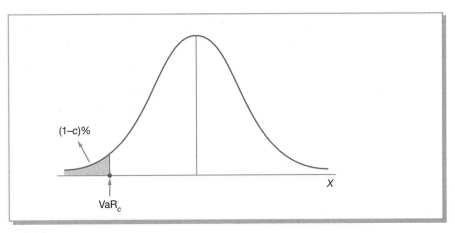

figure 9.1   VaR (value at risk)

Both of these definitions are widely used in practice, but the first one may be deceiving. That actually explains, in case you noticed, the quote marks we've been using around the word 'worst.' Figure 9.1 shows why the first definition is misleading. The calculated VaR is actually *not* the worst possible loss; all the values to the left of the VaR highlighted in the figure represent even higher losses. For this reason, you may want to focus on the second definition of VaR, which is both more accurate and more intuitive.

Take another look at Figure 9.1. Note that VaR is a number on the horizontal axis, and therefore it is measured in the same units as the variable of our interest. If returns are measured in percentages, then VaR is measured in percentages; if revenues or profits are measured in dollars, then VaR is measured in dollars; and so forth.

The calculation of VaR is not necessarily trivial. As you can see from Figure 9.1, we need to calculate the number that leaves $(1–c)\%$ of the distribution to its left. This, in turn, implies that we first need to characterize the distribution, and then estimate this probability, therefore having to calculate an integral (as discussed in Chapters 28 and 29). But don't throw your arms up in despair just yet. If the variable X follows a normal distribution, then calculation of a VaR is very simple indeed. In fact, under normality, VaR is calculated with the expression

$$\text{VaR}_c = AM + z_c \cdot SD \tag{9.3}$$

where AM and SD denote the arithmetic mean and standard deviation of the underlying normal distribution, and z_c is a number that comes from the *standard* normal distribution (discussed in Chapter 28). The values of z_c for the two most widely-used confidence levels, 95% and 99%, are –1.64 and –2.33.

Take a look at Table 9.4, which reports the mean monthly return and monthly standard deviation of four equity markets, based on MSCI indices (in dollars and accounting for capital gains and dividends), between January 2000 and December 2009. The distribution of monthly returns of these four markets is approximately normal, so the assumption underlying expression (9.3) approximately holds.

table 9.4

	Brazil (%)	China (%)	Japan (%)	UK (%)
AM	2.2	1.2	–0.2	0.2
SD	11.0	8.9	5.3	4.9
VaR_{95}	–15.9	–13.4	–8.8	–7.9
VaR_{99}	–23.5	–19.5	–12.4	–11.3
SSD_{AM}	8.2	6.7	3.7	3.7
SSD_0	7.1	6.1	3.8	3.5

Recall that before calculating a VaR we need to select a time horizon and a confidence level. Let's choose a monthly time interval (to make it consistent with the frequency of the returns in Table 9.4) and a confidence level of 95%. And let's focus on the Brazilian market, which between 2000 and 2009 delivered a mean monthly return of 2.2% with a monthly standard deviation of 11%. The 95% monthly VaR for this market is then simply calculated as 0.022–(1.64)(0.11) = –15.9%. In words, the probability of experiencing a monthly loss higher than 15.9% in the Brazilian market is 5%. As simple as that!

What if we change the significance level to 99%? Well, the probability distribution of returns doesn't change, so the mean and standard deviation remain the same. The only change in expression (9.3) is the value of z_c, which will now be –2.33. Therefore, the 99% monthly VaR of the Brazilian market is simply calculated as 0.022–(2.33)(0.11) = –23.5%. In words, the probability of experiencing a monthly loss higher than 23.5% in the Brazilian market is 1%. Note that the higher the confidence level, the lower the VaR; and, the lower the VaR, the more unlikely it is that scenarios worse than the VaR will materialize.

Following the same simple steps you can calculate the rest of the VaRs displayed in Table 9.4. (Try!) Note that, unsurprisingly, the larger VaRs are in the emerging markets of Brazil and China, not in the developed markets of Japan and the UK. Consistent with this, note also that Brazil and China have larger semideviations, both with respect to the mean (SSD_{AM}) and with respect to 0 (SSD_0), than Japan and the UK.

To conclude, one last but *very* important point. The calculations we just ran are valid *exclusively* for variables whose underlying distribution is normal. But of course, whether or not that is the case is an empirical matter that needs to be tested. We cannot simply *assume* normality and always expect it to be an accurate description of the variable of our interest. (Oracle's distribution of returns, for example, is very far from normal.) Importantly, if the underlying distribution is not normal, estimating a VaR is usually more complicated than we discussed. To be sure, the idea behind the calculation remains the same regardless of the underlying distribution; that is, we still need to calculate the number that leaves (1–c)% of the area under the distribution to its left. But the actual calculation may change substantially depending on the type of distribution of the asset considered.

Just as important, note that, in general, many of the distributions we observe in reality have fat tails. (Distributions of daily returns, for example, almost always do.) This means that very high or very low returns are far more likely than what the normal distribution would lead us to expect. And this, in turn, implies that if we calculate a VaR assuming a normal distribution when the actual distribution has fat tails, we'll end up *underestimating* our risk, in many cases by a very substantial margin.

The big picture

Most investors associate risk with negative outcomes. However, one of the most widely used definitions of risk, the standard deviation, does not. Downside risk is an increasingly popular framework and the semideviation is an increasingly popular alternative to traditional measures of risk. It captures the downside that investors want to avoid (but not the upside that investors want to be exposed to) and defines risk as volatility below a chosen benchmark. Plausibly, the benchmark is any number useful for the investor. And importantly, the semideviation highlights the fact that not all volatility is bad; only the volatility below the benchmark is.

VaR, on the other hand, provides investors with an idea of how bad adverse scenarios can be. It is very useful and easy to interpret, and widely used by financial institutions. The normality assumption that yields its simple calculation, however, must be handled with extreme care and tested rather than simply assumed.

Excel section

The semideviation can be calculated in Excel in more than one way. We'll focus here on two ways, emphasizing the first, which is the easier of the two (it takes just one cell). Let's introduce a command that simply counts the number of observations in a series. Suppose you have a series of returns in cells A1:A10.

■ To count the number of observations in the series simply type

=count(A1:A10)

in cell A11 and then hit Enter.

To calculate the semideviation, let's assume that we have entered the 'count' command in cell A11, where we then have the number of observations in the series (10 in our case). Let's also assume that in cell A12 we have entered any benchmark of our interest.

■ To calculate the semideviation with respect to the benchmark in cell A12 type

=sqrt(sumproduct(if(A1:A10–A12<0, A1:A10–A12, 0),

if(A1:A10–A12<0, A1:A10–A12, 0))/A11)

in cell A13 and then press Ctrl+Shift+Enter *simultaneously.*

Two comments about this calculation. First, the expression above is an array, which means that instead of Enter we need to hold down the Ctrl and Shift keys and then press Enter. Second, the 'sumproduct' command generally enables us to multiply, period by period, one variable by another and then to add all the products. In our case, it actually multiplies a variable (each annual 'conditional return') by itself and then adds the products.

There is a longer road to the calculation of the semideviation, which is the step-by-step way outlined in Table 9.1. More precisely, another way of calculating semideviations is:

■ Type =if(A1<A$12, (A1–A$12)^2, 0) in cell B1 and then hit Enter.

■ Copy the previous command all the way down to cells B2 through B10.

■ Type =sqrt(average(B1:B10)) in cell B11 and then hit Enter.

10

Risk and return IV:
Risk-adjusted returns

The financial press often publishes rankings of mutual funds, and many investors read them eagerly. In fact, many even use them to make investment decisions. The problem is, most of these rankings are flawed. More often than not, they focus on short-term past returns, which is problematic on at least two counts: They are not necessarily indicative of future returns and they do not explicitly account for risk. In this chapter we'll discuss how to rank funds properly, and assets in general, on the basis of their long-term risk-adjusted returns.

Returns and good luck

Open a financial newspaper or magazine that features a ranking of mutual funds and you're likely to find that the ranking is based on last year's (or worse, last quarter's) returns. That is at best not very informative, and at worst badly misleading. Furthermore, investors tend to pour their money into the funds at the top of such rankings and withdraw it from the funds at the bottom. That flies in the face of just about everything we know in finance.

It is, of course, important to assess the returns delivered by different funds, but it's just as important to assess the impact of luck and risk on those returns. In fact, a careful analysis must disentangle the effect of three factors on returns: Luck, risk-taking, and ability. Let's consider them one at a time.

Suppose I walk into a casino, head straight to the roulette, bet on 17 ... and win! Would you conclude that I have some special insight on how to beat the casino? What if for the first time in my life I bet on a horse and win? Would you conclude that I do know about horses? Exactly. Why, then, do many investors conclude that the top manager in a list of funds ranked by returns over the last quarter or year is the most competent? Isn't it possible that he just got lucky with a few stock picks?

It sure is. In fact, there's very little (if anything) we can say about a fund manager by observing its return performance over the past quarter or year. Or, put differently, by assessing short-term returns, we just can't rule out the influence of (good or bad) luck on performance. That's why rankings based on three-year returns and five-year returns are more useful, although longer periods would be even better. In short, although there is not really a lot we can do to assess the impact of luck on returns, we can safely say that the longer the evaluation period, the lesser the role luck should play.

And yet, even if we could safely establish that luck was not the reason for which a given fund delivered the best return performance, we could still not conclude that this fund was the best, or that its manager was the most competent. To make that statement, we would first need to account for the effect of one other factor, and that is, precisely, the key issue we discuss in this chapter.

Returns and risk-taking

At the heart of finance theory is the idea that, in the long term, the higher the exposure to risk, the higher is the expected return. This suggests another reason for which a fund may end up at the top of a ranking based on long-term returns: It may simply be a very risky fund. In other words, top-performing managers may be doing something that we could perfectly do ourselves, namely, investing in relatively risky assets to obtain relatively high returns.

Importantly, the risk–return trade-off is open to all investors, and there is no reason to give credit, or to pay fees, to a manager for doing something we could do ourselves. A manager who delivers high returns simply by exposing investors to a high level of risk is adding little or no value. In other words, a proper ranking of performance would need to adjust returns by the impact of luck *and* the level of risk taking. We can address the former by evaluating performance on the basis of long-term returns; and we can address the latter by assessing *risk-adjusted* returns with the magnitudes we'll discuss shortly.

Now, suppose we rank some funds on the basis of their long-term, risk-adjusted returns. Can we now argue that the top-performing funds are the best, or that their managers are the most competent? The short answer is yes. Having accounted for luck and risk on returns, what remains is performance due to superior insight or skill. And putting our money in the top-performing funds of such ranking is, at the very least, a far smarter move than putting it in the funds at the top of any ranking published in the financial press.

An example

Take a look at Table 10.1, which shows the arithmetic mean return (*AM*), standard deviation (*SD*), beta, and semideviation with respect to a benchmark of 0% (SSD_0) of five mutual funds and the S&P 500 for 1990–2009. All magnitudes are annual, and all betas are estimated with respect to the S&P. The five funds considered are the Fidelity Blue Chip Growth (FBGRX), Fidelity Capital Appreciation (FDCAX), Fidelity Select Banking (FSRBX), Fidelity Select Utilities Portfolio (FSUTX), and Franklin Utilities A (FKUTX).

table 10.1

	FBGRX	FDCAX	FSRBX	FSUTX	FKUTX	S&P
AM (%)	11.8	10.3	12.5	10.2	9.5	10.1
SD (%)	16.5	18.4	20.9	15.3	12.6	15.0
Beta	1.04	1.05	1.01	0.75	0.36	1.00
SSD_0 (%)	10.9	12.4	14.5	10.8	8.4	10.2

Note the variability in the risk and return of these funds. Note, also, that the 20-year period we're focusing on seems to be long enough to rule out the effect of luck on returns. If we ranked these five funds by their 20-year mean annual returns, FSRBX would be at the top and FKUTX at the bottom. Should we then put our money in FSRBX and run away from FKUTX?

Not so fast. Although we're assessing returns over a 20-year period and so can rule out luck, we still have to adjust these returns by risk. And, because risk can be assessed in more than one way, so can be risk-adjusted returns. Let's then talk about the methods most widely used to measure it.

Jensen's alpha

Our first measure of risk-adjusted returns is based on a simple comparison between *observed* returns and *required or expected* returns. It goes without saying that in general we'd be happy with any fund that performed above our expectation and unhappy with any fund that did the opposite. Our return expectation may be based on many factors, but a plausible one would be the return we require for bearing the risk of a fund. And we know that the CAPM has been devised precisely for this purpose; that is, to estimate the return investors should require given the risk they are exposed to when the latter is measured by beta.

This brings us to our first measure of risk-adjusted returns. For any fund i, its **Jensen's alpha**, or simply **alpha** (α_i) for short, is given by

$$\alpha_i = R_i - (R_f + MRP \cdot \beta_i) \tag{10.1}$$

where R_i is the *observed* mean annual return of fund i; R_f the risk-free rate; MRP the market risk premium; and β_i the beta of fund i. Note that the expression in parentheses is that of the CAPM and therefore the required or expected return of fund i.

The interpretation of alpha is straightforward. A positive alpha indicates returns above what we required or expected given the risk of a fund, and a negative alpha indicates the opposite. Obviously, the larger the alpha, the better is the risk-adjusted performance of the fund. And, importantly, note that alpha, just as returns, is measured in percentages.

To assess the risk-adjusted returns of the funds in Table 10.1 with alpha, let's assume a risk-free rate of 5.5%, which is the average yield on 10-year Treasury notes over the 1990–2009 period considered in the table. Throughout this chapter, whenever a risk-free rate is needed, we'll use the same 5.5%. Let's also assume a risk premium of 4.6%, which is the average annual difference between the returns of the S&P (10.1%) and the average yield just mentioned over the same 1990–2009 period. (We're being a bit sloppy here. As discussed in Chapter 7, we should calculate the risk premium taking into account the average *return* of bonds, not just the average yield. But if we did that, we'd end up with a 2.4% market risk premium for 1990–2009, very low from a historical perspective. Hence the use of the average yield, which brings the market risk premium somewhat closer to a 'normal' level.)

As expression (10.1) shows, calculating alpha is simple. Take the FBGRX fund, which delivered a mean annual return of 11.8%. Given its beta of 1.04, the required return on this fund according to the CAPM was 0.055+(0.046)(1.04) = 10.3%. Therefore, FBGRX's alpha is just the difference between what the fund delivered and what was required or expected from it; that is, 11.8%–10.3% = 1.5% a year. Intuitive, isn't it?

Table 10.2 shows the alphas of the five funds we've been discussing over the 1990–2009 period. Now, compare the second row of this table with the second row of Table 10.1. Note that a ranking of these funds on the basis of their mean returns would differ from one on the basis of their alphas. In fact, the worst performer in terms of returns (FKUTX) is the best performer (together with FSRBX) in terms of risk-adjusted returns. See the importance of accounting for risk?

table 10.2

	FBGRX	FDCAX	FSRBX	FSUTX	FKUTX	S&P
α_i (%)	1.5	0.0	2.3	1.2	2.3	0.0
T_i	6.0	4.6	6.9	6.2	11.1	4.6
S_i	37.9	26.2	33.3	30.5	31.6	30.7
RAP_i (%)	11.2	9.4	10.5	10.1	10.2	10.1
N_i	107.9	82.8	86.2	94.4	112.5	99.1

Here's one way to think about a ranking of funds on the basis of alpha. Take FSUTX, which delivered a higher mean annual return than FKUTX; in fact, the former outperformed the latter by 0.7% (= 10.2%–9.5%) a year over 20 years. Not bad. But that is an 'unfair' comparison. FSUTX's beta (0.75) was more than twice as high as FKUTX's (0.36). Shouldn't that be taken into account in a proper evaluation? That is exactly what alpha does.

One last thing. Note that with the exception of FDCAX, whose alpha is 0%, the other four funds had a positive alpha and therefore outperformed their expected returns. But it is, of course, possible for a fund to deliver a negative alpha, therefore underperforming its expected return. In fact, if we showed one more decimal place in Table 10.2, we'd see that FDCAX's alpha was –0.03%. And although this is not the place to discuss this issue, it is indeed the case that the ability of fund managers to deliver positive alpha consistently is very much in doubt.

The Treynor index

Alpha is widely used as a measure of risk-adjusted returns but it's not free from problems. Consider two hypothetical funds A and B, with required returns of 10% and 40%, and assume that over the past 20 years their observed mean returns were 15% and 45%. If we assess their risk-adjusted returns with alpha, both funds would be equally attractive; they both delivered an alpha of 5%. But are they *really* equally attractive?

Not really. Think about it this way. Both A and B outperformed their required return by 5 percentage points. In the case of A, 5 points is 50% (= 5%/10%) of its required return, but in the case of B, 5 points is just 12.5% (= 5%/40%) of its required return. Do you still think both funds are equally attractive? The problem with alpha is that it measures outperformance or underperformance in *absolute* terms rather than relative to expected returns. And as the previous example highlights, the same 5 points of outperformance are very different when our expectation is 10% than when it is 40%.

Although alpha is certainly an improvement over a direct comparison of returns, it can also be improved upon; and that is just what our next measure of risk-adjusted returns does. For any fund *i*, the **Treynor index (T_i)** is given by

$$T_i = \frac{R_i - R_f}{\beta_i} \qquad\qquad (10.2)$$

and measures excess returns (that is, returns in excess of the risk-free rate) per unit of beta risk. Before we go back to our example, notice a few things.

First, unlike alpha, which is measured in percentages and therefore easy to understand and communicate, the Treynor index (excess returns per unit of beta risk) is not intuitive. Which brings us to a second point: The Treynor index is mostly used to *rank* funds, and the higher a fund is in the ranking, the better is its risk-adjusted performance. Put differently, the meaning of each fund's Treynor index is less important than the ranking it enables us to make. Third, note that sometimes just for the sake of clarity, expression (10.2) is multiplied by 100; in fact, that is the case with the Treynor indices reported in Table 10.2. Finally, note that Treynor indices are easy to calculate; the Treynor index of the FBGRX fund, for example, is calculated as $100 \cdot (0.118 - 0.055)/1.04 = 6.0$.

Let's now go back to our example and make sure we understand why the Treynor index is an improvement over alpha. Let's compare the FKUTX and FSRBX funds. These funds have betas of 0.36 and 1.01, required annual returns of 7.1% and 10.2% (which you could calculate yourself with the CAPM), observed mean annual returns of 9.5% and 12.5%, and the same alphas of 2.3%. In terms of observed returns, then, FSRBX outperformed FKUTX by 3 percentage points a year, but once we adjust these returns by risk (the beta of the former is almost three times that of the latter), both funds outperformed their respective required returns by the same 2.3 percentage points.

As you're probably thinking by now, the fact that these two funds have the same alpha does not imply that we're equally happy holding one or the other. Note that the 2.3% alpha of FSRBX is less than 23% of its required annual return of 10.2% (2.3/10.2 = 22.8%); the 2.3% alpha of FKUTX, in turn, is almost 33% of its 7.1% required annual return (2.3/7.1 = 32.7%). In other words, FKUTX outperformed FSRBX by a wider margin when we assess alpha relative to each fund's required return than when we do so in absolute terms.

Let's look at this from a different perspective by considering Figure 10.1, which shows the FKUTX and FSRBX funds, as well as the securities markets line (SML) that follows from the CAPM and therefore yields required returns as a function of beta. Alpha is given by the vertical distance between the big dots representing each fund and the SML; and since we know that both funds have the same alpha of 2.3%, then we also know that these two vertical distances are the same.

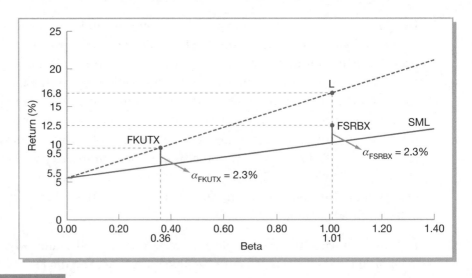

figure 10.1   Alpha and the Treynor index

Now, here's something we could do: We could borrow money at the risk-free rate, invest that money plus whatever our initial capital in the FKUTX fund, and end up with portfolio L, which is just a levered position in FKUTX. By construction, portfolio L has the same risk as FSRBX (a beta of 1.01); but it also has a much higher return (16.8% versus 12.5% for FSRBX). So, by leveraging our position in FKUTX, we end up with a two-asset portfolio (a long position in FKUTX and a short position in the risk-free rate) that outperforms FSRBX on a risk-adjusted basis. In short, although both funds have the same alpha, FKUTX delivered better risk-adjusted returns than FSRBX, which is confirmed by their Treynor indices of 11.1 and 6.9.

Before we move on to our next measure, three quick points. First, note that graphically the Treynor index of a fund is given by the *slope* of a line connecting the risk-free rate and the fund, just like the dashed line that connects the 5.5% risk-free rate and the FKUTX fund in Figure 10.1. Second, note that rankings based on alpha and the Treynor index may differ, as is in fact the case with the funds in Table 10.2; whenever this is the case, and for the reasons just discussed, the ranking based on the Treynor index is methodologically superior. Third, do not let this last fact lead you to underestimate alpha, which is very widely used in practice. The reason alpha is still valuable is because it is typically used to assess the performance of funds *within a similar risk category* (hence with similar required returns) which renders the problem we discussed largely irrelevant.

The Sharpe ratio

The Treynor index adjusts returns by risk measured by beta, but as we know all too well by now, beta is a proper measure of risk once the unsystematic risk has been diversified away and only the systematic risk remains. Put differently, the Treynor index provides an appropriate ranking for investors who are properly diversified *across funds*.

However, many investors diversify *across stocks* by buying one or two broadly-diversified funds, such as the Fidelity Magellan or the Vanguard 500 in the US. In these cases, the unsystematic risk of a fund does not get diversified away and beta becomes a questionable measure of risk. In other words, investors that concentrate their holdings into just one or few funds bear the *total* risk of the fund (rather than just its systematic risk), which is measured by the standard deviation of its returns.

That is, precisely, the insight of our third measure of risk-adjusted returns. For any fund i, the **Sharpe ratio (S_i)** is given by

$$S_i = \frac{R_i - R_f}{SD_i} \tag{10.3}$$

where SD_i is the standard deviation of returns of fund i. As this expression shows, the Sharpe ratio measures excess returns per unit of volatility risk.

The Sharpe ratio shares with the Treynor index three of the characteristics we discussed before for the latter. First, the Sharpe ratio yields a number with little intuition, excess returns per unit of volatility risk, and for this reason the ranking it produces is more important than the actual Sharpe ratio of each fund. Second, Sharpe ratios are often multiplied by 100 for the sake of clarity; that is in fact the way they are calculated in Table 10.2. And third, the calculation of Sharpe ratios is simple; the Sharpe ratio of the FBGRX fund, for example, is calculated as $100 \cdot (0.118-0.055)/0.165 = 37.9$.

Table 10.2 shows that a ranking of funds by the Sharpe ratio may be different from a ranking produced by either alpha or the Treynor index, which at this point in our discussion should come as no surprise. Finally, as is the case with alphas, Sharpe ratios are very widely used in practice; in fact, you can often find them reported in the fact sheets of financial products.

The RAP

The Sharpe ratio is widely used to assess the risk-adjusted performance of funds. However, as we mentioned, excess returns per unit of volatility risk is not a very intuitive idea. This led Nobel-prize-winning economist Franco Modigliani and his granddaughter Leah Modigliani (from Morgan Stanley) to develop the RAP, a measure that preserves the attractive characteristics of the Sharpe ratio but at the same time has a more intuitive interpretation.

For any fund i, its **risk-adjusted performance (RAP_i)** is given by

$$RAP_i = R_f + (R_i - R_f) \cdot \left(\frac{SD_M}{SD_i}\right) = R_f + SD_M \cdot S_i \tag{10.4}$$

where SD_M is the market's standard deviation of returns and S_i is the Sharpe ratio of fund i. In a nutshell, the RAP seeks to adjust the return of each fund in such a way that funds that are riskier than the market are 'punished' with a decrease in their mean return, and those that are less risky than the market are 'rewarded' with an increase in their mean return. Not very clear? Let's look at the numbers.

Let's compare the FDCAX and the FKUTX funds. In terms of mean annual returns, the former outperformed the latter by 0.8% (= 10.3%–9.5%) a year. But by now you should suspect why this comparison is misguided; the volatility of FDCAX (18.4%) was far higher than that of FKUTX (12.6%). In fact, although FDCAX was more volatile than the market, the opposite was the case with FKUTX.

Here's where the RAP comes in, by 'punishing' the returns of FDCAX and rewarding those of FKUTX. Let's calculate the RAPs first. The RAP of the FDCAX fund is equal to

$$0.055 + (0.103 – 0.055) \cdot (0.15/0.184) = 9.4\%$$

and that of the FKUTX fund is equal to

$$0.055 + (0.095 – 0.055) \cdot (0.15/0.126) = 10.2\%$$

which indicates that, contrary to what a direct comparison of returns would suggest, FKUTX outperformed FDCAX based on risk-adjusted returns.

Now, to really understand the RAP, let's look at these figures a little closer. FDCAX is more volatile than the market and the RAP approach suggests that we should 'punish' it by decreasing its mean return. Once we do that, the 10.3% mean annual return is reduced to a 9.4% *risk-adjusted* mean annual return. FKUTX, however, is less volatile than the market and the RAP approach suggests that we should 'reward' it by increasing its mean return. And once we do that we end up with a 10.2% *risk-adjusted* mean annual return. The 0.8% (= 10.2%–9.4%) difference between these two RAPs measures the *risk-adjusted* outperformance of the FKUTX fund.

The rewards and punishments imposed by the RAP on mean returns seek to avoid a comparison between apples and oranges. Funds of different risk are not directly comparable, but once they are punished or rewarded for being more or less volatile than the market, they become comparable among themselves and to the market. In other words, if we compare the returns of different funds we may be comparing apples and oranges, but if we compare the RAPs of different funds we're comparing apples and apples. *And* we're comparing them in percentages, which are easier to grasp than ratios with little intuitive meaning.

Note from Table 10.2 that a ranking of funds by their RAPs is identical to one by their Sharpe ratios. This follows directly from the second equality in equation (10.4), which shows that the RAP is simply a monotonic transformation of the Sharpe ratio. This is just a fancy way of saying that if we multiply Sharpe ratios by a positive number (the standard deviation of the market) and then add another number (the risk-free rate), the ranking of the funds *must* be the same as that produced by the Sharpe ratio. (Note that when calculating RAPs with the second equality in equation (10.4) we need to divide the Sharpe ratios in Table 10.2 by 100. Remember, the multiplication by 100 is only for the sake of expressing Sharpe ratios more clearly but it needs to be undone when using Sharpe ratios to calculate the RAP.)

In short, then, the RAP assesses risk with the standard deviation of returns just like the Sharpe ratio; it preserves the rankings produced by the Sharpe ratio; but it's expressed in percentages and therefore has a more intuitive interpretation than the Sharpe ratio.

The Sortino ratio

Our last measure of risk-adjusted returns is very similar to the Treynor ratio and the Sharpe ratio but uses a different definition of risk, namely, the semideviation of returns with respect to a chosen benchmark. Downside risk in general and the semideviation in particular are discussed in Chapter 9 and, as we argued there, both are becoming increasingly popular among practitioners.

For any fund i, the **Sortino ratio (N_i)** is given by

$$N_i = \frac{R_i - B}{SSD_{Bi}}$$

(10.5)

where B is any benchmark return chosen by an investor and SSD_{Bi} is the semideviation of fund i with respect to the benchmark B. Essentially, the Sortino ratio adjusts the excess returns of the fund with respect to the benchmark B by the volatility of the fund *below* that benchmark. Note that, again only for the sake of clarity, expression (10.5) is often multiplied by 100, which is the case with the Sortino ratios in Table 10.2.

Needless to say, calculating Sortino ratios is easy. Let's consider a benchmark of 0. The semideviation of FBGRX with respect to this benchmark, as Table

10.1 shows, is 10.9%; then, this fund's Sortino ratio is calculated as $100 \cdot (0.118 - 0)/0.109 = 107.9$. Note that, as was the case with the Treynor index and the Sharpe ratio, a Sortino ratio (excess returns per unit of semideviation risk) is not intuitive and the ranking it generates is more important than each individual figure. Also, note from Table 10.2 that a ranking of funds by the Sortino ratio may be different from one based on the other measures of risk-adjusted returns.

Finally, note that one of the appealing characteristics of the Sortino ratio is that it can be tailored to any benchmark return B that is relevant to an investor. Once this benchmark is chosen by the investor, *both* excess returns and downside volatility are measured with respect to that benchmark. And because different investors may have different benchmarks, they may also end up producing different rankings for the same group of funds.

Final thoughts

Not all the rankings of funds in the financial press are flawed. In fact, some take steps to account for the two main factors we discussed in this chapter. To account for luck, besides rankings based on one-quarter or one-year returns, many publications also provide rankings based on three-year and five-year returns. And, to account for risk, most rankings group funds into 'styles' (such as growth, value, small cap, and large cap) with the idea that although risk is quite different *across* styles, it is not so different *within* each style. Having said that, the risk of different funds within a style may in fact vary substantially and the best way to account for this variability is to compare them on the basis of risk-adjusted returns.

Morningstar, the best-known fund-rating company, has popularized the use of a 3 × 3 box with three styles at the top (value, core, and growth) and three styles on the side (large cap, mid cap, and small cap). This yields a square with nine boxes, each representing a different style. Funds are then allocated to the boxes and evaluated only with respect to their peers. A fund that invests in biotech companies and another that invests in utilities have little in common; they would therefore be placed in different boxes and each would be evaluated relative to its own peers. However, note that although comparing the returns of these two funds would be rather pointless (just as comparing apples and oranges), comparing their risk-adjusted returns would be entirely appropriate and, at the end of the day, is the correct comparison to make.

Finally, a brief reference to the widely used and abused expression 'beating the market.' Hopefully by now you will have realized that this expression is more often than not badly misused. Beating the market last year means little because maybe we just got lucky; and beating the market in the long term is always possible if we're willing to take more risk than that of the market. *A rightful claim to beating the market can only be made on the basis of long-term, risk-adjusted returns*; that is quite different from the context in which this expression is typically used. And the evidence on the ability of fund managers to beat the market from this perspective is very, very damning.

The big picture

Ranking funds, or assets in general, on the basis of their returns is rather pointless. A proper ranking must take into account both return and risk; that is, risk-adjusted returns. In fact, a proper ranking must disentangle the effect on returns of luck, risk-taking, and ability. The impact of luck can be removed by assessing returns over a long period of time; the influence of risk can be assessed with the methods discussed in this chapter.

There exist several ways of adjusting returns by risk, largely depending on the relevant definition of risk. These may yield substantially different rankings of assets, which reinforces both the ambiguity and the importance of the concept of risk. Be that as it may, one thing we can say for sure: The only meaningful way to rank assets is on the basis of their long-term risk-adjusted returns.

11

Risk and return V: Portfolio optimization

n Chapter 4 we discussed how to calculate the risk and return of a portfolio. In this chapter we'll discuss how to obtain optimal portfolios. More precisely, we'll look into how to minimize risk; how to minimize risk for any desired level of return; how to maximize expected return for any desired level of risk; and how to maximize risk-adjusted returns. And we'll discuss in detail how to implement all this in Excel. (Before reading this chapter, it's essential that you're familiar with all the concepts discussed in Chapter 4.)

Objectives

We all invest for different reasons and are likely to have different goals; some people save for retirement, others to buy a home, and others to go to college, to name but a few usual reasons. Although the goals are many and varied, we can still put most of the reasons for investing into four groups, all of which we'll discuss in this chapter. And although these four problems are different, they do share at least two characteristics.

First, all problems have the goal of either maximizing or minimizing some target magnitude, usually referred to as the objective function. And second, the maximization or minimization of the objective function is subject to at least one restriction, and often to more than one; the common restriction to all problems is to invest all the capital that has been allocated to the portfolio. This means that optimization problems do not determine how much capital to invest; rather, *given* the capital to be invested, they determine how to optimally allocate it among the assets considered.

So, what are the four problems? Investors are usually interested in:

1 Minimizing the risk of their portfolio;

2 Minimizing the risk of their portfolio subject to a target return;

3 Maximizing the expected return of their portfolio subject to a target level of risk;

4 Maximizing risk-adjusted returns (the ultimate goal).

We'll discuss all these problems shortly, but a bit of notation first. We'll call E_p and SD_p the expected return and risk of a portfolio. We'll call R_f the risk-free rate. And we'll call x_i the proportion of the portfolio invested in asset i; that is, the amount of money invested in asset i divided by the amount of money invested in the portfolio. Finally, as discussed in Chapter 4, the expected return and risk of a portfolio are respectively given by

$$E_p = x_1 \cdot E(R_1) + x_2 \cdot E(R_2) + \ldots + x_n \cdot E(R_n) \tag{11.1}$$

$$SD_p = \left\{ \sum_{i=1}^{n} \sum_{j=1}^{n} x_i \cdot x_j \cdot Cov_{ij} \right\}^{1/2} \quad S \tag{11.2}$$

where $E(R_i)$ denotes the expected return of asset i; Cov_{ij} denotes the covariance between assets i and j; and n is the number of assets in the portfolio.

Inputs and output

All optimization problems require some inputs to produce an output. The inputs consist of expected returns, variances (or standard deviations), and covariances (or correlations). More precisely, for each asset we need its expected return, its variance, and its covariances to the rest of the assets in the portfolio. For a portfolio of n assets, this implies n expected returns, n variances and $(n^2-n)/2$ covariances. (Recall that $Cov_{ij} = Cov_{ji}$.) One of the problems we'll discuss also requires as an input a risk-free rate. And if the problem to be solved involves a target level of risk or return, we'll need those inputs too.

How to estimate the expected returns, variances, and covariances, however, is controversial. We could look back a few years, estimate these elements, and assume (or hope!) that they will remain similar to what they've been in the past. Alternatively, we could use a model to generate forward-looking estimates. The shortcoming of the first approach is that all these parameters fluctuate over time, and history may or may not be a good guide to their future value; the shortcoming of the second approach is that no model exists to reliably estimate the future value of these parameters. One thing is certain, though: A proper portfolio optimization requires the *expected or future* values of these parameters.

The output of the four problems we'll discuss is a set of weights $x_1^*, x_2^*, ..., x_n^*$ that achieve the goal stated in the objective function subject to the relevant restrictions. (In finance and economics the '*' symbol is typically used to denote optimality.) Having obtained these optimal weights, we can then plug them back into the objective function and determine its optimal value.

Minimizing risk

Let's start with the simplest of all problems, which consists of finding the combination of assets that yields the portfolio with the lowest possible risk. Formally, this problem is stated as

$$\text{Min}_{x_1, x_2, ..., x_n} SD_p = \left\{ \sum_{i=1}^{n} \sum_{j=1}^{n} x_i \cdot x_j \cdot Cov_{ij} \right\}^{1/2}$$

$$\text{subject to} \quad \rightarrow x_1 + x_2 + ... + x_n = 1$$

The first line states the goal, which is to minimize the risk of the portfolio measured by its volatility or standard deviation of returns; the '$x_1, x_2, ..., x_n$' between Min and SD_p denotes the endogenous variables, or those that we solve directly for. The second line is the 'allocation restriction' mentioned before, which states that given the capital to be invested, we need to find the optimal allocation to each of the assets considered.

The solution to this problem is a set of weights $x_1^*, x_2^*, ..., x_n^*$ that determines the portfolio with the lowest risk. We can then plug these optimal weights, together with the inputs of the problem, into expressions (11.1) and (11.2) and determine the expected return and risk of this portfolio which, as discussed in Chapter 4, is called the *minimum variance portfolio* (MVP).

Minimizing risk subject to a target return

Investors often have in mind a target return they would like to achieve, and they obviously would like to do it bearing the lowest possible risk. Formally, this problem can be stated as

$$\text{Min}_{x_1, x_2, ..., x_n} SD_p = \left\{ \sum_{i=1}^{n} \sum_{j=1}^{n} x_i \cdot x_j \cdot Cov_{ij} \right\}^{1/2}$$

$$\text{subject to} \rightarrow E_p = x_1 \cdot E(R_1) + x_2 \cdot E(R_2) + ... + x_n \cdot E(R_n) = E^T$$

$$\rightarrow x_1 + x_2 + ... + x_n = 1$$

The first line states the goal, which is (as in the previous problem) to find the portfolio with the lowest risk. The second line states the restriction that the portfolio must have an expected return equal to the target return E^T. And the third line is the allocation restriction we already discussed.

The solution to this problem is a set of weights x_1^*, x_2^*, ..., x_n^* that determines the portfolio with an expected return E^T and the lowest possible risk for that level of return. We can then plug these optimal weights, together with the inputs of the problem, into expression (11.2) and determine the risk of this portfolio.

Maximizing expected return subject to a target level of risk

Some investors may target a maximum level of risk they are willing to bear, and want to find the portfolio that yields the highest expected return for that level of risk. Formally, this problem can be stated as

$$\text{Max}_{x_1, x_2, ..., x_n} E_p = x_1 \cdot E(R_1) + x_2 \cdot E(R_2) + ... + x_n \cdot E(R_n)$$

$$\text{subject to} \rightarrow SD_p = \left\{ \sum_{i=1}^{n} \sum_{j=1}^{n} x_i \cdot x_j \cdot Cov_{ij} \right\}^{1/2} = SD^T$$

$$\rightarrow x_1 + x_2 + ... + x_n = 1$$

The first line states the goal, which is to find the portfolio with the highest expected return. The second line states the restriction that the portfolio must have a target level of risk SD^T. And the third line is the allocation restriction.

The solution to this problem is a set of weights $x_1{}^*$, $x_2{}^*$, ..., $x_n{}^*$ that determines the portfolio with a risk of SD^T and the highest expected return for that level of risk. We can then plug these optimal weights, together with the inputs of the problem, into expression (11.1) and determine the expected return of this portfolio.

Maximizing risk-adjusted returns

The previous three problems state different goals (and restrictions) that investors may have. However, finance theory suggests that the ultimate goal of a rational investor should be to find the portfolio that maximizes risk-adjusted returns; that is, the one that yields the highest possible return per unit of (volatility) risk borne.

We explored the issue of risk-adjusted returns in the previous chapter, so for our current purposes it is enough to highlight two things. First, that the best portfolio is *not* the one that maximizes the expected return. If that were the case, we'd put all our money in the *one* asset with the highest expected return. Needless to say, we don't do that; we do care about risk too and therefore diversify. In other words, we like to earn high returns and to sleep at night too!

Second, although there are many ways to define risk-adjusted returns, one of the most widely-used definitions is the **Sharpe ratio (S_p)** we discussed in the previous chapter, which is given by

$$S_p = \frac{E_p - R_f}{SD_p} \qquad (11.3)$$

Note that an increase in the expected return of the portfolio or a decrease in its risk both increase the Sharpe ratio.

We can now restate the goal of maximizing risk-adjusted returns as finding the portfolio that maximizes the Sharpe ratio. Formally,

$$\text{Max}_{x_1, x_2, ..., x_n} S_p = \frac{E_p - R_f}{SD_p} = \frac{x_1 \cdot E(R_1) + ... + x_n \cdot E(R_n) - R_f}{\left\{ \sum_{i=1}^{n} \sum_{j=1}^{n} x_i \cdot x_j \cdot Cov_{ij} \right\}^{1/2}}$$

subject to $\rightarrow x_1 + x_2 + ... + x_n = 1$

The first line states the goal, which is to find the portfolio with the highest Sharpe ratio, and the second line is the allocation restriction. The solution to this problem is a set of weights x_1^*, x_2^*, ..., x_n^* that determines the portfolio with the highest risk-adjusted return. We can then plug these optimal weights, together with the inputs of the problem, into expressions (11.1), (11.2), and (11.3) and determine the expected return, risk, and Sharpe ratio of this portfolio.

Restrictions

Finally, a comment on the restrictions of all the problems we discussed. Besides the allocation constraint and the other two we considered, we can add to these problems as many constraints as necessary. We could, for example, restrict short-selling by adding the constraint

$$x_1 \geq 0, x_2 \geq 0, ..., x_n \geq 0$$

Or we could limit ourselves to invest not more than, say, 20% of the capital in the portfolio in any single asset by adding the constraint

$$x_1 \leq 0.20, x_2 \leq 0.20, ..., x_n \leq 0.20$$

The possibilities are endless. The optimizer we'll build in the Excel section can solve the four problems we discussed and handle as many restrictions as necessary.

Variations of the standard problems

The four portfolio-optimization problems we discussed are the 'traditional' ones in which risk is defined as the standard deviation of the portfolio returns. There are, however, many other optimization problems. Let's highlight, briefly, two of them.

As we have emphasized several times in this book, risk can be defined in many ways. And we could in principle restate the four optimization problems discussed in this chapter using other definitions of portfolio risk. One such possibility is to assess it with the semideviation of the portfolio returns. We could then think of minimizing this semideviation; or minimizing it subject to a target return; or maximize expected return subject to a target semideviation. And in the case of maximizing risk-adjusted returns, note that the goal would become to maximize the Sortino ratio (see Chapter 10), rather than the Sharpe ratio. To be sure, the solution of all these problems is more complex than that of the problems we discussed in this chapter.

Another interesting approach consists of maximizing the geometric mean return of the portfolio. This criterion amounts to maximizing the rate of growth of the capital invested, thus maximizing the expected terminal wealth. This is usually a very aggressive criterion in the sense that it tends to select portfolios with a low degree of diversification which are therefore very volatile. But it is also a very plausible criterion, with attractive properties and a long history, that unfortunately is not as well known as the 'traditional' problems we discussed in this chapter.

The big picture

The optimization of portfolios cannot be implemented without the aid of spreadsheets or specialized software; even when considering just a few assets, the problems are usually too intractable to solve by hand. All optimizers require the same inputs, which are expected returns, variances or standard deviations, and covariances or correlations. In some cases they will also require a risk-free rate and target levels of risk or return. Given these inputs, the optimizer provides the optimal weights, and the risk and return of the optimal portfolio.

Some investors may want to minimize risk; others may want to minimize risk subject to a target return; others may want to maximize the expected return subject to a target level of risk; and all of them want, at the end of the day, to maximize risk-adjusted returns. The optimizer we discuss in the Excel section will help you solve all these problems.

Excel section

We discuss in this section a simple but powerful optimizer that rapidly and efficiently solves the four optimization problems discussed in this chapter. The set-up is based on a four-asset portfolio but you should have no trouble adapting the spreadsheet to deal with any number of assets. It is also based on the maximization of risk-adjusted returns, but again you should have no trouble adapting the spreadsheet to deal with the other three problems we discussed.

The optimizer we'll build makes use of Excel's Solver, which means that we'll find numerical (rather than analytical) solutions. The advantage of this approach is that the Solver makes it very easy to handle as many restrictions as necessary by making a couple of quick changes in its dialog box.

In a nutshell, these are the three steps we'll follow. First, we'll enter the required inputs (expected returns, standard deviations, variances and covariances, and a risk-free rate); then, we'll make some calculations using those inputs; and finally, we'll use the Solver to find the optimal solution. The end result will be a set of optimal weights (x_1^*, x_2^*, ..., x_n^*) and the risk, return, and Sharpe ratio of the optimal portfolio. Figure 11.1 illustrates the basic set-up, which we can actually use for any of the four problems discussed in this chapter.

	A	B	C	D	E	F	G	H	I
1									
2		Chapter 11							
3		Risk and Return (V): Portfolio Optimization							
4									
5									
6									
7		Rf						Weights	
8									
9			1	2	3	4			
10		ERs							
11									
12		SDs							
13								Ep	
14		Vs-Cs							
15									
16								SDp	
17									
18									
19		Weights						Sp	
20		Sum							
21									
22		ER Vector							
23									
24		V-C Matrix							
25									
26									
27									
28									

figure 11.1   Optimization set-up in Excel spreadsheet

The lightly shaded cells in Figure 11.1 are the ones in which we'll enter the inputs. The cells shaded in darker gray are the ones in which we'll perform calculations. The shaded cells in the H column will display the output; that is, the optimal weights and the expected return, risk, and Sharpe ratio of the optimal portfolio.

For any given four assets, this is, step-by-step, what we need to do to find the portfolio that maximizes the Sharpe ratio:

- Inputs:
    - Enter the *risk-free rate* in cell C7
    - Enter the *expected returns* in cells C10:F10
    - Enter the *standard deviations* in cells C12:F12
    - Enter the *variances and covariances* in cells C14:F17
    - Enter the *weights* to initialize the Solver in cells C19:F19.

- Calculations:
    - Enter =sum(C19:F19) in cell F20.
    - Block cells H8:H11, enter =transpose(C19:F19) and press Ctrl+Shift+Enter simultaneously.
    - Enter =C19*C10 in cell C22 and copy this expression to cells D22:F22.
    - Enter =sum(C22:F22) in cell H14.
    - Enter =C$19*C14*$H8 in cell C24, copy this expression to cells D24:F24, and then copy the range C24:F24 to the range C25:F27.
    - Enter =sqrt(sum(C24:F27)) in cell H17.
    - Enter =(H14-C7)/H17 in cell H20.

- Solver*:
    - Target cell: H20
    - Equal to: Max
    - By changing cells: C19:F19
    - Subject to constraints: F20 = 1.

That's it! Not too bad, is it? Now, before you rush to implement this optimizer, a few important remarks. First, note that our first obvious step is to enter all the required inputs; that is, the risk-free rate, the expected returns, the standard deviations, and all the variances and covariances. But note that the standard deviations are redundant; they are there only to highlight the risk of each individual asset. The reason they are redundant is, as you hopefully

---

*If the Solver option is not visible, it needs to be installed. You do this by clicking on the top left Office Button; then 'Excel Options'; then 'Add-ins'. In the 'Manage' drop-down menu, select 'Excel Add-ins'. Click 'Go'. In the 'Add-Ins available' list, click on the 'Solver Add-in' box, and then click 'OK'. The software will then take you through the installation process.

realized, that we have the variance (the square of the standard deviation) of all the assets in the diagonal of the matrix in C14:F17.

Second, note that to run the optimizer the Solver needs to be initialized with a set of weights. The actual value of these initial weights is largely irrelevant as long as they add up to 1; but a good rule-of-thumb is to enter weights equal to $1/n$, where n is the number of assets in the portfolio. In other words, we initialize Solver by giving it the values of an equally-weighted portfolio; that is, weights of 50% in the two-asset case, of 25% in the four-asset case, of 20% in the five-asset case, and so forth.

Third, to activate the Solver we simply go to the 'Data' tab and click 'Solver' (on the far right). This opens a dialog box where we need to do four things. We first enter the cell where we have the expression for the Sharpe ratio (H20) in 'Set Target Cell.' Then we select 'Max' in the 'Equal to' row, simply because we want to *maximize* risk-adjusted returns. Then we enter the cells that Excel will solve for (the weights in C19:F19) in 'By Changing Cells.' And finally, we add a constraint that forces Excel to find four weights that satisfy our previous requirements *and* that add up to 1. To enter this restriction, we first click 'Add' in 'Subject to Constraints;' then fill the three required boxes (F20 in 'Cell reference;' '=' in the sign box; and '1' in 'Constraint'); and then click 'OK.' Once we're done with these steps, we click 'Solve' and then (when asked whether we want to keep the solution) 'OK.'

Fourth, note that adding more constraints when necessary is very simple. For example, if we wanted to restrict short-selling (that is, if we wanted to restrict the solution to positive weights only), all we need to do in the Solver's dialog box is to click 'Add' in 'Subject to Constraints;' enter 'C19:F19' in 'Cell Reference;' select '>=' in the sign box; enter '0' in 'Constraint;' and finally hit 'OK,' 'Solve,' and 'OK' again. Similarly, if we wanted to restrict the weights to being not larger than, say, 20%, we would click 'Add' in 'Subject to Constraints;' enter 'C19:F19' in 'Cell Reference;' select '<=' in the sign box; enter '0.2' in 'Constraint;' and finally hit 'OK,' 'Solve,' and 'OK' again.

Finally, note that solving the other three problems from this chapter only requires that we change the specifications in the Solver's dialog box; the inputs and intermediate calculations are the same as those we just discussed for the problem of maximizing risk-adjusted returns. Note, also, that the only changes we'd need to introduce are in the target cell (where we'd need to enter the cell for the expected return or risk of the portfolio) and what we want Excel to do with it (maximize or minimize). That's it! Whether we want to minimize risk, minimize risk subject to a target return (which obviously requires an additional constraint specifying the target return), or maximize expected return subject to a target level of risk (which again requires a constraint specifying the target level of risk), it can all be handled with a couple of quick changes in the Solver's dialog box.

Oh, and one last thing: If the whole thing looks messy, don't worry; this is a typical case of 'easier done than said!' Once you use the optimizer a few times, finding optimal portfolios will become a piece of cake. So, just to get yourself familiar with this portfolio-optimization tool, make sure you read and work out the example that follows.

Applying the optimizer

Let's put the optimizer to work by finding the four optimal portfolios discussed in this chapter. Consider four assets: US stocks, EAFE (Europe, Australasia, and the Far East) stocks, EM (emerging markets) stocks, and gold. Panel A of Table 11.1 shows the arithmetic mean monthly returns (*AM*), monthly standard deviations (*SD*), and variance–covariance matrix (Var–Cov) of these four assets over the January 1988–December 2009 period. The performance of US stocks is based on the S&P 500 and accounts for capital gains and dividends; that of EAFE and EM stocks is based on MSCI indices, in dollars and accounting for capital gains and dividends; and that of gold is based on its price per ounce, in dollars.

Panel B of Table 11.1 shows the solutions from our optimizer. Problems 1, 2, 3, and 4 refer to minimizing risk, minimizing risk subject to a target return (1%), maximizing expected return subject to a target level of risk (3%), and maximizing risk-adjusted returns (using a monthly risk-free rate of 0.32%). As the table shows, the weights (x_i) vary substantially depending on the problem, and the same happens with the resulting expected returns (E_p), risk (SD_p), and Sharpe ratio (S_p) of the four portfolios.

table 11.1

Panel A	US	EAFE	EM	Gold
AM (%)	0.85	0.59	1.34	0.37
SD (%)	4.25	5.01	7.01	4.27
Var–Cov				
US	0.0018	0.0015	0.0019	−0.0002
EAFE	0.0015	0.0025	0.0024	0.0003
EM	0.0019	0.0024	0.0049	0.0004
Gold	−0.0002	0.0003	0.0004	0.0018
Panel B	Problem 1	Problem 2	Problem 3	Problem 4
X_{US} (%)	60.4	82.5	69.1	101.7
X_{EAFE} (%)	2.1	−50.7	−18.8	−96.4
X_{EM} (%)	−13.3	35.2	5.7	77.2
X_{Gold} (%)	50.9	32.9	44.0	17.4
E_p (%)	0.5	1.0	0.7	1.4
SD_p (%)	2.8	4.0	3.0	6.1
S_p	0.08	0.17	0.13	0.18

Note that there are a few negative weights, which indicate short positions; that is, situations in which we need to borrow the asset, sell it, and invest the proceeds obtained in the other three assets. If short-selling is not possible or desirable, then all we need to do is to add a constraint in the optimizer restricting the weights to positive values only.

Last, but certainly not least, there is only one way of understanding a tool like this optimizer: using it! There's no substitute for implementing it, making mistakes, and learning from those mistakes. So if you're serious about using this tool, copy into a spreadsheet the general set-up shown in Figure 11.1; then enter in the relevant cells the contents of panel A of Table 11.1; solve the four problems we just discussed; and compare your solutions to those in panel B of Table 11.1. If you get the results right, you'll have a powerful tool in your hands ... and you'll know how to use it!

12

Risk and return VI:
The long term

Most people think that stocks are riskier than bonds, and under some circumstances that is indeed the case. But under some other circumstances that is not so clear. Which brings us to one of the central issues discussed in this chapter: risk is a function of the investment horizon. We'll talk about what that means, we'll take a look at historical trends, and we'll also discuss how to forecast both returns and the probabilities of target returns in chosen holding periods.

Long-term returns

Let's get this straight from the start: In the long term, the compounding power of stocks is *vastly* higher than that of bonds. Want some evidence? In his fantastic book *Stocks for the Long Run*, Jeremy Siegel reports that $1 invested in US stocks in 1802 would have turned into $12.7 *million* by the end of 2006. In comparison, the same dollar invested in US long-term bonds would have turned into $18,235. That is quite a difference!

Now, just in case you're thinking that the differential compounding power of stocks and bonds is something specific to the US market, take a look at Table 12.1, which shows arithmetic (*AM*) and geometric (*GM*) mean annual returns, in both nominal and real terms, for 16 countries and the world market for 1900–2000. Real returns are nominal returns net of inflation and measure changes in purchasing power.

table 12.1

Country	Stocks					Bonds				
	Nominal			Real		Nominal			Real	
	GM (%)	AM (%)	SD (%)	GM (%)	AM (%)	GM (%)	AM (%)	SD (%)	GM (%)	AM (%)
Australia	11.9	13.3	18.2	7.5	9.0	5.2	5.8	11.3	1.1	1.9
Belgium	8.2	10.5	24.1	2.5	4.8	5.1	5.6	10.0	−0.4	0.3
Canada	9.7	11.0	16.6	6.4	7.7	5.0	5.4	8.9	1.8	2.4
Denmark	8.9	10.7	21.7	4.6	6.2	6.8	7.3	11.0	2.5	3.3
France	12.1	14.5	24.6	3.8	6.3	6.8	7.1	8.4	−1.0	0.1
Germany	9.7	15.2	36.4	3.6	8.8	2.8	4.7	13.5	−2.2	0.3
Ireland	9.5	11.5	22.8	4.8	7.0	6.0	6.7	12.2	1.5	2.4
Italy	12.0	16.1	34.2	2.7	6.8	6.7	7.0	9.0	−2.2	−0.8
Japan	12.5	15.9	29.5	4.5	9.3	5.9	6.9	14.9	−1.6	1.3
Netherlands	9.0	11.0	22.7	5.8	7.7	4.1	4.4	7.6	1.1	1.5
S. Africa	12.0	14.2	23.7	6.8	9.1	6.3	6.7	9.5	1.4	1.9
Spain	10.0	12.1	22.8	3.6	5.8	7.5	7.9	10.5	1.2	1.9
Sweden	11.6	13.9	23.5	7.6	9.9	6.2	6.6	9.2	2.4	3.1
Switzerland	7.6	9.3	19.7	5.0	6.9	5.1	5.2	4.5	2.8	3.1
UK	10.1	11.9	21.8	5.8	7.6	5.4	6.1	12.5	1.3	2.3
US	10.1	12.0	19.9	6.7	8.7	4.8	5.1	8.3	1.6	2.1
World	9.2	10.4	16.5	5.8	7.2	4.4	4.7	8.5	1.2	1.7
Average	**10.3**	**12.7**	**23.9**	**5.1**	**7.6**	**5.6**	**6.2**	**10.1**	**0.7**	**1.7**

Source: Adapted from *Triumph of the Optimists: 101 years of global investment returns* by Elroy Dimson, Paul Marsh, and Mike Staunton. Princeton University Press, New Jersey, 2002. Reprinted by permission of Princeton University Press.

The evidence is crystal clear: The mean return of stocks, geometric and arithmetic, nominal and real, is higher than the mean return of bonds in *every* single country, and in most cases by a substantial margin. The difference between the compounding power of both assets can be thought of in more than one way, but here's an interesting one. Take a look at the last row, which shows averages across the 16 countries, and note that the annualized (that is, the mean annual compound) real return of stocks is 5.1% and that of bonds 0.7%. These figures imply that by investing in stocks *purchasing power* would double in just under 14 years. In bonds? It would take more than 98 years!

Risk and the investment horizon

The higher compounding power of stocks relative to bonds is typically referred to as the equity risk premium (or market risk premium, as discussed in Chapter 7), and as Table 12.1 shows, in most countries this difference is fairly large. In fact, because these differences are not easy to explain with standard models of rational behavior and reasonable assumptions on risk aversion, many refer to them as the *equity premium puzzle*.

Now, most people do think that stocks are riskier than bonds, and therefore find plausible the idea that the former should deliver a higher return than the latter. But note that the puzzle is not why stocks deliver a higher return than bonds but *why the difference is so large*. As usual, we will not get into a theoretical discussion here; for our purposes the more relevant question is, why do most people think that stocks are riskier than bonds?

'That's a no-brainer!' If that's more or less what you just thought, then you may be thinking along the lines that stocks are more volatile than bonds. And you'd be right. In fact, as the last row of Table 12.1 shows, over the 1900–2000 period the annual volatility (*SD*) of stock returns in the 16 countries in the table was (on average) around 24%, and that of bond returns was (again on average) around 10%. So, as far as comparing annual volatilities goes, there is no question that stocks are more volatile than bonds.

However, this perception of relative risk is a bit tricky. First, as we discussed more than once in this book, risk can be defined in many ways and volatility is just one of them. Second, different definitions of risk may lead to a different assessment about the relative risk of different assets. (Remember the Oracle and Microsoft comparison in Chapter 9?) And third, the fact that an asset is riskier than another in the short term does not necessarily imply that it is also riskier in the long term.

One way to think about the risk of an asset is to assess the probability of not achieving some target or benchmark return. When investing in any asset an investor may be interested to know how likely is the asset to lose value, or deliver returns below inflation, or below a risk-free rate, or below any other relevant benchmark. This likelihood is usually referred to as *shortfall probability* (that is, the probability that an asset falls short of a benchmark return) and this way of assessing risk is typically referred to as *shortfall risk*. Would the idea that stocks are riskier than bonds change if we assessed risk this way?

Take a look at Figure 12.1, which is based on historical stock and (ten-year) bond returns for the US market over the 1900–2009 period, and let's think of shortfall risk as the (historical) probability that stocks underperform bonds. If we compare the return of these two assets year by year, we'd find that in 35% of the years bonds outperformed stocks, which is what the first bar indicates. Most people think that stocks tend to outperform bonds and typically find this figure surprisingly high. But this is simply what the data show; in over one third of the periods bonds (the less risky or less volatile asset) did outperform stocks (the riskier or more volatile asset).

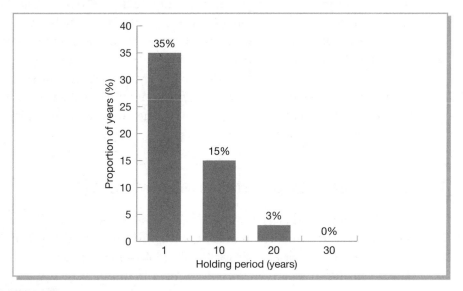

Shortfall risk

Now, what happens if we consider the same market (the US), the same assets (stocks and bonds), and the same period of time (1900–2009) but change the holding period from 1 year to 10 years? As Figure 12.1 shows, the (historical) shortfall probability falls sharply from 35% to 15%; that is, in only 15% of all 10-year periods stocks underperformed bonds.

What happens if we consider again the same market, assets, and period of time but we change the holding period to 20 years? Figure 12.1 shows that the (historical) shortfall probability now falls to 3%, indicating that in only 3% of all 20-year periods stocks underperformed bonds. And if we do it one more time for 30-year periods? Surprise! There has *never* been a 30-year period in which stocks underperformed bonds.

The message from Figure 12.1 is clear: The longer the holding period, the less likely stocks are to underperform bonds. Importantly, as long as we think of risk in terms of shortfall probability, this exhibit also has an important message about the relationship between risk and the investment horizon: *The risk of stocks is decreasing in the length of the holding period.* In other words, the longer the investment horizon, the more likely stocks are to outperform bonds, and therefore the lower is the risk of holding stocks. This leads us to the fact that, in the long term, it is hard to argue that stocks are riskier than bonds.

How can we reconcile, then, the fact that stocks are riskier than bonds because the former are more volatile than the latter, with the fact that stocks are less risky than bonds because the former are very likely to outperform the latter? Simply by focusing on a critical variable, namely, the holding period or investment horizon. More precisely, if we focus on short-term volatility, then clearly stocks are riskier (more volatile) than bonds; if we focus on the long-term shortfall probability, then clearly stocks are less risky (very likely to outperform) bonds.

Time diversification and mean reversion

If you're confused, that's OK. At least draw some comfort from the fact that very sophisticated financial minds have been wrestling with this issue for a very long time, and it is not clear that a final consensus has been reached. And given that risk can be assessed in more than one way, this ambiguity should not surprise you.

Note that perhaps part of the reason why this issue is confusing is because we're saying that in the short term stocks are riskier than bonds, in the long term the opposite is the case, and we're not precisely defining what we mean by the short term and the long term. Yes, we did mention that comparing one-year volatilities stocks are riskier than bonds, and comparing 30-year shortfall probabilities stocks are less risky than bonds. So, is 1 year the short term and 30 years the long term? Yes and no. (As if this issue were not confusing enough!)

'Yes' because most people would agree that as far as investing goes, 1 year is a fairly short period and 30 years is a fairly long period. But 'no' because there is no precise definition of how short is the short term or how long is the long term. Keynes argued that in the long term we're all dead, but that is not of much help for our purposes!

Here's one way to think about this: Forget about trying to put a precise number to the short term and the long term; simply think that the longer the holding period, the more suspect is the statement that stocks are riskier than bonds. In other words, the plausibility of the statement decreases with the length of the holding period. The shorter the term, the more plausible is the idea that stocks are riskier than bonds; the longer the term, the more plausible is the idea that stocks are less risky than bonds.

This discussion brings us to the center of the hotly-debated issue of *time diversification*. Although this concept can be defined in many ways, an intuitive way to think about it is as the idea that *the longer the investment horizon, the more likely is a riskier asset to outperform a less risky asset*. Ring a bell? It should!

Note that this definition of time diversification simply generalizes our previous discussion of the relative risk of stocks and bonds to any two assets. In other words, we could say that the longer the holding period, the more likely value stocks are to outperform growth stocks; or small caps are to outperform large caps; or emerging markets are to outperform developed markets. In all these cases the first asset has a higher short-term volatility than the second, but it also is more likely to outperform in the long term.

Note, also, the important implication that follows from time diversification: given an investor's tolerance for risk, the longer his investment horizon, the higher the exposure he should have to risky assets. This is consistent with the advice financial consultants give to clients and explains why one of the first questions they ask is for how long the client intends to remain invested.

Simple rules of asset allocation are also consistent with the idea of time diversification. Consider an investor who splits a portfolio between stocks and bonds. A rule of thumb is that the proportion of stocks in the portfolio should be equal to 100 minus his age. To illustrate, a 30-year-old investor should have 70% of his portfolio in stocks (and 30% in bonds) and a 60-year-old investor should have 40% in stocks (and 60% in bonds). Regardless of the wisdom of this rule, note that it implies that the younger the investor (that is, the longer his investment horizon), the higher is the proportion he should allocate to stocks.

Now, many theoretical arguments can be (and have been) made in favor of or against time diversification. But just about everybody seems to agree that time diversification holds under *mean reversion*, which is simply *the tendency of an asset to revert to its long-term trend.* Flip a coin a few times, and the proportion of heads can be way off from the expected 50%; but keep flipping the coin, and the larger the number of flips, the more that the proportion of heads will approach 50%. Or spin a roulette a few times, and the proportion of 17s can be way off from its expected proportion of 1/37; but spin the roulette one million times and the proportion of 17s will be very close to 1/37. Mean reversion is as simple as that.

Whether or not there is mean reversion in financial markets is an empirical question, so let's look at some evidence. Figure 12.2 shows the annual returns of the US stock market between 1900 and 2009, and as the picture clearly shows, annual returns have been quite volatile. But the interesting fact to observe is that returns seem to fluctuate around a *constant* trend line (the dashed line), which in this case is the historical mean annual (compound) return of 9.4%.

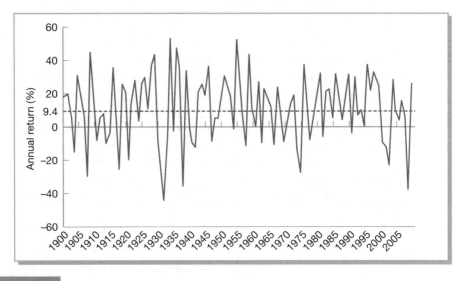

figure 12.2   Mean reversion

Contrast the previous graph with the two graphs in Figure 12.3, both of which are hypothetical (unlike Figure 12.2, which is based on *observed* data for the US market). Note that in Figure 12.3(a) returns fluctuate around an increasing trend line, and in Figure 12.3(b) they fluctuate around a declining trend line. Neither of these graphs displays mean reversion simply because there is no *constant* mean that these returns fluctuate around.

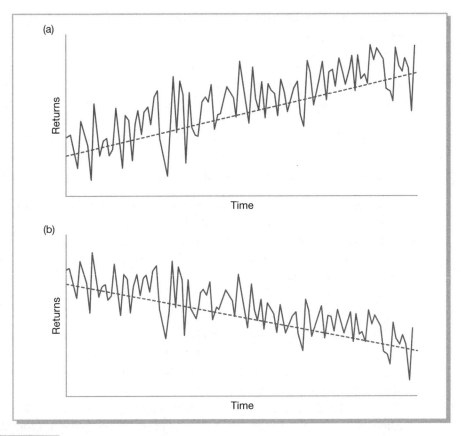

figure 12.3   **No mean reversion**

In short, mean reversion and time diversification are essential concepts in asset allocation and portfolio management and go a long way towards explaining the relationship between risk and the investment horizon. They are also essential in understanding why some argue that stocks are riskier than bonds, whereas others argue the opposite; both arguments may be right and may simply refer to a different holding period.

Forecasting returns: The RDM

Forecasting financial assets is a mix of art and science, with a fair share of sorcery. All investors would like to be able to predict the return of a market, the exchange rate between two currencies, or the price of gold. Unfortunately, we know *very* little about how to forecast these accurately. Having said that, some models are more accurate than others, and some conditions make forecasting more feasible than others. That is what we'll briefly discuss in this section.

Let's start with two conditions. The more diversified the portfolio, and the longer the time period for which the forecast is made, the more likely we are to produce accurate predictions. In other words, we are more likely to get our forecasts right if we focus on markets rather than on individual companies, and if we focus on the medium-to-long-term rather than on the short term. This, of course, does not imply that under these conditions our forecasts are going to be accurate; it only implies that they are *more likely* to be accurate.

Let's focus then on broadly diversified portfolios (markets) and reasonably-long forecasting periods (ten years). And let's focus on a simple but powerful model called the *Returns Decomposition Model*, or RDM for short. This model simply decomposes returns into three components; more precisely, the **RDM** is given by the expression

$$R_1 \approx (D/p)_0 + g_1 + \Delta(P/E)_1 \tag{12.1}$$

where R_1 denotes the annualized return over the forecasting period; $(D/p)_0$ the dividend yield at the beginning of the forecasting period; g_1 the annualized growth of earnings over the forecasting period; and $\Delta(P/E)_1$ the annualized change in the price/earnings ratio during the forecasting period. Note that '0' denotes the present (the moment where we stand when we make the prediction) and '1' the future (the period over which we make our forecast).

In words, the RDM simply states that expected returns can be decomposed into the sum of three components: The dividend yield at the beginning of the forecasting period, the annualized expected growth of earnings over the forecasting period, and the annualized expected change in the P/E during the forecasting period. Note that of the three magnitudes in the right-hand side of equation (12.1), g_1 and $\Delta(P/E)_1$ we have to forecast and $(D/p)_0$ we simply observe. Note, also, that this is an approximation (hence the $\approx$ symbol), but usually a very good one; the exact expression for the RDM is more complicated and yields almost the same results, so we'll stick to the simpler version.

To understand this model, let's apply it right away. And let's do it forecasting the expected annualized return of the world market equity portfolio for 2010–19, which meets the conditions of a broadly-diversified portfolio and a reasonably-long forecasting period. Table 12.2 summarizes some historical data and relevant assumptions for the analysis. All figures are in dollars and returns account for both capital gains and dividends.

table 12.2

Historical (1973–2009)		Assumptions	
Annualized return (%)	10.0	Annualized earnings growth (%)	7.4
Annualized earnings growth (%)	7.4		
Average P/E	17.1	Terminal P/E, scenario 1	17.1
Average dividend yield (%)	2.8	Annualized Δ(P/E), scenario 1 (%)	−1.1
January 1, 2010			
D/P (%)	2.5	Terminal P/E, scenario 2	19.1
P/E	19.1	Annualized Δ(P/E), scenario 2 (%)	0.0

Let's assume we're at the very beginning of 2010. As Table 12.2 shows, the dividend yield at the time was 2.5%; this is the magnitude we observe, the other two we need to forecast. Let's think about the expected growth of earnings first. The evidence shows that this variable tends to be mean reverting; that is, over short periods of time (say, 1 year) the growth of earnings may fluctuate widely, but over longer periods (say, 10 or more years) it tends to revert to its long-term mean. For this reason, let's assume that earnings over the 2010–19 period will grow at the historical annual rate of 7.4% shown in Table 12.2.

So far so good, but here comes the tricky part, which is to forecast the change in the P/E. Because P/Es are often viewed as reflecting the mood of the market (when investors are optimistic P/Es are high, when they are pessimistic P/Es are low), and forecasting moods is nearly impossible, we'll consider two scenarios. In the first, we'll assume that by the end of 2019 the P/E will revert to its historical mean of 17.1 shown in Table 12.2. And for this to happen, starting from a P/E of 19.1 at the beginning of 2010, the P/E needs to fall at the average annual rate of 1.1%; that is, $19.1 \cdot (1-0.011)^{10} = 17.1$. Of course we know that the P/E will not fall linearly at this rate; we expect it to fluctuate widely over time, but on annualized terms this is what *must* happen if our assumption of mean reversion happens to be correct.

The second scenario we'll consider is that by the end of 2019 the P/E will be at its initial starting level of 19.1. The rationale for this is that for variables that fluctuate randomly without any clear pattern that can be exploited to predict its future values, the best forecast is its current value. If this scenario happens to be correct, then the annual change in the P/E will be 0% simply because it will end at the same level at which it began. Again, we do know that the P/E will fluctuate widely over time, but if our forecast is correct, this is what *must* happen in annualized terms.

So, what are the forecasts from the RDM in these two scenarios? In the first case the annualized return we expect is

$$R_1 \approx 2.5\% + 7.4\% - 1.1\% \approx 8.8\%$$

In the second scenario it is

$$R_1 \approx 2.5\% + 7.4\% + 0.0\% \approx 9.9\%$$

In words, given a dividend yield of 2.5% at the beginning of 2010, an annual growth of earnings of 7.4% for 2010–19, and an annual fall in the P/E of 1.1% over the same period, we would expect the world market portfolio to deliver a mean annual (compound) return of 8.8%, a bit lower than the historical average of 10.0%. The reason we expect returns to be a bit lower than the historical average is that the world market at the beginning of 2010 was a bit overpriced, as indicated by its higher-than-average P/E (19.1 as opposed to 17.1) and lower-than-average dividend yield (2.5% as opposed to 2.8%).

In the second scenario, in turn, we expect annual returns almost equal to the historical average simply because we expect no drag in returns from a falling P/E. Note that in the previous scenario the 1.1% annual fall of the P/E pulls returns down by that magnitude; but if we expect the P/E at the end of 2019 to be at its current level, then such drag will not occur and returns of just under 10% a year will follow.

Importantly, do not consider the two scenarios we discussed in terms of the P/E, or the mean reversion assumption for the growth of earnings, as the 'right' assumptions. Ask a hundred investors and you'll probably get as many scenarios. The point to be stressed is that to implement the RDM *some* assumption needs to be made about the growth of earnings and the change in the P/E ratio.

This is, in a nutshell, the essence of the RDM, a model that proves to be fairly accurate in forecasting the medium-to-long-term behavior of markets. Having said that, as you should do with any forecasting model, use it with a healthy dose of skepticism.

Forecasting probabilities

We'll conclude our discussion of the long term with a simple tool designed to answer a question investors often have in mind. Given an asset, a target return, and a target holding period, *how likely* is the asset to deliver at least the target return in the target investment horizon? Say we want to invest in emerging markets, expect to hold the investment for 10 years, and hope to get annual returns of 10%. How likely are we to get annual returns of at least 10%, over the next 10 years, by investing in emerging markets? That is a question this tool is designed to answer.

Let's start with a bit of notation. Let's call AM and SD the (arithmetic) mean and standard deviation of a series of continuously compounded returns (r), and let's assume that these returns follow a normal distribution. This implies that the corresponding simple returns (R) follow a lognormal distribution. (If these concepts are not clear, you may want to read Chapters 1, 28, and 29 before you go on.)

Our goal, then, is to calculate the probability of obtaining *at least* an annualized (that is, mean annual compound) return of R^* over T years. This probability can be calculated with the following two-step procedure

$$\text{Calculate} \rightarrow z^* = \frac{\ln(1 + R^*) - AM}{SD / \sqrt{T}} \tag{12.2}$$

$$\text{Calculate} \rightarrow P(R \geq R^*) = P(z \geq z^*)$$

Note that this procedure basically transforms the lognormal variable $1+R$ into the standard normal variable z, with the purpose of bypassing the lognormal distribution and calculating probabilities out of the more widely used and widely known standard normal distribution. And as the second step indicates, once we find the probability that $z \geq z^*$, $P(z \geq z^*)$, then we have also found the probability that $R \geq R^*$, $P(R \geq R^*)$. Note, also, that we're actually interested in the probability of obtaining target *simple* returns. However, as we discuss in Chapters 1 and 29, continuously compounded returns are a tool we sometimes need to use in the background, and that is exactly the use we'll give them here.

Let's focus again on the world (equity) market, and assume again that we're at the beginning of 2010. Over the 1973–2009 period, the distribution of continuously compounded annual returns had an arithmetic mean of 9.6% and a standard deviation of 15.5%. The distribution of simple annual returns, in turn, had an arithmetic mean of 12.1%, a geometric mean of 10.0%, and a standard deviation of 15.4%. Given this historical behavior, then, what is the probability that the world market returns at least 5% in 2010? That's easy. Using expression (12.2) we get

$$z^* = \frac{\ln(1 + 5\%) - 9.6\%}{15.5\% / \sqrt{1}} = -0.3023$$

and the area *above* this number under the standard normal distribution is 0.619. In other words, there is a 61.9% probability that the world market delivers a return of *at least* 5% in 2010.

What about the probability of an annualized return of at least 5% over the next twenty years? Again, very simple. Using expression (12.2) we get

$$z^* = \frac{\ln(1 + 5\%) - 9.6\%}{15.5\% / \sqrt{20}} = -1.3518$$

and the area *above* this number under the standard normal distribution is 0.912. In other words, there is an 91.2% probability that the world market delivers *at least* an annualized return of 5% over the next 20 years.

Finally, what is the probability that the world market returns *less* than 8% over the next 30 years? Same story. Using expression (12.2) we get

$$z^* = \frac{\ln(1 + 8\%) - 9.6\%}{15.5\% / \sqrt{30}} = -0.6606$$

and the area *below* this number under the standard normal distribution is 0.254. In other words, there is a 25.4% probability that the world market delivers an annualized return of 8% *or less* over the next 30 years.

We could go on, but hopefully you see that this tool is relatively easy to implement. In any case, you may want to calculate probabilities for several target returns over several holding periods to get familiar with it. And if you want to double-check your results, you could use the target returns and holding periods shown in Table 12.3, and then compare your results to those displayed there. All figures in this table are based on the same parameters just discussed for the world market, and indicate the probability of obtaining *at least* the specified target returns in the specified holding periods.

table 12.3

Target return	Holding period (years)						
	1 (%)	5 (%)	10 (%)	15 (%)	20 (%)	25 (%)	30 (%)
−5%	82.8	98.3	99.9	100.0	100.0	100.0	100.0
0%	73.1	91.6	97.4	99.2	99.7	99.9	100.0
5%	61.9	75.0	83.0	87.9	91.2	93.5	95.1
10%	50.1	50.2	50.3	50.4	50.4	50.5	50.5
12%	45.5	39.9	35.9	33.0	30.5	28.4	26.6
14%	41.0	30.5	23.5	18.9	15.4	12.7	10.6
16%	36.7	22.3	14.1	9.4	6.4	4.4	3.1
18%	32.6	15.7	7.7	4.1	2.2	1.2	0.7
20%	28.8	10.6	3.9	1.5	0.6	0.3	0.1
25%	20.6	3.3	0.5	0.1	0.0	0.0	0.0
30%	14.1	0.8	0.0	0.0	0.0	0.0	0.0

Tables such as 12.3 help to evaluate the potential of investing in different assets and more generally to make investment decisions. The two-step procedure that generates is very versatile and, as you hopefully agree, easy to implement.

The big picture

There is little question that in the long term the compounding power of stocks is vastly higher than that of bonds. And there is little question that in the short term stocks are more volatile than bonds. What is more controversial is whether stocks remain riskier than bonds in the long term. If we think of risk in terms of shortfall probability, then as the holding period increases, stocks become less risky relative to bonds; or, put differently, the longer the holding period, the more likely stocks are to outperform bonds and therefore the lower is the risk of holding stocks.

The discussion about the relative risk of stocks and bonds is part of the broader issue of time diversification; that is, the idea that the longer the holding period, the more likely is a riskier asset to outperform a less risky asset. Time diversification holds under mean reversion, and the latter is clearly present in the data. These two concepts help to explain why financial consultants recommend to their clients a higher exposure to risky assets the longer is the clients' investment horizon.

As for forecasting, well, that is not something we know a whole lot about. Some models are better than others, some assumptions are more plausible than others, and some conditions may favor or hinder the accuracy of our predictions. That being said, the RDM is a useful tool to assess the *long*-term behavior of *markets*, though it is far less useful when forecasting the returns of individual companies and short-term returns in general. Like any tool, handle it with care.

Excel section

The Excel section of Chapter 28 discusses how to calculate probabilities out of the normal distribution; the Excel section of Chapter 29 does the same for the lognormal distribution. Forecasting the probabilities discussed in this chapter can be done with the tools discussed at the end of both chapters.

part

2

Valuation

13

Stocks I: The dividend discount model

There are many models of equity valuation, some based on discounted cash flow and others based on various ratios. Many academics and practitioners portray the dividend discount model as the simplest of the discounted cash flow models. That's a mistake. If you learn one thing from this chapter, let it be this: The dividend discount model is far from simple, it can easily be misused, and its implementation is much more difficult than is usually believed.

First things first

There are three distinctions to keep in mind when discussing valuation. One is general and applies to the valuation of all assets, and the other two are specific to equity valuation. The first is the distinction between price and value; the second between fundamental analysis and technical analysis; and the third between absolute valuation and relative valuation. Let's take one at a time.

Although we're usually sloppy when talking about them, there is a distinction between *price* and *value*. The former simply indicates the amount of money you have to take out of your pocket to buy an asset. There is no arguing about it; it is what the computer screen says it is. Period. The latter, often referred to as *intrinsic value*, is more subtle and refers to the amount of money you *should* take out of your pocket to buy an asset. And how much you should pay for an asset, obviously, depends on what you expect to get from it. Problem is, expectations may (usually do) differ among investors, which makes intrinsic value a *subjective* concept; price, in turn, is an *objective* concept. For any given asset at any given point in time, intrinsic value and price may be similar or widely different; and the same is true for the estimates of intrinsic value across investors.

Models of equity valuation can be split into fundamental analysis and technical analysis. Fundamental analysis refers to a valuation technique that focuses on the *fundamentals* or *value drivers* of a company. It involves the analysis of a company's financial statements, financial ratios, market, competitors, and many other factors that ultimately determine its value. Technical analysis, on the other hand, focuses on the past prices of a stock. It does not really attempt to value a company; rather, it involves the extrapolation of trends and patterns from past prices to extract clues as to where the price may be headed in the near future. Fundamental analysis focuses on the long term, technical analysis on the short term.

Finally, models of equity valuation can be split into models of *absolute valuation*, sometimes referred to as *discounted cash flow* models, or *DCF* models for short; and models of *relative valuation*, sometimes referred to as *multiples*. The former refer to models that assess the value of a company on the basis of its own fundamentals; the latter refer to those that assess the value of a company relative to one or more benchmarks. The former assess intrinsic value by discounting expected cash flows at a rate that reflects their risk; the latter do it by comparing ratios. Both types of models belong to the category of fundamental analysis.

The dividend discount model (DDM), the weighted-average cost of capital (WACC) model, the adjusted present value (APV) model, and the flows-to-equity (FTE) model are all versions of DCF models. Price-to-earnings (P/E), price-to-book (P/B), price-to-cash flow (P/CF), and price-to-dividend (P/D) ratios are some of the most widely used multiples in relative valuation.

Last but not least, something essential to keep in mind. We often abuse language and talk about stock pricing or bond pricing when we should really talk about stock *valuation* or bond *valuation*. All DCF models and multiples yield an estimate of *intrinsic value*; they yield what we *should* pay for a stock or bond. Again, the price is what it is. The point of valuing an asset is to assess whether it is worth what its market price indicates. If our estimate of its intrinsic value is higher than its price, then the asset may be undervalued and we should consider buying it; if the opposite is the case, then the asset may be overvalued and we should avoid it. And we say 'may' because, remember, intrinsic value depends on our expectations about the future, and our best guess about it may be wrong.

Discounted cash flow models

All DCF models involve the calculation of a present value (discussed in Chapter 21). They all require the analyst or investor to estimate expected cash flows and discount them at the appropriate rate. The differences across DCF models are given by the type of cash flows estimated and the rate used to discount them. Yes, there is more than one definition of cash flow; actually, there are at least three.

In terms of cash flows, in this chapter we'll deal with dividends (we'll discuss the other two definitions in the next chapter), so keep this in mind. Some people view dividends as 'simpler' than other definitions of cash flow, perhaps because the former are observed directly whereas the latter have to be calculated from financial statements. But this obviously applies to past values. Looking ahead, all cash flows need to be forecast and it's not all that clear that forecasting dividends is any easier than forecasting other types of cash flow.

When forecasting any type of cash flow, analysts typically make assumptions about their expected growth rate. These assumptions may range from constant growth to two or more stages of growth. We'll have more to say about this shortly. Also, analysts typically estimate a **terminal value**; this is the last cash flow to be discounted and attempts to summarize in a single number all the cash flows expected from that point on. The most widely used options for estimating a terminal value are a **growing perpetuity** (an infinite sequence of cash flows growing at a constant rate) or a **multiple** of some fundamental variable (such as earnings or cash flow). Again, more on this shortly.

In terms of the discount rate, keep in mind its underlying idea: It should capture the risk of the cash flows discounted. That's why DCF models that differ on the cash flows they consider also differ on their discount rate. The discount rate of some DCF models is the cost of equity, whereas that of some others is the cost of capital. The appropriate rate for discounting dividends is the cost of *equity*.

The dividend discount model: Theory

The underlying idea behind the DDM is both simple and plausible: A share of a company is worth the present value of all the cash flows an investor expects to pocket from it. And what does an investor pocket from a share?

Dividends (if the company pays them) for as long as he holds the stock, and a final cash flow given by the price at which the investor sells the share. It can't really get much simpler than that, which may be one of the reasons why, mistakenly, the DDM is usually thought of as a 'simple' model. However, as we'll discuss below, the devil is in the details.

But let's leave the details for later and focus on the formal expression of the DDM

$$V = \frac{E(D_1)}{(1+R)} + \frac{E(D_2)}{(1+R)^2} + \frac{E(D_3)}{(1+R)^3} + ... + \frac{E(D_T) + E(p_T)}{(1+R)^T} \tag{13.1}$$

where V denotes the intrinsic value of (or what an investor *should* pay for) a share; $E(D_t)$ the expected dividend per share in period t; $E(p_T)$ the expected share price at time T, often thought of as the terminal value; R the discount rate; and T the number of periods for which dividends are forecast. The period from 1 to T is often referred to as the *forecasting period*.

A couple of remarks about this expression are in order. First, note that the cash flows we're discounting, dividends, end up in the pocket of shareholders who are then the ones bearing their risk. The discount rate, then, must reflect the return shareholders require from holding shares of the company. This required return on equity, sometimes referred to as the cost of equity, can be estimated with many models, the most popular of which is the CAPM (discussed in Chapter 7). Therefore, the discount rate is usually estimated as $R = R_f + MRP \cdot \beta$, where R_f, MRP, and β denote the risk-free rate, the market risk premium, and the company's beta.

Second, note that it is possible, though in no way essential, to forecast $E(p_T)$ as a function of the dividends expected to be received from time T on; that is, $E(p_T) = f\{E(D_{T+1}), E(D_{T+2}), E(D_{T+3}), ...\}$. In that case, expression (13.1) turns into the present value of an infinite sequence of dividends; that is

$$V = \frac{E(D_1)}{(1+R)} + \frac{E(D_2)}{(1+R)^2} + ... + \frac{E(D_T)}{(1+R)^T} + \frac{E(D_{T+1})}{(1+R)^{T+1}} + \frac{E(D_{T+2})}{(1+R)^{T+2}} + ... \tag{13.2}$$

You may find the idea of an 'infinite' sequence of dividends a bit hard to grasp. But although no investor is going to hold a share 'forever,' the life of the company is in principle unlimited. If it makes your life easier, just think of expression (13.2) as the present value of a 'very long' sequence of dividends. You can even drive this thought home by noting that dividends very far into the future add very little to V.

The dividend discount model: Versions

The DDM is typically not used in practice as stated in expression (13.1) or (13.2). Its usual implementation imposes some structure on the expected growth of dividends, with different assumptions generating different versions of the DDM. It's important to keep in mind that an assumption about the way dividends are expected to evolve is a statement about the company's expected dividend policy. This policy, in turn, depends on the expected profitability of the company, the existence of various uses for the company's profits (investment opportunities), and many other factors. This is one of the reasons why, however simple some versions of the DDM may appear to be, its proper implementation is far from trivial: Because the impact of a wide variety of important factors must all be summarized in a sequence of dividends, which is 90% art and 10% science.

No growth

The simplest assumption we could make about expected dividends is that they will remain constant at the level of the last dividend paid by the company (D_0); that is, $E(D_1) = E(D_2) = E(D_3) = \ldots = D_0$. Substituting this stream of dividends into (13.2) we get

$$V = \frac{D_0}{(1+R)} + \frac{D_0}{(1+R)^2} + \frac{D_0}{(1+R)^3} + \ldots = \frac{D_0}{R} \tag{13.3}$$

Now, if you've never dealt with this model before or are not trained in math, the second equality may surprise you. But it is indeed the case that if we discount an infinite sequence of constant cash flows (D_0 in our case), then the sum of the infinite terms collapses into the constant cash flow divided by the discount rate. Mathematically, this is called a *perpetuity*. Whether or not it leads to a good pricing model we'll discuss later.

Constant growth

A second possibility is to assume that dividends will grow at a constant rate g beginning from the last dividend paid by the company; that is, $E(D_1) = D_0 \cdot (1+g)$, $E(D_2) = D_0 \cdot (1+g)^2$, $E(D_3) = D_0 \cdot (1+g)^3$, and so on. Substituting this stream of dividends into expression (13.2) we get

$$V = \frac{D_0 \cdot (1+g)}{(1+R)} + \frac{D_0 \cdot (1+g)^2}{(1+R)^2} + \frac{D_0 \cdot (1+g)^3}{(1+R)^3} + \ldots = \frac{D_0 \cdot (1+g)}{R-g} \tag{13.4}$$

Again, the second equality may surprise you. But here too an infinite sum of terms collapses into something relatively simple. Mathematically, this is called a *growing perpetuity* and holds as long as $R > g$.

Whether the assumption that dividends will grow at a constant rate in perpetuity is a plausible one we'll discuss later. But it's important to note that this assumption shouldn't be thought of as implying that dividends are expected to grow year after year at the rate g; that would be naive. Rather, g should be thought of as an *average* growth rate of dividends. In other words, in some periods dividends may grow at more than g and in some others at less than g, but on average we expect them to grow at g.

Two stages of growth

A third possibility is to assume that dividends will grow at a rate g_1 over the first T periods, and at a rate g_2 from that point on, usually (but not necessarily always) with $g_1 > g_2$. Imposing this assumption on expression (13.1) or (13.2) we get the scary expression

$$V = \frac{D_0 \cdot (1 + g_1)}{(1 + R)} + \frac{D_0 \cdot (1 + g_1)^2}{(1 + R)^2} + \dots + \frac{D_0 \cdot (1 + g_1)^T}{(1 + R)^T} + \frac{\dfrac{\{D_0 \cdot (1 + g_1)^T\} \cdot (1 + g_2)}{R - g_2}}{(1 + R)^T} \quad (13.5)$$

Let's think about this expression. The first T terms of the right-hand side simply show a sequence of dividends growing at the rate g_1 during T periods. In the last ('funny-looking') term, the numerator is the terminal value and therefore an estimate of the value of a share at time T. Note that this numerator is basically the same as expression (13.4) but set at time T rather than at time 0. If dividends grow at the rate g_1 over T periods, the dividend in period T will be $D_0 \cdot (1 + g_1)^T$; and if beginning from that level dividends grow at g_2 from that point on (in perpetuity), then at time T the intrinsic value of the share would be

$$\frac{\{D_0 \cdot (1 + g_1)^T\} \cdot (1 + g_2)}{R - g_2}$$

Now, that's the expected value of a share at time T, but we're performing the evaluation today. Then, we need to discount the above by its appropriate rate, which is where the $(1+R)^T$, the denominator of the last term of expression (13.5), comes in.

The first growth rate (g_1) is usually thought of as a period of relatively faster growth in dividends; the second (g_2) as one of relatively slower growth in dividends, after the company matures. The number of periods for which dividends are expected to grow at g_1 (T) in principle depends on each individual company, its stage of growth, and its dividend policy. However, in practice, $T = 5$ and $T = 10$ are popular choices, though not necessarily for any particularly good reason.

Other possibilities

Analysts might consider it appropriate to model three or even more stages of growth in dividends; or they may estimate the terminal value with a multiple. The possibilities are endless. But note this. Although it may seem that by considering more stages of growth we're making the model more precise, each stage of growth opens two questions. First, for how long will it last? Second, at what rate will dividends grow during that stage? In other words, the more stages of growth we consider, the more assumptions we need to make. Then, there's a trade-off between the more flexibility brought on by several stages of growth and the more elements we have to estimate to implement the model. As the saying goes, there are no free lunches!

The dividend discount model: An example

In 2009, General Electric (GE) delivered a profit of $11 billion on revenues of $157 billion. Its earnings per share (EPS) and dividends per share (DPS) were $1.01 and $0.61, implying a dividend-payout ratio (DPR) of just over 60% (=$0.61/$1.01). By the end of the year, GE's stock price, market cap, and P/E ratio were $15.13, $161 billion, and 15 (=$15.13/$1.01).

Throughout our analysis we'll assume that we're assessing the value of GE at the end of 2009, or what is the same, at the very beginning of 2010. Standing at that point in time, then, how much *should* an investor pay for a share of GE? That is the question we'll attempt to answer with the DDM.

Before we get to the numbers, keep one thing in mind: Our goal is to go over different versions of the DDM and discuss their pros and cons, *not* to make a strong statement about GE's intrinsic value. This implies that we'll be making assumptions about how dividends could be expected to grow over time, effectively making an 'if, then' analysis; that is, *if* the dividends were to evolve this way, *then* GE's intrinsic value would be $x. This is obviously not the way analysts implement the DDM, or any other model. Analysts do not go over version after version of a model as we'll do here for illustrative purposes; rather, they consider what they think is the most plausible scenario, perhaps complementing it with some sensitivity analysis, and base their opinion on it.

It's also important to keep in mind that it's fundamentally wrong to make a set of assumptions, get an estimate of intrinsic value, compare that with the market price, and determine from the comparison whether *our assumptions* are right. That defeats the very purpose of the analysis! Stock pricing is about coming up with what we believe is a plausible set of assumptions, getting an estimate of intrinsic value that follows from those assumptions, and then deciding whether to buy, hold, or sell based on the comparison between our estimate of intrinsic value and the market price. *Never* compare an estimate of intrinsic value to a market price to assess the plausibility of your assumptions! Always use assumptions that you believe to be plausible to start with.

The discount rate

As discussed above, the discount rate for the DDM is the required return on equity, which is typically (but not exclusively) estimated with the CAPM. At year-end 2009 the yield on 10-year US Treasury notes was 3.9%; and GE's beta, based on data from the previous 5 years, was 1.6. For the market risk premium we can fall back on the widely-used estimate of 5.5% (see Chapter 7). Putting these three numbers together we get a cost of equity for GE at year-end 2009 of $0.039+(0.055)(1.6) = 12.7\%$. That will be our estimate of the discount rate.

No growth

Let's assume that our best estimate of GE's expected dividends is that they will remain constant at the level of the last dividend paid by the company ($0.61). According to expression (13.3), our best estimate of GE's intrinsic value would be $0.61/0.127 = \$4.8$. The calculation is trivial, but is this version of the DDM, and its implied value for a share of GE, plausible?

Not really. Note that a constant nominal dividend implies that real dividends will steadily decrease over time; that is, inflation will continuously erode the purchasing power of the dividends. That doesn't sound like a plausible dividend policy for a company to follow. Constant nominal dividends may be plausible for a few years, but certainly not in the long term.

Unsurprisingly, then, our estimate of GE's intrinsic value is much lower than its price. Given that GE has a long history of increasing its dividends (by roughly 9% a year over the past 35 years, even taking into account that the company more than halved its dividend in 2009 with respect to 2008), the market is plausibly factoring some dividend growth into GE's price. In short, because our assumptions are not very plausible, neither is our estimate of GE's intrinsic value.

Constant growth

Let's now assume a more plausible dividend policy for GE. Let's assume that we expect the company to keep the purchasing power of its dividend constant over time. If we expect inflation to run at an annual rate of 3% (roughly the long-term average), and GE to increase its annual dividend at that rate in the long term, then according to expression (13.4), our best estimate of GE's intrinsic value would be $0.61·(1.03)/(0.127–0.03) = 6.5. If we think that our assumption of 3% constant growth in dividends is plausible, then we should conclude that GE, trading at $15.13, is overvalued.

What if we expected GE to increase its dividend at the annual rate of 6% in the long term instead? Then according to expression (13.4), our best estimate of GE's intrinsic value would be $0.61·(1.06)/(0.127–0.06) = 9.7, and we should still conclude that GE is overvalued. Note that under both assumptions our estimate of intrinsic value is much lower than the market price. Should we then conclude that the market is expecting a much higher *long-term* growth in dividends?

Hardly. The reason is that the constant-growth model makes an assumption about the growth of dividends 'as far as the eye can see.' In that very long term, the growth in dividends, the growth in earnings, and the growth of the company itself must align. In addition, this growth rate cannot outpace the growth of the overall economy, simply because the growth of a component factor (a company) cannot forever outpace that of the aggregate (the economy). In other words, what may be plausible in the short term is not necessarily plausible in the long term.

Historically, the US economy has grown at an annual rate of roughly 6%, 3% in real terms plus 3% inflation. That becomes an upper bound for any plausible estimate of the *long-term* growth of dividends. Put differently, whenever we use the constant-growth model, or any model in which the terminal value is expressed as a growing perpetuity, it is simply not plausible to assume a long-term growth much higher than 6%. Other economies may of course have different long-term growth rates, but it is hard to make a plausible case for rates much higher than 6% or so. (Yes, China has been growing at almost 10% a year for several years. But do you think it will be able to keep up that growth in the *long* term? Exactly.)

Two stages of growth

The main problem with the constant-growth model is its lack of flexibility. What if we expected GE to increase its dividends at, say, 15% a year over the next five years, but at a much lower rate in the long term? Well, tough luck, because the constant-growth model does not allow changes in the growth rate of dividends. Here's where the added flexibility of the two-stage model becomes valuable.

At the end of 2009, analysts were expecting GE to increase its EPS roughly at the annual rate of 11% for the following five years. Let's then assume that dividends will grow at the same 11% rate during that period, and that from that point on they will grow at a long-term rate of 6% a year. According to expression (13.5) our best estimate of GE's intrinsic value would be

$$V = \frac{\$0.61 \cdot (1.11)}{(1.127)} + ... + \frac{\$0.61 \cdot (1.11)^5}{(1.127)^5} + \frac{\dfrac{\{\$0.61 \cdot (1.11)^5\} \cdot (1.06)}{0.127 - 0.06}}{(1.127)^5} = \$11.9$$

If we think our assumptions are correct, then we'd still conclude that GE was overvalued. Our estimate of its intrinsic value ($11.9) is lower than its current market price ($15.13), and then from this perspective GE does not look like a good buy.

Terminal value as a multiple

Finally, let's consider a DDM in which we model the terminal value as a multiple rather than as a growing perpetuity. When using multiples, it is standard to forecast both the ratio and the fundamental variable that goes with it. For example, if we thought that T years down the road a company would have a P/E of (P/E)*, then we'd forecast the EPS in period T (EPS$_T$) and multiply that figure by the expected multiple. As a result, our estimate of the terminal value would be given by $(P/E)^* \cdot (EPS_T)$.

Now, let's assume that over the next five years dividends will grow at the 11% we assumed in our previous scenario. Let's also assume that over the next five years EPS will grow at that same 11% annual rate, which is what analysts are expecting; that would imply EPS of $(\$1.01) \cdot (1.11^5) = \$1.70$ five years down the road. Finally, let's assume that at that point in time GE's P/E ratio remains at its current 15, thus implying a terminal value of $25.5 (=$15·1.70). According to expression (13.1), our estimate of the value of a share of GE is

$$V = \frac{\$0.61 \cdot (1.11)}{(1.127)} + \ldots + \frac{\$0.61 \cdot (1.11)^5}{(1.127)^5} + \frac{(15) \cdot (\$1.70)}{(1.127)^5} = \$16.9$$

If we believe that our assumptions are plausible, we'd conclude that GE, trading at $15.13, is *under*valued, an opposite conclusion from the one we arrived at with the previous versions of the DDM. Note that most of the difference in intrinsic value between our current estimate and the previous one ($11.9) comes from the terminal value. In our previous scenario the terminal value calculated from the growing perpetuity was $16.3, which discounted back to the present added $8.9 to our estimate of intrinsic value. In the current scenario, the terminal value calculated from the P/E multiple is $25.5, which discounted back to the present adds $14 to our estimate of intrinsic value.

The big picture

At this point you may be wondering, 'So, where's the catch?' No part of our discussion appears to pose any great challenge, and you may be tempted to join the camp of those who argue that the DDM is a simple model. That would be a mistake.

Recall the 'if, then' nature of our analysis. Essentially what we did was to make assumptions and come up with the intrinsic values that followed from those assumptions. That's not difficult to do. *The problem is, precisely, how to come up with a set of plausible assumptions to estimate the expected dividends.*

Note that for the DDM to yield an accurate estimate of intrinsic value, everything that is relevant for the valuation of a company must be summarized in a sequence of dividends. Managerial strategies, the evolution of the competitive landscape, expected innovations in technology, possible changes in management, the economic environment, ... you name it. That and much more must *all* come down to one or two numbers that summarize the expected growth in dividends. Do you think that's an easy task? Not at all! The DDM *appears to be* simple, but it's far from it.

Besides, the constant-growth DDM almost invariably yields an estimate of intrinsic value below the market price; often, in fact, way below. The same goes for the two-stage DDM with a growing perpetuity as a terminal value. And this problem is severe in companies that have low dividend payout ratios. Does the market consistently overprice these companies or is the DDM inappropriate in these cases? Most likely the latter.

One of the really tricky issues when implementing the DDM is how to properly model the reinvestment of the earnings not paid out as dividends. Where does that money go? How does it alter the future growth of dividends or the terminal value? It's not trivial to account properly for that in the model. And the lower the dividend payout ratio is, the more severe this problem becomes. Throwing numbers into a formula is easy; dealing with this issue appropriately is not at all.

Ultimately, the DDM is useless in assessing the value of companies that pay little or no dividends. It's far more useful for mature companies that grow more or less in line with the economy and pay a good chunk of their earnings out as dividends. And, importantly, it's also useful in valuing markets as a whole.

In short, the DDM is a model with an impeccable logic behind it: Don't pay more for a share of a company, or don't demand any less, than the present value of the cash flows an investor is expected to pocket from the share. But the details are tricky and far from trivial. This may perhaps help explain why, however plausible the DDM may be, the WACC model discussed in the next chapter is far more widely used.

14

Stocks II: The WACC model

- Earnings and cash flow

- Cash flow and cash flow

- Valuation with the WACC model: Overview

- Valuation with the WACC model: An example

- The big picture

There is little question that the discounted cash flow (DCF) model is the technically-correct method to assess the value of a company. As discussed in the previous chapter, there is no reason to pay more, or demand less, than the present value of the cash flows expected to be delivered by the company. And as we also discussed, this model has variations that depend on the way cash flows are defined and the rate used to discount them. In this chapter we'll discuss the weighted-average cost of capital (WACC) model, arguably the most widely-used version of the DCF model.

Earnings and cash flow

It is often said that earnings are an opinion and cash flows are a fact. And it is largely true. In fact, the accounting scandals of the early 2000s (think Enron) did nothing but reinforce this idea. Regardless of what accountants report, at the end of the day investors care about the ability of companies to generate cash. And that is the ultimate goal of all DCF models: To forecast the generation of cash, to account for the risk and timing of that cash through a discount rate, and to bring both together into the estimation of an intrinsic value.

Let's start then by taking a look at Table 14.1. The left column shows a simplified *income statement*. It begins with the revenue a company generated over any given period; then subtracts all operating costs (a big bag that includes cost of goods sold; selling, general, and administrative expenses; and much more stuff we don't really need to bother with here); then subtracts depreciation and amortization; then subtracts the interest expense (if any); and finally subtracts taxes to arrive at the company's *net income*. That is what accountants usually refer to as the company's earnings, or the bottom line.

table 14.1

Revenue	Net income
– Operating costs	+ Depreciation and amortization
– Depreciation and amortization	– Net capital expense
= Earnings before interest and taxes (EBIT)	– Increase in net working capital
– Interest expense	**= Equity free cash flow (EFCF)**
= Earnings before taxes	+ After-tax interest
– Taxes	**= Capital free cash flow (CFCF)**
= Net income	

Now, there are many reasons why this net income is not a proper measure of cash generation. For starters, depreciation and amortization are non-cash charges; that is, they reduce earnings but not cash flow. And changes in fixed capital or working capital, which do affect cash flow, are not reflected in the income statement. (There are many other items that affect cash flow, but these three will do for our purposes.) In short, if we want to estimate the cash generated by a company we can't rely on its net income; we need to adjust it appropriately.

Take a look now at the right column of Table 14.1. To account for the inflows and outflows of cash, we start by adding back to the net income the non-cash charge of depreciation and amortization. Then we subtract the net capital *expense*, which is the difference between investments in and sales of fixed assets. And then we subtract the *increase* in net working capital, which are cash contributions to the day-to-day operations. (But note that, if a company sells more fixed assets than it invests in, the difference will increase cash flow; and the same will happen if it decreases its net working capital.)

The end result of the previous three adjustments to the net income is, as Table 14.1 shows, what we'll call the **equity-free cash flow** (EFCF), also called the *levered free cash flow*. And if beginning from this EFCF we add the after-tax interest payments, the end result is, as Table 14.1 also shows, what we'll call the **capital-free cash flow** (CFCF), also called the *unlevered free cash flow*.

Cash flow and cash flow

Let's think a bit about these two definitions of cash flow. We can think of the EFCF as the cash available *to the shareholders* of a company. More precisely, this is the cash available to shareholders after the company has taken care of all relevant costs and claims to its cash flow, including fixed capital and working capital requirements. We can also think of the EFCF as the largest dividend the company could afford to pay with the cash generated in any given period.

The CFCF, on the other hand, is the cash available *to all the capital providers* after the company has taken care of all relevant costs and claims to its cash flow, including fixed capital and working capital requirements. If a company is financed only by debt and equity, this would be the total cash available to both shareholders and debt holders. If the company raised capital through additional sources of financing, such as (say) convertible debt, then the CFCF would also include the cash available to these capital providers. (In that case, we would have to make two adjustments to Table 14.1, one to reflect the interest payment in the income statement, and another to add the after-tax cost back between the EFCF and the CFCF.) Note, then, that the main difference between CFCF and EFCF arises from claims to cash from non-equity holders.

There is another way to think of the difference between CFCF and EFCF which has to do with leverage and cash flows. Put briefly, the EFCF depends on the company's capital structure (that is, on its combination of debt and equity) whereas the CFCF does not. To see this, take a look at Table 14.2, which displays the calculation of a company's EFCF and CFCF under three capital structures. This company borrows at 5% and pays taxes at a corporate rate of 35%.

Note that the more the company borrows, the higher is the interest expense, and the lower are both the net income and the EFCF. But note that the decrease in both net income and EFCF is *not* equal to the full amount of the interest payment; rather, it is equal to the *after-tax* interest payment and therefore accounts for the tax shield provided by debt. This after-tax interest payment is calculated simply as $(1-t_c)\cdot(\text{Interest})$, where t_c is the corporate tax rate.

table 14.2

	0% debt ($)	20% debt ($)	40% debt ($)
Debt	0	2,000	4,000
Equity	10,000	8,000	6,000
Capital	10,000	10,000	10,000
Income statement	*($)*	*($)*	*($)*
Revenues	10,000	10,000	10,000
Operating costs	–6,000	–6,000	–6,000
Depreciation and amortization	–1,000	–1,000	–1,000
EBIT	3,000	3,000	3,000
Interest expense	0	–100	–200
Earnings before taxes	3,000	2,900	2,800
Taxes	–1,050	–1,015	–980
Net income	1,950	1,885	1,820
FCF calculation	*($)*	*($)*	*($)*
Net income	1,950	1,885	1,820
Depreciation and amortization	1,000	1,000	1,000
Net capital expense	–1,000	–1,000	–1,000
Increase in net working capital	–500	–500	–500
EFCF	**1,450**	**1,385**	**1,320**
After-tax interest	0	65	130
CFCF	**1,450**	**1,450**	**1,450**

The last line of the table shows that the CFCF, the cash available to all capital providers, is independent from leverage. Therefore, one way to think of the CFCF is as the free cash flow delivered by a company, independent from its capital structure; or, similarly, as the free cash flow of an unlevered company.

Valuation with the WACC model: Overview

As discussed in the previous chapter, the underlying idea behind all DCF models is to discount expected cash flows at a rate consistent with their risk, which means that given the definition of cash flow the appropriate discount rate follows. The dividend discount model (DDM) we discussed in the previous chapter discounts expected dividends at the cost of equity. The

WACC model we discuss in this chapter discounts expected *capital free cash flows* at the *cost of capital*; or, more precisely, at the weighted-average cost of capital, which is where the name of this method comes from.

Formally, the WACC model can be expressed as

$$V = D + E = \frac{E(CFCF_1)}{(1 + R_{WACC})} + \frac{E(CFCF_2)}{(1 + R_{WACC})^2} + ... + \frac{E(CFCF_T) + TV}{(1 + R_{WACC})^T} \qquad (14.1)$$

where V denotes the value of the company; D and E the value of the company's debt and equity; $E(CFCF_t)$ the expected capital-free cash flow in period t; TV the terminal value; R_{WACC} the (weighted-average) cost of capital; and T the number of periods for which cash flows are forecast.

The cost of capital, in turn, is given by

$$R_{WACC} = (1 - t_c) \cdot x_D \cdot R_D + x_E \cdot R_E \qquad (14.2)$$

where R_D and R_E denote the required return on debt and the required return on equity; x_D and x_E the proportions of debt and equity in the company's capital structure, measured at market value; and t_c the corporate tax rate. The debt considered for the estimation of the cost of capital is only the interest-bearing (usually long-term) debt. Both the CAPM, the model most widely used to estimate the required return on equity, and the cost of capital are discussed in Chapter 7.

Before we apply this model to the valuation of a company, there are a few things worth mentioning. First, as discussed in the previous chapter, the terminal value is the last cash flow to be discounted and attempts to summarize in a single number all the cash flows expected from that point on. It can be estimated in more than one way, and (as also discussed in the previous chapter) a growing perpetuity and a multiple of some fundamental variable are the two most widely used methods.

Second, the standard implementation of the WACC model consists of estimating one or more short-term growth rates for the cash flows as well as the terminal value just mentioned. Although short-term growth rates can be as high as it may be plausible to assume given the characteristics of a company at a given point in time, when the terminal value is estimated as a growing perpetuity, the '6% restriction' discussed in the previous chapter applies. In other words, in the very long term, it doesn't make a lot of sense to assume that a company's cash flows will grow faster than the overall economy. True, strictly speaking, the 6% figure is relevant for the US economy, but it would not be easy to make a case for a much higher number (*in the very long term*) for other economies.

Third, it's essential to note that expression (14.1) does not yield the value of the company's equity but the value of the *equity plus debt*. Note that the CFCFs we're discounting are those that could be distributed to shareholders *and* debt holders; therefore, the present value we're calculating is that of equity *and* debt. The important implication of this is that after arriving at an estimate of the value of the *company* using expression (14.1), to estimate the value of the company's *equity* we need to subtract the market value of the long-term debt outstanding. To drive this point home, think that if you buy a house valued at $500,000, but the owner has a mortgage outstanding for $200,000, you would only pay $300,000; the remaining $200,000 is the debt you would be assuming.

Finally, although the DDM is typically used in a way that yields the value of a company's *share*, the WACC model is typically used in a way that yields the value of the company's *equity*. Therefore, to estimate the intrinsic value of an individual share, we need to divide our estimate of the intrinsic value of equity by the number of shares outstanding. Piece of cake!

Valuation with the WACC model: An example

In fiscal-year 2009, Starbucks delivered a profit of $391 million on revenues of almost $10 billion. By the end of September 2009, when Starbucks' 2009 fiscal year ended, the company's market cap was just over $15 billion and its stock price just over $20 a share. Our goal in the remainder of this chapter is to apply the WACC model to assess the value of Starbucks as of the end of September 2009. Standing at that point in time, then, how much *should* an investor pay for a share of Starbucks? That is the question we'll attempt to answer with the WACC model.

Before we get to the numbers, keep this in mind: Similar to what we've done in the previous chapter, our goal here is to illustrate the use of the WACC model, not to make a statement about Starbucks' intrinsic value. For the latter we would have to think long and hard about the most appropriate assumptions for the analysis. The assumptions we'll discuss below may be plausible but are not necessarily those that a more thorough analysis of the company would yield. Again, our goal is to illustrate, step-by-step, the implementation of the WACC model.

Let's start by taking a look at Table 14.3, which shows the most relevant items of Starbucks' balance sheet and income statement, as well as two additional relevant cash flows, all of them for 2009. Consistent with our goal, although all the numbers are accurate and coming straight out of the company's annual report, their presentation has been simplified.

table 14.3

Balance sheet	($m)	Income statement	($m)
Cash and equivalents	599.8	Revenue	9,774.6
Other current assets	1,436.0	Cost of revenue	4,324.9
Total current assets	2,035.8	Operating expenses	3,689.5
Net fixed assets	2,536.4	Other expenses	785.4
Other long-term assets	1,004.6	Depreciation and amortization	534.7
Total assets	**5,576.8**	Other income	158.2
Accounts payable	267.1	EBIT	598.3
Other current liabilities	1,313.9	Interest expense	39.1
Total current liabilities	1,581.0	Earnings before taxes	559.2
Long-term debt	549.3	Taxes	168.4
Other long-term liabilities	400.8	**Net income**	**390.8**
Total liabilities	2,531.1	*Other relevant cash flows*	*($m)*
Equity	3,045.7	Net capital expense	403.1
Total liabilities and equity	**5,576.8**	Increase in net working capital	−116.4

Free cash flow estimation

Our first step will be to estimate Starbucks' CFCF from the company's financial statements. The calculation, based on our previous discussion, and final result are shown in Table 14.4. After adjusting the company's net income by depreciation and amortization, the net capital expense, the change in net working capital, and the after-tax interest, we end up with a CFCF of $664.2 million; that will be the starting point of our calculations. But before we get to those calculations, there are a couple of things worth mentioning.

table 14.4

	($m)
Net income	390.8
+ Depreciation and amortization	534.7
− Net capital expense	403.1
− Increase in net working capital	−116.4
EFCF	**638.8**
+ After-tax interest	25.4
CFCF	**664.2**

First, note that Starbucks actually *decreased* its working capital by more than $116 million, which has a *positive* impact on its CFCF. We'll get back to this point later, but for now note that this is more likely to be a one-off rather than a trend. Second, the after-tax interest is calculated as (1–0.35)·($39.1) = $25.4m; that is, based on a statutory corporate tax rate of 35%. However, as you can check for yourself from Table 14.3, Starbucks' ratio of taxes to earnings before taxes during fiscal-year 2009 was around 30%. There are reasons we don't need to bother with for which Starbucks paid taxes at a rate lower than 35%, but we're calculating the tax-shield (and the cost of capital in a minute) based on the full statutory rate.

OK, now we have to make some assumptions about how the CFCFs are going to evolve. Let's assume that over the first five years (September 2009–September 2014), Starbucks' CFCFs will increase at an annual rate of 14%, which is roughly the rate at which the company's earnings grew during the 2000s. Let's also assume that growth over the following five years (2014–19) will slow down to 10% a year. And let's finally assume that from that point (September 2019) on, Starbucks' cash flows will grow along with the economy at the annual rate of 6%. The expected CFCFs that follow from these assumptions, which you should have no trouble calculating yourself, are shown in Table 14.5.

table 14.5

Fiscal year	CFCF ($m)	Fiscal year	CFCF ($m)
Sep 09 – Sep 10	757.2	Sep 14 – Sep 15	1,406.8
Sep 10 – Sep 11	863.2	Sep 15 – Sep 16	1,547.5
Sep 11 – Sep 12	984.1	Sep 16 – Sep 17	1,702.2
Sep 12 – Sep 13	1,121.8	Sep 17 – Sep 18	1,872.4
Sep 13 – Sep 14	1,278.9	Sep 18 – Sep 19	2,059.7
		Sep 19 on	48,753.6

Note that the last number in the table, almost $49 billion, is the terminal value and is calculated as the present value of CFCFs growing at 6% in perpetuity from September 2019 on. If you read the previous chapter, after estimating Starbucks' cost of capital (which we'll do immediately below), you should have no trouble calculating this terminal value yourself.

Cost of capital estimation

Having an estimate of the expected CFCFs we now have to estimate the discount rate that captures their risk; that is, Starbucks' cost of capital. All the figures relevant for its calculation are in Table 14.6.

table 14.6

Long-term debt		Equity	
Book value	$549.3m	Risk-free rate	3.3%
Interest rate	6.25%	Market risk premium	5.5%
Market value	$593.8m	Beta	1.35
Yield to maturity	5.14%	Stock price	$20.46
Maturity	August 2017	Shares outstanding	742.9m

Let's start with the debt. Starbucks has only one interest-bearing (long-term) instrument relevant for the calculation of the cost of capital. It's a 6.25% senior debt note that matures in August 2017 and is rated BBB by Standard & Poor's. At the end of September 2009, this note has a book value of

$549.3 million and a market value of $593.8 million; its interest rate is 6.25% and its yield to maturity 5.14%. The relevant values to keep in mind for the calculation of the cost of capital are the market value of debt ($593.8 million) and the required return on debt (5.14%).

As is usually done, we'll estimate the cost of equity with the CAPM. The 3.3% figure in Table 14.6 is the yield on 10-year Treasury notes at the end of September 2009. The 5.5% market risk premium is the mid-point of the widely-used 5–6% interval for the US. The beta of 1.35 was estimated relative to the S&P 500 and on the basis of the 60 months to the end of September 2009. Given this information, Starbucks' cost of equity based on the CAPM is $(0.033)+(0.055)(1.35) = 10.8\%$.

Finally, we need to calculate the proportions of debt and equity at market value. We already know we have $593.8 million of debt. The market value of equity is calculated by multiplying the number of shares and the price per share in Table 14.6, which yields $15,199.7 million, or just under $15.2 billion. Then, the total amount of capital, the sum of debt and equity, is $15,793.5 million; and the proportions of debt and equity are 3.8% (=$593.8m/$15,793.5m) and 96.2% (=$15,199.7m/$15,793.5m). These figures indicate that Starbucks is almost fully financed by equity, with just a little bit of debt.

Now, putting together the required returns on debt and equity, the proportions of debt and equity, and a corporate tax rate of 35%, we get Starbucks' cost of capital (R_{WACC}), which is, roughly

$$R_{WACC} = (1-0.35) \cdot (0.038) \cdot (0.0514) + (0.962) \cdot (0.108) = 10.5\%$$

Therefore, unsurprisingly given the very low level of debt, Starbucks' cost of capital is very similar to its cost of equity.

So, at this point we have the expected cash flows and their appropriate discount rate. The next step is to put them together and calculate a present value. Discounting the expected CFCFs in Table 14.5 at the cost of capital just calculated, we get the value of the company (V)

$$V = D + E = \frac{\$757.2m}{(1.105)} + \frac{\$863.2m}{(1.105)^2} + ... + \frac{\$2,059.7m + \$48,753.6m}{(1.105)^{10}} = \$25,486.5m$$

or just under $25.5 billion.

Importantly, remember that this is the value of Starbucks' equity *plus debt*. Then, to get our estimate of the intrinsic value of Starbucks' *equity*, we need to subtract the $593.8 million of long-term debt, which yields E = $25,486.5m–$593.8m = $24,892.7m. Finally, if we want to calculate intrinsic value per share, we only need to divide this figure by the number of shares; that is, $24,892.7m/742.9m, which yields $33.5. Given that Starbucks is trading at around $20.5, then, we find it undervalued and likely to be a great buy.

Two more things and we'll be done. First, note that the present value of the terminal value, $17,998.8m = $48,753.6m/(1.105)^{10}$, accounts for 72.3% of the total value of equity. Although this figure may be higher than usual, it's not unusual to find that the present value of the terminal value accounts for over 50% or 60% of the total value of equity. Therefore, it does pay to think about *when* we should have the terminal value (that is, after how many periods), and *at what rate* we should expect cash flows to grow in the very long term.

Second, remember that when calculating our first CFCF, in Table 14.4, we added $116.4 million to the net income because Starbucks had reduced its net working capital by that amount. As we mentioned briefly before, that is not likely to be a trend, particularly in the case of a growth company like Starbucks. Now, we could think long and hard about how much should the company increase its net working capital over time (thus decreasing its CFCF accordingly), but let's take a shortcut here and at least assume no change in net working capital; that is, replace the –$116.4 million in Table 14.4 by $0. In that case, the CFCF falls from the $664.2 million we estimated before to $547.8 million.

We're not going to go through the rest of the calculations, but here's a challenge: Beginning with this CFCF, apply the same growth assumptions as before; re-estimate all the expected cash flows; re-calculate their present value by discounting them at the same cost of capital we calculated; subtract the market value of debt; and divide the resulting equity value by the number of shares. If you do all that correctly, you should find an intrinsic value of $27.5 a share, $6 lower than our previous estimate. Under this more (but still not totally) realistic assumption Starbucks still looks undervalued, but certainly a lot less than before.

The big picture

The WACC model is the most widely used version of the DCF model, and for good reasons. Unlike the DDM, the WACC model enables analysts to perform a detailed analysis and forecast different components of a company's financial statements, and to assess their impact on both free cash flows and intrinsic value. This may be a reason why spreadsheets have become an inseparable component of valuation with the WACC model.

All versions of the DCF model discount free cash flows at a rate that appropriately captures their risk. The WACC model, in particular, discounts CFCFs at the cost of capital. This implies that it yields the value of the whole company, not just the value of the equity. And this in turn implies that the market value of the claims of non-equity holders must be subtracted from the present value of CFCFs to find the intrinsic value of the company's equity.

Although in theory all versions of the DCF model should yield the same value of a company's equity, in practice implementing one version is typically easier than implementing some others. That's why it pays to discuss two other versions of the DCF model, which is what we'll do in the next chapter.

15

Stocks III: Other DCF models

n theory, given the company and the point in time, all discounted cash flow (DCF) models should yield the same intrinsic value. In practice, however, that is rarely the case. Plus, implementing one version of the DCF model is typically easier than implementing another. That's why in this chapter we'll discuss the flows-to-equity (FTE) and the adjusted present value (APV) models, two versions of the DCF model that, although less widely used than the WACC model, may be easier to apply in some cases. (Before you start reading this chapter, make sure you're clear about all the concepts and figures discussed in the previous chapter.)

The FTE model

You may recall from the previous chapter that the weighted-average cost of capital (WACC) model discounts capital free cash flows at the cost of capital. The calculated present value is therefore the intrinsic value of debt and equity, which implies that to find the value of the company's equity, we need to subtract from the calculated present value the market value of long-term debt.

The flows-to-equity (FTE) model is simpler than the WACC model on two counts. First, it estimates the value of the equity directly, so there is no need to subtract the long-term debt. Second, the discount rate is a bit easier to estimate because, being the cost of equity, it is just one component of the company's cost of capital.

Before we formally characterize the FTE model it is important to recall the difference between the equity free cash flow (EFCF) and the capital free cash flow (CFCF): The EFCF is the cash available to shareholders after the company has taken care of all relevant costs and claims to its cash flow, including fixed capital and working capital requirements; the CFCF, in turn, is the cash available to all the capital providers after the company has taken care of all relevant costs and claims to its cash flow, including fixed capital and working capital requirements. Also, recall that the CFCF is independent of the company's capital structure but the EFCF is not.

Note that the EFCFs belong to shareholders, who are the ones bearing their risk. The appropriate discount rate for these cash flows, then, is the company's required return on equity. Therefore, the FTE model discounts EFCFs at the cost of equity and can be formally expressed as

$$E = \frac{E(EFCF_1)}{(1+R_E)} + \frac{E(EFCF_2)}{(1+R_E)^2} + ... + \frac{E(EFCF_T) + TV}{(1+R_E)^T} \qquad (15.1)$$

where E denotes the value of the company's equity; $E(EFCF_t)$ the expected equity free cash flow in period t; R_E the required return on equity; TV the terminal value; and T the number of periods for which cash flows are forecast. The required return on equity is usually (but not exclusively) estimated with the CAPM (Chapter 7).

As mentioned above, the FTE model yields the value of the company's equity directly. Therefore, there is no need for the additional step of subtracting the value of long-term debt from the result of expression (15.1). Also, as should be obvious by now, if we want to estimate the intrinsic value per share, the figure resulting from expression (15.1) must be divided by the number of shares outstanding.

Finally, as we discussed in the previous chapter, the terminal value can be estimated in different ways, the two most widely used being a growing perpetuity and a multiple of some fundamental variable. In the first case, it is important to keep in mind that it is not plausible to assume a *long*-term growth rate for the cash flows higher than that for the economy, which limits this rate to not much more than 6% or so a year.

Valuation with the FTE model: An example

Let's apply the FTE model to the valuation of Starbucks, the company we used to illustrate the WACC model in the previous chapter. Recall that during fiscal-year 2009 Starbucks delivered a profit of $391 million on revenues of almost $10 billion. By the end of September 2009, when the company's fiscal-year 2009 ended, its market cap was just over $15 billion and its stock price just over $20 a share. Our goal is to assess the value of Starbucks at that point in time using the FTE model.

Table 14.4 in the previous chapter shows our calculation of Starbucks' EFCF and CFCF during fiscal-year 2009. The $638.8 million EFCF will be the starting point of our calculations. Beginning from this figure, let's assume that Starbucks' EFCFs will grow over the next five years (September 2009–September 2014) at an annual rate of 14%; over the following five years (September 2014–September 2019), at an annual rate of 10%; and from that point (September 2019) on, at the long-term annual rate of 6%. (These are, as you probably noticed, the same assumptions we made on the expected growth of CFCFs in the previous chapter.) The expected EFCFs that follow from these assumptions are shown in Table 15.1.

table 15.1

Fiscal year	EFCF ($m)	Fiscal year	EFCF ($m)
Sep 09 – Sep 10	728.2	Sep 14 – Sep 15	1,353.0
Sep 10 – Sep 11	830.2	Sep 15 – Sep 16	1,488.2
Sep 11 – Sep 12	946.4	Sep 16 – Sep 17	1,637.1
Sep 12 – Sep 13	1,078.9	Sep 17 – Sep 18	1,800.8
Sep 13 – Sep 14	1,230.0	Sep 18 – Sep 19	1,980.9
		Sep 19 on	44,140.2

Note that the last number in the table, just over $44 billion, is the terminal value and is calculated as the present value of EFCFs growing at 6% in perpetuity from September 2019 on. Note, also, that these EFCFs are very similar to the CFCFs shown in Table 14.5 in the previous chapter. This is the case simply because Starbucks is almost fully financed by equity, which means that its interest payments are very small, and so is the difference between CFCFs and EFCFs.

In the previous chapter we estimated Starbucks' cost of equity using the CAPM and arrived at a figure of 10.8%. Therefore, discounting the EFCFs in Table 15.1 at this required return on equity we can obtain the intrinsic value of Starbucks' equity, which is

$$E = \frac{\$728.2m}{(1.108)} + \frac{\$830.2m}{(1.108)^2} + \ldots + \frac{\$1,980.9m + \$44,140.2m}{(1.108)^{10}} = \$22,990.7m$$

Finally, dividing this figure by the number of shares outstanding (742.9 million), we obtain $30.9, which is our estimate of Starbucks' intrinsic value per share. As we concluded in the previous chapter, then, given that Starbucks is trading at around $20.5, we still find it undervalued and likely to be a good buy.

Note that our estimate of intrinsic value from the FTE model, $30.9 a share, is not too far from the estimate we obtained from the WACC model in the previous chapter ($33.5). There are at least two reasons for this. First, remember, all DCF models *must* yield the same estimate of intrinsic value. Unfortunately, that cannot be the only reason because, as any analyst knows, in practice that is rarely the case. And that brings us to the second reason: Starbucks has very little leverage, which means its EFCFs are very similar to its CFCFs, and its cost of equity is very similar to its cost of capital.

The APV model

The last DCF model we'll discuss, the adjusted present value (APV) model, estimates the value of a company by adding two sources of value, one that stems from the company's business and the other that stems from its capital structure. Formally, the APV model is expressed as

$$V = D + E = \frac{E(CFCF_1)}{(1+R_U)} + \ldots + \frac{E(CFCF_T) + TV_E}{(1+R_U)^T} + PV(NID) \tag{15.2}$$

where V denotes the value of the company; D and E the value of the company's debt and equity; $E(CFCF_t)$ the expected capital free cash flow in period t; R_U the required return on unlevered equity (defined below); TV_E the terminal value of equity; $PV(NID)$ the present value of the net impact of debt; and T the number of periods for which cash flows are forecast.

In principle, the last term of the right-hand side should account for the present value of the *net* impact from debt; that is, for both the benefits *and the costs* of debt on the company's value. Unfortunately, when implementing this model in practice, *only the benefits* of debt are typically taken into account. (More on this below.) In that case, the APV model can be expressed as

$$V = \frac{E(CFCF_1)}{(1+R_U)} + \ldots + \frac{E(CFCF_T) + TV_E}{(1+R_U)^T} + \frac{t_c \cdot I \cdot D_0}{(1+I)} + \ldots + \frac{t_c \cdot I \cdot D_{T-1} + TV_D}{(1+I)^T} \tag{15.3}$$

where t_c denotes the corporate tax rate; D_t the (interest-bearing) debt in period t; I the interest rate paid on the debt; and TV_D the terminal value of debt. Finally, if it is reasonable to assume that the amount of debt will remain constant over time at a level D, then expression (15.3) simplifies to

$$V = \frac{E(CFCF_1)}{(1+R_U)} + ... + \frac{E(CFCF_T) + TV_E}{(1+R_U)^T} + t_c \cdot D \qquad (15.4)$$

Let's first think a bit about expression (15.3). The first half of the right-hand side is the present value of the expected CFCFs discounted at the unlevered cost of equity. We can think of this part as the value of a company fully financed by equity, and more intuitively as the value the company generates from its business activity, independent from the effect of debt on its value.

The second half of the right-hand side, in turn, represents the present value of the tax shields generated by the interest payments on the debt. Each annual tax shield is given by $t_c \cdot I \cdot D_{t-1}$ and their discount rate is the interest rate paid on the debt. (This is actually controversial, but we'll ignore this rather technical issue.) The terminal value of the debt (TV_D) is the present value of debt tax shields from period T on.

Essentially, then, the APV model estimates the value of an unlevered company and adds to it the benefits of debt measured by the present value of the tax shields it provides. Expression (15.4) expresses the same idea as (15.3) but under the assumption that the amount of debt remains constant at a level D. In that case, the tax shields become a perpetuity and their present value can be calculated as $(t_c \cdot I \cdot D)/I = t_c \cdot D$.

Finally, the APV model estimates, just as the WACC model does, the value of both equity and debt. Therefore, to estimate the value of a company's equity, we need to subtract from the figure calculated from either expression (15.3) or (15.4) the market value of the long-term debt outstanding. If, in addition, we want to estimate the intrinsic value of an individual share, then we need to divide the resulting intrinsic value of equity by the number of shares outstanding.

The required return on unlevered equity

The (systematic) risk of any company can be thought of as the sum of two components, business risk and financial risk. The former is inherent to the industry in which the company operates and is related to its business activity; the latter stems from leverage and increases with the company's level of indebtness. (This should not really be so, but more on this below.)

As long as a company is partially financed with debt, the beta we observe and estimate is a *levered* beta. Put differently, as long as a company has debt on its capital structure, its beta will reflect both its business risk *and* its financial risk. Under some assumptions which we won't get into, we can actually strip from this levered beta the financial risk and obtain an unlevered beta that reflects only business risk. Technically, the relationship between the unlevered beta (β_U) and the levered beta (β_L) is given by

$$\beta_U = \frac{\beta_L}{1 + (1 - t_c) \cdot (D/E)} \tag{15.5}$$

where D/E is the company's current debt/equity ratio, measured at market value. Note that because the denominator of this expression is larger than or equal to 1, then the unlevered beta is always lower than or equal to the levered beta. This makes intuitive sense because the levered beta reflects both business risk and financial risk, whereas the unlevered beta reflects only business risk.

So, having estimated a company's levered beta, and then having unlevered it by using expression (15.5), we can calculate the company's required return on unlevered equity simply by plugging our estimate of β_U into the CAPM expression. Therefore, the required return on unlevered equity (R_U) can be calculated as

$$R_U = R_f + MRP \cdot \beta_U \tag{15.6}$$

where R_f and MRP denote the risk-free rate and the market risk premium.

Valuation with the APV model: An example

Let's apply the APV model to assess (again) the value of Starbucks at the end of September 2009. If we can plausibly assume that Starbucks will keep its current *level* of long-term debt more or less constant over time, then we can base our estimation of intrinsic value on expression (15.4). And if we do that, then we need to estimate Starbucks' expected CFCFs, a terminal value for unlevered equity, the required return on unlevered equity, and the present value of the debt tax shields. Hands on, then!

There is only one thing to do with the CFCFs we estimated in the previous chapter, shown in Table 14.5. As you probably remember, those cash flows were estimated under the assumptions of 14% annual growth over the five years beginning in September 2009; 10% annual growth over the following five years; and 6% annual growth from that point (September 2019) on. It is only in this last cash flow where we need to make a little change. In the previous chapter we calculated the growing perpetuity with a discount rate of 10.5% (the cost of capital), and obtained a final cash flow of $48,753.6 million; now we have to calculate the growing perpetuity with a discount rate of 10.6% (the unlevered cost of equity), and when we do that we obtain a slightly different terminal value of $47,676.8 million. So, the 10 cash flows of the forecasting period are the same as those of the previous chapter, and the terminal value is the one we just mentioned. Done with the cash flows, then!

To discount these cash flows we need Starbucks' required return on unlevered equity, for which we need the company's unlevered beta. Remember that we do know its levered beta from the previous chapter (1.35), so all we need to do is to unlever it by using expression (15.5). To do that we need Starbucks' current D/E ratio at *market* value, which based on the figures in Table 14.6 we can easily estimate as $593.8m/$15,199.7m = 0.039. Therefore, Starbucks' unlevered beta is

$$\beta_U = \frac{1.35}{1+(1-0.35)\cdot(0.039)} = 1.32$$

Unsurprisingly, this unlevered beta is just a bit lower than the levered beta. This is the case because Starbucks is pretty much an unlevered company.

Having obtained this unlevered beta we now plug it into the expression for the CAPM, using the same parameters we used before, which yields a required return on unlevered equity of

$$R_U = (0.033) + (0.055)\cdot(1.32) = 10.6\%$$

Unsurprisingly again, there is little difference between Starbucks' required return on levered equity (the 10.8% we estimated in the previous chapter) and its required return on unlevered equity. As before, this is because Starbucks uses little debt. The 10.6% cost of unlevered equity is the rate we'll use to discount the company's CFCFs.

Now on to the debt part of expression (15.4), which is simple. We only need the corporate tax rate, which is 35%; and the *book* value of the long-term debt, which is the $549.3 million shown in Table 14.6. (Note that we need the *book* value of debt because interest is paid based on the book, not on the market, value of the debt outstanding.) Then, multiplying one figure by the other we obtain the present value of debt *benefits*, which amounts to $(0.35) \cdot (\$549.3m) = \$192.3$ million. (Remember, we're following the unfortunate standard practice of accounting only for the benefits, and not for the costs, of debt. In our defense, Starbucks' very low level of debt implies that this assumption may actually be plausible in this case.)

So, plugging into expression (15.4) the expected CFCFs we estimated in the previous chapter, the required return on unlevered equity we estimated above, and the present value of debt benefits we just calculated, we obtain

$$V = D + E = \frac{\$757.2m}{(1.106)} + \ldots + \frac{\$2,059.7m + \$47,676.8m}{(1.106)^{10}} + \$192.3m = \$25,082.7m$$

Recall, however, that this is the value of Starbucks' equity *and* debt. Therefore, subtracting from this figure the *market* value of long-term debt outstanding we get the intrinsic value of Starbucks' equity, which is $\$25,082.7m-\$593.8m = \$24,488.9m$. Finally, dividing this figure by the number of shares outstanding we get $\$24,488.9m/742.9m = \$33.0$. And given that, as we know, Starbucks is trading at around $\$20.5$, we still find it undervalued and likely to be a good buy.

Note that the intrinsic value per share we just estimated ($\$33.0$) is very similar to those we estimated from the WACC model in the previous chapter ($\$33.5$) and from the FTE model in this chapter ($\$30.9$). This is for the same two reasons we discussed before. First, although in practice they rarely do, in theory we would expect all DCF models to yield the same result. Second, because Starbucks has very little debt, its CFCFs are very similar to its EFCFs; its cost of capital, cost of levered equity, and cost of unlevered equity are all very similar to each other; and the present value of debt tax shields are a relatively small amount.

Some loose ends

We'll conclude this chapter with a few comments and remarks on the four DCF models we covered in this chapter and the previous two. There are many other issues we could discuss, but we'll stick to our guns and ignore some topics that would probably be discussed in a 700-page book. Ah, the trade-offs in life!

Consistency across models

We have mentioned a couple of times that all DCF models (DDM, WACC, FTE, and APV), if consistently applied, should yield exactly the same value of a company's equity. Although we will not prove this statement here, we can at least discuss why this equivalence should exist.

Let's compare the WACC and the APV models first. The APV model discounts CFCFs at the cost of unlevered equity, and adds to that the benefit of using debt. The WACC model also discounts CFCFs, but instead of accounting for the benefit of debt in a separate term, it does so by lowering the discount rate. (Note that the cost of capital is always lower than or equal to the cost of unlevered equity.) In other words, both models seek to quantify the same benefits of debt but do so in different ways. Then, when properly implemented, both models should yield the same intrinsic value.

The WACC and the FTE models, however, seem to be quite different because they discount different free cash flows at different rates. However, the only difference between them is, again, how they deal with debt. The WACC model does it by lowering the discount rate, as we have just discussed; the FTE model, in turn, does it by lowering the cash flows (EFCFs are always lower than or equal to CFCFs) and increasing the discount rate (the cost of equity is always higher than or equal to the cost of capital).

Finally, both the FTE and the DDM models use the same discount rate, the cost of equity, but discount different cash flows. The obvious condition under which these two models yield the same intrinsic value of equity is that dividends equal the EFCFs. However, there is a second (and more subtle) condition under which the equality between these models holds: When the excess free cash flows (the difference between EFCFs and dividends) are invested in projects with zero net present value.

When to use each model

Given that in theory it doesn't make any difference which DCF model we choose, the reasons for preferring one over another in any given situation can only be practical. Let's think about this.

Consider a company that is expected to maintain its debt *ratio* more or less constant over time. In other words, assume that the company intends to maintain a constant capital structure, therefore fixing the *proportions* of debt and equity. In this case, the WACC and the FTE models are easier to implement than the APV model. The reason is that when the proportions of debt and equity are constant over time, so are both the cost of equity and the cost of capital, and therefore the discount rates of the WACC and the FTE models. (This argument assumes that the business risk of the company will not change substantially over time.)

Consider now a company that is expected to maintain its *level* of debt more or less constant. This implies that the *proportions* of debt and equity are likely to change over time, and so are the cost of equity and the cost of capital. In this case, the APV model becomes easier to apply for at least two reasons. First, because the cost of unlevered equity is independent of the company's capital structure and therefore constant over time; and second, because the impact of debt can easily be calculated as the product between the corporate tax rate and the constant level of debt. (This argument again assumes that the business risk of the company will not change substantially over time.)

Now that we're at it, note that in the expressions we used in this chapter and the previous two, we never used a *t* subscript for the discount rate; that is, we never assumed a time-varying discount rate. It is possible to do so, though it is not often done in practice for at least two reasons. First, the present value calculations become more cumbersome; and second, we usually have little ability to foresee how the discount rate will change over time. This second point helps explain why, when using constant discount rates, we should at best expect to get the average right; that is, in most periods the actual discount rate will be higher or lower than our estimate, but we still aim to be right on average.

Back to our main point in this section, keep this in mind: If the *proportions* of debt and equity are expected to remain more or less constant over time, then the WACC and the FTE models are easier to implement; if the *level* of debt is expected to remain more or less constant over time, then the APV model is easier to implement.

A practical limitation of the APV model

Expression (15.2) shows that the APV model adds to the value of the unlevered company the present value of the *net* impact from debt. Although, in theory, this implies accounting for both the benefits and the costs of debt, in practice it's almost always the case that only the benefits of debt, typically summarized by the present value of tax shields, are explicitly considered.

This is unfortunate for several reasons but one of them is obvious. If we take expressions (15.3) and (15.4) at face value, both of which incorporate only the benefits of debt, the APV model is implicitly saying that the higher the amount of debt, the higher the value of the company. This obviously doesn't make a lot of sense. Increasing the level of debt reduces the cost of capital, and therefore increases the value of a company, *but only up to a point*; beyond that point, the opposite is the case. Debt, like many other things, is beneficial in prudent amounts but detrimental in excessive amounts. Unfortunately, the usual implementation of the APV model ignores this fact.

Market value weights and target weights

It may sound strange that to estimate the value of a company's equity with the WACC model we have to use the value of the company's equity as an input. If this takes you by surprise, notice that this is exactly what we do when considering the proportions of debt and equity at *market* value for the calculation of the cost of capital, which then becomes our discount rate. It may sound like a contradiction to use the market value of equity to estimate the intrinsic value of equity; it's pretty much like saying that we believe the market price is right, but we're actually assessing the value of a company because we do not really believe that the market price is right!

There is indeed a circularity problem in the standard application of the WACC model. Essentially, we use the market value of equity to come up with our own estimate of the intrinsic value of equity. This issue gets very technical very quickly so let's just make one point: The best way around this circularity is to use *target* values for the proportions of debt and equity. The idea behind this argument is that we should first figure out what is the company's optimal capital structure, and then use the proportions of debt and equity in *that* capital structure to estimate both the cost of capital and the intrinsic value of equity.

Last but not least

Here are two final issues worth mentioning. First, implementing any version of the DCF model always implies having to make a call about how many stages of growth in the cash flows we will model, how long each will last, and at what rate cash flows are expected to grow in each. We may know little about these things, and sometimes we may find ourselves making arbitrary assumptions, but that's the way it is. With experience, the arbitrary assumptions will evolve into more and more educated guesses.

Second, keep in mind that terminal values typically do account for a large proportion of the intrinsic value estimated. Figures of 50% or 60% are not unusual. Given the importance of the terminal value in our assessment of value, then, sensitivity analysis becomes essential. If we use a multiple of a fundamental variable, we need to know how our valuation is affected by changes in the multiple; if we use a growing perpetuity instead, we need to know how our valuation is affected by changes in the perpetual growth rate of cash flows. As mentioned before, this is one of the reasons why spreadsheets have become essential when implementing valuation models.

The big picture

The FTE and the APV models are two versions of the DCF model. The former yields the value of equity directly, whereas the latter yields the value of the company. The former is preferred when the proportions of debt and equity are expected to be constant over time, whereas the latter is preferred when the level of debt is expected to be constant over time.

All DCF models require the analyst to estimate free cash flows and the proper rate to discount them. The FTE model discounts EFCFs at the cost of equity; the APV model discounts CFCFs at the cost of unlevered equity and then adds the present value of the net impact of debt. In theory, both models yield the same value; in practice, this is only the case when the relevant assumptions are applied very carefully and consistently, which is rarely the case.

16

Stocks IV: Reverse valuation

All discounted cash flow (DCF) models require the analyst to forecast cash flows and to estimate their proper discount rate. Estimating cash flows, however, is a mix of art and science, with a fair share of sorcery. But there is a way around. We can reverse-engineer market prices to infer the market's expectations for the growth rate of a company's cash flows. We can then evaluate the plausibility of those expectations, and finally assess the value of the company. Read on, it's less difficult than it sounds.

What is this all about?

The idea behind reverse valuation is to expose the assumptions implicitly built into a stock price to evaluate their plausibility, and from there assess the value of a company. The technique goes like this: 'If this and that happen, then this stock is fairly valued at the current market price. Now, are this and that likely to happen?'

Essentially, reverse valuation is a type of 'if, then' analysis. That is, *if* some conditions are met, *then* the company is fairly valued at the current market price. Or, put differently, reverse valuation is a technique that enables us to compare the things that *must* happen for the stock to be fairly valued at the current market price with the things that *are likely* to happen.

Reverse valuation requires us to start with a model. Given the model, some of its inputs, and a market price, we solve for one of the variables that summarizes the market's expectations. We then compare what the market is expecting with what we believe the company can be reasonably expected to deliver. If what the market is expecting is above what we believe the company can deliver, then we conclude that the stock is overvalued; if the opposite is the case, then we conclude that the stock is undervalued.

A simple example

Consider a company that has just delivered a free cash flow of $10 million. The company has no debt and its cost of equity (and cost of capital) is 12%. The expected annual growth of free cash flows over the long term is 5%. We could then use the constant-growth version of a DCF model to estimate the intrinsic value of this company. More precisely, we could use the expression

$$V = E = \frac{FCF_0 \cdot (1+g)}{R-g} \tag{16.1}$$

where V denotes the value of the company; E the value of the company's equity (equal to V in our simple example because the company has no debt); FCF_0 the observed free cash flow; g the expected long-term growth rate of cash flows; and R the discount rate. Using this expression and the assumptions above it's trivial to determine that the intrinsic value of this company is $V = E = (\$10m)\cdot(1.05)/(0.12-0.05) = \$150m$.

Nothing new here. We put together expected cash flows and their discount rate within a specific version of the DCF model and estimated a company's intrinsic value. That is the standard way of implementing a valuation by DCF, in which we input all the terms of the right-hand side to solve for the variable on the left-hand side.

Note that the previous analysis requires us to form an expectation of the rate at which the free cash flows will grow. Most of the time, though, accurately determining one or more expected growth rates for the cash flows is far from trivial. That's where the mix of art, science, and sorcery comes in. And that is, precisely, where reverse valuation is helpful.

Suppose we observe that the company we've been discussing has a market capitalization of $270 million. An interesting question we could ask, then, is the following: At what annual rate do its free cash flows need to grow in the long term for this company to be fairly valued at $270 million?

Formally, the answer to this question can be found by solving for g from the expression

$$\$270m = \frac{\$10m \cdot (1+g)}{0.12-g} \tag{16.2}$$

where we input the *observed* market value on the left-hand side, and we have the unknown on the right. In this case, solving for *g* analytically is simple. Alternatively, we could find a numerical solution by using the Solver in Excel. Either way, we should find that the *g* that solves the expression is 8%. Paraphrasing our statement above, we could now say: *If* this company grows its free cash flows at the annual rate of 8% in the long term, *then* it is fairly valued at $270 million.

But solving expression (16.2) doesn't mean in any way that we're done. Having found that *g* is equal to 8% is just *the beginning* of the analysis. In fact, we have only found the condition that sustains the market valuation. In other words, if this company is valued at $270 million, then the market must be expecting a long-term growth of free cash flows of 8% a year. And now comes the hard part: Is this plausible? Are free cash flows likely to grow at that rate? Will they do so at a higher rate? Or at a lower rate? Only by answering these questions can we finally determine whether the company is overvalued, undervalued, or fairly valued.

It is essential to note that reverse valuation does not say that the company *will* grow its free cash flows at the annual rate of 8%. Reverse valuation says that *if* the company grows its free cash flows at the annual rate of 8%, *then* it is fairly valued at $270 million. The difference is subtle but critical. Remember, reverse valuation is an 'if, then' analysis.

Note, also, that reverse valuation basically involves two steps. In the first we find the expectations built into market prices; in the second we determine the plausibility of those expectations. The first step is purely mathematical; it's in the second step where the analyst's skill comes in.

Incidentally, it should be clear by now where the name 'reverse valuation' comes from. We're reverse-engineering a market price to solve for one of the components that determines it. Note that we're not solving (as usual) for the variable on the left-hand side of the expression; rather, we're solving for one of the components of the right-hand side.

A more realistic set-up

The constant-growth model we have just used to illustrate the essence of reverse valuation is not widely used in practice. As discussed in Chapter 13, this model gives no flexibility to accommodate different stages of growth. A more widely-used option is the two-stage model, in which we forecast cash flows for the first T periods and then add a terminal value that summarizes the cash flows from that point on.

The two-stage version of a DCF model with a terminal value expressed as a growing perpetuity can be written as

$$V = \frac{FCF_0 \cdot (1+g_1)}{(1+R)} + ... + \frac{FCF_0 \cdot (1+g_1)^T}{(1+R)^T} + \frac{\dfrac{\{FCF_0 \cdot (1+g_1)^T\} \cdot (1+g_2)}{R-g_2}}{(1+R)^T} \qquad (16.3)$$

where g_1 is the expected growth rate of free cash flows during the first T periods, and g_2 the expected growth rate of free cash flows from period T on. A standard DCF analysis would require the analyst to come up with estimates for all the terms on the right-hand side to obtain the left-hand side (the intrinsic value of the company).

A reverse valuation analysis, in turn, would require the analyst to calculate the last free cash flow generated by the company (FCF_0), to estimate the proper discount rate (R) and the long-term growth of cash flows (g_2), and to observe the current market value of the company (V). The unknown in expression (16.2), then, would be g_1; that is, the expected annual growth rate of free cash flows over the first T periods.

Let's go back to our hypothetical company that has just delivered a free cash flow of $10 million, is unlevered, has a cost of equity of 12%, and has a market value of $270 million. Let's assume now that its free cash flows from year 5 on can be plausibly expected to grow at the annual rate of 5%. We can then ask: At what annual rate would its free cash flows need to grow over the next five years for this company to be fairly valued at $270 million?

Formally, the answer to this question can be found by solving for g_1 from the expression

$$\$270m = \frac{\$10m \cdot (1+g_1)}{(1.12)} + ... + \frac{\$10m \cdot (1+g_1)^5}{(1.12)^5} + \frac{\dfrac{\{\$10m \cdot (1+g_1)^5\} \cdot (1.05)}{0.12 - 0.05}}{(1.12)^5} \qquad (16.4)$$

Obviously, solving for g_1 now is a lot more complicated than in expression (16.2). Still, the Solver in Excel can find a numerical solution for this expression in the blink of an eye, which in this case is, roughly, $g_1 = 19.7\%$. So, *if* this company grows its free cash flows over the next five years at 19.7% a year, and at 5% a year from that point on, *then* it is fairly valued at $270 million.

Note that this more realistic set-up comes at a price: It is now mathematically more difficult to uncover the market's expectations; that is, solving for g_1. But it is still the case that the critical part of the analysis is to evaluate the plausibility of the solution. In other words, although the set-up is different, the essential step remains to determine whether the company can plausibly be expected to grow its free cash flows at the annual rate of 19.7%.

Hands on: Yahoo!

On April 12, 1996, Yahoo! traded publicly for the first time. At the end of its first day of trading, its stock closed at a (split-adjusted) price of $1.38. As shown in Figure 16.1(a), between then and January 3, 2000, its all-time high, Yahoo!'s stock price increased by 8,505%, closing the day at $118.75. It was pretty much all downhill from there. Between then and July 30, 2010, Yahoo! lost over 88% of its value. Figure 16.1(b) displays the performance of Yahoo! between its first day of trading and the end of July 2010, at which point the stock was trading for $13.88 a share.

Let's apply the reverse valuation methodology to Yahoo! at the end of 1999, just one day before its high. Table 16.1 shows the calculation of the company's free cash flow for the year 1999. Because Yahoo! was at the time fully financed by equity, its capital free cash flow (CFCF) is equal to its equity free cash flow (EFCF), and its cost of capital is equal to its cost of equity. As the table shows, during 1999 Yahoo! generated a free cash flow of $166.8 million and its cost of equity was 25.5%.

table 16.1

Free cash flow estimation	($m)	Cost of capital estimation	
Net income	61.1	Risk-free rate (%)	6.5
+ Depreciation and amortization	42.3	Market risk premium (%)	5.5
− Net capital expense	49.5	Beta	3.4
− Increase in net working capital	−59.2	**Cost of equity = Cost of capital (%)**	**25.5**
+ Other relevant cash flows	53.6		
EFCF = CFCF	**166.8**		

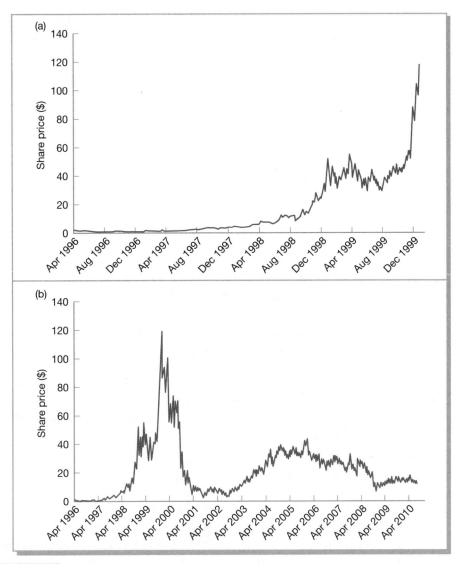

figure 16.1   Yahoo!'s rise and fall

The market capitalization of Yahoo! at the end of 1999 (just one day before its high) was $115,267.7 million, or over $115 billion. However outrageous that figure may seem to be now, many (if not most) investors at the time seemed to feel comfortable about it. This is a perfect situation, then, to use reverse valuation to pose the critical question: at what rate would Yahoo!'s free cash flows needed to grow to justify such valuation?

To answer this question, let's use a two-stage DCF model, and let's assume a long-term growth of cash flows of 5% after a 10-year forecasting period. The more precise question then becomes: At what rate would Yahoo!'s free cash flows need to grow between the years 2000 and 2009 to justify a market capitalization of $115,267.7 million?

Formally, the answer to this question can be found by solving for g_1 from the expression

$$\$115,267.7m = \frac{\$166.8m \cdot (1+g_1)}{(1.255)} + ... + \frac{\$166.8m \cdot (1+g_1)^{10}}{(1.255)^{10}}$$

$$+ \frac{\dfrac{\{\$166.8m \cdot (1+g_1)^{10}\} \cdot (1.05)}{0.255 - 0.05}}{(1.255)^{10}} \qquad (16.5)$$

Using Excel, we can quickly find, roughly, g_1 = 95.5%. So, *if* Yahoo!'s free cash flows grow at the annual rate of 95.5% a year between 2000 and 2009, and at 5% a year from that point on, *then* Yahoo! is fairly valued at $115.3 billion. (You may laugh at the 95.5% figure now, but at the beginning of 2000 many investors would have found it plausible or even modest!)

This, of course, should not be the end but the beginning of the analysis. Now we would have to get into the hard part; that is, assessing whether or not those growth expectations built into the market price are realistic. In other words, to justify its market value, Yahoo!'s free cash flows would need to grow at the annual rate of 95.5% between 2000 and 2009 (and at 5% from 2009 on). *But is Yahoo! likely to deliver such growth?*

As usual, our goal is to illustrate the use of a technique rather than passing judgment on the valuation of a company. But still, let's push the analysis further. To evaluate the plausibility of the growth rate embedded in the price, we would first need to find the conditions that would make this growth possible, and then to evaluate the plausibility of such conditions. Note that this implies that we would first determine the condition that sustains the market valuation; to evaluate the plausibility of that condition we would try to find the conditions that make the first condition plausible; and then we would evaluate the plausibility of this second set of conditions. A good analyst would go through as many rounds of conditions and plausibility of conditions as necessary until the relevant questions were answered.

In our example, having established that Yahoo! needs to increase its free cash flows at the annual rate of 95.5% a year between 2000 and 2009 (and at 5% a year from 2009 on), we should ask what are the conditions that would make this growth possible. We may find, for example, that if Yahoo!'s advertising revenues grow at the annual rate of x% between 2000 and 2009, then an annual growth of free cash flows of 95.5% during the same period is plausible. The question would then become whether we can plausibly expect Yahoo! to increase its advertising revenues at x% a year during 2000–09.

We could go on, but by now you surely got the point. Reverse valuation pushes us to go through as many rounds of conditions–plausibility as necessary until we can ultimately and reliably answer whether or not the expectation that sustains the market valuation is plausible.

A few comments

It may be useful to conclude this discussion with a few caveats and comments. First, note that reverse valuation requires us to specify a valuation model. If we choose a model that is not appropriate for the situation, the results from a reverse valuation analysis will be misleading. Using a constant-growth version of a DCF model for a growth company, for example, will most likely lead us to conclude that the company is overvalued, particularly if the company is in its early stages of growth. The problem here is simply the model's inability to accommodate high growth in the short term.

Second, the solution of a reverse valuation problem depends on the rest of the values we put into the model, as well as on the model's specification. If we input implausible estimates for the discount rate or the long-term growth rate of free cash flows, then the growth of cash flows in the forecasting period implied by the model will also be implausible. In addition, our growth estimate for the forecasting period will depend on how long (5 years, 10 years, or any other number of years) we assume this period to be.

Third, reverse valuation does not spare us from having to estimate expected cash flows. To evaluate the plausibility of the growth of cash flows expected by the market we need to have a good idea of what the company can actually deliver. It may be easier to assess the plausibility of a given rate of growth than estimating a specific one, but still, reverse valuation does not imply that we don't have to deal with expected cash flows at all.

The big picture

The main obstacle to a proper implementation of DCF models is forecasting the expected cash flows correctly. This is, as mentioned above, a mix of art, science, and sorcery. But there is no way around; if we want to value a company using a DCF model, we need to both forecast expected cash flows and assess their risk.

Or maybe there actually is a way around. The idea behind reverse valuation is to expose the conditions that sustain a market price and to evaluate the plausibility of those conditions. This technique pushes the analyst to evaluate as many rounds of conditions and plausibility of conditions as necessary until he can reliably answer whether or not the assumptions built into the market price are plausible.

It may have been close to impossible to forecast the growth of internet companies such as Yahoo! by the end of the 1990s. However, exposing that the market was basically expecting Yahoo! to double its cash flows year after year, for 10 years in a row, should have probably led many investors to question the valuation of this company. And that is exactly the type of situation in which reverse valuation is particularly useful.

17

Stocks V: Relative valuation

E instein taught us that everything is relative. Perhaps that's one of the reasons why analysts use tools of relative valuation so widely. This type of analysis, based on ratios usually referred to as multiples, is often misinterpreted as being a simple comparison between two numbers. But far from that being the case, relative valuation can be just as complicated as DCF valuation. Read on and you'll see why.

Definition and issues

Relative valuation tools assess the value of a company relative to a benchmark. Implementation of these tools involves three steps: First, comparing a ratio for the company of interest to a benchmark; second, determining the reasons why the ratio and the benchmark may differ; and third, assessing whether the company is cheap, expensive, or fairly valued relative to the benchmark.

An analyst using relative valuation tools has two issues to deal with: Determining the appropriate benchmark; and deciding why the ratio for the company of interest and the benchmark may differ. To understand these issues and how they fit into the valuation process, we first need to consider the most widely-used ratios and benchmarks.

Multiples

Most of the ratios used in relative valuation, usually called *multiples*, consist of a share price divided by a fundamental variable expressed on a per-share basis. Price-to-earnings (P/E) ratios, price-to-book (P/B) ratios, price-to-sales (P/S) ratios, and price-to-dividend (P/D) ratios are some of the most widely used. Table 17.1 shows these ratios for ten companies in the pharmaceutical industry as of early July 2010. (We'll discuss the difference between P/E-T and P/E-F, and the meaning of g_{+5} and PEG, in a moment.)

These ratios are called multiples simply because they express the number of dollars that investors must pay per dollar of the fundamental variable. Abbott's P/E of 14, for example, indicates that investors have to pay $14 per $1 of the company's earnings per share; the company's P/B of 3.5, in turn, indicates that investors have to pay $3.5 per $1 of the company's book value per share. Obviously, these multiples mean very little when considered in isolation; they provide useful information only when compared with something else.

Before we go any further, an important remark. There is little to discuss about the numerator of all these multiples; it is simply the current market price of a share. The denominator, however, can be tricky. There may be little to argue about sales per share or dividends per share, which are straightforward figures. But take, for example, the widely used and abused P/E ratio.

Those earnings per share can be observed or expected, the former often being those that the company delivered over the past four quarters, and the latter those that the company is expected to deliver over the next four quarters. P/E ratios based on observed earnings are usually called *trailing* P/Es and are shown in the second column of Table 17.1 (P/E-T); those based on expected earnings are usually called *forward* P/Es and are shown in the third column of the table (P/E-F). As you can see, the numerical differences between them are far from negligible in many cases.

table 17.1

Company	P/E-T	P/E-F	P/B	P/S	P/D	g_{+5}	PEG
Abbott	14.0	10.3	3.5	2.3	29.1	9.7%	1.4
Amgen	10.9	9.4	2.2	3.5	N/A	8.8%	1.2
Bristol Myers Squibb	4.6	11.0	2.9	2.6	20.3	2.7%	1.7
Eli Lilly	8.9	7.8	3.7	1.7	17.7	−4.3%	N/A
GlaxoSmithKline	10.1	10.9	5.5	2.0	17.3	3.7%	2.8
Johnson & Johnson	12.7	11.6	3.2	2.7	30.2	6.4%	2.0
Merck	7.7	9.2	1.9	2.7	23.3	5.6%	1.4
Novartis	12.0	10.3	2.0	2.4	24.8	3.8%	3.1
Pfizer	13.5	6.5	1.3	1.9	21.5	2.5%	5.5
Sanofi Aventis	11.4	7.1	1.3	2.0	18.3	1.3%	8.8

To make matters worse, trailing and forward earnings may not necessarily refer to the last and the next four quarters but to the last and the next calendar year. And to make matters even worse, when calculating earnings, some analysts use the net income as stated in a company's income statement whereas others subtract one-time charges. Pick a company, go to three websites and you may find three different values for its P/Es. And this typically does not imply a mistake in the calculation; more likely than not it only indicates that the P/Es are calculated using different definitions of earnings.

Need more? OK then, besides all of the above, when valuing companies from different countries, different accounting standards make the comparison of earnings and P/E ratios more often than not a comparison between apples and oranges. In fact, it's not unusual to read about companies that earned billions of dollars under European accounting standards and at the same time *lost* billions of dollars under American accounting standards. Same company, same year, different ways of calculating a company's earnings. Remember, earnings are an opinion!

Importantly, none of this means that multiples are useless for valuation. Nothing of the sort. What this means is that you should be careful enough to find out the exact definition of the denominator of a multiple, particularly in the case of P/E ratios, where earnings can be defined in many different ways. Never be shy to ask what the 'E' part of a P/E really is!

Benchmarks: Basics

Consider the trailing P/E ratio of GlaxoSmithKline (GSK) shown in Table 17.1. Sure, we can immediately see that an investor who buys GSK shares is paying about $10.1 per $1 of the company's trailing earnings per share (EPS). But in terms of valuation, what does that mean? Is GSK stock cheap, expensive, or fairly valued?

Considering only this P/E, we just can't tell. That's why this and other ratios are tools of relative valuation; because we need to evaluate this information *relative to* something else. Which begs the question, in relation to what? Here is, precisely, where the issue of benchmarks comes in.

One, rather narrow, possibility is to benchmark GSK against some other pharmaceutical company. For example, we might argue that GSK (P/E = 10.1) is expensive relative to Merck (P/E = 7.7) and cheap relative to Abbott (P/E = 14). But that does not provide a great deal of insight. If all it took to value a company was to establish that a number is higher or lower than another, then we'd all be analysts! That comparison requires no expertise whatsoever. Relative valuation is a lot more complicated than that.

For now, let's go back to consider other benchmarks we could use to compare to GSK's P/E to assess the value of this company. There are three standard benchmarks, the first two typically more widely used than the third. We'll refer to the first as a *temporal* or *historical* benchmark; to the second as a *cross-sectional* or *peer-based* benchmark; and to the third as a *theoretical* benchmark.

A *historical* benchmark aims to assess the current value of a company relative to its historical valuation. This benchmark, calculated simply as the average multiple for the company over the previous several years, is then compared with the company's current multiple. To illustrate, consider that over the 1989–2009 period GSK's P/E averaged 18.8. Therefore, given its current P/E of 10.1, the company appears to be substantially cheaper than it's been in the past. For reasons to be discussed below, we're not drawing any conclusions at this point regarding whether this implies that GSK is currently undervalued.

A *peer-based* benchmark aims to assess the current value of a company relative to the current value of 'comparable' companies. (For the time being, let's say that a comparable company is one that's in the same industry or sector as the company of our interest. It's actually a bit more complicated than that, but we'll get back to this shortly.) This benchmark, calculated simply as the average current multiple of companies in the same industry or sector as the company we're interested in, is then considered against the company's current multiple. To illustrate, consider that in early July 2010, the average P/E of the companies in the healthcare sector was 11.6 (not reported in Table 17.1). Therefore, given its P/E of 10.1, GSK appears to be a bit cheaper than its peers. As before, we're not drawing any conclusions at this point regarding whether this implies that GSK is undervalued.

Finally, a *theoretical* benchmark aims to assess the current value of a company relative to the value the company *should* have, given its fundamentals. In this case, we would first need to determine the relevant fundamentals; then estimate a (regression) model that relates the selected multiple to those fundamentals; then use this estimated model to determine the multiple the company of interest *should* have; and finally compare this benchmark with the current multiple of the company of interest. A simple example is discussed in the next section.

Benchmarks: A few comments

Relative valuation with a historical benchmark implicitly states that if the fundamentals of a company haven't changed much over time, neither should its valuation. When performing this type of analysis, it's important to assess whether we're comparing apples with apples. It may well be the case that a company today has little to do with what it's been in the past, and therefore comparing current and historical multiples may make little sense. Think, for example, of European telecommunication companies that until a few years ago were local monopolies in one line of business and nowadays are companies offering an array of products and services both at home and abroad.

This brings us to one of the issues we must wrestle with when using historical benchmarks: How many years should we go back when calculating the average multiple? It is obviously impossible to come up with a 'magic number' that would fit all purposes. Here is where a good analyst may provide a valuable insight. Ideally, we want to go back enough years to obtain an average that is not heavily influenced by a couple of very good or very bad years. But at the same time we don't want to go so far back that the average is mostly made up of years in which the company was very different from what it is now. That's a tricky trade-off, but one we have to live with.

Relative valuation with a peer-based benchmark implicitly states that comparable companies should have similar valuations. This makes sense as long as we can precisely define what a comparable company really is. Obviously, we can never expect to find companies identical to the one we're analyzing, so the question is what differences in size, growth prospects, and risk (to name but a few variables) we are willing to tolerate and still consider a company as comparable to the one we're valuing. That's obviously very hard to say. To make matters worse, should we calculate an average multiple based on a few companies very similar to the one we're interested in, or should we instead use a large number of companies (say, all those in the same industry or sector), many of which may be quite different from the one we're interested in? Again, very hard to say. And here again a good analyst may provide a valuable insight.

Also, when using peer-based benchmarks it's important to assess whether the whole industry or sector is, at least roughly, fairly valued. Think, for example, of internet companies during the 1997–99 period. Had we compared the multiple of such a company with the average multiple of companies in the technology sector, we could have found that our company was a bit more or less expensive than its peers. And yet, this naive comparison would have missed the fact that *the whole sector* was grossly overvalued.

Finally, to illustrate a theoretical benchmark, consider a simple framework, the sometimes-called Fed Model. This model states that the forward P/E of the S&P 500 should be equal to the inverse of the yield on 10-year Treasury notes (y_{10}); that is, $P/E = 1/y_{10}$. The theoretical benchmark, or the value the P/E *should* have according to this model, then, is $1/y_{10}$. Therefore, if $P/E > 1/y_{10}$, the model indicates that the market is overvalued and expected to decline; and if $P/E < 1/y_{10}$, it indicates that the market is undervalued and expected to rise.

It's important to note that using one of these three benchmarks does not preclude the use of the other two. Quite the contrary. In fact, a thorough analysis should include all three or at least both the temporal and the cross-sectional benchmarks. It's also important to note that we shouldn't always expect all three comparisons (or even two of them) to point in the same direction. In fact, it's not unusual to find that a company may be expensive relative to its historical performance but cheap relative to its peers, or the other way around.

The second issue

We mentioned before that an analyst using relative valuation has two critical issues to deal with, namely, determining the appropriate benchmark and determining why a multiple and the benchmark may differ. We have just discussed the first issue and by now you probably agree that properly estimating the value of one or more benchmarks is less trivial than may seem at first sight. Well, get ready because the second issue is even more difficult.

Let's go back to assessing the value of GSK (P/E = 10.1) using Abbott (P/E = 14) as a benchmark. A naive analysis would simply compare these two ratios and conclude that GSK was cheap relative to Abbott. Now, how much would you pay an analyst to make this 'analysis' for you? Exactly. There is no insight whatsoever gained from this comparison. Putting these two numbers together should be *the beginning*, not the end of the analysis.

Our next and essential step should be to ask why these two multiples differ. That is, to explore whether there's any reason why GSK *should* be cheaper than Abbott. It is at this point that a good analyst may add value by looking into the fundamentals of both companies, and assessing whether these fundamentals justify the difference in valuation revealed by the multiples. If they do, then there is no trading opportunity; that is, these two companies belong to the same industry and have a different valuation but both still are properly priced. If they do not, then there may be a trading opportunity; that is, it may be a good time to buy GSK and (short-)sell Abbott.

If we compare the multiple for a company with a temporal or a cross-sectional benchmark instead, the steps to follow are basically the same. In the first case we would ask whether the current fundamentals of the company justify a different valuation from the company's historical valuation. In the second case, we would ask whether the current fundamentals of the company justify a valuation different from that of its peers in the industry.

Now you can hopefully see why relative valuation is only *seemingly* simple. Assessing the fundamentals that may explain differences in valuations is not easy and requires the same skills as those necessary for implementing a proper DCF valuation. So, far from being a simple comparison of two numbers, a multiple and a benchmark, relative valuation is a tool that uses this comparison only as *the starting point* of the inquiry.

Now, if you're wondering what fundamentals we should consider to try to explain the difference between a multiple and a benchmark, you're certainly asking the right question. But also a very difficult one to answer! Here again a good analyst may be able to pinpoint the most relevant fundamental variables that should be explored. Some fundamentals, such as growth and risk, may immediately come to mind; others may depend on the multiple used in the analysis or on the type of company being considered.

We're not going to bother with the underlying theory here, so let's just say that a P/E ratio can be written as

$$P/E = \frac{DPR \cdot (1+g)}{(R-g)} \tag{17.1}$$

where DPR denotes the dividend payout ratio (the ratio between dividend and earnings); g the expected growth in EPS; and R the required return on equity, which is a function of the company's risk. This expression neatly shows that differences in P/E ratios could be due to differences in dividend payout ratios, expected growth, and risk. The last two variables, in particular, are two of the most important fundamentals typically used to explain differences between P/Es.

Growth prospects and risk are not the only fundamentals we should look at, but at the very least they are a good place to start. Assessing differences in growth prospects, in particular, is both essential and widely done. In fact, there is a popular multiple, the PEG ratio, that's been designed for the specific purpose of adjusting P/E ratios by expected growth.

The PEG ratio

Let's go back once again to GSK and Abbott. The former, with a P/E of 10.1, seems to be substantially cheaper than the latter, which has a P/E of 14. But it should be clear by now that rushing to conclude that GSK is a better buy would be foolish. The question we should ask right away is whether this difference in valuation can be explained by differences in the fundamentals of these two companies.

Expression (17.1) shows that differences in P/Es may be explained by differences in growth prospects. Now, as Table 17.1 shows, the expected annual growth in EPS over the five years following July 2010 (g_{+5}), is much lower for GSK (3.7%) than for Abbott (9.7%). Can we then really say that GSK is cheaper than Abbott? We can answer this question with the help of the PEG ratio, which is nothing but a P/E ratio adjusted by expected growth.

Formally, the PEG ratio is defined as

$$PEG = \frac{P/E}{g}$$

(17.2)

where g denotes the expected growth in EPS. As often happens with ratios, the definition of the PEG is not clear cut. Besides the possibilities for the P/E we discussed, the expected growth in EPS may be for the next four quarters, for the next calendar year, or annualized for the next five years. Again, when dealing with ratios you'd better make sure you know the exact definition of their components.

As expression (17.2) shows, calculating a PEG ratio is simple. The PEG ratios in Table 17.1 are calculated by dividing the second column (P/E-T) by the seventh column (g_{+5}), with the growth rate multiplied by 100. To illustrate, the PEG for GSK is calculated as 10.1/3.7 = 2.8 and for Abbott it is 14.0/9.7 = 1.4.

Importantly, when comparing companies on the basis of their PEGs, the *lower* the figure, the better. This is because a lower PEG indicates a less expensive valuation, or a higher expected growth, or both. And very importantly, note that once we adjust the P/Es by their different growth prospects, GSK is actually more expensive than Abbott, *the opposite* than what a simplistic comparison of P/Es indicates.

This is, precisely, the useful insight provided by the PEG ratio: differences in P/Es may reflect differences in expected growth. In our case, the lower P/E of GSK relative to that of Abbott may be (partially or fully) justified by the fact that, as Table 17.1 shows, the market is expecting GSK to grow its EPS far more slowly than Abbott (3.7% versus 9.7%). So, once we adjust for these growth prospects, GSK turns out to be more expensive than Abbott.

Importantly, a thorough analysis would not end here. It would go on to look at other fundamentals that may explain the differences between P/Es; and then on to consider another benchmark; and then on to consider another multiple. But hopefully you still got the point. There may be good reasons why the P/Es of two companies may differ, and growth prospects and risk are two of the suspects we should look into.

Some analysts look for GARP (growth at a reasonable price) in stocks with a PEG lower than 1; that is, in stocks whose P/E is lower than the expected annual growth rate of the company's earnings. This rule was made popular by Peter Lynch, the venerable former manager of the Fidelity Magellan fund, and is used, at least informally, by some analysts. However, this rule has little or no support from theory. If you see it used as a full justification to buy a stock, you may want to do a lot more research before calling your broker!

The big picture

Relative valuation seeks to value companies and markets relative to a benchmark. This tool should be thought of not as a substitute but as a *complement* of absolute valuation. In fact, a thorough analysis should involve both multiples and DCF analysis.

Relative valuation is only seemingly simple. Far from being a comparison between two numbers, such comparison is only the beginning of the analysis. Determining the appropriate benchmark, and determining the factors that may explain the difference between a multiple and a benchmark, are not trivial tasks. In fact, a proper analysis of relative valuation is not necessarily less difficult than DCF valuation.

18

Bonds I: Prices and yields

S ome people think that bonds are boring, some others think they're for wimps. Whatever you think about them, the truth is that bonds are an asset class that financial markets could hardly live without. In this and the next two chapters we'll discuss issues that will help you understand their risk and return characteristics, as well as many of those things you probably always wanted to know about bonds but were afraid to ask.

The basics

A bond is just a loan in which the issuer is the borrower and the buyer is the lender. The *maturity date* is the time at which the bond expires and the issuer returns the amount borrowed, called the *principal* or *face value*. Between the time when the bond is issued and the maturity date most bonds make periodic interest payments based on the bond's *interest rate* (also called the *coupon*), which is expressed as a percentage of the bond's face value. All the relevant terms of the loan agreement between the borrower and the lender are contained in a contract called the bond's *indenture*.

To illustrate, consider a 10-year bond with a face value of $1,000 and an interest rate of 10%. The holder will receive $100 in annual coupon payments during 9 years, and the final coupon payment ($100) plus the principal ($1,000) in the 10th year. Because most bonds pay interest semiannually, the buyer of this bond would actually receive two interest payments of $50 a year.

Bonds can be floated (that is, issued) by governments, states, municipalities, and corporations, among others. In fact, just about anybody can issue a bond. Rock stars David Bowie and the late Michael Jackson, for example, both issued bonds, the former in 1997 and the latter in 1998. (And at good rates too! David Bowie raised $55 million with a 10-year bond issued with an interest rate of 7.9%, just 1.5% more than the US government was paying at the time. Jackson's bond eventually defaulted.)

Not all bonds have a fixed interest rate. *Floating-rate bonds* have an interest rate that is adjusted over time (typically twice a year) and is usually linked to a benchmark rate, such as a government bond rate. Also, not all bonds have a fixed principal; *inflation-protected bonds* (such as Treasury Inflation-Protected Securities, or TIPS), for example, have a principal that is adjusted periodically (typically twice a year) by inflation. This implies that although the interest rate of these bonds is fixed, their coupon payments are not because the principal on which they are calculated changes over time.

Depending on their maturity, US government bonds are classified into *bills*, maturing in 1 year or less; *notes*, maturing in 2 to 10 years; and *bonds*, maturing in more than 10 years. US corporate bonds, in turn, are classified into *short term*, maturing between 1 and 5 years; *medium* (or *intermediate*) *term*, maturing between 6 and 12 years; and *long term*, maturing in more than 12 years.

Secured bonds are those backed by assets pledged by the issuer. Should the issuer not meet its obligations, the collateral can be liquidated and the proceeds distributed among the debt holders. *Unsecured bonds* (also called *debentures*), in turn, are backed only by the good name of the issuer, which means that no assets are pledged and therefore there is nothing to liquidate if the issuer defaults.

Bearer bonds are those belonging to whoever holds them. They are traded without any record of ownership, and have coupons that must be clipped and sent to the issuer to receive the scheduled payments. *Registered bonds*, on the other hand, are those belonging to the registered holder. The issuer keeps a record of ownership and automatically sends the scheduled payments.

Convertible bonds are issued by corporations and can be converted into a specified number of shares in the company at specified times during the bond's life. The terms of the conversion (basically the number of shares per bond and the times at which the exchange can be made) are specified in the bond's indenture. Given that this option is valuable for investors, these bonds offer a lower return than identical bonds without a conversion option.

Callable bonds are those that the issuer can call (that is, buy back) before maturity. The terms of the call provision (basically when the bonds can be called and at what price) are specified in the bond's indenture. In general, the call provision does not apply to the first few years of the bond's life; during this time the bond is said to be *call protected*. Given that this option is valuable for issuers (because they exercise it only when they can replace outstanding bonds by new bonds with a lower interest rate), these bonds offer a higher return than identical bonds without the call option.

Consols are bonds that make perpetual coupon payments but never return the principal. They never mature and therefore have an infinite life. The Bank of England issued consols in the eighteenth century and they still trade nowadays; the US government issued consols to finance the construction of the Panama Canal but eventually retired them. *Zero-coupon bonds* (or *zeros*), in contrast, don't make any coupon payments and only return the principal at maturity. Curiously, taxes have to be paid on the annual interest accrued (but not received!) by these bonds. All US Treasury bills are zero-coupon bonds.

Bond valuation

It is important to note from the outset that price and principal (or face value) are different concepts. The principal, as we discussed, is the amount the issuer promises to pay to the bondholder at maturity. The price, on the other hand, is simply the number of dollars you have to take out of your pocket to buy the bond at a given point in time. For reasons we'll explore in a minute, most of the time these two figures differ.

In fact, although the price of a bond fluctuates almost continuously, its face value remains constant. (This is true for most, but not all, bonds. As mentioned before, the face value of inflation-protected bonds is indexed to inflation.) A bond with a face value of $1,000 may sell in the market for $900, $1,100, or any other price (including $1,000). It may also sell at one price at 10.30 am and at a different price a minute later.

When the bond's price is higher than its face value, the bond is said to sell *at a premium*. Conversely, when the bond's price is lower than its face value, the bond is said to sell *at a discount*. (Note that zero-coupon bonds always sell at a discount. Think why!) Finally, when the bond's price and face value are the same the bond is said to sell *at par*.

Let's start by considering a coupon bond; that is, one that makes periodic coupon payments and has a maturity date. Its pricing is actually fairly straightforward, simply involving the calculation of a present value. Formally, the intrinsic value of this bond (V) is given by

$$V = \frac{C}{(1+R)} + \frac{C}{(1+R)^2} + ... + \frac{C+P}{(1+R)^T} \tag{18.1}$$

where C denotes the bond's coupon payment; P the bond's principal or face value; R the discount rate (or required return on the bond); and T the number of periods until maturity. Note that this expression yields what an investor *should* pay for a bond (that is, the bond's intrinsic value), which may or may not be equal to the bond's current market price. (The difference between price and intrinsic value is discussed in Chapter 13.)

Expression (18.1) is a discounted cash flow (DCF) calculation, and therefore a present value calculation. Note that it involves discounting the cash flows the bondholder will receive from the bond (that is, the coupon payments and the principal) at a rate consistent with their risk. (Yes, bonds *are* risky and we'll explore the sources of risk in the next chapter.) From this perspective, the main difference between stock and bond valuation is that the bond's cash flows are not expected but (at least contractually) certain.

As an example, let's consider again the 10-year bond with a face value of $1,000 and an interest rate of 10%, and let's assume (until we say otherwise) that it makes annual coupon payments. This means that the holder of this bond will receive $100 in annual coupon payments during 9 years, and the final coupon payment ($100) plus the principal ($1,000) in the 10th year. Let's assume that the proper discount rate for this bond is 12%. (We'll discuss shortly why the discount rate and the interest rate may differ.) Then, the intrinsic value of this bond would be

$$V = \frac{\$100}{(1.12)} + \frac{\$100}{(1.12)^2} + ... + \frac{\$100 + \$1,000}{(1.12)^{10}} = \$887.0$$

Note, first, that if the bond were trading at this price (that is, if the market price properly reflected the bond's intrinsic value), the bond's price and principal would differ from each other. Note, also, that although the bond's interest rate is 10%, its required return (or discount rate) is 12%. So, for the time being, keep in mind that a bond's price and face value can be (usually are) different, and so can be (again, usually are) the bond's interest rate and required return.

Zeros and consols

There is little mystery in the pricing of zero-coupon bonds. They deliver only one cash flow, at maturity, and make no coupon payments before that date. Therefore, the intrinsic value of a zero is given by

$$V = \frac{P}{(1+R)^T} \tag{18.2}$$

For example, a five-year zero with a face value of $1,000 and a discount rate of 8% should be priced at

$$V = \frac{\$1,000}{(1.08)^5} = \$680.6$$

Note that, as suggested before, these bonds *must* sell at a discount. In other words, if a bondholder expects to receive $1,000 T years down the road and no coupon payments before that date, the only way to obtain a positive return from this bond (if held until maturity) is to pay less than $1,000 today.

And there is, again, little mystery in the pricing of consols. Formally, a consol is a perpetuity (briefly discussed in Chapter 13) and therefore its intrinsic value is given by

$$V = \frac{C}{(1+R)} + \frac{C}{(1+R)^2} + \frac{C}{(1+R)^3} + ... = \frac{C}{R} \tag{18.3}$$

For example, an 8% consol (that is, one that makes perpetual coupon payments of $80) with a discount rate of 6% should be priced at $80/0.06 = $1,333.3.

Prices, interest rates, and discount rates

It should be clear by now that the price and the face value of a bond are different concepts and can also be numerically different. The three bonds discussed in the previous section all had a face value of $1,000 but they all had prices different from this face value. However, if you are unfamiliar with bonds, the difference between a bond's interest rate and discount rate may be less clear. As you may have noticed, these two numbers are different from each other in the three bonds we discussed. Let's see why.

The interest rate or coupon of a bond plays only one role: determining the amount of the periodic coupon payment. As discussed above, in most cases this rate is fixed throughout the life of the bond. What is the discount rate, then? It is the return *required* by investors as a compensation for bearing the risk of a bond. And it's not difficult to see why it may differ from the bond's interest rate.

Consider an airline that two years ago issued a five-year bond with a 10% interest rate, which was the return investors required as a compensation for the risk of this bond at that time. By now, two years after the bond was issued, many things could have changed; the economy, the airline industry, and the company itself may all be in a vastly different shape. Would you, as an investor, require the same return from this bond as you did two years ago?

Obviously not. If the economy, the airline industry, or the airline itself are in worse shape, you'd require a higher return to compensate you for the higher risk; if the opposite is the case, then you'd require a lower return. Another way to say the same thing is that, as the risk of the bond increases, your willingness to pay for the same cash flows decreases; and as its risk decreases, your willingness to pay for them increases.

Let's go back to our 10-year bond with a face value of $1,000 and an interest rate of 10%. As we saw above, if investors required an annual return of 12%, this bond should trade at $887.0. However, if the economic outlook improves and that makes the issuer more likely to pay its debt, then investors would lower their required return. If, for example, they required 11%, then this bond should trade at

$$V = \frac{\$100}{(1.11)} + \frac{\$100}{(1.11)^2} + ... + \frac{\$100 + \$1,000}{(1.11)^{10}} = \$941.1$$

If, on the other hand, the outlook for the company worsens and that makes the issuer less likely to pay its debt, then investors would increase their required return. If, for example, they required 13%, then this bond should trade at

$$V = \frac{\$100}{(1.13)} + \frac{\$100}{(1.13)^2} + ... + \frac{\$100 + \$1,000}{(1.13)^{10}} = \$837.2$$

It should come as no surprise that, given fixed cash flows, if the discount rate increases the bond price falls, and if the discount rate falls, the bond price increases. In other words, *there is an inverse relationship between bond prices and required returns (or discount rates).* And this should also come as no surprise: Everything else being equal, an increase in risk must be compensated by a higher return which, given fixed cash flows, can only be obtained if current prices fall.

In short, then, the face value and interest rate of most bonds are set when the bonds are issued and remain fixed all the way to maturity. Their price and required return (or discount rate), in turn, fluctuate almost continuously and always do so in opposite directions.

The yield to maturity

Take another look at expressions (18.1) to (18.3), or at those we used to calculate intrinsic values in the previous sections. They all have at least one thing in common: The 'causality' runs from the right-hand side to the left-hand side. In other words, if we input the bond's cash flows and discount rate, we obtain the bond's intrinsic value as a result.

But what if instead of estimating a bond's intrinsic value we want to calculate the bond's *return* instead? We could calculate it in more than one way, but by far the most widely used magnitude is the bond's **yield to maturity (*y*)**, which formally solves from the expression

$$p_M = \frac{C}{(1+y)} + \frac{C}{(1+y)^2} + ... + \frac{C+P}{(1+y)^T} \qquad (18.4)$$

where p_M denotes the bond's current market price.

Now, you may be wondering what the difference is between (18.4) and (18.1). Have we only changed the notation of the price and the discount rate? No. The change is more fundamental than that and goes back to the 'causality' mentioned above. In expression (18.1) we input the bond's cash flows and discount rate and find the bond's intrinsic value as a result. In (18.4), however, we input the bond's cash flows *and current market price,* and solve *for the discount rate or required return*; that is, for the yield to maturity.

Before we define this concept more precisely, let's go back once again to our ten-year bond with a face value of $1,000 and an interest rate of 10%, and let's suppose that it's currently trading at $950. Then, this bond's yield to maturity solves from the expression

$$\$950 = \frac{\$100}{(1+y)} + \frac{\$100}{(1+y)^2} + ... + \frac{\$100 + \$1{,}000}{(1+y)^{10}}$$

and is equal to 10.8%. Let's think about this.

First, what exactly is 10.8%? It is the *mean annual compound return* we get from buying this bond *at \$950* and holding it *until maturity*. (Chapter 2 defines the concept of mean compound return.) It is essential to note that the return we get depends on how much we pay for the bond; that is, because the cash flows to be received are always the same, different prices determine different returns. It is also important to note that this is the return we'll obtain if, and only if, we hold the bond until maturity. If we buy a 10-year bond and sell it after a year (or, in fact, any time before maturity), our return doesn't have to be anywhere close to the yield to maturity.

Second, note that a bond's yield to maturity is identical to what in capital budgeting we refer to as a project's internal rate of return (discussed in Chapter 21). In fact, we could perfectly define the yield to maturity as a bond's internal rate of return. Third, from a mathematical point of view, the calculation of a bond's yield to maturity is much more complicated than the estimation of a bond's intrinsic value. Still, as usual, Excel delivers in the blink of an eye.

Fourth, the yield to maturity implicitly assumes that all cash flows received are reinvested at this rate. This may or may not be actually possible (usually it's not), which gives way to the so-called reinvestment risk. We discuss this issue in the next chapter, so for the time being let's just say that to obtain the return given by the yield to maturity, we must be able to reinvest all coupons at exactly this rate. (Don't worry if this is not clear at this point; we'll get back to it in the next chapter.)

Fifth, the yield to maturity is widely used to describe a bond's return. In fact, typically you don't even have to calculate it; you will find it right next to a bond's price in the financial pages. Sixth, this yield to maturity is also used as the required return on debt when calculating a company's cost of capital (discussed in Chapter 7). Seventh, if markets do a good job at pricing bonds, then higher yields reflect higher risk, thus implying that the yield to maturity provides information not only about the return of a bond *but also about its risk*. In other words, if we compare two bonds with different yields, the one with the higher yield not only offers a higher return but also exposes investors to more risk.

Eighth, it's important not to confuse the yield to maturity with the *current yield*. The latter is simply calculated as the coupon payment divided by the current market price; that is, C/p_M. (This is similar to the dividend yield of a stock, which is simply the annual dividend payment divided by the current market price.) The current yield of the 10-year bond we've been discussing, when priced at $950, is $100/$950 = 10.5\%$, slightly different from the yield to maturity of 10.8%. In fact, the current yield can be thought of as a 'quick-and-dirty' yield to maturity but, importantly, the former is not nearly as widely used as the latter to characterize a bond's return. For this reason, whenever most people refer to the 'yield' of a bond, they are implicitly referring to the bond's yield to maturity.

Finally, now that we're at it, let's define the *yield curve* as the relationship between the yield to maturity of government bonds and the time to maturity. To illustrate, Table 18.1 shows the yield curve for US bonds on July 1, 2010.

table 18.1

1 month	6 months	1 year	5 years	10 years	30 years
0.16%	0.22%	0.32%	1.80%	2.96%	3.88%

As you can see, the yields increase as the maturity increases, which implies an upward-sloping yield curve. This is the most typical, but not necessarily the only possible, shape of this curve.

The effective yield to maturity

Unlike what we've been assuming so far, most bonds make semiannual coupon payments. When this is the case, the calculation of a bond's intrinsic value and yield to maturity are just slightly different from what we discussed. Let's start with the intrinsic value, which with semiannual coupon payments is calculated as

$$V = \frac{C/2}{(1+R/2)} + \frac{C/2}{(1+R/2)^2} + ... + \frac{C/2+P}{(1+R/2)^{2T}} \tag{18.5}$$

Comparing expression (18.5) with (18.1), it's easy to see that the adjustments are straightforward: We halve the coupon; we halve the discount rate; and we double the number of periods. To illustrate, if our 10-year bond with a face value of $1,000, an interest rate of 10%, and a discount rate of 12% made semiannual coupon payments (instead of annual payments as we've been assuming), its intrinsic value would be

$$V = \frac{\$50}{(1.06)} + \frac{\$50}{(1.06)^2} + ... + \frac{\$50 + \$1,000}{(1.06)^{20}} = \$885.3$$

The calculation of the yield to maturity requires a similar adjustment. Formally, the yield to maturity of a bond that makes semiannual coupon payments solves from the expression

$$p_M = \frac{C/2}{(1+y/2)} + \frac{C/2}{(1+y/2)^2} + ... + \frac{C/2+P}{(1+y/2)^{2T}} \tag{18.6}$$

where it's important to keep in mind that the current market price (p_M) is an input (just as C, P, and T) and that we're actually solving for the annual yield (y).

Comparing (18.6) and (18.4) it's easy to see that the adjustments are again straightforward: Halve the coupon; halve the yield; and double the number of periods. And if we define the *semiannual yield to maturity* (y_S) as half of the annual yield to maturity (that is, $y_S = y/2$), then we can rewrite (18.5) as

$$p_M = \frac{C/2}{(1+y_S)} + \frac{C/2}{(1+y_S)^2} + ... + \frac{C/2+P}{(1+y_S)^{2T}} \tag{18.7}$$

This is simply to highlight that when dealing with semiannual coupons, we'll ask Excel to solve for the semiannual (rather than for the annual) yield. (This does not have to be the case; more on this in the Excel section.)

Let's go back once again to our 10-year bond, again assuming that it makes semiannual coupon payments, and let's assume that it's currently trading at $950. Then, its yield to maturity would solve from the expression

$$\$950 = \frac{\$50}{(1+y_S)} + \frac{\$50}{(1+y_S)^2} + ... + \frac{\$50+\$1,000}{(1+y_S)^{20}}$$

and would be equal to 5.4%. Note, again, that this is a semiannual yield to maturity, but we typically prefer to discuss annual magnitudes. Then, according to our previous definition, the annual yield to maturity would be (2)(5.4%) = 10.8%, which is obviously the same figure we had calculated in a previous section when we assumed annual coupon payments.

Importantly, this annual yield ignores compounding. Note that with semiannual coupon payments, the $50 we get half way into the year earns interest on interest. (This is a bit tricky; here again the assumption implicit in the calculation of the yield to maturity, that all cash flows are reinvested at this yield, comes into play.) To take into account compounding, we need to calculate the **effective annual yield to maturity** (y_E), which is given by

$$y_E = \left(1 + \frac{y}{2}\right)^2 - 1 = (1 + y_S)^2 - 1 \tag{18.8}$$

In our case, then, $y_E = (1 + 0.054)^2 - 1 = 11.1\%$. Note that this effective annual yield is higher than the annual yield (10.8%). This is always the case, simply because the effective yield takes into account the compounding (the interest earned on the coupon payments we get half way into each year) that the annual yield ignores.

An example

To wrap up and make sure we keep our feet firmly on the ground, let's briefly consider the 3.5% US 10-year Treasury note that matures in May 2020. In early July 2010, this note has an annual required return of 2.99%. Then, according to expression (18.5) its intrinsic value is given by

$$\frac{\$17.5}{(1 + 0.0299 / 2)} + \frac{\$17.5}{(1 + 0.0299 / 2)^2} + \dots + \frac{\$17.5 + \$1,000}{(1 + 0.0299 / 2)^{20}} = \$1,044.1$$

Note that this note makes semiannual coupon payments and therefore the $35 it pays annually is split into two semiannual payments of $17.5. And note that the annual coupon payment of $35 is simply calculated by multiplying the annual coupon (3.5%) by the principal ($1,000).

Now let's take it from the other end. If, half way into 2010 we know that the 3.5% US 10-year Treasury note that matures in May 2020 is trading for $1,044.1, how would we calculate its return? Well, if we input the market price and cash flows into expression (18.6) or (18.7) we would obtain

$$\$1,044.1 = \frac{\$17.5}{(1 + y_S)} + \frac{\$17.5}{(1 + y_S)^2} + \dots + \frac{\$17.5 + \$1,000}{(1 + y_S)^{20}}$$

and solving for y_S we would get a semiannual yield to maturity of 1.49%. Then, the annual yield would be $(2)(1.49\%) = 2.99\%$, and the effective annual yield would be $(1 + 1.49)^2 - 1 = 3.01\%$.

The big picture

Bonds are an essential asset class. They may receive less attention than stocks in the financial press, but they provide issuers with a critical source of financing and investors with a relatively predictable source of income. Federal, state, and local governments, as well as corporations, could hardly live without them.

The price of a bond is given by the present value of its coupon payments and principal, discounted at a rate that reflects their risk. A bond's return, in turn, is most properly summarized by its yield to maturity. In most cases, although the face value and interest rate are fixed throughout a bond's life, its price and yield to maturity fluctuate almost continuously.

Finally, if markets price bonds properly, the yield to maturity summarizes both a bond's return *and* risk; that is, bonds with different yields are also bonds of different risk. Yes, bonds are risky, and that is precisely the issue we'll discuss in the next chapter.

Excel section

Calculating intrinsic values and yields to maturity is easy in Excel, as long as you're aware of a few quirks. Let's suppose you have 10 semiannual coupon payments in cells A2 through A11, the last being the semiannual coupon plus the principal. (Leave cell A1 empty for now.)

To calculate the bond's intrinsic value, type

    =NPV(DR, A2:A11)

where DR is a numerical value for the (semiannual) discount rate or required return, and then hit Enter. (Note that what Excel calls NPV is really a *present value*, which is what you actually need to calculate an intrinsic value.)

There is an easier way to calculate intrinsic values and that is by using the 'price' function. The advantage of this is that you don't have to lay out the bond's cash flows to calculate its price. You do, however, have to input some relevant information. Suppose you input the date on which you want to calculate the price in cell B1; the maturity date in cell B2; the annual interest rate in cell B3; the annual discount rate in cell B4; 100 in cell B5;

and the number of coupon payments per year in cell B6. To calculate the bond's intrinsic value, type

    =price(B1, B2, B3, B4, B5, B6)

and then hit Enter.

A couple of comments are in order. First, Excel requires you to enter both the day of evaluation and the maturity date. This can be a nuisance if you want to calculate the price of some hypothetical bond for which you care about its time to maturity but not about specific dates. There's an easy way around, though. If you want to price, say, a five-year bond, you can enter '1/1/2010' as the date of evaluation and '1/1/2015' as the maturity date; Excel will then interpret that this bond is five years away from maturity. More generally, if you don't care about specific dates, you can always fool Excel by entering any two dates that are as far apart as the time to maturity of your bond.

Second, the reason for entering '100' in B5 is because Excel calculates a price for each $100 of face value. For this reason also, if you want to calculate the price of a bond with a face value of $1,000, you must multiply the value resulting from the 'price' function by 10.

To calculate a (semiannual) yield to maturity, you need to input the bond's current market price. In fact, you need to input *minus* the market price, so that Excel understands that this is the money you take *out* of your pocket (the equivalent of your initial investment in a project). Once you do that in cell A1, to calculate the *semiannual* yield to maturity, type

    =IRR(A1:A11)

and then hit Enter.

This is, again, a semiannual yield. If you want to calculate the annual yield, you multiply the previous result by 2; and if you want to calculate the effective annual yield, you can use expression (18.8).

Again, there's an easier way to calculate a bond's yield to maturity that has the advantage that you don't have to lay out the bond's cash flows. But again, you still have to input some relevant information. Suppose you enter the date on which you want to calculate the price in cell C1; the maturity date in cell C2; the annual interest rate in cell C3; the bond price in cell C4; 100 in cell C5;

and the number of coupon payments per year in cell C6. To calculate the *annual* yield to maturity, type

=yield(C1, C2, C3, C4, C5, C6)

and then hit Enter.

A couple of comments are again in order. First, Excel calculates the yield for each $100 of face value. This means that if your bond has a face value of $1,000, you must enter one-tenth of its price. Second, Excel asks you to input the date of the evaluation and the maturity date, but if you don't care about specific dates, you can again fool Excel by entering any two dates that are as far apart as the time to maturity of your bond. Finally, note that Excel gives you the annual yield. Therefore, to calculate the effective annual yield, you can use expression (18.8).

19

Bonds II: Default risk and market risk

I t may come as a surprise to some people but, yes, bonds are risky; and, yes, money can be lost by investing in bonds, even in those of the safest kind. The sources of risk are many and varied but we'll focus on the main two, default risk and market risk. (Before you start reading this chapter, make sure you're clear about all the concepts discussed in the previous chapter.)

Sources of risk

Suppose we buy a corporate bond that matures in five years and we intend to hold it for only one year. What can go wrong? What are the sources of risk we face? Can we actually *lose* money? In a nutshell, many things can go wrong, because bonds are risky in more than one way; and yes, we can lose money by investing in this or in any other bond. To make this clear from the start, note that even investors in US Treasury bonds, widely perceived as one of the safest assets in the world, can lose money. Over the past two decades, the 1990s and the 2000s, investors in 10-year Treasuries lost 7.3% in 1994, 7.5% in 1999, and 9.5% in 2009. (We'll see how in a minute.)

The first and obvious source of risk is related to whether the issuer will meet its obligations. In the case of a corporate bond, we can never be certain that the company will make the promised coupon payments and return the principal. And the same goes for any other issuer, including governments. We'll discuss this possibility in more detail below, but for the time being let's call this *default risk*; that is, the uncertainty about whether the issuer will make the promised payments.

But in fact, things do not have to get that bad for us to lose money on a bond. In the case of a corporate bond it may be the case that, during the year we hold it, the general level of interest rates goes up, which as we discussed in the previous chapter, will push bond prices down. Our bond will then suffer a capital loss, and if this capital loss is larger than the coupon payment, we would lose money on our bond. We'll also discuss this possibility in more detail below, but for the time being let's call this *market risk* or *interest-rate risk*; that is, the uncertainty about the price at which we'll sell a bond; or the uncertainty about whether we'll suffer a capital loss; or the uncertainty about our return if we sell the bond any time before maturity. (This is, by the way, the reason investors in default-free US bonds lost money in 1994, 1999, and 2009; the decrease in prices more than offset the coupon payments.)

What else can go wrong? Well, in some cases it may not be easy to find a buyer for our bond. If we buy a government bond from a developed country, or a corporate bond from a solid company, selling the bond should not be a problem. Those bonds change hands very frequently and buyers and sellers are always easy to find. However, many bonds trade less frequently, buyers and sellers may be scarce, and finding a buyer may not be trivial. Let's call this *liquidity risk*; that is, the uncertainty about our ability to find a buyer for our bond at the current market price. To illustrate, both German and Austrian bonds have a negligible probability of default. However, at the same maturity, Austrian bonds typically have a yield a tiny bit higher than German bonds. The difference between these two yields is a compensation for the lower liquidity of Austrian bonds.

To introduce two other sources of risk, let's assume that instead of holding our corporate bond for just one year we hold it until maturity (five years down the road). Let's also assume that the issuer is a blue-chip company, and therefore neither default risk nor liquidity risk is an issue. And let's finally assume that the bond's yield to maturity is 4%. Now, what if, unexpectedly, over the next five years inflation runs at an annual rate of 5%? Well, that would be too bad because we're only earning 4% on the bond. And although the 4% return is certain, we will suffer a loss in real terms; that is, our purchasing power will fall. Let's call this *inflation risk*; that is, the uncertainty about whether the nominal return we will obtain will keep up with inflation. (But recall that the TIPS do enable investors to lock a *real* return, therefore eliminating this inflation risk and the uncertainty about future purchasing power.)

Finally, recall that the calculation of the yield to maturity implicitly assumes that the cash flows generated by the bond are reinvested at that rate. (We'll discuss an example in the next section.) However, that may or may not be possible, which brings us to the so-called *reinvestment risk*; that is, the uncertainty about the rate at which we'll be able to reinvest the coupon payments made by the bond.

In short, then, bonds are far from risk-free. Their sources of risk are many and varied, and those we just discussed are not an exhaustive list. Therefore, since any required return (R), including that of bonds, is the sum of a risk-free rate (R_f) plus a risk premium (RP), we can think of a bond's risk premium, and hence its required return, as being *positively* affected by these (and other) sources of risk; that is

$$R = R_f + RP(\text{default risk, market risk, liquidity risk, inflation risk, reinvestment risk ...})$$

In other words, the higher these sources of risk, the higher the risk premium, the higher the required return, and, everything else being equal, the lower the price of a bond.

Now, before we go deeper into the two most relevant types of risk, default risk and market risk, let's briefly discuss the reinvestment assumption implicitly built into the calculation of the yield to maturity. (For simplicity, throughout this chapter we'll assume that bonds make annual, as opposed to semiannual, coupon payments.)

Yield to maturity: The hidden catch

Let's consider a five-year bond with a face value of $1,000, a 6% coupon, and a current price of $920. Assuming that this bond makes annual coupon payments, at the end of each of the first four years we'll receive $60, and at the end of the fifth and final year we'll receive $1,060. You know by now how to calculate yields to maturity, so if you run the calculation you should find that it is 8.0%.

We argued before that this 8% yield hides an implicit reinvestment assumption. What does that mean? Let's think about it this way. Let's say we get the first coupon payment of $60 at the end of the first year, and that we put it in the bank at 8% a year over four years. Then, by the time the bond matures, the $60 will have turned into $60·(1.08)^4 = $81.6.

Let's do something similar for the rest of the coupon payments. When we receive the second $60 two years down the road, we put it in the bank at

8% a year over three years, which by the time the bond matures will have turned into $60·(1.08)^3 = $75.6. When we receive the third $60 we put it in the bank at 8% a year over two years, which will turn into $70.0 by the time the bond matures. And when we get the fourth $60 we put it in the bank at 8% for one year, which will turn into $64.8 by the time the bond matures. Finally, five years down the road, we'll receive $1,060 which is the last coupon payment plus the principal.

So, what do we get in five years? We get the sum of all the cash flows calculated above; that is, $81.6 + $75.6 + $70.0 + $64.8 + $1,060 = $1,352. And here comes the clincher. Remember the bond's price of $920? Well, what would we get if we deposited $920 in the bank at the annual rate of 8% and came back five years later to cash in? Surprise! We'd get exactly $1,352! In other words, to turn $920 into $1,352 by investing at the annual rate of 8% over five years, *all interest payments must be reinvested at 8%*.

The problem is, that is hardly ever possible. First, if our investment is small the coupon payment may not be large enough to buy another bond, even if we could find one that has the same yield as the one we already have. Second, finding a bond of similar quality to the one we already have, and which also pays the same yield, is typically far from trivial. And third, even if we could get around the previous two problems (that is, we can find another bond of similar risk and the same yield, and our coupon payment is large enough to buy it), once the new bond makes a coupon payment, we'd have the same problems all over again.

All this in no way means that the yield to maturity is a flawed measure of a bond's return. In fact, the calculation of the internal rate of return of an investment project has the same built-in reinvestment assumption, and yet this tool is routinely used by corporations to evaluate projects. But it's always important to know the limitations of, and the hidden assumptions behind, the financial tools we use very often. (Chapter 21 discusses the internal rate of return as a tool for project evaluation.)

Default risk

Not all bond issuers are equally likely to meet their promises. Governments of developed countries and blue-chip companies are almost certain to honor their obligations to bondholders; governments of emerging markets or less reliable companies not necessarily are. The government of Argentina, for example, defaulted on over $80 billion of debt in December 2001 (the largest sovereign default in history); Michael Jackson, as mentioned in the previous chapter, also defaulted on his bond. The job of rating agencies is, precisely, to assess the likelihood of such events.

The two largest rating agencies are Standard & Poor's (S&P) and Moody's. These agencies provide investors with ratings that indicate the likelihood of default. The rating system used by S&P, as well as the meaning of each rating, is shown in Table 19.1.

Bonds rated AAA, AA, A, and BBB are called *investment grade* bonds and are very unlikely to default. Bonds rated BB and below are called *high-yield* (or *junk*) bonds and are speculative in the sense that, although they offer high yields, they also have a relatively high probability of default. (In fact, some organizations such as pension funds are prohibited from buying bonds of quality lower than investment grade.) Companies that achieve investment grade status, then, have a substantially lower cost of debt than companies that do not.

Rating agencies are usually criticized for being slow to downgrade issuers whose fundamentals deteriorate rapidly. Many times, in fact, rating agencies have downgraded companies or governments to junk status *after* a critical situation became public news. In 2001, Enron, for example, filed for bankruptcy on December 2, but S&P downgraded the company to junk status only four days earlier, on November 28. Lehman Brothers was also rated investment grade until a few days before it filed for bankruptcy.

In the long term, however, credit ratings are far more reliable; that is, they do predict quite accurately the probability of default. Table 19.2 displays 'mortality rates' between the years 1971 and 2003. The figures show the proportion of US companies that defaulted 5 and 10 years after being rated. As the table clearly shows, the lower the rating (and therefore the riskier the company), the higher the mortality rate; that is, the higher the proportion of companies that did default.

table 19.1	

S&P	Description
AAA	The highest rating assigned by Standard & Poor's. The obligor's capacity to meet its financial commitment on the obligation is extremely strong.
AA	Differs from the highest-rated obligations only to a small degree. The obligor's capacity to meet its financial commitment on the obligation is very strong.
A	More susceptible to the adverse effects of changes in circumstances and economic conditions than obligations in higher-rated categories. However, the obligor's capacity to meet its financial commitment on the obligation is still strong.
BBB	Exhibits adequate protection parameters. However, adverse economic conditions or changing circumstances are more likely to lead to a weakened capacity of the obligor to meet its financial commitment on the obligation.
BB	Less vulnerable to nonpayment than other speculative issues. However, it faces major ongoing uncertainties or exposure to adverse business, financial, or economic conditions, which could lead to the obligor's inadequate capacity to meet its financial commitment on the obligation.
B	More vulnerable to nonpayment than obligations rated 'BB', but the obligor currently has the capacity to meet its financial commitment on the obligation. Adverse business, financial, or economic conditions would be likely to impair the obligor's capacity or willingness to meet its financial commitment on the obligation.
CCC	Currently vulnerable to nonpayment, and dependent upon favorable business, financial, and economic conditions for the obligor to meet its financial commitment on the obligation. In the event of adverse business, financial, or economic conditions, the obligor is not likely to have the capacity to meet its financial commitment on the obligation.
CC	Currently highly vulnerable to nonpayment.
C	Obligations that are currently highly vulnerable to nonpayment, obligations that have payment arrearages allowed by the terms of the documents, or obligations of an issuer that is the subject of a bankruptcy petition or similar action which have not experienced a payment default.
D	In payment default. The 'D' rating category is used when payments on an obligation are not made on the date due even if the applicable grace period has not expired, unless Standard & Poor's believes that such payments will be made during such grace period. The 'D' rating also will be used upon the filing of a bankruptcy petition or the taking of similar action if payments on an obligation are jeopardized.

The ratings from AA to CCC may be modified by the addition of a plus or minus sign to show relative standing within the major rating categories.

Source: 'Standard & Poor's Ratings Definitions', © August 2010, published by Standard & Poor's. Reproduced with permission of Standard & Poor's Financial Services LLC.

table 19.2

S&P rating	5 years (%)	10 years (%)
AAA	0.04	0.07
AA	0.44	0.51
A	0.20	0.66
BBB	6.44	7.54
BB	11.90	19.63
B	27.54	36.80
CCC	46.26	59.02

Source: Adapted from Edward Altman and Brenda Karlin, 'Defaults and returns in the high-yield bond market: the year 2007 in review and outlook,' working paper, 2008. Reproduced with permission of E. Altman.

This being the case, it should come as no surprise that, the lower the rating, the more issuers have to pay to convince investors to buy their bonds. In other words, the lower the rating, the higher the risk, and the higher the yield. Table 19.3 shows the bond yields of several companies in different rating categories in early July 2010, as well as the yield of a US Treasury note with similar maturity. (All bonds mature sometime between June 2018 and July 2020.)

table 19.3

Bond	S&P rating	Yield (%)	Spread (%)
US Treasury	N/A	3.00	N/A
Microsoft	AAA	3.08	0.08
Wal-Mart	AA	3.63	0.63
AT&T	A	3.99	0.99
Time Warner	BBB	4.45	1.45
Omnicare	BB	7.39	4.39
MGM Mirage	B	8.61	5.61
Beazer Homes	CCC	10.95	7.95

As Table 19.3 shows, yields increase as the credit rating worsens. The last column shows the spread over US Treasury notes, which is often thought of as reflecting expectations about the economy. When the economy is expected to grow at a fast pace, spreads tend to shrink, reflecting a lower probability of corporate default. Conversely, and for the opposite reason, when the economy is expected to perform poorly these spreads tend to widen. (The same goes for emerging markets bonds, whose spreads over Treasuries tend to tighten or widen depending on the good or bad growth prospects for these economies.)

In short, then, rating agencies assess the fundamentals of issuers and assign a rating on their bonds. These ratings quite accurately predict the long-term probability of default, and therefore investors require a higher yield the lower the rating of the issuer. In the short term, however, rating agencies seem to be slow to react and typically trail the actions of bond traders. Finally, the cost of debt of investment-grade issuers is substantially lower than that of 'junk' issuers.

Market risk

Investors who buy government bonds from developed markets are almost free from default risk and face a rather low liquidity risk. However, they are still subject to both inflation risk and reinvestment risk, as well as the market risk that is the focus of this section.

It should be clear from the discussion in the previous chapter that a bond's discount rate and its price move in opposite directions. It should also be clear that discount rates may change because of changing expectations about the performance of the issuer and that of the overall economy.

Let's consider a 5-year bond and a 10-year bond, both with a face value of $1,000, a 10% coupon, and a discount rate of 10%. It is straightforward to calculate that both bonds should sell at par; that is, for $1,000. The relevant question for us now is what happens to the price of these bonds if the general level of interest rates (and therefore the discount rate of both bonds) increases by, say, 1 percentage point. We know that the price of both bonds should fall, but the question is *by how much*.

Again, by now we know how to perform the relevant calculations. It is easy to determine that given an 11% discount rate, the 5-year bond should trade at $963 and the 10-year bond at $941.1. Note, then, that the bond with the longer maturity falls by more (5.9%) than does the one with shorter maturity (3.7%).

What if the general level of interest rates (and therefore the discount rate of both bonds) were to fall by, say, 1 percentage point? Then, given a 9% discount rate, the 5-year bond should trade at $1,038.9 and the 10-year bond at $1,064.2. Note, then, that the bond with the longer maturity rises more (6.4%) than does the one with shorter maturity (3.9%).

What this simple example shows is that, everything else being equal, given two bonds of different maturity, the one with the longer maturity will be more sensitive to changes in interest rates. In other words, the longer a bond's maturity, the more its price will be affected by changes in discount rates; or, similarly, the higher its price (or return) volatility.

To drive this point home, Figure 19.1 shows the prices of 30 bonds (all with a face value of $1,000, a 10% coupon, and maturities between 1 and 30 years) at discount rates (DR) of 9% and 11%. As is clear from the exhibit, the longer a bond's maturity, the larger the change in price (both upwards and downwards) for any given change in discount rates. Or, in other words, *the longer the maturity, the higher a bond's market risk.*

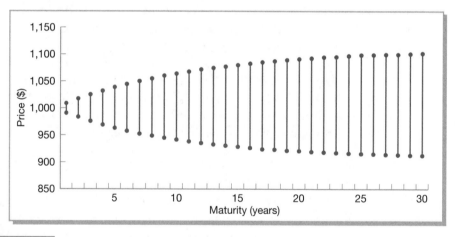

figure 19.1   Market risk

The intuition behind this result is straightforward. The longer we are locked into a contract that pays 10% when the required return is only 9%, the more we stand to gain. Conversely, the longer we are locked into a contract that pays 10% when the required return is 11%, the more we stand to lose. Therefore, the longer a bond's maturity, the more we stand to gain *and* lose when interest rates change and we remain locked into the bond's interest rate.

It is important to note that this result applies only when we compare two bonds identical in every way except for their yields to maturity. In other words, if we compare two bonds with the same face value, coupon, and discount rate, but with different maturity, the one with the longer maturity *must* have a higher market risk. However, if we compare two bonds with different maturity, but also with different coupon and/or discount rate, it does *not necessarily* follow that the one with the longer maturity will have the higher market risk.

Market risk is also related to the size of the coupons. In fact, everything else being equal, *the larger the coupon, the lower a bond's market risk*. Table 19.4 shows three bonds with different coupons but the same $1,000 face value and five-year maturity, as well as their price at a discount rate (DR) of 5%. Because all bonds have different initial prices, it makes sense to think of price volatility as the *percentage* (rather than the absolute) change in prices.

When the discount rate falls from 5% to 4%, the prices of the bonds with a 2% coupon and a 10% coupon increase by 4.7% and 4.2%. Similarly, when the discount rate increases from 5% to 6%, the prices of the bonds with a 2% coupon and a 10% coupon fall by 4.4% and 3.9%. Then, everything else being equal, the higher the coupon, the lower the market risk.

table 19.4

DR	2% coupon	6% coupon	10% coupon
4%	4.7%	4.4%	4.2%
5%	$870.1	$1,043.3	$1,216.5
6%	−4.4%	−4.1%	−3.9%

Finally, market risk is also related to the yield (or discount rate). In fact, everything else being equal, *the higher the yield, the lower a bond's market risk*. Table 19.5 overleaf shows three bonds with different yields but the same $1,000 face value, 10% coupon, and five-year maturity, as well as their price at their actual yields. Because all bonds have different initial prices, it makes sense again to think of price volatility as the percentage (rather than the absolute) change in prices.

When the discount rate falls by one percentage point, the prices of the bonds with a 3% yield and a 15% yield increase by 4.3% and 3.6%. Similarly, when the discount rate increases by one percentage point, the prices of the bonds with a 3% yield and a 15% yield fall by 4.0% and 3.5%. Then, everything else being equal, the higher the yield (discount rate), the lower the market risk.

table 19.5

	3% yield	9% yield	15% yield
Yield – 1%	4.3%	3.9%	3.6%
Actual yield	$1,320.6	$1,038.9	$832.4
Yield + 1%	–4.0%	–3.7%	–3.5%

In short, then, bond prices react to changes in the factors that affect discount rates and expose investors to price volatility. This market (or interest-rate) risk is the main source of risk for bonds that are very unlikely to default, and more generally a critical source of risk for all bonds. Everything else being equal, this market risk is increasing in a bond's maturity, decreasing in a bond's coupon, and decreasing in a bond's yield.

The big picture

Bonds, like just about all financial assets, are risky. Their sources of risk are many and varied and, as long as markets price bonds properly, higher levels of risk translate into higher yields. Liquidity risk, inflation risk, and reinvestment risk are all positively related to a bond's yield, but default risk and market risk are the key determinants of differences in yields across bonds.

Default risk is related to the uncertainty about whether the issuer will make the bond's promised payments. It is assessed by rating agencies and captured in credit ratings, which are widely used and quite reliable in the long term. Investment grade bonds are very safe and a timely payment of their promised cash flows is almost certain. High-yield bonds, on the other hand, are much more likely to default and therefore compensate investors with higher yields. Market (or interest-rate) risk is related to price (or return) volatility, and therefore to uncertainty about future bond prices. This market risk increases with a bond's maturity, decreases with its coupon, and decreases with its yield.

20

Bonds III: Duration and convexity

A t this point we know how to price bonds and how to assess their default risk and market risk. The former is evaluated by rating agencies and summarized in credit ratings. The latter can be assessed as we discussed in the previous chapter, as well as with two critical tools widely used by bond traders, duration and modified duration, both of which we discuss in this chapter.

Maturity reconsidered

We discussed in the previous chapter that one of the most important sources of a bond's risk is its market (or interest-rate) risk, which measures the bond's price (or return) volatility. We also discussed that, everything else being equal, this market risk is increasing in a bond's maturity. However, when bond traders think about volatility, they hardly ever relate it to a bond's maturity; almost invariably they relate it to its duration. Is there any relationship, then, between maturity and duration? There sure is.

The lifetime of a bond is given by its maturity, which is the number of years until the bond returns the principal. However, this is not a good measure of a bond's *effective* lifetime. To see why, compare a five-year zero with a five-year bond with a 10% coupon, both with a face value of $1,000. Note that although we have to wait five years to get a cash flow from the first bond, by the end of the fourth year the second bond will have paid almost 27% (=$400/$1,500) of the total cash flows it will deliver. In fact, note that with this second bond we receive its cash flows, on average, after three years: $(1 + 2 + 3 + 4 + 5)/5 = 3$.

Three years, however, is not a good measure of the second bond's effective maturity. The reason is that we receive a much larger cash flow in the fifth year ($1,100) than in any of the previous years ($100). Should we then give a larger weight to five years than to any other time to receive cash flows? Yes. Should we then assign these weights according to the cash flows paid by the bond? No.

The reason is that if we do so we would give the same weight to both one year and two years because in both cases we receive $100. However, $100 after one year is more valuable than $100 after two years. This suggests that the best way to assign weights to each time to receive cash flows is to weight them by *the present value* of the cash flows to be received.

By definition, then, a bond's *duration* is the weighted-average time to receive a bond's cash flows, with the weights being the present value of each cash flow relative to the bond's price. Do I hear you saying ... *what?!*

Duration: An example

Let's go again, this time step by step. It's actually less difficult than it sounds. Let's go back to our five-year bond with a face value of $1,000 and a 10% coupon, and let's assume that the required return on this bond is 8%. For the sake of simplicity, throughout this chapter we'll assume that bonds make annual, as opposed to semiannual, coupon payments. Then, this bond will pay $100 at the end of each of the first four years and $1,100 at the end of the fifth year. What is this bond's duration?

Take a look at Table 20.1. The first column shows the times to receive cash flows (*t*) measured in years and ranging from 1 to 5. The second column shows the actual cash flows (CF) paid by the bond. The third column shows the present value of each cash flow (PVCF), discounted at the required return of 8%; the sum of these present values is of course equal to the bond's current price ($1,079.9). The fourth column shows the present value of each cash flow relative to the bond's price (RPVCF); these weights obviously add to 1. The last column shows the product of the first and the fourth columns (*t*·RPVCF); that is, each time to receive cash flows multiplied by the relative present value of each cash flow. The sum of these numbers (4.20) is, finally, the duration of our bond.

table 20.1

t	CF ($)	PVCF ($)	RPVCF (%)	t·RPVCF
1	100	92.6	8.6	0.09
2	100	85.7	7.9	0.16
3	100	79.4	7.4	0.22
4	100	73.5	6.8	0.27
5	1,100	748.6	69.3	3.47
Sum		**$1,079.9**	**100.0**	**4.20**

Let's think about this. If we buy a five-year zero, we have to wait five years to get a cash flow. In this case, the maturity of the zero is a good measure of its effective lifetime simply because the time to receive the final cash flow (five years) has a weight of 1. In fact, unsurprisingly, the duration and maturity of zero-coupon bonds always coincide.

If we buy our five-year coupon bond instead, we receive a $100 cash flow at the end of each of the first four years, and a much larger cash flow ($1,100) at maturity. Because we don't have to wait the whole lifetime of the bond to get all of its cash flows, its duration is lower than its maturity. In fact, *duration is lower than maturity for all coupon bonds*, simply because these bonds pay out some cash flows before they mature. In the case of our bond, 4.2 years indicates the (weighted-)average maturity of the bond's cash flows.

Look at it this way. The first $100 'mature' after one year; the second $100 after two years; the third $100 after three years; the fourth $100 after four years; and the final $1,100 after five years. We already know why we shouldn't calculate the average maturity of these cash flows simply as (1 + 2 + 3 + 4 + 5)/5. And we also know that we should weight each of these 'maturities' by the relative present value of each cash flow. If we take into account each 'maturity' *and* the appropriate weights, then we get the duration of 4.2 years, which represents the weighted-average maturity of the bond's cash flows.

Formally, a bond's **duration (D)** is given by

$$D = \left(\frac{1}{P_M}\right) \cdot \left(\frac{1 \cdot CF_1}{(1+R)} + \frac{2 \cdot CF_2}{(1+R)^2} + \ldots + \frac{T \cdot CF_T}{(1+R)^T}\right) \tag{20.1}$$

where T denotes the time to maturity; CF_t the cash flow paid by the bond at the end of period t; R the discount rate (or yield to maturity); and p_M the bond's current market price. Applying expression (20.1) to our five-year coupon bond we get

$$D = \left(\frac{1}{\$1,079.9}\right) \cdot \left(\frac{1 \cdot \$100}{1.08} + \frac{2 \cdot \$100}{1.08^2} + ... + \frac{5 \cdot \$1,100}{1.08^5}\right) = 4.2 \text{ years}$$

which is the same as the result we calculated in Table 20.1.

It should be clear by now what is the idea behind the concept of duration. It attempts to capture the effective maturity of a bond by taking into account not only the different times to receive the bond's cash flows but also the size of each cash flow relative to the bond's price. The duration of our five-year coupon bond, 4.2 years, is lower than five years simply because the bond pays some cash flows before maturity; and it's higher than three years simply because most of the bond's cash flows are paid at maturity.

Finally, note that, as Table 20.1 shows, only 8.6% of the bond's price is recovered at the end of the first year; therefore, the first cash flow contributes very little (less than 9% of a year, or just over one month) to the bond's duration. Conversely, 69.3% of the price is recovered at maturity; therefore, this last cash flow contributes almost 3.5 years to the bond's duration of 4.2 years.

Determinants of duration

We started this chapter by arguing that when bond traders think about price volatility they usually relate it to a bond's duration. So at this point you may fairly ask what does duration have to do with market risk? After all, our discussion so far seems to suggest that duration simply measures the effective maturity of a bond, taking into account both the timing of the bond's cash flows and their relative present value.

We argued in the previous chapter that, everything else being equal, market risk is directly related to a bond's maturity, and inversely related to its coupon and discount rate. Well, it turns out to be the case that a bond's duration also is directly related to its maturity and inversely related to its coupon and discount rate.

To illustrate, consider the four bonds in Table 20.2, the first of which is the five-year bond we've been discussing. Let's use this bond as a reference and ask what happens to its duration as we change, *one at a time*, its maturity (Bond 2), its coupon (Bond 3), and its discount rate (Bond 4). As the table shows, if the bond's maturity increases, its duration also increases; if its coupon decreases, its duration increases; and if its discount rate decreases, its duration increases. Therefore, as already mentioned, a bond's duration is directly related to its maturity and inversely related to its coupon and discount rate.

table 20.2

	'Our' bond	Bond 2	Bond 3	Bond 4
Face value	$1,000	$1,000	$1,000	$1,000
Maturity	5 years	6 years	5 years	5 years
Coupon	10%	10%	6%	10%
Coupon paid	Annually	Annually	Annually	Annually
Discount rate	8%	8%	8%	4%
Price	$1,079.9	$1,092.5	$920.1	$1,267.1
Duration	4.2 years	4.8 years	4.4 years	4.3 years

The direct relationship between duration and maturity is intuitively obvious. After all, the former is just a 'more sophisticated' way of thinking about the latter. The relationship between these two, however, is not linear. For the bond we've been discussing, Table 20.3 shows that, everything else being equal, as maturity increases, duration also increases but at a lower rate. Note, for example, that when maturity increases by a factor of 10, from 5 years to 50 years, duration only increases by a factor of just over 3, from 4.2 to 13.1.

table 20.3

Maturity (years)	5	10	20	30	40	50
Duration (years)	4.2	7.0	10.2	11.8	12.6	13.1

The intuition behind this result is that, as maturity increases, later cash flows are discounted more heavily than earlier cash flows; that is, very distant cash flows have a very small present value. As a result, duration increases with maturity but at a lower rate. This is in fact the case for all coupon bonds. In the case of zeros, however, duration and maturity are always the same and therefore both increase at the same rate.

The inverse relationship between a bond's duration and its coupon is also intuitive. Larger coupon payments increase the percentage of cash flows received before maturity, which obviously decreases duration. Finally, the inverse relationship between a bond's duration and its discount rate is explained by the fact that, as the discount rate increases, the discount factor of later cash flows increases more than that of earlier cash flows.

Modified duration

You may still be wondering, what does duration have to do with market risk? But, hey, we have made *some* progress! We have established in the previous section that the same factors that affect market risk also affect duration, and that they do so in the same direction; that is, both market risk and duration increase as maturity increases, coupons decrease, and discount rates decrease. As a result, there is a direct relationship between a bond's duration and its market risk; that is, the larger a bond's duration, the higher its price (or return) volatility.

In fact, tweaking slightly the definition of duration we've been discussing (often referred to as *Macaulay's duration*), we can obtain a measure of a bond's sensitivity to changes in interest rates. More precisely, a bond's **modified duration (D_M)** is given by

$$D_M = \frac{D}{(1+R/n)} \tag{20.2}$$

where n is the number of coupon payments per year (hence, $n = 1$ for annual coupons and $n = 2$ for semiannual coupons). This expression yields an *approximation* to the percentage change in a bond's price given a change in the bond's discount rate.

Let's go back to our five-year coupon bond which, as we calculated, has a duration of 4.2 years. At a discount rate of 8%, the modified duration of this bond is $D_M = 4.2/1.08 = 3.9$. What does this number indicate? It says that if the bond's discount rate were to change by 1%, then its price would change by 3.9% (obviously, in the opposite direction). Modified duration, then, is a measure of a bond's price sensitivity to changes in its discount rate and, therefore, a measure of a bond's market risk. So, finally, we have linked duration and market risk!

There is a little problem, though ...

Convexity

Let's put it this way. We know that when the discount rate is 8%, our five-year coupon bond should trade at $1,079.9. If the discount rate increases from 8% to 9%, the bond should sell for $1,038.9 for a decrease of 3.8%. If, on the other hand, the discount rate falls from 8% to 7%, the bond should sell for $1,123.0 for an increase of 4.0%. Note that, in both cases, the percentage change in the bond's price is close, but not exactly equal, to the 3.9% change predicted by its modified duration of 3.9. That's why we said before that modified duration is an approximation to the sensitivity of a bond's price to changes in its discount rate.

How good is the approximation? That depends on two factors, the size of the change in the discount rate and the so-called *convexity* of the bond. To understand the latter, let's first consider small changes in the discount rate. The first column of Table 20.4 shows discount rates (DR) ranging between 7.5% and 8.5%. The second column shows the price (p) of our five-year coupon bond at the discount rates in the first column. The third column shows the percent changes (%Δ) in price with respect to the initial price of $1,079.9. The fourth column shows the prices implied by a duration of 3.9 (p^*). And the final column shows the percentage change in the implied prices, again with respect to the initial price of $1,079.9. Note that the numbers in this last column are all calculated as the product of the modified duration (3.9) and the change in the discount rate; for example, 1.95% = 3.9(0.08–0.075).

table 20.4

DR (%)	p ($)	%Δ	p^* ($)	%Δ
7.5	1,101.1	1.97	1,100.9	1.95
7.6	1,096.8	1.57	1,096.7	1.56
7.7	1,092.6	1.18	1,092.5	1.17
7.8	1,088.3	0.78	1,088.3	0.78
7.9	1,084.1	0.39	1,084.1	0.39
8.0	1,079.9	N/A	1,079.9	N/A
8.1	1,075.7	−0.39	1,075.7	−0.39
8.2	1,071.5	−0.77	1,071.4	−0.78
8.3	1,067.3	−1.16	1,067.2	−1.17
8.4	1,063.2	−1.54	1,063.0	−1.56
8.5	1,059.1	−1.92	1,058.8	−1.95

Table 20.4 shows that the actual changes in price and those predicted by a modified duration of 3.9 are the same for small departures from 8%. As the change in the discount rate gets larger, the differences between these two percentage changes also get larger, although they remain very low. In other words, for small changes in the discount rate, a bond's modified duration is a very good predictor of the expected change in the bond's price.

Figure 20.1, however, shows that as the changes in the discount rate get larger (still beginning from 8%), the approximation provided by modified duration worsens. The dotted line shows the actual prices at different discount rates, and the solid line the prices predicted by a modified duration of 3.9. Note that the predicted prices fall along a straight line whereas the actual prices fall along a *convex* line. In other words, modified duration estimates prices assuming a linear relationship between a bond's price and its discount rate, but the actual relationship between these two variables is convex.

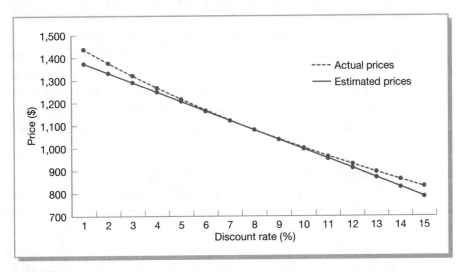

figure 20.1   Convexity

Note that if the discount rate of our bond increases from 8% to 15%, the bond's price falls by 22.9%; using modified duration, however, we would predict a fall of 27.2%. If, on the other hand, the discount rate of our bond falls from 8% to 1%, the bond's price increases by 33.1%; using modified duration, however, we would predict an increase of 27.2%. In other words, as the graph makes clear, the larger the change in the discount rate, the larger the error we would make when predicting (changes in) prices using modified duration.

How large can these errors be? That depends on the convexity of the dotted line. That is, in fact, what the issue of convexity is all about: The more convex the line representing the relationship between actual prices and discount rates, the larger the differences between the actual prices and those predicted on the basis of modified duration.

It remains the case, however, that for small changes in the discount rate, modified duration accurately predicts the change in price. Note that the straight line is tangent to the convex line at the initial discount rate of 8%. This implies that, at that point of intersection, the slope of both lines is the same. Mathematically speaking, then, modified duration always provides an accurate prediction of the price change when the change in the discount rate is *very* small.

This is not, however, as limiting as it may sound. Note that, as Table 20.4 shows, even for changes as large as half a percentage point up or down, modified duration provides a very good approximation to the actual changes in price. Swings in interest rates as large or larger, needless to say, hardly ever happen over short periods of time. Note, also, that very large changes in interest rates, such as those swings of 7 percentage points (from 8% to 15%, or from 8% to 1%) discussed above, are almost unheard of and only occur over very long periods of time. For practical purposes, then, modified duration provides a fairly good approximation to a bond's market risk.

Finally, because the accuracy of the predicted prices based on modified duration decreases with the convexity of the relationship between actual prices and discount rates, then you may be wondering what determines the degree of convexity. In a nutshell, a bond's convexity is increasing in its maturity (and duration) and decreasing in its coupon and discount rate. In other words, modified duration predicts better the market risk of bonds with, everything else equal, shorter maturity, higher coupon, and higher discount rate.

Applications

Both duration and convexity are essential tools for managers of bond portfolios and are the heart of *immunization strategies*. These are strategies that seek to protect bond portfolios from their main source of risk, changes in interest rates, and can be divided into two categories: income immunization and price immunization.

Income immunization strategies seek to ensure that a stream of assets is sufficient to meet a stream of liabilities; these strategies are largely based on duration. A pension fund, for example, has a predictable stream of liabilities and needs to invest its assets in such a way as to be able to meet future cash outflows. In response, bond managers typically seek to match the duration of assets and liabilities to minimize the probability of a shortfall.

Price immunization strategies, on the other hand, seek to ensure that the market value of assets exceeds that of liabilities by a specified amount; these strategies are largely based on convexity. Bond managers may seek to match the duration of assets and liabilities, and at the same time achieve a convexity of assets larger than that of liabilities. With this strategy, if interest rates increase, the value of the assets will increase by more than that of the liabilities; and if interest rates decrease, the value of the assets will decrease by less than that of the liabilities.

These tools can also be used to immunize a bond portfolio from the influence of changing interest rates. By setting the portfolio's duration equal to the investor's holding period, if interest rates increase, the capital loss on the value of the bonds is offset by the higher rate at which the bonds' cash flows will be reinvested. If, on the other hand, interest rates fall, the lower rate at which the bonds' cash flows will be reinvested is offset by the capital gain in the value of the bonds.

Finally, these tools can be used to either enhance or protect the value of a bond portfolio given an expected change in interest rates. If a bond manager expects interest rates to fall, he would increase the duration of his portfolio to leverage the expected capital gain. If, on the other hand, he expects interest rates to increase, he would reduce the duration of his portfolio to mitigate the effect of the expected capital loss.

The big picture

Duration and convexity are two essential concepts that every bond investor needs to understand. They are also widely used by bond managers to both protect and enhance the value of their portfolios.

The duration of a bond measures its effective maturity by taking into account both the timing of the bond's cash flows and their relative present value. A bond's modified duration, in turn, measures the sensitivity of the bond's price to changes in the discount rate and is used to assess a bond's market risk.

Modified duration, however, provides only an approximation to a bond's market risk. The accuracy of the approximation depends on two factors, the size of the change in the discount rate and the convexity of the relationship between the bond's price and its discount rate. For most practical purposes, the approximation is good enough and therefore modified duration is widely used to assess the price (or return) volatility of bonds.

Excel section

You already know how to calculate both bond prices and bond yields in Excel. Calculating a bond's duration is just as simple. Suppose you have the date on which you want to calculate the duration in cell A1; the maturity date in cell A2; the annual coupon rate in cell A3; the annual discount rate in cell A4; and the number of coupon payments per year in cell A5. Then, to calculate the bond's duration, type

=duration(A1, A2, A3, A4, A5)

and hit Enter.

The calculation of a bond's modified duration requires exactly the same inputs. To calculate the bond's modified duration, type

=mduration(A1, A2, A3, A4, A5)

and hit Enter.

Note that Excel requires you to enter both the date on which you are making the calculation and the bond's maturity date. As discussed in Chapter 18, if specific dates are irrelevant for your purpose, you can always enter any two dates just as far apart as the time to maturity of the bond you're dealing with.

part 3

Other important topics

21

NPV and IRR

know, you do know and may even use frequently the concepts of NPV and IRR. But these two essential tools, as well as a few related ideas, are the backbone of many calculations in finance and just too important not to discuss in any desktop companion. There are some things worth reviewing and refreshing, and that's exactly what we'll do in this chapter.

Basic principles

Let's start with three questions whose answers will lead us to three basic principles or ideas implicitly built into many financial tools. First question: Would you rather have $100 today or next year? No contest there, you prefer them today. (If not, just send me your $100 bills and I'll return them to you in a year ... Promise!)

Inflation erodes the purchasing power of money. That's why we don't keep our money under the mattress but in a bank, where we earn interest on the capital deposited. The interest paid by the bank protects us against the expected loss of purchasing power. This brings us to another way of seeing why we prefer the $100 today: Because we can deposit it in a bank, earn interest, and withdraw more than $100 in the future.

Second question: Would you rather have $100 one year from now or two years from now? Again, no contest, you prefer the $100 one year from now. The reason is again obvious and follows from the argument above; that is, the more time passes by, the more purchasing power we lose. In other words, given a fixed amount of money, the sooner we get it, the better.

Third and final question: Would you rather have $100 for sure, or accept the outcome of a coin flip such that heads you get $200 and tails you get nothing? This one depends on your degree of risk aversion, but most people will pocket the certain $100, though the expected value of the flip of the coin is also $100. (In fact, *all* risk-averse individuals should choose the certain $100. Risk-loving individuals would go for the coin toss, and risk-neutral individuals would be indifferent.) Just in case you're hesitating a bit on this one, change the $100 to $1 million and the $200 to $2 million. What would you choose now?! Exactly.

Now for the basic principles, which follow from the answers to the three questions above. First, $1 today is worth more than $1 in the future. Second, $1 in the future is worth more than $1 in a more distant future. And third, both now and in the future, a certain $1 is worth more than an uncertain (or risky, or expected) $1. All basic common sense; and yet essential to understand the idea of present value, a central concept in finance.

Present value

The idea of discounting is central to many financial calculations. It follows from the fact that, as mentioned above, inflation erodes the purchasing power of money, which means that dollars received at different times in the future have different purchasing power. Therefore, adding dollars to be received one and two years from today is a bit like adding apples and oranges.

To add apples and apples we need to turn the oranges into apples. That sounds impossible, but not so much when it comes to turning future dollars into current dollars. That's where *discounting*, a simple but powerful idea, comes in. Consider this: How much money should you ask for today (x) to be indifferent between receiving x today or $100 a year from now?

The answer depends on the interest rate (I) you could earn in the bank. Given I, you would be indifferent between these two propositions when $x(1+I) = \$100$, from which it follows that $x = \$100/(1+I)$. In words, x is the *present value* of $100. If the interest rate were 5%, then you'd be indifferent between receiving $95.2 (= \$100/1.05$) now or $100 one year from now, simply because you could deposit today the $95.2 at 5% and withdraw $100 one year down the road.

What about a two-year framework? That is, how much money should you ask for today (x) to be indifferent between receiving x today or $100 two years from now? Again very simple. You'd be indifferent between these two propositions when $x(1+I)^2 = \$100$, that is, $x = \$100/(1+I)^2$. Again, x is the present value of $100. And if the interest rate were 5%, then you'd be indifferent between receiving $90.7 now or $100 two years from now, simply because you could deposit today the $90.7 at 5% and withdraw $100 two years down the road.

And how much money should you ask for today ($x) to be indifferent between receiving $x today or $100 one year from now *plus* $100 two years from now? You only need to add the present value of $100 one year from now and the present value of $100 two years from now; that is, $x = $100/(1+I) + $100/(1+I)^2$. And with interest rates at 5% you should ask for $185.9.

We could go on but hopefully you already appreciate the two points we're getting at. First, the present value of $1 to be received T years from now is given by $x = $1/(1+I)^T$. And second, present values are additive, which follows from the fact that when we divide any amount to be received T years from now by $(1+I)^T$, we're effectively turning all future dollars into current dollars (that is, oranges into apples).

One more thing. So far in this section we haven't really dealt with risk. All those $100 we've been talking about are sure things, which is why we've been discounting them at a rate that is risk free. In other words, when we deposit money in the bank, we know exactly how much we will be withdrawing T years down the road. (Well, after the 'real estate crisis,' it's not clear how truthful this last statement really is!)

And yet, as mentioned in the previous section, you're not indifferent between $100 for sure and the 50-50 chance of $200 or nothing given a coin flip. Between those two, you would prefer $100 for sure. Which is just another way of saying that, given a certain amount $x to be received T years from now, and a gamble with an expected value of $x also to be received T years from now, the present value of the gamble is lower than the present value of the certain amount. (Read this last sentence again and make sure you understand it.)

Note that, mathematically, this can only be the case if you discount the gamble at a rate higher than I. That is, $x/(1+I)^T > $x/(1+R)^T$ only if $R > I$, where R is the discount rate for the gamble. The intuition here is clear: Everything else being equal, the riskier the proposition, the lower the value you place on it. Or, in other words, the riskier the proposition the higher the discount rate you apply to it.

So, finally, we arrive at one of the most useful and widely-used expressions in finance. Given any investment expected to deliver the cash flows CF_1, CF_2, ..., CF_T in periods 1, 2, ..., T, the **present value (PV)** of the investment is given by

$$PV = \frac{CF_1}{(1 + DR)} + \frac{CF_2}{(1 + DR)^2} + ... + \frac{CF_T}{(1 + DR)^T} \qquad (21.1)$$

where DR is a discount rate that captures the risk of the investment. Think of this discount rate as a hurdle rate; that is, the minimum return that a company requires to invest in a project, or that an investor requires to put his money in an asset. (In capital budgeting, this discount rate is usually a company's cost of capital. This, and more generally how to properly adjust the discount rate for risk, are discussed in Chapter 7.)

Net present value

Going from present value to net present value is straightforward. The latter only 'nets' from the former the initial investment required to start a project. Therefore, the **net present value (NPV)** of an investment is given by

$$NPV = CF_0 + \frac{CF_1}{(1 + DR)} + \frac{CF_2}{(1 + DR)^2} + ... + \frac{CF_T}{(1 + DR)^T} \qquad (21.2)$$

Often, CF_0 is expressed as a strictly negative cash flow representing the upfront investment required to start the project. There are, however, projects in which the first cash flow can be positive (an example is considered below), so let's keep expression (21.2) as general as possible and think that all cash flows can be positive or negative.

Now, how do we decide whether or not to invest in a project by using the NPV approach? The rule is simple and you've surely seen it (and probably used it) before: Calculate the NPV of the project using the expression above, and then

■ If $NPV > 0$ ⇒ Invest

■ If $NPV < 0$ ⇒ Do not invest

The intuition is straightforward: A positive NPV indicates that the present value of the project's cash flows outweighs the necessary investments (that is, the project pays its way); a negative NPV indicates the opposite.

If two competing (mutually exclusive) projects are evaluated, then the one with the higher NPV should be selected. That is, given any two competing projects i and j, calculate the NPV of both and then

■ If $\text{NPV}_i > \text{NPV}_j$ ⇒ Invest in i

■ If $\text{NPV}_i < \text{NPV}_j$ ⇒ Invest in j

Throwing a bunch of numbers into a formula and coming up with another number is not difficult. The difficult task is, obviously, to estimate correctly the cash flows to be generated by the project; and, to a lesser degree, to capture the risk of those cash flows appropriately in the discount rate.

The internal rate of return

There are many rules for project evaluation, some of which are so simplistic that we don't even bother to review them here. (Some of these include the payback period, the discounted payback period, and the average accounting return.) The main contender of the NPV approach is the **internal rate of return (IRR)**, which is defined as the discount rate that sets the NPV of a project equal to 0

$$\text{NPV} = CF_0 + \frac{CF_1}{(1+\text{IRR})} + \frac{CF_2}{(1+\text{IRR})^2} + \dots + \frac{CF_T}{(1+\text{IRR})^T} = 0 \tag{21.3}$$

Note that although it is not trivial to solve this expression for the IRR, as we'll see at the end of the chapter, Excel calculates this number in the blink of an eye. Note, also, that the IRR does not depend on 'external' parameters such as a specific discount rate; rather, it depends exclusively on the cash flows of the project considered.

How do we decide whether or not to invest in a project using the IRR approach? Again, the rule is simple: Calculate the IRR of the project and then:

■ If IRR > DR ⇒ Invest

■ If IRR < DR ⇒ Do not invest

The intuition of this rule is also straightforward. Recall that the discount rate is also the hurdle rate, or the minimum required return (and that in capital budgeting this is usually the cost of capital). Then, the rule says that if the return of the project is higher than the minimum required return, we should invest in it; otherwise, we should not. If we finance our investments at 10%, then we should not invest in any project from which we expect any less than a 10% return. Makes sense?

Finally, if two competing (mutually exclusive) projects are evaluated, then the one with the higher IRR should be selected. That is, given any two projects i and j, calculate the IRR of both and then, assuming that both IRRs are higher than the discount rate

■ If $IRR_i > IRR_j$ ⇒ Invest in i

■ If $IRR_i < IRR_j$ ⇒ Invest in j

Note, however, that as we'll discuss in a moment, this statement is not always true.

Applying NPV and IRR

Consider the projects in Table 21.1, all being considered by a company whose hurdle rate is 12%. You should have no difficulty in calculating the NPVs reported in the next-to-last line and concluding that all projects but B are beneficial for the company, G being the most valuable (the one with the highest NPV) and D the least valuable (the one with the lowest positive NPV). Project B has a negative NPV and is therefore detrimental for the company.

table 21.1

Period	A ($m)	B ($m)	C ($m)	C' ($m)	D ($m)	E ($m)	F ($m)	G ($m)
0	−100	100	−200	−100	−100	100	−100	−100
1	150	−150	280	130	260	−300	150	50
2					−165	250	25	150
NPV ($m)	**33.9**	**−33.9**	**50.0**	**16.1**	**0.6**	**31.4**	**53.9**	**64.2**
IRR (%)	**50.0**	**50.0**	**40.0**	**30.0**	**10.0***	**N/A**	**65.1**	**50.0**

* Project D has another IRR equal to 50%

Let's focus for a moment on project A, which has both a positive NPV ($33.9m) and an IRR (50%) higher than the discount rate (12%); therefore, the company should go for it. Figure 21.1 shows the relationship between NPV and IRR for this project and highlights three points. First, that whenever the discount rate is lower than the IRR, the NPV of the project is positive. (The opposite occurs when the discount rate is higher than the IRR.) Second, that the lower the discount rate with respect to the IRR, the higher is the NPV of the project. And third, when the discount rate is equal to the IRR, the NPV of the project is 0.

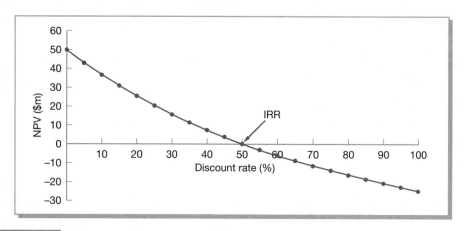

figure 21.1   NPV and IRR

Now, before you get too excited about the consistency between NPV and IRR, consider projects A and B in Table 21.1. The NPV rule would lead us to accept A and reject B, whereas the IRR rule would lead us to accept both. Not good. Now consider projects B and D. The NPV rule would lead us to accept D and reject B, whereas the IRR rule would lead us to do the opposite. Oh well, the consistency was fun while it lasted!

Problems of the IRR approach

What, then, should a company do in situations in which the NPV and the IRR criteria point in different directions? The answer is unequivocal: *Follow the NPV approach.* This is due to some potential problems inherent in the IRR approach, which we now turn to.

Multiple IRRs

Consider project D, which is depicted in Figure 21.2(a). As you can see, this project has two IRRs, 10% and 50%. If you're curious, this is due to the structure of the cash flows, which go from negative to positive and back to negative. These two changes in sign imply that there can be up to two IRRs. (In general, according to Descartes' rule, if a sequence of cash flows has *n* changes of sign, then the project could have up to *n* different IRRs.) And do not rush to think that changes in a sign in a project's cash flows are unusual; think, for example, of projects that require large subsequent investments after the start-up phase.

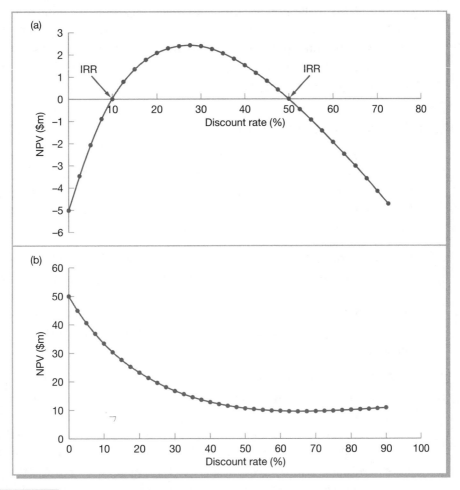

figure 21.2   Problems with the IRR

Now, note that the first IRR is lower than the hurdle rate (12%) and the second IRR is higher than the hurdle rate. So what should a company do? Focus on the first IRR (10%) and reject the project, or focus on the second (50%) and go for the project? Unfortunately, the IRR cannot be used in this or similar cases, and the decision of whether or not to go ahead with the project must be made with the NPV approach. (And because the NPV is positive, the company should accept the project.)

No IRR

Consider now project E. As you can see in Figure 21.2(b), this project has a positive NPV for all discount rates, and, therefore, it has no IRR. (Remember, the IRR is the discount rate for which the NPV of a project is equal to 0.) For this reason, the IRR approach cannot be used in this or similar cases, and the decision must be made with the NPV approach. (And given that the project has a positive NPV, the company should accept it.)

Lending versus borrowing

Consider now projects A and B. Note that B has a peculiar sequence of cash flows, beginning with an inflow and followed by an outflow. This is unusual but not necessarily hypothetical. In executive-education courses run by business schools, the participants often pay in advance and the schools incur the costs of delivering at a later date.

Consider project A first. Both approaches, NPV and IRR, point in the same direction and suggest that the company should accept the project. In the case of project B, however, the NPV approach suggests that the company should reject the project, but the IRR approach suggests the opposite. How can the NPV approach reject a project in which the IRR of 50% is so much higher than the hurdle rate of 12%?

Note that project A consists of an outflow followed by an inflow. If you think about it, this sounds similar to depositing money in a bank, with the negative cash flow being the deposit (money out of our pocket) and the positive cash flow being the withdrawal (money into our pocket). Similarly, we can think of the company as 'lending' money to project A. And, in these cases, the higher the IRR (with respect to the discount rate), the better. After all, when we lend money, don't we want to receive the highest possible rate?

Now think about project B. Doesn't it sound like *borrowing* money from a bank, with the inflow coming first when the loan is received (money into our pocket) and the outflow coming later when the loan is repaid (money out of our pocket)? Importantly, in these cases, the IRR rule must be reversed. A project must be accepted when the IRR is *lower* than the hurdle rate, and rejected when the IRR is *higher* than the discount rate. After all, when we borrow money, don't we want to pay the *lowest* possible rate?

Scale problems

Consider now projects A and C and assume they are mutually exclusive; that is, if we invest in one, we cannot invest in the other. Based on the NPVs, the company should go for project C; but based on the IRRs, the company should go for project A. What is going on? And what should the company do?

As mentioned above, when the NPV and the IRR approaches conflict, the company should base its decision on the NPV approach. In this case, that means going for project C. There are two ways of seeing why this is the right decision, both of them based on the idea of *incremental* cash flows; that is, the difference between the cash flows from project C compared with those of project A, which is exactly what 'project' C' shows.

First, note that the NPV of the incremental cash flows is positive. In words, given a discount rate of 12%, it pays to invest $100 million more in project C (with respect to the investment in project A), to get an additional $130 million (again, with respect to project A). Second, note that the incremental cash flows have an IRR of 30%, which given a hurdle rate of 12% would also lead the company to accept the project.

The 'problem' here is that the IRR is biased toward accepting projects with a small upfront investment. This is the case because the smaller an investment is, the easier it is to get a high return from it. To see this, consider these two options: I offer to borrow $1 from you today and return $2 to you in one month; or to borrow $1 million from you today and return $1.9 million to you in one month. Which one would you choose? Exactly. And yet the IRR of the first option (100%) is higher than that of the second option (90%).

272 Other important topics

Timing problems

Consider now projects F and G. Note that in this case we have a problem similar to the previous one; that is, the NPV criterion suggests that the company should accept one project (G) whereas the IRR criterion suggests the company should accept the other (F). What is going on and what should the company do?

Take a look at Figure 21.3, which depicts the NPV of both projects at several discount rates. Note that, at 'low' discount rates project G is better, and at 'high' discount rates project F is better. At a discount rate of 25% both projects are equally profitable. This is not surprising. Project G delivers the high cash flows relatively late, and late cash flows are more valuable the lower the discount rate is. (Note that at a discount rate of 0%, the value of $x today and in five years is the same; at a discount rate of 20%, however, $x are much more valuable today than in five years.)

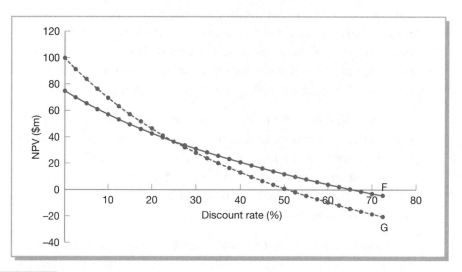

figure 21.3   **More on problems with the IRR**

This example shows that projects that deliver large cash flows relatively early in the project's life are more valuable when discount rates are high; and projects that deliver large cash flows relatively late in the project's life are more valuable when discount rates are low. Having said that, *given* the discount rate, the NPV approach always selects the right project. In our case, at a 12% discount rate, the company should select project G.

Time-varying discount rates

Finally, let's consider what happens if the appropriate discount rate for the project is expected to vary over time. This may happen when changes are expected in interest rates, or in the company's capital structure, or in some other factors that affect the risk of the company over the project's life.

So, let's say we have computed the IRR of our project. Then, to decide whether or not to invest in it, we need to compare it with a discount rate. But which one? The one expected for next year? The one for the year after? An average of the expected rates over the project's life? It's not clear. In other words, when discount rates change over time, the IRR approach loses its intuitive appeal.

The NPV approach, however, can still be applied, though not without an additional cost. Now we can no longer raise those (1+DR)s to the power of 2, 3, ..., T, as the periods go by. If discount rates change over time, the discount factor for any period becomes the *product* of 1 plus the discount rate in each period; that is

$$\text{NPV} = CF_0 + \frac{CF_1}{(1+DR_1)} + \frac{CF_2}{(1+DR_1)\cdot(1+DR_2)} + \ldots + \frac{CF_T}{(1+DR_1)\cdot\ldots\cdot(1+DR_T)} \qquad (21.4)$$

This expression is more difficult to handle than expression (21.2), which may explain why, more often than not, companies do not use time-varying discount rates unless they have a good reason to expect a substantial change over the project's life. Having said that, spreadsheets have made the implementation of expressions like (21.4) easier to deal with.

The big picture

Make no mistake about it: The IRR is very useful and very widely used, and for good reasons. Therefore, do not consider the previous discussion a dismissal of the IRR approach. Far from it. Rather, consider it a warning sign. The IRR does have shortcomings and practitioners need to be aware of them. In particular, practitioners should carefully inspect the expected cash flows of the projects considered and ask whether those cash flows may be subject to some of the problems discussed.

Also, avoid the erroneous consideration that the IRR is useful because it summarizes a project in a single number, which follows exclusively from the project's cash flows, and is independent from 'external' parameters such as a discount rate. True, to calculate the IRR we only need the project's cash flows; but *to make an investment decision*, we do need a discount rate to compare to the IRR.

In short, then, the NPV approach is the theoretically correct method to evaluate investment projects, perhaps properly complemented by the real options approach (discussed in the next chapter). The IRR is also a very valuable tool, but remember to handle it with care.

Excel section

Calculating NPVs and IRRs is simple in Excel, though you must be aware of a few quirks. Suppose you have a series of 10 cash flows of a given project in cells B1 through B10, the first being a current (positive or negative) cash flow, and the rest being the project's (positive or negative) expected cash flows. Suppose, also, that the proper discount rate for the project is in cell A1. Then, to calculate the project's NPV, type

=B1+NPV(A1, B2:B10)

and hit Enter.

To calculate the project's IRR, type

=IRR(B1:B10)

and hit Enter.

Note that what Excel calls NPV is really a present value (without the 'net' part). This is because Excel assumes that the first cash flow comes one period down the road. Therefore, if you need to consider a current cash flow, *you must add it* to Excel's NPV calculation; that's exactly what the 'B1' in the NPV calculation above represents. Note, however, that the IRR function does assume that the first cash flow is a current one.

Finally, note that when calculating the IRR, Excel uses an iterative process that starts with a guess. Excel actually gives you the opportunity to make this guess yourself, but you might as well ignore this opportunity. If you just type what is suggested above, Excel will make the guess for you.

Having said that, note that in cases with several IRRs, Excel returns *just one* IRR; if you want to calculate the others, the best strategy is the following. First, plot the NPV for many discount rates (like the figures in this chapter); then, visually determine the approximate values of the other IRRs; and finally, get Excel to calculate them, in each case making a guess close to the numbers that result from your visual inspection. In each of these cases, you should type

=IRR(B1:B10, Guess)

where Guess is a value close to the IRR you determine from your visual inspection, and then hit Enter.

22

Real options

I n the previous chapter we discussed the two tools most widely used in project evaluation, net present value (NPV) and internal rate of return (IRR). As we'll discuss in this chapter, however, NPV typically undervalues projects because it does not account for the value of flexibility. The real options approach does, and therefore enables companies to make better investment decisions. But, as we'll also discuss, this useful tool can easily be (and often is) misused.

A caveat

The incorporation of real options into the evaluation of investment opportunities is a relatively new development. As we discuss below, it is both plausible and necessary to assess the value of the real options embedded in projects to make correct investment decisions. But, unfortunately, the actual implementation is far from trivial.

Companies that use this tool must wrestle with two issues. First is understanding the concept of a real option, the types of options embedded in projects, the role they play in project evaluation, and the possible misuses of this tool. Second, the valuation of these options; this is a very technical topic (more for PhDs than for MBAs, so to speak), which requires not only a good grasp of option pricing theory but also knowledge of the twists and turns necessary to adapt this theory to the valuation of real options. Given our goals, we'll focus here only on the first issue.

What's wrong with NPV?

Think about the way companies typically make investment decisions. Given the project considered, a company first forecasts its cash flows; then discounts the expected cash flows at a rate that reflects the risk of those cash flows (typically, the company's cost of capital); and finally subtracts the value of the initial investment required to start the project. Then, if the project has a positive NPV, the company goes ahead with it; and if the project has a negative NPV, it does not.

As we discussed in the previous chapter, obstacles to the implementation of this tool include the correct estimation of cash flows and, to a lesser degree, the proper assessment of their risk. And yet, that is not the only reason why NPV is less than perfect for project evaluation.

To see why, think of a company considering a project to extract copper from a mine in a developing country. The company can buy the exclusive rights to exploit the mine during the next 10 years for $5 million; after these 10 years the rights will expire. The local government will buy all the copper extracted at an agreed price, which will remain fixed during the 10 years. This fixed price is in local currency and the main source of uncertainty for the company is the exchange rate.

The developing country is currently negotiating a stand-by loan with the International Monetary Fund (IMF). If the negotiations are successful, stable economic conditions and fast growth will imply a strong local currency, in which case the project will deliver $30 million a year. If the negotiations fail, uncertainty and sluggish growth will imply a weak local currency, and the project will deliver only $10 million a year. As of today, the chances of successful negotiations are 50:50. The project requires an initial investment on equipment of $150 million and the company's hurdle rate is 10%. Should the company invest in this project?

Well, we know by now how to estimate NPVs. Given that high and low cash flows are equally likely, the *expected* cash flow is $20 million during each of the 10 years, as shown in the second column of Table 22.1. Discounting those expected cash flows at 10% we get a present value of $122.9 million, and subtracting the initial investment of $150 million we get an NPV of –$27.1 million. Therefore, the company should not buy the rights to extract copper from the mine.

table 22.1

			Cash flows		
Year	Expected ($m)	Low ($m)	High ($m)	Low ($m)	High ($m)
0	−150	−150	−150		
1	20	10	30	−150	−150
2	20	10	30	10	30
3	20	10	30	10	30
4	20	10	30	10	30
5	20	10	30	10	30
6	20	10	30	10	30
7	20	10	30	10	30
8	20	10	30	10	30
9	20	10	30	10	30
10	20	10	30	10	30
NPV-0	−27.1	−88.6	34.3		
NPV-1				−92.4	22.8

But wait a minute. The third column of Table 22.1 shows that with annual cash flows of $10 million, the NPV of the project is −$88.6 million. But with annual cash flows of $30 million, the fourth column shows that its NPV is $34.3 million. (The −$27.1 million NPV of the project is obviously the equally weighted average of these two numbers.) Therefore, if the company could wait a bit and get a better idea of the exchange rate that will prevail during the life of the contract, it could make a much better investment decision. That is, it would invest in the project if the exchange rate was high and would not invest if the exchange rate was low.

The thing is, the company *can* wait. Let's assume the company buys the right to exploit the mine for $5 million but doesn't make any investment during the first year. By the end of the year, with the country's negotiations with the IMF finished, the company will have a much better idea of the economic outlook and therefore of the expected exchange rate. Then, if the exchange rate is expected to be low, the company will refrain from investing in the mine. Note that, as the fifth column of Table 22.1 shows, investing $150 million at the end of the first year to get cash flows of $10 million during nine years has an NPV of −$92.4 million (at the end of the first year).

If, however, the exchange rate is expected to be high, the last column of the table shows that investing $150 million at the end of the first year to get annual cash flows of $30 million during nine years has an NPV of $22.8 million. But, of course, the relevant issue is, what should the company do *today*? Should it pay $5 million for the rights?

Well, if the negotiations with the IMF fail, which happens with a probability of 50%, the company will reject this project, neither making the initial investment in equipment nor receiving any cash flows. But if the negotiations succeed, which happens with a probability of 50%, the company could invest in a project with an NPV of $22.8 million *at the end of the first year*. Then, the expected value of this project *today* is given by

$$(0.5) \cdot \left(\frac{\$22.8m}{1.10} \right) + (0.5)(\$0m) = \$10.4m$$

Therefore, it is worth paying $5 million for the rights to extract copper from the mine.

So, what is wrong with NPV? Simply that it fails to account for the value of flexibility. Note that a static NPV calculation based on expected cash flows leads the company to reject the mining project. However, this calculation ignores the fact that the company can choose to wait for one year until the uncertainty disappears, and then decide whether it's worth investing $150 million to extract copper (which it would do only if the exchange rate is high). In other words, once the company takes into account the flexibility given by the option to delay the investment decision, it turns a project with a negative NPV into one with a positive NPV.

Importantly, note that the company considers acquiring the *right* (not the obligation) to exploit the copper mine. That flexibility to choose *whether* to exploit the mine is valuable, and yet that value is ignored by a static NPV analysis. In other words, the NPV approach fails to account for the value of the right to take certain actions and, as a result, it usually *undervalues* investment projects.

What is a real option?

You may have gotten the idea by now, but let's take a walk before we run and first define a few important option-related terms. Regardless of whether they are financial or real, options can be classified into calls and puts. A *call* option gives its owner the right to *buy* the underlying asset at a fixed price at (or up until) a given point in time. A *put* option, on the other hand, gives its owner the right to *sell* the underlying asset at a fixed price at (or up until) a given point in time. In both cases the option holder has the right, not the obligation, to buy (in the case of calls) or sell (in the case of puts) the underlying asset.

The price at which the option holder can buy (in the case of calls) or sell (in the case of puts) the underlying asset is called the *exercise* (or *strike*) *price*. The last day in which the option can be exercised is called the *expiration date*. Depending on when calls and puts can be exercised, both can be either *American* options, which can be exercised at any time up to the expiration date; or *European* options, which can be exercised only on the expiration date. Finally, the underlying asset can be either financial, such as shares of stock, or real, such as an investment project.

A **real option**, then, is the *right* to take an action on a *non-financial asset* at a *given cost* during a *given period of time*. Several parts of this definition are important. First, a real option (like all options) gives a right, not an obligation, which means that the option can be exercised or discarded. In the example we discussed, the company can choose whether to extract copper from the mine and when it will start to do so.

Second, the underlying asset of a real option is not financial, and the right is not to buy or sell the asset. Rather, these are options in the sense of choice, meaning that the owner can choose to take an action, such as delaying, abandoning, expanding, or scaling back a project, to name but a few. In the example we have discussed, the company has the option to delay (up to 10 years) the extraction of copper from the mine.

Third, exercising real *call* options is usually costly in the sense that the company has to pay to take the action contemplated in the option. In the example we discussed, the company can exercise the option to extract copper from the mine by investing $150 million. When exercising a *put* option, on the other hand, the company usually gets a benefit. A company that abandons a project can sell the remaining assets, and one that scales back a project can reallocate resources to more productive activities.

Finally, the right to take an action is usually limited to a specific period of time. In the example we discussed, the company has the option to delay the extraction of copper for up to 10 years, after which period the right expires.

Types of real options

There are many types of real options, basically differing on the type of choice they provide the owner with. An *option to delay* gives its owner the right to delay taking an action. Technically, this option is an American call with the value of the underlying asset being the present value of the project and the exercise price being the initial investment required to start the project. In the example we have discussed, the rights to exploit the copper mine give the company the ability to begin extraction at any time during the length of the contract. This is valuable because the company can wait until uncertainty about the exchange rate is resolved and then decide whether to invest.

An *option to expand* gives its owner the right to increase the size of a project. Technically, this option is an American call with the value of the underlying asset being the present value of the project and the exercise price being the investment required to expand the project. Note that a project may be unattractive at a small scale but attractive at a larger one, and yet the larger scale might make sense only under certain conditions. Setting up an institute for executive education may not be profitable at a small scale. However, a small project may be valuable to test demand for the institute's programs, and if this demand proves to be high, the institute could expand and operate profitably. Alternatively, a pharmaceutical company can make a small investment in developing an AIDS vaccine, and if the vaccine clears the first tests, then the project can be expanded for full clinical trials.

An *option to abandon* gives its owner the right to close down a project. Technically, this option is an American put with the underlying asset being the present value of the project and the exercise price being the liquidation value (if any). If the demand for executive-education programs at the institute above proves disappointing, the institute could close and realize the liquidation value, such as, for example, selling the property where it operated. Alternatively, if the AIDS vaccine of the pharmaceutical company above fails any of the clinical trials, the operation could be shut down and its resources redeployed.

You can probably imagine many other types of real options, such as the option to scale back an operation, or to shut down and restart an operation. All of them are characterized by the fact that they provide the right but not the obligation to take an action; or, put differently, they provide *flexibility*. This flexibility is valuable and should be incorporated into the evaluation of projects, which is what the NPV approach fails to do.

Valuation of real options

Valuing financial options is no trivial matter, but valuing real options is even harder. Financial options are usually valued with the Black–Scholes model (discussed in Chapter 24), which is far from trivial. And yet, because the underlying asset (shares of stock) trades in a market and has observable prices, the inputs of this model are not hard to come by. What makes the valuation of real options particularly difficult is that these are options on a *non-traded* asset; therefore, the value and volatility of this asset are much harder to determine.

Rather than attempting the daunting task of pricing a real option, we'll discuss the factors that affect its value and how they do so. The five factors we'll discuss are those necessary to price a financial option using the Black–Scholes model. These are the value of the underlying asset, the exercise price, the volatility in the value of the underlying asset, the time to expiration, and the risk-free rate.

In the case of financial options, the value of the underlying asset is the price of the stock on which the option is written. In the case of real options, the value of the underlying asset is given by the present value of a project's cash flows. The effect of this variable on the value of a real option depends on whether we are valuing a call or a put. In the case of a call, the higher the value of the asset, the higher the value of the real option; in the case of a put, the opposite is the case.

The exercise price also has a different impact on the value of a real option depending on whether we are valuing a call or a put. In the case of a call, the exercise price is the cost of the investment required to start or expand a project and is inversely related to the value of the real option. In the case of a put, the exercise price is the liquidation value of the project and is directly related to the value of the real option.

The value of a real (call and put) option is directly related to the volatility in the value of the underlying asset. It may sound strange that an increase in volatility makes an asset more (rather than less) valuable. However, note that the buyer of an option can never lose more than the price he paid for it. Therefore, given a limited downside, a higher volatility implies a higher probability that the value of the underlying asset will move in the direction favorable to the option holder.

The time to expiration is the period of time during which the owner of a real option can take an action on a project. The value of a real (call and put) option is directly related to the time to expiration. This is, again, because the loss of an option holder is limited to the price he paid for it. Therefore, given a limited downside, the longer the time to expiration, the more time the underlying asset has to move in the direction favorable to the option holder.

Finally, the risk-free rate mainly affects the present value of the exercise price and has a different influence on the value of real call and put options. In the case of a call, the higher the risk-free rate, the lower the present value of the exercise price, and the higher the value of the real option. In the case of a put, the opposite is the case.

Problems in the valuation of real options

As mentioned above, valuing a financial option is not trivial, and valuing a real option is even harder. To start with, the approach most widely used to value a financial option, the Black–Scholes model, is far from appropriate for real options. This model requires, for example, continuous (trading and) prices for the underlying asset. This requirement, largely fulfilled in the case of shares, is hardly fulfilled in the case of investment projects.

Second, although the value of a financial option rests on a certain value for the underlying asset, the market price of a share, the value of a real option rests on a value which is much more difficult to assess, the value of an investment project. This value, in fact, is not only more difficult to assess but also much more subjective. After all, different individuals evaluating the same investment opportunity can come up with very different assessments of a project's potential and the advisability of investing in it.

Third, although it is trivial to estimate the volatility of a stock's returns, there is nothing trivial about estimating the volatility in the value of a project. Because this value is not observed periodically and a history of its past values cannot be collected, calculating its volatility usually involves a wild guess. Often, the best course of action is to try to reduce the sources of uncertainty in the value of a project to one *tradable* factor, and then infer from the volatility of this factor the volatility in the value of the project. Another possibility is to outline some relevant scenarios, to assign a probability to each, and to estimate the expected cash flows of each. The standard deviation of the project's cash flows can then be estimated. Both approaches require a good mix of art, science, and sorcery.

Fourth, although in the mining example the company had a clear time frame to exercise its option (10 years), this is not always the case. Legal rights may have a clear expiration date but not all expiration periods are based on legal considerations. A company assessing the value of an option to expand a project may find it has no specific time limit. However, the entry of competitors, or the introduction of better technology, may render this flexibility worthless at *some* point in the future. This further complicates the valuation of real options.

This list is not exhaustive; there are many other complications that companies face when assessing the value of a real option. But it should give an idea of why the task is far from trivial. And the problem is that, the more uncertain the value of a real option is, the more uncertain is the actual value of an investment opportunity. It is for this reason, precisely, that real options can easily be misused.

Misuses of real options

The danger of real options should be obvious at this point. Recall that a real option can only *add* to the NPV of a project. Recall, also, that the value of a real option is uncertain and may be subject to a variety of assessments. Then, as you have probably guessed, real options can be used by managers to justify investing in projects that a conventional NPV analysis would reject.

This is not necessarily wrong. The whole point of considering real options is to properly assess the value of investment projects. In many cases, these projects do come with valuable real options embedded, and in some cases the value of these options turn a project with negative NPV into one with positive NPV. That was precisely the case in the mining example and, again, this is the whole point of considering real options.

But the potential for misuse is ample. This problem is particularly serious when the uncertainty about the value of the real option is high, and when the NPV of a project *without* incorporating the value of real options is close to 0. In the first case, a manager who wants to invest in a pet project will find it easier to justify the investment by adding to the project's negative NPV an arbitrarily high value for a real option. In the second case, even a low value of a real option may turn an unprofitable project into a profitable one. It is in these situations that real options may cease to be an asset and turn into a liability instead.

The big picture

The incorporation of real options into the evaluation of investment projects is a relatively new development. Many projects do come with options embedded and the rights they create to take future actions are valuable. The traditional and static NPV analysis ignores the value of this flexibility and, as a result, it typically undervalues investment opportunities.

But, however plausible the incorporation of real options into the evaluation of investment projects may be, the problem lies in properly assessing the value of these options. Standard models for the valuation of financial options need to be twisted and turned to value real options. This usually creates high uncertainty about their actual value, which in turn lends itself to the potential misuse of this very useful tool. Real options, like most tools, must be handled with care.

23

Corporate value creation

Whether managers create or destroy shareholder value is critical for companies and their shareholders. It is also critical for managers because, very often, their compensation is (or aims to be) tied to their performance. The problem is, there isn't an undisputed way to define value creation. In this chapter we discuss some definitions and pay special attention to both residual income and its most well-known variation, EVA.

What should be the goal of management?

On the face of it, this appears to be a simple question. We could argue that the goal of managers should simply be to maximize the value of the capital invested by the shareholders of a company, which would translate into maximizing the company's stock price. But some would beg to disagree. They would argue that focusing *only* on shareholders is very restrictive.

Managers, many argue, should take into account the interest of *all* their constituencies, such as shareholders, employees, and suppliers, to name a few. This view is often referred to as the stakeholder theory. In this view, managers are not supposed to focus only on the wellbeing of the company's shareholders but more broadly on the wellbeing of all the company's stakeholders.

However interesting and important this debate may be, it will not be the focus of this chapter. We'll restrict our focus on the goal of maximizing shareholder value and discuss ways of defining this concept. And this for at least two reasons. First, although there are several ways to assess whether managers create shareholder value, there is no accepted way to assess (much less to quantify) whether they are creating stakeholder value.

Second, it is difficult to see how a manager can create shareholder value without taking care of the company's stakeholders. In the long term, a manager will hardly be able to make shareholders better off by mistreating employees, suppliers, or any other constituency that has a role to play in value creation. In other words, in the long term, a manager can only create shareholder value by creating stakeholder value. For this reason, the either–or characterization of this issue (a manager can maximize either shareholder value or stakeholder value) is exaggerated.

We'll use as a working hypothesis, then, that the goal of managers is to maximize shareholder value. And although this concept doesn't have an undisputed definition, we can agree that a manager who invests in projects with positive NPV creates value for shareholders. If, in addition, markets price securities properly, investing in projects with positive NPV should have a positive impact on the company's stock price. This is essentially why value creation is usually associated with the goal of maximizing a company's share price.

Accounting profits and economic profits

Consider a company with $100 million in capital, $50 million of debt and $50 million of equity. Its cost of debt is 8%, its cost of equity 12%, and the corporate tax rate 35%. Its earnings before interest and taxes (EBIT) are $10 million. Is this company profitable?

Accountants define profit in a variety of ways. One measure of accounting profit is a company's *net income*, which in the case of our very simple company would be

	($m)
EBIT	10.0
– Interest	4.0
Pretax income	6.0
– Taxes	2.1
Net income	**3.9**

From an accounting point of view, then, this company is profitable. But does it make enough profit to compensate its shareholders? Well, shareholders require a 12% return on $50 million of invested equity, so the company needs to make at least $6 million (= 0.12 · $50m) to satisfy the return required by shareholders. Therefore, being $2.1 million short of that target, the company is not profitable from an *economic* point of view.

Another accounting measure of profitability is a company's *net operating profit after taxes* (NOPAT), which in the case of our company is

	($m)
EBIT	10.0
– Interest	4.0
Pretax income	6.0
– Taxes	2.1
Net income	3.9
+ After-tax interest	2.6
NOPAT	**6.5**

This NOPAT, which can also be calculated as EBIT after taxes (0.65 · $10m = $6.5m), can be thought of as the (accounting) profit of the company independent from the composition of its capital. In other words, NOPAT highlights the profitability of the capital invested regardless of who provided the capital. (It's easy to see that different capital structures would affect the company's net income but would leave NOPAT unchanged. Try!)

Given a NOPAT of $6.5 million, the company is profitable from an accounting point of view. But does it make enough profit to appropriately compensate its capital providers? Not really. Given a cost of capital of 8.6% (= 0.65 · 0.5 · 0.08 + 0.5 · 0.12)) and the $100 million of capital invested, the company should make at least $8.6 million. Therefore, being $2.1 million short of this amount, the company is not profitable from an *economic* point of view.

Importantly, note that in both cases the company is $2.1 million short of appropriately compensating shareholders in the first case and capital providers in the second case. This is no coincidence. Note that debt holders receive interest payments based on their required return on debt; that is, debt holders are appropriately compensated for lending capital to the company. Therefore, any shortage of cash after interest payments to debt holders and tax payments to the government is born by the residual claimants; that is, by the shareholders. (Conversely, if the company makes accounting profits larger than its cost of capital, the extra profits flow into the pockets of shareholders.)

In short, then, regardless of whether we look at our company exclusively from the point of view of shareholders, or that of all capital providers, we can say that the company is profitable from an accounting point of view but unprofitable from an economic point of view. Or, put differently, *this company did not create shareholder value.*

Residual income

The main reason why net income (or NOPAT for that matter) cannot be considered a good measure of corporate performance should be clear by now. A positive net income may or may not compensate shareholders appropriately for investing their capital in the company. And this is precisely where the measure of residual income comes in.

Residual income (RI), sometimes called *economic profit*, can be defined as

$$RI = \text{Net income} - (\text{Equity}) \cdot (\text{COE}) \tag{23.1}$$

where COE denotes the cost of equity; or, equivalently, as

$$RI = \text{NOPAT} - (\text{Capital}) \cdot (\text{COC}) \tag{23.2}$$

where COC denotes the cost of capital, and capital is the sum of debt and equity, both measured at book value. (More generally, a company's capital can be defined as the sum of all its sources of financing, thus including preferred stock, convertible debt, and other sources of capital.) The second term of the right-hand side of expression (23.1), (Equity)·(COE), is usually called the *equity charge*; and the second term of the right-hand side of expression (23.2), (Capital)·(COC), is usually called the *capital charge*.

Finally, note that if we define return on capital (ROC) as the ratio of NOPAT to capital (that is, ROC = NOPAT/Capital), then we can also define residual income as

$$RI = (\text{ROC} - \text{COC}) \cdot (\text{Capital}) \tag{23.3}$$

Now, let's think a bit about the meaning of residual income. According to expression (23.1), residual income is what's left for shareholders *after* they have been appropriately compensated for providing the company with equity capital. Similarly, according to expression (23.2), residual income is what's left for shareholders *after* all capital providers have been appropriately compensated for providing capital to the company. Note that, in both cases, we are defining an *economic* profit, in the sense that we label a company profitable or unprofitable only if it generates accounting profits *in excess of* those required by the capital providers.

Here's another way to look at this. Note that expression (23.1) subtracts from the company's net income the equity charge. Essentially, then, managers are being 'charged' for using equity at the return required by shareholders to 'lend' money to the company. Similarly, expression (23.2) subtracts from the company's NOPAT the capital charge, indicating that managers are being 'charged' for using capital at the average return required by the capital providers. Only after generating enough accounting profits to cover these charges can a company be thought of as profitable from an economic point of view.

Expression (23.3) expresses the same idea in a different way. It says that residual income is created when the return on invested capital is larger than the cost of that capital. In other words, if the company manages to invest capital in activities that generate a return higher than the cost of obtaining the funds to invest in them, then it will create economic profit. Makes sense, doesn't it?

Well, if it does, then we can go one step further and argue that:

- If RI > 0 ⇒ The company has *created* shareholder value

- If RI < 0 ⇒ The company has *destroyed* shareholder value

To drive this point home, let's go back to the company in the previous section and, first, note that its ROC is 6.5% (= $6.5m/$100m). Then, its residual income is given by

$$
\begin{aligned}
RI &= \$3.9m - (\$50m)\cdot(12.0\%) \\
&= \$6.5m - (\$100m)\cdot(8.6\%) \\
&= (6.5\%-8.6\%)\cdot\$100m \\
&= -\$2.1m
\end{aligned}
$$

In words, this company has been $2.1 million short from appropriately compensating its capital providers and, more precisely, its shareholders. We can then say that, based on the concept of residual income, this company has destroyed shareholder value.

In short, then, residual income measures the creation or destruction of value by subtracting from a company's accounting profits the return required by capital providers. Therefore, a company creates value only when it makes accounting profits *in excess of* those required to compensate capital providers; or, similarly, when it invests capital in activities whose return is larger than the cost of the capital invested in them.

Some evidence

It should be clear from the previous section that calculating residual income is fairly simple, consisting of magnitudes easy to either obtain or estimate. Using expression (23.3), Table 23.1 calculates the residual income of 10 US industries and the market as a whole as of the end of 2009. The second column displays returns on capital; the third column, costs of capital; the fourth column, the book value of the capital invested; and the last column, residual incomes.

table 23.1

Industry	ROC (%)	COC (%)	Capital ($bn)	RI ($bn)
Advertising	12.9	9.1	42.6	1.6
Biotechnology	12.5	8.5	26.6	1.1
Entertainment/ technology	2.7	9.3	16.9	−1.1
Financial services	6.6	7.4	1,354.9	−10.2
Hotel/gaming	10.8	9.3	94.5	1.4
Internet	33.8	8.4	43.2	11.0
Securities brokerage	22.5	7.0	474.0	73.5
Semiconductor	28.6	10.4	96.0	17.5
Telecom services	23.0	8.1	965.3	144.5
Wireless networking	14.6	9.8	30.7	1.4
Total market	**18.0**	**8.2**	**14,289.0**	**1,402.4**

Source: These figures are based on information from Aswath Damodaran's web page
http://pages.stern.nyu.edu~adamodar

The table shows that two industries (entertainment/technology and financial services) have a return on capital lower than their respective cost of capital, and, therefore, a negative residual income. Based on this concept, then, these industries destroyed shareholder value during 2009. The other eight industries (and the market as a whole), however, delivered positive residual income and, therefore, created value for their shareholders.

Note that in this framework value creation is a function of both the spread (between the return on capital and the cost of capital) and the capital invested. Therefore, any given level of residual income may be obtained from investing a little capital at a large spread, or lots of capital at a small spread, or any combination in between. To illustrate, note that the wireless networking industry and the hotel/gaming industry have the same residual income but very different levels of capital and spreads; the former has far less capital invested at a much higher spread than the latter.

EVA and MVA

The concept of residual income is far from new. In fact, it is usually acknowledged that General Motors implemented a similar measure to evaluate its performance in the early 1920s. That being said, the renewed interest in residual income is due in no small part to Stern Stewart. The company's trademarked variation of residual income, introduced in the early 1980s and called **economic value added (EVA)**, is defined as

$$EVA = NOPAT^* - (Capital^*) \cdot (COC) \tag{23.4}$$

where NOPAT* and Capital* denote *adjusted* NOPAT and *adjusted* capital. Just as was the case with residual income, in this framework a company is said to create value when its EVA is positive, and to destroy it when its EVA is negative.

What are the differences between residual income and EVA? At the end of the day, not many. In fact, EVA is just a variation of residual income. Having said that, Stern Stewart emphasizes that to turn accounting profits into economic profits both the NOPAT and the capital need to go through several adjustments.

Which ones? Unfortunately, although Stern Stewart has identified more than a hundred potential adjustments, only a few of them are publicly known; the rest are the company's trade secret. A well-known adjustment, however, is the proper treatment of research and development (R&D). From an accounting point of view, R&D is an expense. From an economic point of view, Stern Stewart argues, R&D should be treated as a capital investment. This implies, first, that R&D is capitalized rather than expensed; and, second, that the accounting charge for R&D is added back to (and the depreciation of capital subtracted from) earnings for the calculation of the adjusted NOPAT.

Closely associated with EVA is the concept of **market value added (MVA)**, which can be defined as

$$MVA = Market\ Value\ of\ Capital - Book\ Value\ of\ Capital \tag{23.5}$$

Essentially, MVA is the difference between what capital providers have put into the company (and given up in the form of retained earnings) and what they can get out of the company by selling their claims. Obviously, then, the larger this is, the better the *cumulative* performance of the company.

In this framework, EVA can be thought of as a tool that serves the ultimate goal of maximizing a company's MVA. Formally, the link between these two magnitudes is given by the fact that MVA is the present value of expected EVAs, discounted at the company's cost of capital, which explains their direct relationship.

Stern Stewart has made EVA the centerpiece of an integrated framework of performance evaluation and incentive compensation. The company claims that EVA can be used to measure value creation, take managerial decisions, motivate managers through compensation schemes, and (perhaps stretching the concept) change the mindset of the whole corporation. It also publishes a well-known annual ranking of corporate value creators and destroyers in which companies are ranked on the basis of their MVAs.

Other measures of value creation

Many consulting companies offer trademarked techniques designed to assess corporate value creation and set executive compensation. These, plus some other non-commercial tools, form a crowded field of options for companies to choose from. We briefly review three of them here.

Cash flow return on investment (CFROI), originally developed by Holt Associates, is the internal rate of return of inflation-adjusted cash flows. To evaluate corporate performance, CFROI is compared with a company's inflation-adjusted (or real) cost of capital. If the former is larger than the latter, the company has created shareholder value; if the opposite is the case, the company has destroyed shareholder value.

Cash value added (CVA) is similar to EVA and also a measure of economic profit. It adjusts NOPAT by depreciation, adding back depreciation and subtracting *economic* depreciation, and then subtracts a capital charge. The economic depreciation represents an annual amount invested in a sinking fund, earning a return equal to the cost of capital, and set aside to replace plant and equipment; capital, in turn, is measured as the full cash invested in the business. In this framework, a positive CVA indicates that the company has created shareholder value, and a negative CVA indicates the opposite.

Total shareholder return (TSR) is simply the sum of a stock's capital gain/loss and dividend yield in any given period, just as the simple or arithmetic return we calculated in Chapter 1. This return must then be compared with the stock's required return, calculated from a pricing model such as the CAPM (discussed in Chapter 7). If the total return is larger than the required return, then the company has created shareholder value; if the opposite is the case, the company has destroyed shareholder value.

These three measures far from exhaust the possibilities. TBR (total business return), SVA (shareholder value added), and RAROC (risk-adjusted return on capital) are just three more among many other performance measures that companies can choose from.

The big picture

Managers create shareholder value when they invest in projects with positive NPV. No argument in this chapter contradicts this well-established fact. Our discussion focused instead on different ways of defining shareholder value creation. And although there is no undisputed way to determine whether a company has created or destroyed value, once a company has chosen to assess performance based on one particular measure, then executive compensation can be linked to that measure.

The concept of residual income attempts to measure economic (as opposed to accounting) profit. This means that a company is profitable from an economic point of view only when accounting profits exceed the compensation required by capital providers.

Several other measures of shareholder value creation exist. EVA, the best known and most widely used of them, is a modification of residual income that adjusts accounting profit and capital to assess economic profitability. Other well-known measures of performance include CFROI, CVA, TBR, SVA, and RAROC.

Competition and shareholder activism are increasing around the world and there is increasing pressure on managers to create shareholder value. The challenge is not so much *what to do* to create this value (investing in projects with positive NPV would do); the real challenge is to devise a system *that gives managers the incentive* to make the right decisions and therefore to create shareholder value.

24

Options

The world of investing is not limited to stocks and bonds; there are many other financial instruments investors can choose from. Derivatives, which are assets that derive their value from the value of an underlying asset, are one of them; and options are one type of derivative. In this chapter we'll discuss the basics of this financial instrument, including how they are priced and how they can be used to enhance returns or limit risk.

The basics

We have already discussed real options, so in this chapter we'll focus on *financial* options. As the name suggests, in this case the underlying asset is not a project but a financial asset, such as shares of a company, an index, or a currency. Financial options can be classified into calls and puts. A *call option* gives its owner the right to *buy* the underlying asset at a fixed price at (or up until) a given point in time; a *put option* gives its owner the right to *sell* the underlying asset at a fixed price at (or up until) a given point in time. In both cases the option holder has the right, not the obligation, to buy (in the case of calls) or sell (in the case of puts) the underlying asset.

The price at which the option holder can buy or sell the underlying asset is called the *exercise* (or *strike*) *price*. The last day the option can be exercised is called the *expiration date*. And depending on when they can be exercised, options can be either *American*, which can be exercised at any time up to the expiration date, or *European*, which can be exercised only on the expiration date.

At any time before expiration, a call option is *in the money* when the asset price is higher than the exercise price, and *out of the money* when the opposite is the case. A put option, on the other hand, is in the money when the asset price is lower than the exercise price and out of the money when the opposite is true. Both calls and puts are *at the money* when the asset price and the exercise price coincide.

The price of an option (which is expressed on a per-share basis when the option is on stock) is called the option *premium*. Note that the premium is paid by the buyer and received by the seller, who is *not* the company behind the asset. Options are issued *by investors*, not by companies. Finally, note that although the option buyer has the right (not the obligation) to buy or sell the underlying asset, the option seller does have the obligation (not the right) to buy or sell the asset. In other words, the buyer pays to acquire a right, and the seller is paid for committing to take an action (buying or selling the underlying asset) at some point in time in the future.

Option valuation at expiration

From this point on, to streamline the discussion, we'll focus on options on a company's stock. Importantly, note that these options give the holder the right to buy or sell 100 shares; then, a premium of $5 indicates that we have to pay $500 for the option.

Let's introduce some notation and denote the current price of the stock with S; the exercise price of both options with X; the call premium with C; and the put premium with P. Also, let's consider a call and a put written on the same stock and with an exercise price of $50. And let's ask how valuable are these call and put options *on* the expiration date?

Well, that's not hard to figure out. The call option gives us the right to buy the stock at $50 a share, so it will be valuable only if the stock trades for more than $50. If on the expiration date the stock is trading at $60 a share, we could exercise our right to buy shares at $50, sell them right away at $60, and pocket a profit of $10 a share (before transaction costs). Then, on the expiration date, this call has a value of $1,000 ($10 for each of the 100 shares).

If, on the other hand, the stock is trading at $35 on the expiration date, then we are better off by letting the call expire. No point exercising an option to buy shares at $50 when we could buy those same shares in the market at $35. Therefore, in this situation, our call would be worthless.

What about the put option? Just as simple. In this case we have the right to sell the stock at $50 a share, which will be valuable only if the stock trades for less than $50. If on the expiration date the stock is trading at $35 a share, we could buy shares in the market at that price and exercise our right to sell them at $50, for a profit of $15 a share (again, before transaction costs). Then, on the expiration date this put has a value of $1,500 ($15 for each of the 100 shares).

If, on the other hand, the stock is trading at $60, we are better off by letting the put expire without exercising it. No point exercising an option to sell shares at $50 when we can sell those same shares in the market at $60. Therefore, in this case, our put would be worthless.

To formalize this a bit, we can say that on the expiration date a call option is worth the greater of $S-X$ and 0, and a put option is worth the greater of $X-S$ and 0. Or, even more formally, on the expiration date

$$C = \text{Max}\,(S-X,\, 0) \tag{24.1}$$
$$P = \text{Max}\,(X-S,\, 0) \tag{24.2}$$

It is obvious, then, that if we expect a company's stock price to rise we would buy calls (or sell puts), and if we expect its stock price to fall we would buy puts (or sell calls).

Option valuation before expiration

As it's hopefully obvious from the previous discussion, calculating the value of an option on the expiration date is trivial. The interesting and far more complicated issue, however, is to determine the value of an option any time *before* the expiration date. Let's start with the five variables that influence this value:

- the value of the underlying asset;
- the exercise price;
- the volatility in the value of the underlying asset;
- the time to expiration;
- the risk-free rate.

We have discussed the effect of the value of the underlying asset (the stock price) and the exercise price on the value of calls and puts on the expiration date. And we know that the larger the difference between S and X, the more valuable the call will be on this date. For this reason, the larger the difference $S-X$ at any time before expiration, the more likely that $S>X$ on the expiration date, and, therefore, the higher the value of the call. Similarly, because on the expiration date a put is valuable only when $X>S$, then the larger the difference $X-S$ at any time before expiration, the more likely that $X>S$ on the expiration date, and, therefore, the higher the value of the put.

The value of both calls and puts is directly related to the volatility in the value of the underlying asset (the stock). Although this may sound strange, note that the buyer of an option can never lose more than the premium he paid for it. This implies that the owner of a call has an unlimited upside (the higher $S-X$, the higher the value of the call) but a limited downside (the premium paid).

Conversely, although the buyer of a put does not have an unlimited upside (on the expiration date he can never make more than X, which he would only if $S=0$), he does benefit from large movements of S below X, but still can't lose more than the premium he paid when S increases with respect to X. The combination of a substantial upside and a limited downside, then, makes volatility valuable for the owner of *both* calls and puts.

The value of both calls and puts is also directly related to the time to expiration. This is the case, again, because the potential loss suffered by an option holder is limited to the premium he paid for it. Therefore, given a limited downside, the longer the time to expiration, the more time the stock price has to move in the direction that benefits the option holder.

Finally, the risk-free rate mainly affects the present value of the exercise price and has a different impact on the value of calls and puts. Note that the option buyer pays the exercise price (if he exercises at all) on the expiration date, and that before expiration the present value of the exercise price decreases as the risk-free rate increases. (More intuitively, the ability to defer a payment is more valuable as the risk-free rate increases.) Therefore, the higher the risk-free rate, the higher the value of a call.

In the case of a put, the opposite is the case. The owner of a put will not receive the exercise price (if he exercises at all) until the expiration date, and the present value of the exercise price decreases as the risk-free rate increases. (Again, more intuitively, having to wait for a payment is more costly as the risk-free rate increases.) Therefore, the higher the interest rate, the lower the value of a put.

Table 24.1 summarizes the impact of these five variables on the value of both calls and puts before expiration. Importantly, note that before the expiration date, the only variable that will not change for sure is the exercise price. For this reason, the third row of the table should be interpreted as saying that if we compare two calls (on the same stock) with different exercise prices, the one with the lower exercise price will be the more valuable. Conversely, if we compare two puts (on the same stock) with different exercise prices, the one with the higher exercise price will be the more valuable.

table 24.1

Increase in ...	Effect on C	Effect on P
Value of the underlying asset	Increases	Decreases
Exercise price	Decreases	Increases
Volatility in the value of the underlying asset	Increases	Increases
Time to expiration	Increases	Increases
Risk-free rate	Increases	Decreases

The Black–Scholes model

There is a good chance that, if you were unfamiliar with options, at this point you may be thinking that this stuff is not so hard after all. It's not too difficult to understand what an option is and how the relevant variables affect its value. Unfortunately, the fun ends (though some would say it actually begins!) when we try to put a *precise dollar figure* on the value of an option *anytime before expiration*.

The Black–Scholes model, the standard framework to value options, is given by a horrifying expression we'll discuss shortly. But before we get to that, a quick digression on the so-called *binomial model*, which is usually discussed on the way to introducing Black–Scholes. The binomial framework assumes that the stock price can take only two values (hence its name). This simplifying assumption is useful to show how we could replicate the payoffs of buying a call with a strategy of borrowing money and buying stock. Because both strategies would have the same payoffs, they would have to cost the same; therefore, by determining the cost of the 'borrow-money-and-buy-stock' strategy, we could indirectly determine the value of the call. The Black–Scholes model essentially values the call this way, adjusting continuously over time.

Now, without any further delay, the expression to calculate the value of a *call* option according to the **Black–Scholes model** is given by

$$C = S \cdot N(d_1) - X \cdot e^{-T \cdot R_f} \cdot N(d_2) \tag{24.3}$$

where

$$d_1 = \frac{\ln(S/X) + \left[R_f + (1/2) \cdot \sigma^2\right] \cdot T}{\sigma \cdot \sqrt{T}} \tag{24.4}$$

$$d_2 = d_1 - \sigma \cdot \sqrt{T} \tag{24.5}$$

where C denotes the value of the call; S the price of the underlying stock; X the exercise price; T the time to expiration (in years); R_f the (continuously compounded) annual risk-free rate; σ the annualized standard deviation of (continuously compounded) returns of the underlying stock; and $e = 2.71828$. $N(d_1)$ and $N(d_2)$ denote the probability that a variable following the standard normal distribution takes a value lower than or equal to d_1 and d_2. Still think that this stuff is not so hard?

A couple of points before using this model to value an option. First, don't try to make a lot of sense out of these three expressions; they're not intuitive. (The model behind them is, but we'll wave our hands on that discussion.) Second, note that the value of a call option depends on the same five factors we discussed before: The stock price, the exercise price, the volatility in the stock price, the time to expiration, and the risk-free rate. And third, note that, however complicated the model may seem, it's not demanding in terms of the inputs it requires.

Hands on now! Let's consider a call option with an exercise price of $30 and six months away from expiration. The call is written on a stock that is currently trading at $35 a share and has a historical annual volatility (standard deviation of returns) of 25%. The annual risk-free rate is 4%. How much should we pay for this call?

Again, do not look for much intuition behind this process. Better to throw these inputs into the expressions and see what we get. First step, let's calculate d_1 and d_2, which, using expressions (24.4) and (24.5) are equal to

$$d_1 = \frac{\ln(\$35 / \$30) + \left[0.04 + (1/2) \cdot (0.25)^2\right] \cdot 0.5}{0.25 \cdot \sqrt{0.5}} = 1.0735$$

$$d_2 = d_1 - \sigma \cdot \sqrt{t} = 1.0735 - 0.25 \cdot \sqrt{0.5} = 0.8968$$

What is the area under the standard normal distribution *below* these numbers? Using either a table of cutoff points (such as that at the end of Chapter 28), or the 'normsdist' command in Excel, we find that $N(1.0735)=0.8585$ and $N(0.8968)=0.8151$. Finally, substituting these values into (24.3) we get

$$C = \$35 \cdot 0.8585 - \$30 \cdot e^{-(0.5 \cdot 0.04)} \cdot 0.8151 = \$6.1$$

So, a call option with an exercise price of $30, six months away from maturity, written on a stock with a historical annual volatility of 25% and currently trading at $35, when interest rates are at 4%, is worth $6.1. Note that this premium is higher than the difference between the current stock price and the exercise price ($5 = $35–$30), indicating that investors find value in the upside potential of the stock.

Put–call parity

Are you wondering whether valuing a put is even more difficult than valuing a call? Fear not! In a way, valuing a put is less difficult, *if* the put is on a stock which also has a call with the same exercise price and time to maturity, *and* we have already valued the call. Under these conditions, the put and the call must be priced in such a way as to avoid arbitrage opportunities.

More precisely, given a call and a put with the same exercise price, the same time to maturity, and written on the same stock, arbitrage opportunities do not exist only if the call and the put meet the condition

$$C - P = S - X \cdot e^{-T \cdot R_f}$$

(24.6)

This relationship, called **put–call parity**, is one of the most important in option pricing. If it doesn't hold, arbitrage opportunities exist and implementing a trading strategy to exploit them is relatively simple. (If the right-hand side is larger than the left-hand side, we would buy the stock and the put and sell the call; if the opposite is the case, we would short-sell the stock, sell the put, and buy the call.)

In equilibrium, then, put–call parity must hold and the value of a put is obtained simply by rearranging terms in (24.6); that is

$$P = C - S + X \cdot e^{-T \cdot R_f} \qquad (24.7)$$

Returning to our example above, the value of a put with an exercise price of $30 and six months away from expiration (written on the same stock with an annual volatility of 25% and currently trading at $35, and with interest rates at 4%) would be equal to

$$P = \$6.1 - \$35 + \$30 \cdot e^{-(0.5 \cdot 0.04)} = \$0.5$$

Note, then, that investors seem to assign a very low probability to the stock price falling below $30 within the next six months. As a result, the right to sell the stock at $30 has very little value.

Having explored the pricing of both calls and puts, we can now confirm more formally the qualitative results in Table 24.1. Table 24.2 displays the value of the call and the put after changing, one at a time, the value of the five relevant parameters, each time beginning from the base case we've been discussing. The numbers in parentheses indicate the value of the parameters in this base case and their implied call and put premiums.

table 24.2

	S ($35)		X ($30)		σ (25%)		T (0.50)		R_f (4%)	
	$40	$30	$35	$25	35%	15%	1.00	0.25	6%	2%
Call ($6.1)	$10.7	$2.4	$2.8	$10.5	$6.7	$5.7	$7.2	$5.5	$6.3	$5.8
Put ($0.5)	$0.1	$1.8	$2.1	$0.0	$1.1	$0.1	$1.0	$0.2	$0.4	$0.5

To illustrate, beginning with the parameters of the base case, if the stock price increases from $35 to $40, the call premium increases from $6.1 to $10.7, and the put premium decreases from $0.5 to $0.1. If, on the other hand, the stock price falls from \$35 to \$30, the call premium decreases from \$6.1 to \$2.4, and the put premium increases from \$0.5 to \$1.8. This confirms the direct relationship between the price of a call and the stock price, and the inverse relationship between the price of a put and the stock price. If you go over the rest of the numbers in Table 24.2, you'll see that they confirm the qualitative results we anticipated in Table 24.1.

Why options?

There are many and varied reasons for buying and selling options. Of those, we'll briefly discuss here the two most important, leverage and protection. Interestingly, the former is implemented with the goal of increasing risk (and obviously expected return), and the latter with the goal of limiting it.

Options can be used to magnify the (risk and) reward of trading directly in stock because of the leverage they provide. Note that by investing in options an investor can control a capital much larger than the one he takes out of his pocket. In the example we've been discussing, an investment of \$610 (the cost of buying the call) enables an investor to control a capital of \$3,500 (the market price of a hundred shares).

What are the consequences of this leverage? Let's go back to our example and look at the bright side first. If the stock price increases from \$35 to \$40, an investor in the stock would obtain a 14.3% return; an investor in the call, however, would obtain a whopping 75.9% return (=\$10.7/\$6.1–1). This is what leverage is all about. But don't rush to call your broker to buy options just yet! Note that if the stock price falls from \$35 to \$30, the investor in the stock would lose 14.3%; the investor in the call, however, would lose 60.5% (=\$2.4/\$6.1–1). Leverage, then, is a double-edged sword; it amplifies *both* expected gains *and* expected losses.

This leverage is obviously not restricted to calls and can also be obtained through puts. An investor who believes that a company's stock price will fall can profit by either short-selling the stock or buying a put. Going back to our example, if the stock price falls from \$35 to \$30 a short-seller would make a 14.3% return by short-selling at \$35 and buying back at \$30 to close the short position. The investor in the put, however, would obtain a return of 273% (=\$1.8/\$0.5–1)!

But puts also are a double-edged sword. If the stock price happens to rise to $40, the short-seller in the stock would lose 14.3%. The investor in the put, however, would lose 79.4% (=$0.1/$0.5–1). In short, then, although options amplify *both* the reward and risk of investing directly in stock, investors who hope to leverage gains (rather than losses!) can find in options a useful tool.

The other good reason for buying options is protection. Let's see how this would work. Consider an investor that, believing in an imminent rise, buys 100 shares of the stock we've been discussing at its current price of $35. And let's assume that, against his expectations, the stock takes a dive to $10, delivering a 71.4% capital loss ($2,500 on a $3,500 investment). How could options have helped this investor?

Easy. At the same time he bought shares at $35 he could have also bought a put with an exercise price of $30. This way, he would have preserved all the upside, and at the same limited his downside (at a cost of $0.5 according to the Black–Scholes model). Note that, when the stock falls to $10, the investor could limit his $2,500 loss by selling the put at $19.4 according to Black–Scholes (realizing a gain of $1,892 on the put). Alternatively, he could wait six months until maturity and, if the stock price remains below $30, exercise the put and then sell the shares received at $30 each.

Protection can also be obtained with calls. Consider another investor that, believing in an imminent fall, short-sells 100 shares of the same stock we've been discussing at its current price of $35. What would happen if, against his expectations, the stock rises to $60? In this case the investor would suffer a 71.4% loss. (He pocketed $3,500 by short-selling 100 shares and now would have to spend $6,000 to buy them back to close the short position.) Would trading in options have helped this investor to limit his downside?

Absolutely. At the same time he sold the 100 shares short at $35 he could have bought a call with an exercise price of $40 (at a cost of $1.0 according to the Black–Scholes model). By doing this, the investor could have preserved his upside in case the stock fell and protected his downside if it rose. Note that if the stock rises to $60, the investor could limit his $2,500 loss by selling the call at $20.8 according to Black–Scholes (realizing a gain of $1,979 on the call). Alternatively, he could wait six months until maturity and, if the stock price remains above $40, exercise the call and buy the shares at $40 to cover his short position.

Finally, there are good reasons for selling options too. The main difference with buying them is, obviously, that an investor who buys an option has to pay for it, but one who sells an option is paid for it. In other words, an option writer (seller) is paid to bear the risk of committing to either buy or sell shares of stock at a predetermined price. If conditions move against the option writer, he will incur a loss for which, at least in principle, he has already been compensated with the premium he received.

The big picture

Investing in options enables investors to enhance returns or limit risk. If that sounds too good to be true, do keep in mind, first, that options magnify both gains and losses; and, second, that limiting risk does have a cost, which is given by the option premium.

The framework most widely used to price options is the Black–Scholes model, which values them based on the price and volatility of the underlying stock, the exercise price and time to expiration of the option, and the risk-free rate. Interestingly, according to this model, volatility, which is harmful for investors in stock, is valuable for investors in options.

Importantly, options are only one financial instrument of the many available to enhance returns or limit risk. Futures and forwards are also widely used for these purposes and we'll discuss them in the next chapter.

25

Futures and forwards

O ptions, which we discussed in the previous chapter, are one type of derivative; futures and forwards, which we discuss in this chapter, are two others. These markets are rather complex and definitely not for inexperienced investors. Still, the essentials of how futures and forwards are priced, and how they can be used for hedging and speculating, are not difficult to understand. These are, precisely, the focus of this chapter.

Basic definitions

You've probably done it many times. You go into a shop and that hot CD or book has already flown off the shelves. So what do you do? You order it, pay a small good-faith deposit, the seller promises to deliver the CD or book around a given date, at which time you pay the balance due and take the CD or book home. That is, more or less, what futures and forwards are all about.

More precisely, *futures* and *forwards* are contracts that specify an agreement to buy or sell a given quantity of an asset, at a given price, at a given point in time in the future. The asset can be real (commodities such as corn, cattle, coffee, or gold) or financial (such as currencies, bonds, or indices). In the case of commodities, the quality of the asset and the place of delivery are also specified in the contract. In the case of indices, which have no physical counterpart, the contract is settled in cash.

Futures and forwards differ from options in one critical aspect: Options give their owners the *right* to buy or sell the underlying asset; futures and forwards, however, *compel* the parties to buy or sell the underlying asset as specified in the contract. This does not imply, as we discuss below, that all transactions in these markets involve delivering an asset; in fact, the vast majority of transactions are offset before delivery.

Futures and forwards differ from each other in several aspects. Futures are standardized contracts specified by (and traded in) organized exchanges. They are highly liquid and enable traders to undo a position simply by making an offsetting transaction. Forwards, in turn, are contracts whose terms are set by agreement between the involved parties (usually financial institutions and corporations), are traded in over-the-counter markets (basically a network of traders), and can be undone only by consent of the involved parties. Therefore, although forwards are more flexible than futures regarding the specification of contract terms, they are also more difficult to undo.

Participants in these markets can take long or short positions. A party with a *long* position agrees to *receive* (buy) the underlying asset under the terms specified in the contract; a party with a *short* position, in turn, agrees to *deliver* (sell) the underlying asset under the terms specified in the contract. Delivering or taking delivery of an asset, however, are not the main reasons for participating in these markets. In fact, most participants do it to hedge or speculate.

Hedgers and speculators

There are two kinds of participants in futures and forwards markets, hedgers and speculators. *Hedgers* buy or sell contracts with the goal of protecting themselves from adverse movements in the price of an asset; *speculators* buy and sell contracts hoping to profit from short-term changes in prices. Hedgers, then, trade to reduce their risk; speculators, in turn, hope to make a profit by exposing themselves to that risk.

Both hedgers and speculators can take long and short positions. Hedgers take long positions seeking protection from an increase in the price of an asset, and short positions seeking protection from a decrease in the price of an asset. An airline that buys oil (future or forward) contracts, for example, seeks protection against increases in the price of one of its most critical inputs; a farmer who sells corn (future or forward) contracts, for example, seeks protection against decreases in the price of the product he sells.

Speculators who take long positions expect the price of the underlying asset to increase; those who take short positions expect the price of the underlying asset to fall. In both cases, speculators do not seek to receive or deliver an asset. Rather, they only seek to profit from changes in prices.

In fact, as anticipated above, most of the transactions in futures and forwards markets are not made by parties interested in delivering or accepting delivery of an asset. Rather, the vast majority of positions are offset before delivery. All a party needs to do to close a long position in a contract is to take a short position of the same size in the same contract. Conversely, a party closes a short position in a contract simply by taking a long position of the same size in the same contract. In fact, even hedgers usually close their positions before delivery and then sell the underlying asset in the spot market (that is, the market for current delivery).

Peculiarities of futures markets

Futures markets are different from bond and stock markets in several aspects. We briefly discuss here two of these aspects, margins and leverage. Individuals who want to operate with futures are required to open a *margin account*. These accounts require an *initial margin*, which is a minimum initial deposit required to operate in futures. The amount of the initial margin is set by the exchange, depends on the type of futures the individual intends to trade, and is a small percentage (usually around 5%) of the market value of the relevant contract. It also depends on whether the account is opened by a hedger or a speculator; the latter is required to deposit a higher initial margin. In most cases, the cash in a margin account earns interest. Also, in most cases, individuals can deposit securities instead of cash, but these are usually accepted at less than their face value.

Margin accounts have a *maintenance margin*, which is the minimum amount that must be kept in the account (usually around 75% of the initial margin). When the amount of cash in the account falls below this margin, even in the absence of any transaction, the individual gets a *margin call*; that is, a request to make a deposit in the account to bring it back to the initial (not to the maintenance) margin. If you're wondering why, in the absence of any transaction, the amount of money in a margin account may fall below the maintenance margin, or why it may fall at all, you're asking the right question.

Futures are *marked to market*, which means that daily gains and losses caused by price fluctuations are credited or debited to the account. In other words, changes in the value of futures contracts are realized each day. (Forwards are not marked to market but settled in full at the end of their life.) The main reason for marking futures to market daily is to reduce the probability of default when the contract expires.

To illustrate, let's suppose we buy one June contract on the Dow Jones Industrial Average during the month of March, when this index is at 10,000. Futures on the Dow trade at 10 times the value of the index; therefore, the price of one contract is $100,000. But we don't need that much money to trade in Dow futures; we only need to deposit an initial margin, which let's assume is 5% of the value of the contract ($5,000). What happens if by the end of the next day the Dow rises 2% to 10,200?

Well, the value of the contract will increase to $102,000 and therefore $2,000 would be credited to our account, for a closing balance of $7,000. We have made no transactions the day after opening the account and yet we have *realized* a $2,000 gain! Not bad! That's simply because our account has been marked to market.

But wait. What if the next day the Dow falls by 5%, closing at 9,690? Well, the value of the contract will fall to $96,900 and therefore $5,100 (= $102,000–$96,900) would be debited from our account, for a closing balance of $1,900. So, in this case, we made no transactions and still lost over $5,000. That *is* bad! But it's also the way futures markets work. Even worse, at this time we'd probably get a margin call from our broker asking us to deposit $3,100 to get our account back to the initial $5,000. This illustrates, briefly, the dynamics of margin accounts and the practice of marking to market.

Futures markets also exhibit another important characteristic, which is the leverage they provide. The investment of a small amount of capital to control much larger capital, which is what leverage is all about, increases both the return and the risk of investing in futures relative to investing directly in the underlying asset. This is not too different from the leverage provided by options (discussed in the previous chapter), but let's illustrate it by going back to the example we've been discussing.

Let's compare two strategies, one consisting of buying an index fund that mimics the behavior of the Dow, and the other consisting of investing in Dow futures. On the day the Dow rises 2%, our index fund would also rise 2%. However, we have seen that if we buy one futures contract on the Dow, on that same day we'd get a $2,000 deposit in our margin account, for a return of 40% (= $2,000/$5,000). That's quite a difference. Thumbs up to leverage!

But wait. Before you rush to buy futures, consider what happens the next day. When the Dow goes down 5%, our index fund would also fall by that amount. But our margin account in the Dow futures, as we have seen, would be debited by $5,100, for a return of –72.9% (= –$5,100/$7,000). Big thumbs down to leverage! Still, that's what leverage is all about; it amplifies *both* the returns *and* the risk of investing in the underlying asset.

Futures pricing

The valuation of futures contracts is, from a technical point of view, slightly different from that of forward contracts. However, for most practical purposes, given the same asset and delivery date, it is safe to assume that the price of both contracts is the same. (To streamline the discussion we'll focus below on the valuation of futures, although we could have almost the same discussion on the valuation of forwards.) This price, as we'll discuss in a moment, follows from the critical assumption of no arbitrage opportunities.

The framework to value futures contracts is the cost-of-carry model, which links the futures price of an asset with the spot (or current) price of that asset. More precisely, the **cost-of-carry model** states that

$$F = S \cdot e^{(c-y) \cdot T} \tag{25.1}$$

where F and S denote the futures price and the spot price of the underlying asset; c and y the cost of carry and the convenience yield (both expressed as a proportion of the spot price); T the time to delivery (in years); and e=2.71828. This model essentially says that the value of a futures contract is equal to the spot price of the underlying asset, adjusted by the net cost of carrying the asset for the relevant period of time. This requires some explanation.

Let's introduce, first, a relevant distinction between consumption assets (such as corn, oil, and coffee) and investment assets (such as gold, currencies, or stock). The former are held primarily for consumption purposes, the latter for investment purposes. This distinction is important because the type of asset underlying the futures contract determines both the cost of carry and the convenience yield. So, you may ask, what are these?

The *cost of carry* (c) is the cost of holding the asset for the relevant period of time. This cost may include financing costs, storage costs, insurance costs, and transportation costs, all of which depend on the type of asset underlying the futures contract. For consumption assets such as corn or coffee, all these costs may be relevant; for investment assets such as stock or currencies, only the financing cost is relevant.

The *convenience yield* (*y*) is the benefit for holding the underlying asset, and arises because ownership of a physical asset may provide benefits not provided by a futures contract. Storing coffee, for example, enables Starbucks both to keep its coffee shops going and to prevent disruption in operations should coffee become scarce. This convenience yield largely depends on the market's expectations about the future availability of a commodity; the greater the probability of shortages, the larger the benefit of holding the physical asset, and the higher the convenience yield. (Although the convenience yield, strictly speaking, applies only to consumption assets, the income generated by some investment assets can be *thought of* as a convenience yield. More on this below.)

Note that, in general, the cost of carry is larger than the convenience yield (that is, *c*>*y*) and, therefore, *F*>*S*. This situation is usually referred to as *contango*. At times, however, when inventories of a physical asset are low and the probability of shortages is high, it may be the case that the convenience yield is high enough to offset the cost of carry (that is, *c*<*y*) and, therefore, *F*<*S*. This situation is usually referred to as *backwardation*. Note, finally, that as time goes by, the futures price and the spot price tend to converge until, on the settlement date, both values become the same.

Confused? That's OK, the examples below should clarify the idea behind the cost-of-carry model and the role its components play in the valuation of futures contracts on assets.

Some examples

Let's start by considering an investment asset, shares in a company, and let's assume that this company pays no dividends. Let's also assume that the stock currently trades at $50 a share and that the (continuously compounded) annual risk-free rate is 4%. What should be the price of a six-month futures contract to buy one of these shares?

Note, first, that because we're dealing with a futures contract on a share, there are no storage, insurance, or transportation costs; the cost of carry, then, is given only by the financing cost. Also, note that because the stock pays no dividends, there is no convenience yield. According to expression (25.1), then, the futures contract to buy one share in six months (half a year) should be valued at

$$F = \$50 \cdot e^{(0.04) \cdot 0.5} = \$51.0$$

But that is just throwing numbers into a formula. It is useful to think about why the futures *must* trade at this price.

Let's consider what would happen if the futures traded at $55. Well, in this case, clever as we are, we could borrow $50 for six months at the annual rate of 4%; buy one share; and take a short position in a futures contract (committing to deliver one share in six months in exchange for $55). What would happen at that time? We would use the share we bought to deliver the one we're committed to deliver; get $55 for this delivery; and use $51 (= $50·$e^{0.04·0.5}$) to pay back the loan. That would leave us with a *certain* profit of $4.

What if the futures traded at $45 instead? Well, in this case we could sell one share short and receive $50; invest that at the annual rate of 4% during six months; and take a long position in a futures contract (to take delivery of one share in six months in exchange for $45). What would happen at that time? We would get $51 (= $50·$e^{0.04·0.5}$) from our six-month investment at 4%; take delivery of the share and pay $45 for it; and use that share to cover the short position. That would leave us with a *certain* profit of $6.

Needless to say, we're not the only clever ones that can figure this out. The market is populated by thousands of clever investors looking for the tiniest of these opportunities, and therefore these arbitrage profits are not easy to find. That's why the futures contract must be priced at $51. Because if it's not, arbitrageurs would jump in, trade seeking to obtain arbitrage profits, and the resulting change in prices would quickly eliminate the mispricing.

What would be different if the stock paid dividends? Simply that this dividend would be a benefit of holding the stock, and we can then think of the stock's dividend yield as the convenience yield in expression (25.1). Therefore, in the case of a dividend-paying stock, we have a cost of carry equal to the financing cost and a convenience yield equal to the stock's dividend yield. If the stock we've been discussing in this section had an annual (continuously compounded) dividend yield of 2%, then a futures contract to buy one share in six months should be valued at

$$F = \$50 \cdot e^{(0.04-0.02)\cdot0.5} = \$50.5$$

Finally, what about futures on consumption assets such as corn, coffee, or oil? Two main differences arise. First, besides financing costs, there would also be costs associated with storing and transporting the asset; and, if there is a risk that the asset can be damaged or spoiled, insurance costs would also add to the cost of carry. Second, for the reasons discussed above, all consumption assets have a positive convenience yield; that is, a benefit derived from having the physical asset readily available. In short, then, when valuing a futures contract on a consumption asset, we must take into account a cost of carry that is the sum of financing, storage, transportation, and insurance costs, as well as a positive convenience yield.

Hedging with futures

We have discussed the fact that many participants in futures and forwards markets are hedgers who seek protection from changes in the price of an asset. We have also discussed long hedges, which involve buying a futures contract seeking protection against price increases, and short hedges, which involve selling a futures contract seeking protection against price decreases. Positions that enable a hedger to eliminate the risk associated with price changes are called *perfect hedges* and are rare in practice.

Hedges can be static or dynamic. A *static hedge* is a position that is taken and left unchanged until the end of the position's life. A *dynamic hedge*, in turn, is a position that is taken and subsequently monitored and adjusted as frequently as necessary. The discussion below involves a static hedge. To simplify, we'll ignore the daily settlement of futures contracts and treat them as forwards contracts; the basic points to be made remain the same and are more easily conveyed this way.

Let's see how futures on the Dow can be used to hedge the risk of a portfolio. Let's assume we have a $2 million equity portfolio and we want to protect it for the next three months. Let's also assume that the (continuously compounded) annual risk-free rate is 4%; that the beta of our portfolio with respect to the Dow is 1; that the Dow has a (continuously compounded) annual dividend yield of 2%; and that it is now trading at 10,000.

Let's consider first what would happen to the unhedged portfolio if three months down the road the Dow closes down 5% at 9,500. Because the annual dividend yield of this index is 2%, the three-month dividend yield of 0.5% mitigates the loss and leaves it at 4.5%. And because our portfolio has a beta of 1 with respect to the Dow, it would also lose 4.5%, and end up with $1,910,000, for a loss of $90,000. Using the same reasoning, we can easily determine that if, three months down the road, the Dow closes up 5% at 10,500, then our portfolio will end up with $2,110,000 (up 5.5%), for a gain of $110,000.

How can we use futures contracts on the Dow to reduce (and at the limit, eliminate) the variability in the value of our portfolio? Note that because we have a long position in the equity portfolio, our hedge involves taking a *short* position on Dow futures. So the first thing we need to determine is how many contracts we need to sell. That's easy. Because each futures contract on the Dow trades at 10 times the value of the index, and the index is trading at 10,000, each contract is worth $100,000. And because we need to hedge a $2 million portfolio, then we need to sell 20 contracts.

What is the fair value of a three-month futures contract on the Dow? Using expression (25.1) we can determine that $F = \$10,000 \cdot e^{(0.04-0.02) \cdot 0.25} = \$10,050.1$, which means that three months down the road we'll receive $100,501.3 (= 10·$10,050.1) for each of the 20 contracts we sell today.

What if the Dow closes at 9,500 then? Well, we know that in this case we'll suffer a loss of $90,000 in our portfolio. But, at the same time, we'll gain $110,025.0 from our short position in Dow futures. This is calculated as the difference between the price at which we'll deliver each contract in three months ($100,501.3) and the actual value of each contract at the time ($95,000), multiplied by the number of contracts we sold (20); that is, ($100,501.3–$95,000)·(20). If we combine our loss on the portfolio with our gain in the Dow futures, then, we obtain a total gain of $20,025.

Before we think a bit about this, let's consider what happens if the Dow closes at 10,500 instead. We know that in this case our portfolio will end up with a gain of $110,000. But we'll lose on the futures this time. Note that we'll receive $100,501.3 per contract delivered when the actual value of each contract will be $105,000. Therefore, we'll lose $4,498.7 per contract, for a total loss of $89,975. If we now combine our gain on the portfolio with our loss in Dow futures, we obtain a total gain of ... $20,025!

Magic? Not really; it's called *hedging*. This is, in fact, what hedging is all about. We built a portfolio consisting of a long position in equities and a short position in futures, and the value of this portfolio is independent of the performance of the market or that of the stocks in the portfolio. This is exactly what hedgers seek to obtain by participating in the futures market. And obviously they can protect not only the value of equity portfolios, but also the value of wheat, coffee, gold, oil, or currencies, to name a few possibilities.

Importantly, note that the $20,025 we get regardless of the closing value of the Dow in three months is almost exactly what we would obtain by depositing $2 million (the value of our equity portfolio) at the (continuously compounded) risk-free rate of 4% during three months ($20,100.3). The only reason why these two numbers are not equal to each other is because, just to simplify the discussion, we've been a little sloppy when dealing with compounding. Had that not been the case, the total gain in our portfolio of equities and forward contracts would have been *exactly* equal to the gain from investing the value of our equity portfolio safely at the risk-free rate. In other words, because the hedge eliminated all risk, we can gain no more than the risk-free rate.

Note, also, that we assumed that the beta of our portfolio with respect to the Dow is 1. What if this beta is anything but 1? In that case, the return on our portfolio would be calculated as $R_p = R_f + (R_M - R_f) \cdot \beta$, where R_p, R_f and R_M denote the returns of our portfolio, the risk-free rate (for the appropriate length of time, which is three months in our case), and the returns of the market (the Dow in our case). In addition, the number of contracts to trade (N) would be given by $N = \beta \cdot (V_p/V_F)$, where V_p and V_F denote the value of our portfolio and the value of the stocks underlying one contract (ten times the value of the Dow in our case).

Table 25.1 displays the relevant numbers of the case we have discussed (in the second and third columns), as well as a similar case (in the fourth and fifth columns) for a portfolio of the same value ($2 million) but with a beta of 1.5 with respect to the Dow. In the first column, 0 denotes the present time and 1 denotes the future time (three months down the road in our example).

table 25.1

	$\beta = 1$		$\beta = 1.5$	
S (0)	$10,000.0	$10,000.0	$10,000.0	$10,000.0
c	4.0%	4.0%	4.0%	4.0%
y	2.0%	2.0%	2.0%	2.0%
T	0.25	0.25	0.25	0.25
F (0)	$10,050.1	$10,050.1	$10,050.1	$10,050.1
Dow (0)	10,000	10,000	10,000	10,000
Dow (1)	9,500	10,500	9,500	10,500
R_M	−4.5%	5.5%	−4.5%	5.5%
Beta	1.0	1.0	1.5	1.5
Portfolio (0)	$2,000,000	$2,000,000	$2,000,000	$2,000,000
R_p	−4.5%	5.5%	−7.3%	7.8%
Portfolio (1)	$1,910,000.0	$2,110,000.0	$1,855,000.0	$2,155,000.0
Gain/loss	−$90,000.0	$110,000.0	−$145,000.0	$155,000.0
F (0)	$10,050.1	$10,050.1	$10,050.1	$10,050.1
F (1) = S (1)	$9,500	$10,500	$9,500	$10,500
N	20	20	30	30
Gain/loss	$110,025.0	−$89,975.0	$165,037.6	−$134,962.4
Total gain/loss	$20,025.0	$20,025.0	$20,037.6	$20,037.6

Why hedging?

Perhaps you're wondering why any investor would bother to hedge a portfolio if, at the end of the day, he would fare just as well by selling the portfolio and investing the money safely at the risk-free rate. There are at least two reasons for doing so.

First, if an investor is confident in his portfolio but less so in the expected performance of the market, hedging would enable him to remove the risk arising from market swings and still remain exposed to the risk of the portfolio relative to the market. Second, if an investor is confident in his portfolio as a long-term investment but for some reason needs to protect it in the short term, hedging is quite likely to be better than selling the portfolio, investing its proceeds temporarily at the risk-free rate, and eventually buying back the portfolio, which would involve incurring transaction (and possibly tax) costs.

Second, recall that participants in futures markets hedge all sorts of assets, not just financial portfolios. Airlines hedge against increasing oil prices, farmers against falling corn prices, and exporters against falling local currencies, to name just a few examples. Hedging, then, enables them to focus on their main business and avoid surprises from variables they can hardly control or predict.

The big picture

Futures and forwards may not be for the faint of heart. Although the essentials of these markets are not difficult to understand, hedging and speculating can be extremely complex. For this reason it should come as no surprise that the derivatives departments of investment banks are populated by PhDs in physics and mathematics rather than by MBAs! And yet, these markets play an essential role: They enable companies to focus on their core business without being distracted by the swings of variables they do not control.

Futures and forwards are similar in some ways and different in others. Essentially, these markets enable hedgers to lock prices at which assets can be delivered in the future, enabling them to reduce uncertainty. And hedgers can do this only because speculators provide liquidity by exposing themselves to the risk of price fluctuations with the hope of making a short-term profit. This, in a nutshell, is what futures and forward markets are all about.

26

Currencies

You're familiar with interest rates and inflation; you're likely to be familiar with traveling, exchanging money, and exchange rates; and perhaps you're somewhat less familiar with forward contracts (which are discussed in the previous chapter). In this chapter we'll bring all these variables together and relate them to each other. And, when so doing, perhaps we'll understand a bit better their influence on the international flows of capital, a topic of daily coverage in financial newspapers.

A word of caution

The *international parity conditions* are a set of equilibrium relationships involving exchange rates, forward exchange rates, interest rates, and inflation rates that make up the backbone of international finance. These parity conditions hold under some assumptions, such as no transactions costs; no barriers to trade (such as tariffs or quotas); and competitive markets. Not much like the world we know, to be sure.

We don't have to take these or any other assumptions at face value; they are merely useful devices to focus on the relevant insights provided by the parity conditions. And when the discussion grants it, we'll consider the impact of relaxing some of these assumptions. As usual, a solid theory plus a fair bit of common sense go a long way toward understanding reality.

The exchange rate

Most people like to travel, particularly when it's cheaper abroad than at home. And what determines whether nice hotels, good meals, and rental cars are cheaper at home or abroad? Many factors, including one that plays a central role in the discussion of this chapter: The exchange rate between currencies.

However familiar you might be with traveling, exchanging money, and exchange rates, before we go any further let's formally define this last concept. And we'll do it mostly for one reason: The exchange rate can be defined in two ways, and *both* of them are frequently used. This often is, needless to say, a source of confusion.

The exchange rate, which is simply the price of one currency in terms of another, can be defined as units of domestic currency per unit of foreign currency, or as units of foreign currency per unit of domestic currency. Throughout our discussion we'll use the former and therefore define the **nominal exchange rate (*E*)** as

$$E = \frac{\text{Units of domestic currency}}{1 \text{ unit of foreign currency}} \tag{26.1}$$

Given this definition, when the euro was launched in 1999, Americans would have said that the exchange rate was (roughly) 1.15, meaning that they needed $115 to buy €100. Europeans, in turn, would have said that the exchange rate was (roughly) 0.87, meaning that for each €87 they took out of their pockets they could buy $100.

The rate at which currencies can be exchanged changes over time. A *depreciation* of the local currency consists of a decrease in its purchasing power, which implies that more local currency is needed to buy a given amount of foreign currency. An *appreciation* of the local currency, in turn, consists of an increase in its purchasing power, which means that less local currency is needed to buy a given amount of foreign currency.

Given the way we have defined the exchange rate, then, a depreciation consists of an *increase* in the exchange rate, and an appreciation of a *decrease* in the exchange rate. To illustrate, between the launch of the euro at the beginning of 1999 and the summer of 2001, the dollar appreciated with respect to the euro, going from 1.15 in January 1999, to 0.85 in July 2001. Between that time and the end of 2003, however, the dollar depreciated with respect to the euro, going from 0.85 in July 2001, to 1.20 in December 2003. Table 26.1 illustrates these changes in the dollar/euro parity during the first five years of the euro's life, all viewed from the perspective of Americans.

Table 26.1

Jan 1999		Jul 2001		Dec 2003
	Revaluation		Devaluation	
$E = \dfrac{\$1.15}{€1}$	$\xrightarrow{\hspace{2cm}}$	$E = \dfrac{\$0.85}{€1}$	$\xrightarrow{\hspace{2cm}}$	$E = \dfrac{\$1.20}{€1}$

Depreciations and appreciations of a currency affect its purchasing power. Even if the price of a sporty Mercedes had remained unchanged at, say, €50,000, Americans buying this car at the end of 2003 would have spent 41% more than those who bought it in the summer of 2001 ($60,000 compared with $42,500). Conversely, even if the daily rates of a nice hotel in Paris had remained unchanged at, say, €200, Americans traveling to Europe in the summer of 2001 would have spent 26% less than those traveling at the beginning of 1999 ($170 compared with $230).

Therefore, European goods become cheaper for Americans when the dollar appreciates, and more expensive when the dollar depreciates. In contrast, US goods become cheaper for Europeans when the dollar depreciates, and more expensive when the dollar appreciates.

The law of one price

No conscientious shopper would pay more for an item at one store if he could buy the same item at a cheaper price at another store. Unless, of course, it's too much trouble to get the item from the latter. If we replace the word 'store' by 'country' we get the law of one price. This relationship states that if an item sold in two countries is expressed in a common currency, its price should be the same.

Formally, the **law of one price (LOP)** states that

$$p_D = E \cdot p_F \qquad (26.2)$$

where p_D and p_F denote the domestic and the foreign price of an item. From this point on we'll assume that the US is home and Europe is abroad, and, therefore, that domestic and foreign prices refer to American and European prices.

Consider a laptop that costs $1,000 in the US and €1,100 in Europe, and assume that the exchange rate is 0.909 dollars per euro. Americans could buy the laptop in the US for $1,000, or take the same $1,000, exchange them for €1,100, and buy the laptop in Europe. Similarly, Europeans could buy the laptop in Europe for €1,100, or take the same €1,100, exchange them for $1,000, and buy the laptop in the US. If the law of one price holds, then, Americans and Europeans are indifferent between buying the laptop at home or abroad.

What would happen if the laptop were priced at $1,000 in the US and at €1,300 in Europe? Simply that Europeans would be better off by exchanging €1,100 for $1,000 and buying the laptop in the US, thus saving €200. This would put upward pressure on the price of the laptop in the US, or downward pressure on the price of the laptop in Europe, or downward pressure in the exchange rate. (As Europeans demand more dollars to buy laptops in the US, the dollar will strengthen with respect to the euro and E will fall.) So, if $p_D < E \cdot p_F$, then p_D must rise, or p_F must fall, or E must fall until the equality in (26.2) is restored.

What would happen, in turn, if the laptop were priced at $1,200 in the US and at €1,100 in Europe? In this case Americans would be better off by exchanging $1,000 for €1,100 and buying the laptop in Europe, thus saving $200. This would put upward pressure on the price of the laptop in Europe, or downward pressure on the price of the laptop in the US, or upward pressure in the exchange rate. (As Americans demand more euros to buy laptops in Europe, the euro will strengthen with respect to the dollar and E will rise.) So, if $p_D > E \cdot p_F$, then p_D must fall, or p_F must rise, or E must rise until the equality in (26.2) is restored.

As it has surely crossed your mind, in reality things don't work out that way. We know that laptops are usually cheaper in the US than in Europe. And here is, precisely, where some of those things we assumed away come in: For the law of one price to hold, transaction costs have to be zero, or at least fairly low. Because if that's not the case, the shipping costs (and perhaps a tax) may offset the price differential and therefore discourage Europeans from buying laptops at a US store. To make matters worse, even in the presence of low shipping costs, Europeans trying to buy a laptop online from a US store are likely to get a little message that, paraphrasing, may say something like, "Sorry, we don't ship this stuff to Europe, but please do buy from our site there." (Talk about price discrimination!)

There may be other considerations that lead Europeans to buy at home if the price differential is not too large. Some consumers find that buying a laptop at home has the advantage that all programs come in the local language, and the keyboard is set up according to local custom. In other words, the law of one price holds when transaction costs are low enough *and* the items are identical (or very similar). Besides, note that although laptops can be bought at home or abroad, lunch at noon, heating for the bedroom, and the monthly fee for the gym are bought and consumed at home; that is, the law of one price applies only to *tradable* goods and services.

In short, then, although the law of one price may not be a very accurate description of relative prices across countries, it is still a useful tool to think about price differentials across countries. And, as we discuss below, in the *long* run and in terms of *changes* in prices and exchange rates, it actually does hold quite well empirically.

Purchasing power parity

When the law of one price is applied to aggregate price indices rather than to the price of an individual item, it receives the name of *absolute purchasing power parity*. This is not, however, the PPP that you may have heard much about. Before we get to that one, let's formally define **absolute purchasing power parity** as

$$P_D = E \cdot P_F \tag{26.3}$$

where P_D and P_F denote the domestic and foreign aggregate price indices. You may want to think of them as consumer price indices, which are used to measure inflation rates.

As you can see from a comparison between expressions (26.2) and (26.3), the only difference between the law of one price and absolute purchasing power parity is that the former refers to the price of an individual item and the latter to the aggregate price of a basket of goods and services. Thus, absolute purchasing power parity states that when the same basket of goods and services in two different countries is expressed in a common currency its price should be the same. Or, put differently, one unit of a currency should have the same purchasing power across countries; one dollar, for example, should buy the same goods in the US than abroad.

Now for the PPP you probably heard about. Let's start with a formal definition. **Purchasing power parity (PPP)** is given by

$$\frac{E_1 - E_0}{E_0} = \frac{1 + \pi_D}{1 + \pi_F} - 1 \approx \pi_D - \pi_F \tag{26.4}$$

where E_0 and E_1 denote the exchange rate at the beginning and the end of a period, and π_D and π_F the domestic and foreign rates of inflation during the same period. The term after the 'approximately equal' sign ($\approx$) is an approximation that works well when the magnitudes involved are small. (We'll find similar approximations in this chapter and you should interpret them all as just mentioned.)

PPP can be thought of as the dynamic version of absolute PPP. It states that when prices in one country increase at a faster rate than prices in another country, the currency of the country with higher inflation must depreciate with respect to the currency of the country with lower inflation just enough to offset the inflation differential.

Or think about it this way. If inflation in the US increases relative to that in Europe, American goods become relatively more expensive to Europeans; therefore, the dollar gets cheaper to offset the higher prices and make American goods just as desirable to Europeans as they were before. At the same time, European goods become relatively cheaper to Americans, but the more expensive euro just offsets the decrease in relative prices; therefore, European goods remain just as desirable to Americans as they were before.

To clarify these ideas, let's consider an example. Suppose we start from an absolute PPP equilibrium in which the dollar/euro exchange rate is 1.2, and over the course of one year prices increase by 10% in the US and by 5% in Europe. According to expression (26.4), the absolute PPP equilibrium would be restored when the dollar depreciates 1.10/1.05–1 = 4.76% to 1.257. Let's make sure we understand why this must be the case.

Consider the situation from the point of view of Americans first. Prices in the US have increased by 10%. Has it become cheaper for Americans to shop in Europe, given that European prices have increased by only 5%? Not really. To shop in Europe, Americans need to exchange dollars for euros and euros have become 4.76% more expensive. Then, for Americans, the cost of shopping in Europe has increased by a factor of (1.05)(1.0476)–1 = 10.0%. In other words, Americans remain indifferent between shopping in the US or in Europe.

Consider now the situation from the point of view of Europeans. Prices in the US have increased by 10%. At the same time, the euro/dollar exchange rate went from 0.833 (=1/1.2) to 0.795 (=1/1.257), thus decreasing by 4.55%. Then, for Europeans, the cost of shopping in the US has increased by (1.10) (1–0.0455)–1 = 5.0%. Therefore, Europeans remain indifferent between shopping in Europe or in the US.

Note that expression (26.4) can be used to calculate the *level* of the exchange rate consistent with PPP after an inflation differential distorts relative prices. By manipulating this expression we get

$$E_1 = E_0 \cdot \left(\frac{1 + \pi_D}{1 + \pi_F} \right) \tag{26.5}$$

which is usually referred to as the *PPP exchange rate*. Applying (26.5) to the example we just discussed, we'd get that the PPP dollar/euro exchange rate is equal to $E_1 = (1.2)(1.10/1.05) = 1.257$, which is the same as the number we calculated before.

By the way, what we've just done is very similar to what *The Economist* does with its 'Big Mac index,' which is, precisely, PPP at work. As you may know, *The Economist* compares the prices of Big Macs in different countries, and assuming that they should cost the same everywhere, calculates the implied equilibrium (PPP) exchange rates; it then compares those exchange rates with current exchange rates to predict the direction in which the parities will move. To illustrate, say a Big Mac costs €3 in Europe and $3 in the US. Then, the implied PPP rate is $3/€3 = 1.0. So, if the actual exchange rate is $1.25 per €1, then the dollar would be expected to appreciate by 20% (1.0/1.25–1 = –20%) with respect to the euro. Or, similarly, since the actual exchange rate is €0.80 per $1, then the euro would be expected to depreciate 25% (1.0/0.80–1 = 25%) with respect to the dollar.

As for empirical evidence, the consensus on PPP seems to be the following. Although short-term inflation differentials do not seem to explain variations in exchange rates well, in the long term the opposite is the case; that is, long-term variations in exchange rates are largely explained by inflation differentials. Or, put differently, in the long term, exchange rates do tend to revert to the levels predicted by PPP.

The Fisher effect

Let's say we deposit $100 in the bank at the annual rate of 4%. One year down the road we withdraw $104. Are we better off or worse off? It depends. Remember that the ultimate reason for saving is to increase future *consumption*. And whether $104 in one year enables us to consume more or less than $100 today depends on the rate of inflation. If during the year we kept our money in the bank at 4% prices increased by 2%, our purchasing power would have increased; if prices increased by 6% instead, our purchasing power would have decreased.

Let's put it another way: What investors really care about is the rate at which they can exchange current consumption for future consumption, which is given by the *real* interest rate. The rate at which current dollars can be exchanged for future dollars, in turn, is given by the *nominal* interest rate. More formally, the **nominal interest rate (*I*)** is given by

$$I = (1+i) \cdot (1+\pi) - 1 \approx i + \pi \tag{26.6}$$

and, therefore, the **real interest rate (*i*)** is given by

$$i = \frac{1+I}{1+\pi} - 1 \approx I - \pi \tag{26.7}$$

where, as before, π denotes the rate of inflation. Expression (26.6) is often referred to as the **Fisher effect (FE)**.

Given that investors care about their purchasing power, which depends on the real return they obtain from their investments, expression (26.6) states that if inflationary expectations increase, so will the demand for a nominal return to keep purchasing power constant. Expression (26.7), in turn, says that purchasing power depends on the difference between the nominal interest rate and the rate of inflation; if $I > \pi$, purchasing power increases, and if $I < \pi$, purchasing power decreases.

Ultimately, what investors compare are real returns, and they are willing to jump from country to country to obtain the highest possible. As a result, real interest rates tend to the same level (and, in equilibrium, are equalized) across all countries.

The international Fisher effect

The only way to get to the equilibrium just described is by moving money around from country to country until differences in real interest rates are eliminated. But we cannot take our money from one country and invest it in another without first exchanging one currency for another, which will alter exchange rates.

That brings us to the **international Fisher effect (IFE)**

$$\frac{E_1 - E_0}{E_0} = \frac{1 + I_D}{1 + I_F} - 1 \approx I_D - I_F \tag{26.8}$$

where I_D and I_F denote the domestic and foreign nominal interest rates. In words, the international Fisher effect states that when nominal interest rates are higher in one country than in another, the currency of the country with the higher interest rate must depreciate with respect to the currency of the country with the lower interest rate. Or, put differently, differences in nominal interest rates are offset by changes in the exchange rate. Let's see why this must be the case.

Let's assume that nominal (annual) interest rates are 13% in the US and 8% in Europe, and that the dollar/euro exchange rate is 1.2. According to expression (26.8), then, the dollar must depreciate with respect to the euro by 1.13/1.08–1 = 4.63% to 1.256. If that's the case, Americans could invest $100 in the US at the annual rate of 13% and get $113 one year down the road. Alternatively, they could exchange $100 for €83.3 (at the current exchange rate of 1.2); invest them in Europe at the annual rate of 8%; get €90 in one year; convert them back into dollars at the rate of 1.256 dollars per euro; and end up with the exact same $113. In other words, Americans are indifferent between investing in the US or in Europe.

What about Europeans? Well, they could invest €100 in Europe at the annual rate of 8% and get €108 one year down the road. Alternatively, they could exchange €100 for $120 (at the current rate of 1.2 dollars per euro); invest them for a year at 13% in the US; get $135.6 in one year; convert them back to euros at the rate of 0.796 euros per dollar (=1/1.256); and end up with the exact same €108. In other words, Europeans are indifferent between investing in Europe or in the US.

To formalize this example, note that by manipulating expression (26.8) we get

$$(1 + I_D) = \left(\frac{E_1}{E_0}\right) \cdot (1 + I_F) \tag{26.9}$$

In words, the return from investing at home is equal to the return from investing abroad, the latter being the compound return of investing in a foreign currency and at a foreign interest rate. And because investing at home and abroad yield the same return, the equilibrium is such that there is no incentive to keep moving money around.

Note, also, that if we combine expressions (26.4) and (26.8) we get

$$\frac{1 + I_D}{1 + I_F} = \frac{1 + \pi_D}{1 + \pi_F} \approx I_D - I_F \approx \pi_D - \pi_F \tag{26.10}$$

which basically says that if one country has a rate of inflation higher than another, it must also offer a higher interest rate to compensate investors for the faster loss of purchasing power. In equilibrium, then, differences in inflation are fully compensated by differences in interest rates.

Finally, reshuffling terms in expression (26.10) gives

$$\frac{1 + I_D}{1 + \pi_D} = \frac{1 + I_F}{1 + \pi_F} \approx i_D \approx i_F \tag{26.11}$$

where i_D and i_F denote the domestic and foreign real interest rate, which formalizes a result we informally discussed before; that is, real interest rates tend to the same level (and, in equilibrium, are equalized) across all countries.

Interest rate parity and forward parity

As discussed in the previous chapter, a forward is a contract that specifies an agreement to buy or sell a specified quantity of an asset, at a specified price, at a specified time in the future. For our current purposes, the relevant forward contract consists of an agreement to exchange a given amount of one currency for another, at a given exchange rate, at a given time in the future.

The **interest rate parity (IRP)** relationship states that

$$\frac{F - E_0}{E_0} = \frac{1 + I_D}{1 + I_F} - 1 \approx I_D - I_F \tag{26.12}$$

where F is the forward exchange rate. Note that by manipulating expression (26.12) we get

$$F = E_0 \cdot \frac{1 + I_D}{1 + I_F} \tag{26.13}$$

In words, the forward exchange rate is the current exchange rate adjusted by the difference in interest rates. Or, put differently, the currency of a country with higher interest rates is expected to depreciate with respect to the currency of a country with lower interest rates. Or, put yet another way, interest rate differentials are fully offset by changes in exchange rates.

The IRP relationship is an equilibrium condition in the sense that, if it doesn't hold, then arbitrage opportunities exist. To see this, let's go back to the example we've been discussing in which nominal (annual) interest rates in the US and Europe are 13% and 8%, and the dollar/euro exchange rate is 1.2. According to (26.13), then, the one-year forward rate should be 1.256; that is, the dollar is expected to depreciate by 4.63% (= 1.256/1.2–1) with respect to the euro. Let's consider first what would happen if the forward rate were lower than indicated by IRP; let's assume $F = 1.2$.

In this case, clever as we are, we could borrow €100 at the annual rate of 8%; turn them into $120 and lend them at 13%; and buy a forward to get €108 in one year in exchange for $129.6 (=€108 · 1.2). One year down the road we'd get $135.6 from our investment at 13%; use $129.6 to buy €108 under the forward contract; pay off the loan in euros (€108); and obtain a *riskless* profit of $6. Not bad, huh? How about doing that with €100 *million*?!

Let's consider now a forward rate higher than indicated by IRP; let's assume $F = 1.4$. In this case, we could borrow $100 at 13%; turn them into €83.3 and lend them at 8%; and buy a forward to get $113 in one year in exchange for €80.7 (= $113/1.4). One year down the road we'd get €90 from our investment at 8%; use €80.7 to buy $113 under the forward contract; pay off the loan in dollars ($113); and obtain a *riskless* profit of €9.3. And that's another round of trades we'd rather make with $100 million!

You can see now why the futures *must* be priced at 1.256: Any other value will give us the opportunity to obtain a riskless profit. Unfortunately, as we trade to exploit this opportunity, we'll push all the variables involved just enough to restore the equilibrium in (26.13) and the arbitrage opportunity will disappear.

Finally, the **forward parity (FP)** is given by

$$F = E_1^e \qquad\qquad (26.14)$$

where E_1^e denotes the expected exchange rate at the end of a period. This parity condition simply states that forward rates are unbiased predictors of future exchange rates. Which is not to say, that they are perfect (or even good) predictors. It simply says that, on average, forward rates do not systematically overestimate or underestimate future spot rates.

The big picture

The international parity conditions are a set of equilibrium relationships widely used to understand the linkages among interest rates, inflation rates, exchange rates, and forward exchange rates. We have already discussed each relationship separately; Figure 26.1 shows how they relate to each other.

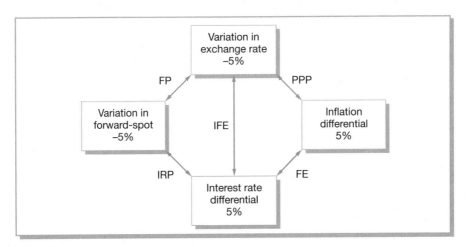

figure 26.1 International parity conditions

Suppose that next year inflation in the US is expected to be 5% higher than in Europe. Then, according to PPP, the dollar should depreciate by roughly 5% against the euro; and according to the Fisher effect (FE) nominal interest rates in the US should be 5% higher than in Europe. According to interest rate parity (IRP), then, the one-year forward dollar/euro exchange rate should be 5% higher than the dollar/euro spot rate, implying a 5% depreciation of the dollar against the euro; and given the forward parity (FP), this 5% depreciation gives an unbiased prediction of the dollar/euro spot rate one year down the road. Finally, the international Fisher effect (IFE) reaffirms that, with a 5% interest rate differential, the dollar is expected to depreciate 5% against the euro.

part

4

Statistical background

27

Stats I: Summary statistics

- Random variables

- Summarizing information

- The mean

- The median

- The mode

- The variance

- The standard deviation

- The covariance

- The correlation coefficient

- The big picture

- Excel section

know, you don't like stats. You are also likely to have had your share of it at school but barely remember the stuff. Well, the goal of this chapter is to get you back up to speed. Don't worry, we'll not go into any details, it will all be basic stuff. But a warning first: Like any other tools in statistics or finance, the ones discussed in this chapter should be used with caution. Although many decisions should never be made without them, they will hardly ever give us, by themselves, all the relevant information we need to make a decision.

Random variables

Finance and uncertainty are two concepts inevitably linked to each other. Just about all the variables we deal with in finance are characterized by our imperfect knowledge about their future values. In fact, most of what we usually know about them is their historical behavior and whatever we can make out of it to estimate the likelihood of some scenarios that may interest us.

This is one way of saying that in finance we deal with **random variables**, which are variables that take values determined by the outcome of a random process. They can be *discrete* or *continuous*, the former indicating that the variable can take a finite (or a countably infinite) number of values, and the latter indicating that the variable can take an infinite (not countable) number of values.

Consider the roll of a dice, which can take only 6 values but we don't know beforehand which one will occur on any given roll. Or roulette, which can take 37 values (0 to 36) but again we don't know which one will occur before spinning the wheel. Or consider the temperature, which can take an infinite number of values. Or the returns of a stock, which again can take an infinite number of values with a minimum of –100%. All of these are random variables, the first two discrete and the last two continuous.

Note that the fact that the outcome of a process is uncertain doesn't mean that we're completely ignorant about it. When we roll a dice or spin a roulette we do know beforehand both the possible outcomes and their probabilities (1/6 for each of the possible outcomes in a dice and 1/37 for each of the possible outcomes in a roulette). And from historical data and past experience we know that it is quite unlikely, though not impossible, for a summer day to be 10°F, or for a stock to return 700% in any given year.

Summarizing information

There's little doubt that staring at, for example, ten years of monthly returns will help us little in characterizing the behavior of any asset. The same would happen, in general, if we wanted to assess whether two assets were closely related or not. That's where the magnitudes we discuss in this chapter come in: They help us summarize information in a single number.

Before we jump into numbers and statistics, though, a quick comment on two related concepts. A **population** is the *complete* set of observations on any variable of our interest; a **sample**, on the other hand, is a *subset* of the population. To illustrate, if we are interested in the performance of every mutual fund manager in New York for 2009, and collect information on each and every one of them, we will have obtained the population. If, alternatively, we choose to collect information on a subset of only a hundred of them, we will have obtained a sample.

The main reason for working with a sample is obvious: It's a lot less costly to obtain a sample than the whole population. Having said that, the only purpose of obtaining a sample is to make inferences about what is really going on in the population. In other words, a sample is just a convenient tool that is used for the purpose of learning something about the population.

table 27.1

Year	Dow (%)	Footsie (%)
2000	−4.8	−8.2
2001	−5.4	−14.1
2002	−15.0	−22.2
2003	28.3	17.9
2004	5.3	11.2
2005	1.7	20.8
2006	19.0	14.4
2007	8.9	7.4
2008	−31.9	−28.3
2009	22.7	27.3

Let's start by taking a look at the numbers in Table 27.1, which contains the returns of the Dow and the Footsie (the familiar names of the Dow Jones Industrials Average and the FTSE-100, two indices often used to describe the behavior of the American and UK stock markets) between 2000 and 2009. Now, if we wanted to characterize the behavior of these markets, or explore how they behave relative to each other, staring at these numbers would help little; calculating some statistics, however, would.

The mean

The arithmetic mean, often referred to simply as the mean, is perhaps the most widely used measure of central tendency. You do remember this one, of course. We calculate averages all the time, and at the end of the day the mean is just that, an average. More formally, the **arithmetic mean (AM)**, or simply the mean, is the sum of all the relevant observations, divided by the number of observations

$$AM = (1/T) \cdot \sum_{t=1}^{T} R_t \tag{27.1}$$

where R_t represents returns in period t, and T the number of observations. Given this definition, the mean annual return of the Dow over the 2000–09 period is

$$(-4.8\% - 5.4\% + \dots - 31.9\% + 22.7\%)/10 = 2.9\%$$

In terms of interpretation, the mean is just an average and there is not much more to it than that. If you look at the performance of the Dow in Table 27.1 you'll see that some returns were high, some low, some positive, some negative, and on average they happened to be 2.9%. End of the story.

Remember, however, that there is an important distinction, very relevant in finance, between the arithmetic mean and the geometric mean; both means and the relationship between them are discussed in detail in Chapter 2. What we are calling simply the mean in this chapter is, as stated above, the *arithmetic* mean (hence the notation *AM*).

Easy as it may be to calculate and interpret, the mean has at least one problem: It may be markedly affected by extreme values, particularly when the number of observations is small. To illustrate, let's hypothetically assume that the return of the Dow in 2009 had been 300% (you wish!) instead of 22.7%. If we recalculated the mean, we'd find that it becomes 30.6%, substantially different from our previously calculated value of 2.9%. In other words, the introduction of an extreme value in our small sample causes our measure of central tendency to increase by more than ten times! Enter then our next statistic.

The median

The median is another measure of central tendency and its importance can be grasped with a simple example. Consider what would happen if Warren Buffett moved to a poor and small town. Clearly, the mean wealth of the town would increase (very!) substantially. This mean wealth, however, would give us now a very distorted picture (way too rosy) of the prosperity of the 'average' person in town. In cases like this it is, precisely, where our next statistic becomes very useful.

The best way to define the **median** is to understand the way we calculate it. First, arrange all the observations in increasing order; then, if the number of observations is odd, the median is the value in the middle; if the number of observations is even, the median is the average of the two values in the middle. To illustrate, if we arrange in increasing order the ten annual returns of the Dow between 2000 and 2009 we obtain

−31.9%, −15.0%, −5.4%, −4.8%, 1.7%, 5.3%, 8.9%, 19.0%, 22.7%, 28.3%

The median of these returns is 3.5% (the average of 1.7% and 5.3%), and it can easily be interpreted as the return such that half of the returns are higher, and half of the returns lower, than this value.

If we added to the 10 returns just considered the return of the Dow in 1999 (27.2%, not shown in Table 27.1), and reordered all 11 returns, we would obtain

   −31.9%, −15.0%, −5.4%, −4.8%, 1.7%, 5.3%, 8.9%, 19.0%, 22.7%, 27.2%, 28.3%

The median of these returns now would be 5.3% (the value in the middle), and again half of the returns would be above, and half below, this number.

To appreciate one of the main characteristics of the median as a measure of central tendency, let's go back to the 10 returns of the Dow between 2000 and 2009 and assume again that the return in 2009 had been 300% instead of 22.7%. As we saw above, that increases the mean from 2.9% to 30.6%. Does it change the median by much? Not at all. You can check for yourself (by reordering the returns and taking the average of the two in the middle) that the median remains at its previous value of 3.5%.

In short, then, in cases in which extreme observations affect the mean substantially and its figure would give us a distorted picture of the average we intend to interpret, the median is preferred over the mean. And if this is not yet entirely clear, just think whether the mean wealth or the median wealth would give us a better description of the prosperity of the 'average' person in the town we mentioned above after Warren Buffett moves in. Got it now?

The mode

Our final measure of central tendency is not widely used in finance. The **mode** is simply the value that occurs most frequently. If you look again at the returns of the Dow between 2000 and 2009, you'll see that no return appears more than once; hence, this series simply has no mode. However, suppose that we consider those same returns but in round numbers (without decimals). In that case, the returns become

   −5%, −5%, −15%, 28%, 5%, 2%, 19%, 9%, −32%, 23%

and the mode would be −5%, which is the round return that occurred most often (twice) during this period.

Although, again, this statistic is not widely used in finance, it may actually be useful in other areas. Consider a manufacturer of tennis shoes looking at the distribution of sizes of the shoes he sells. It would obviously be of interest to this entrepreneur to know what is the size in heaviest demand. That number, precisely, would be given by the mode.

The variance

Consider two hypothetical assets, both with the same mean return of 10%. Would you consider these two assets equally desirable if the observed returns of the first asset were tightly clustered between 9% and 11%, whereas those of the second asset were widely dispersed with values as low as –50% and as high as 70%? Of course not. In other words, *dispersion* around the mean matters, and that is precisely what the variance intends to capture.

Now, there's a problem with simply measuring the average distance to the mean. The problem is that if we take the average of the differences between each observation and the mean, above-average distances and below-average distances may cancel out. Consider, for example a mean return of 10% and two returns of –10% and 30%. If we subtract the mean from each return we get –20% in the first case and 20% in the second case; and if we take the average of these two differences we'll get 0%. However, it is obvious that this number would be misleading as a measure of dispersion.

A possible solution is to simply take the average of the *squared* differences between each return and the mean. And that is precisely what the **variance** (*V*) measures, the average of the squared deviations from the mean. More formally, the variance is given by

$$Var = (1/T) \cdot \sum_{t=1}^{T} (R_t - AM)^2 \tag{27.2}$$

Because the variance is an average of non-negative numbers, it is itself a non-negative number.

Calculating a variance is easy in Excel (as we'll see at the end of the chapter), but just to make sure you understand what's behind the number that Excel throws back at you, take a look at Table 27.2. The second column (*R*) shows the returns of the Dow taken from Table 27.1; the third column simply subtracts the mean from the returns in the second column; and the fourth column squares the numbers in the third column. If we take the average of the numbers in this last column, we will obtain the variance of returns (0.0300 in our case).

table 27.2

Year	R (%)	R–AM (%)	(R–AM)²
2000	−4.8	−7.7	0.0060
2001	−5.4	−8.3	0.0069
2002	−15.0	−17.9	0.0320
2003	28.3	25.4	0.0646
2004	5.3	2.4	0.0006
2005	1.7	−1.1	0.0001
2006	19.0	16.2	0.0262
2007	8.9	6.0	0.0036
2008	−31.9	−34.8	0.1211
2009	22.7	19.8	0.0393
Average	**2.9**		**0.0300**

Not too difficult, huh? Two brief comments, then. First, you may occasionally see an expression for the variance in which the sum of squared differences from the mean is divided by $T–1$ instead of by T. Obviously, this has little effect when the number of observations is large, as is usually the case in finance (though not in the tables of this book!). When the number of observations is small, however, dividing by either T or $T–1$ may lead to fairly different estimates. In these cases, it is convenient to calculate the variance with respect to $T–1$. (The reasons why this is the case are purely statistical and we won't bother with them here. Just hold on to the fact that in finance we usually deal with a large T and therefore whether we divide by T or $T–1$ is largely irrelevant.)

Second, as a measure of dispersion, the use of the variance is straightforward: The larger this number, the larger the dispersion around the mean. And yet, by looking at the last column of Table 27.2, you couldn't be blamed for wondering, 'And what is a percent squared?' That is, precisely, the problem with the variance as a measure of dispersion: It is not measured in the same units as those of the variable we consider. In the case we're discussing, the variance gives us a percent squared, which does not have a straightforward interpretation. But don't throw your arms up in despair just yet; we're only one step away from arriving at a more intuitive measure of dispersion.

The standard deviation

The **standard deviation (SD)** is simply the square root of the variance (that is, $SD = V^{1/2}$), and is measured in the same units as those of the variable we are considering. If we take the square root of 0.0300 we will obtain 0.1733 or, roughly, 17.3%. The standard deviation is also discussed in Chapter 3 and for our current purposes it suffices to highlight that, just as was the case with the variance, the higher the standard deviation, the higher the dispersion around the mean. And, obviously, because the standard deviation is the square root of a non-negative number, it is itself a non-negative number.

The covariance

So far we have focused on summary statistics for a single variable. And yet, in finance, we're often interested in the *relationship* between two variables. We could ask, for example, whether the Dow and the Footsie tend to move closely or loosely together, or whether they tend to move in the same or in opposite directions.

The **covariance** between two variables i and j (Cov_{ij}) measures the strength of the linear association between them. Formally, it is defined as

$$Cov_{ij} = (1/T) \cdot \sum_{t=1}^{T}(R_{it} - AM_i) \cdot (R_{jt} - AM_j) \qquad (27.3)$$

Just in case the notation is messy, let's think a bit about this expression. It basically says that, for each period t, we need to take the difference between the value of each variable and its respective mean (that is, $R_{it} - AM_i$ and $R_{jt} - AM_j$); multiply these two differences; do the same for all the periods; and take the average of these products. Too messy? OK, take a look at Table 27.3.

table 27.3

Year	Dow		Footsie		Product
	R (%)	R–AM (%)	R (%)	R–AM (%)	
2000	−4.8	−7.7	−8.2	−10.9	0.0084
2001	−5.4	−8.3	−14.1	−16.7	0.0139
2002	−15.0	−17.9	−22.2	−24.8	0.0443
2003	28.3	25.4	17.9	15.3	0.0388
2004	5.3	2.4	11.2	8.6	0.0021
2005	1.7	−1.1	20.8	18.2	−0.0021
2006	19.0	16.2	14.4	11.8	0.0191
2007	8.9	6.0	7.4	4.7	0.0029
2008	−31.9	−34.8	−28.3	−31.0	0.1077
2009	22.7	19.8	27.3	24.7	0.0489
Average	**2.9**		**2.6**		**0.0284**

The second and fourth columns of this exhibit show the returns of the Dow and the Footsie taken from Table 27.1. The third and fifth columns show these returns minus the mean of each respective market. And the last column is simply the product of the third and the fifth columns. The average of the numbers in this last column is, precisely, the covariance (0.0284).

What does this number mean? Here comes the problem. In fact, there are *two* problems with the covariance. The first is that it depends on the units in which the variables are measured. For example, suppose we wanted to assess the relationship between the height and weight of the students on a corporate finance course. If we took all the heights measured in feet and all the weights measured in pounds, and calculated the covariance, we would obtain a number. However, if we were to rescale all the weights from pounds to kilos, and recalculated the covariance between height and weight, we would obtain a different number. Of course, nothing fundamental has changed in the relationship (the students' heights and weights are still the same), and yet the covariance has changed. Not good.

The second problem is that the covariance is unbounded; that is, it has neither an upper limit nor a lower limit. This implies that the number we just calculated (0.0284) doesn't clearly tell us whether the relationship between the Dow and the Footsie is weak or strong. We can tell that these two markets are positively related (that is, when the Dow goes up the Footsie tends to go up, and vice versa), but not how strong this relationship is. Too discouraging? Don't worry, help is just around the corner. Enter our next (and final) statistic.

The correlation coefficient

Both problems of the covariance can be solved by a simple modification, which will lead us to the last summary statistic for this chapter. The **correlation coefficient** between two variables i and j ($Corr_{ij}$) is obtained by dividing the covariance between the two variables by the product of the standard deviation of each variable. Formally, the correlation coefficient is given by

$$Corr_{ij} = \frac{Cov_{ij}}{SD_i \cdot SD_j} \tag{27.4}$$

This coefficient is also discussed in Chapter 5 and for our current purposes it suffices to highlight a few things. First, it measures the strength of the *linear* relationship between two variables. In other words, two variables may be very closely related in a nonlinear way, and yet the correlation coefficient may indicate a very weak or nonexistent relationship. This is, again, because the correlation coefficient aims to assess linear relationships only.

Second, it can take a maximum value of 1 and a minimum value of –1. When the correlation is positive, the two variables tend to move in the same direction, whereas when it is negative they tend to move in opposite directions. A correlation of 1 indicates a perfect positive linear relationship between two variables, and a correlation of –1 indicates a perfect negative linear relationship between them. A correlation equal to 0, in turn, indicates no *linear* relationship between them.

Perhaps the most intuitive way of thinking about the extreme values of this coefficient is the following. When the correlation between two variables is either 1 or –1, by knowing the value of one variable, we could *perfectly* predict the value of the other. This is so because in these cases we could always write the linear equation that deterministically relates the two variables. The lower the absolute value of the correlation between two variables, however, the less precisely we'd be able to predict the value of one variable by knowing the value of the other. In the particular case when the correlation between two variables is 0, there is nothing we can say about the value of one variable by knowing the value of the other (as long as we try to relate the variables in a linear way).

Finally, going back to the Dow and the Footsie, what does the correlation coefficient tell us about them? According to expression (27.4), all we need to compute it is the covariance between these two markets (0.0284, calculated in the previous section), and the standard deviation of returns of both markets (17.3% for the Dow, which we calculated earlier, and 18.4% for the Footsie, as you could check for yourself). Then, the correlation between the American and the UK markets is equal to 0.0284/(0.173·0.184) = 0.89. In other words, there is a *very* close positive (linear) relationship between these two markets, which indicates that they tend to move very much in sync.

The big picture

In finance we deal with random variables and information about them must be summarized to be interpreted. Measures of central tendency such as the mean and the median are essential to financial analysis, and so are measures of dispersion such as the variance and the standard deviation. But we do not always analyze variables in isolation. Sometimes it's important to assess the sign and strength of the relationship between two variables, in which case the concepts of covariance and correlation become essential too.

All these statistics are extremely useful in making financial decisions. But again, they are tools, and for this reason they should be used with caution.

Excel section

Calculating the summary statistics discussed in this chapter in Excel is simple. Suppose you have a series of 10 returns of an asset in cells A1 through A10 and a series of 10 returns of another asset in cells B1 through B10. Then, choose any empty cell and do the following:

■ To calculate the *mean* of the first asset, type =average(A1:A10) and hit Enter.

■ To calculate the *median* of the first asset, type =median(A1:A10) and hit Enter.

■ To calculate the *mode* of the first asset, type =mode(A1:A10) and hit Enter.

■ To calculate the *variance* of the first asset, type =varp(A1:A10) and hit Enter.

■ To calculate the *standard deviation* of the first asset, type =stdevp(A1:A10) and hit Enter.

■ To calculate the *covariance* between the assets, type =covar(A1:A10, B1:B10) and hit Enter.

■ To calculate the *correlation* between the assets, type =correl(A1:A10, B1:B10) and hit Enter.

As mentioned above, it is not unusual to see an expression for the variance in which the sum of squared deviations from the mean is divided by $T-1$ instead of by T. Excel provides a way to estimate both the variance and the standard deviation in this way:

■ To calculate the *variance* of the first asset, type =var(A1:A10) and hit Enter.

■ To calculate the *standard deviation* of the first asset, type =stdev(A1:A10) and hit Enter.

28

Stats II: Normality

H ave you read the previous chapter? If yes, then you have refreshed your memory with some statistics that provide invaluable help when summarizing financial information. Which means you're ready for the second step of our crash course in stats. The heart of this chapter focuses on the widely-used (and abused) normal distribution and a very important (and potentially dangerous to your wallet!) application, the prediction of returns.

Frequencies and histograms

In the previous chapter we argued that not much can be learned by staring at 10 years of monthly returns of any given asset, and that it's far better to calculate some summary statistics. Having said that, a convenient grouping and subsequent visual display of the data may occasionally be helpful.

Suppose we have a sample and we want to learn some of its characteristics. Here's something we could do. First, we could group the data in convenient ranges; then we could count the number of observations in each range; and finally we could display this information in a bar graph. We'll get to the graph in a minute, but before that let's draw a distinction between the **absolute frequencies** (the number of observations in each range) and the **relative frequencies** (the number of observations in each range relative to the total number of observations in the sample).

To drive these points home, take a look at Table 28.1. The data in the table consist of the monthly returns of the MSCI All Country World Index (the most widely used benchmark for the world market equity portfolio) between January 1988 and December 2009. The first and fourth columns display the ranges in which the data are arranged; these ranges are usually chosen depending on the purpose at hand, and those in the table are convenient enough for our purpose. The second and fifth columns show the number of returns in each interval; that is, the absolute frequencies (AFs). Finally, the third and sixth columns show the number of returns in each interval relative to the total number of observations (264); that is, the relative frequencies (RFs).

table 28.1

Range (%)	AF	RF (%)	Range (%)	AF	RF (%)
(-∞, -10)	5	1.9	(0, 1)	24	9.1
(-10, -9)	3	1.1	(1, 2)	26	9.8
(-9, -8)	5	1.9	(2, 3)	32	12.1
(-8, -7)	1	0.4	(3, 4)	28	10.6
(-7, -6)	6	2.3	(4, 5)	17	6.4
(-6, -5)	5	1.9	(5, 6)	13	4.9
(-5, -4)	10	3.8	(6, 7)	8	3.0
(-4, -3)	8	3.0	(7, 8)	3	1.1
(-3, -2)	20	7.6	(8, 9)	4	1.5
(-2, -1)	20	7.6	(9, 10)	3	1.1
(-1, 0)	19	7.2	(10, ∞)	4	1.5

The symbol ∞ denotes infinity

A quick glance at the table shows, for example, that almost two-thirds of the returns (169, or 64%) fall in the interval between –3% and 4%. It also shows that, as the returns depart more and more from the mean (0.7%, not shown in the table), the number of returns in the intervals tends to decrease. High frequencies around the mean, and decreasing frequencies as returns depart more and more from the mean, are widely observed in reality, including in the returns of many financial assets.

A **histogram** is a graphical representation of ranges and (either absolute or relative) frequencies. An example is shown in Figure 28.1. This bar chart shows the ranges on the horizontal axis and the absolute frequencies on the vertical axis, both corresponding to the figures in Table 28.1.

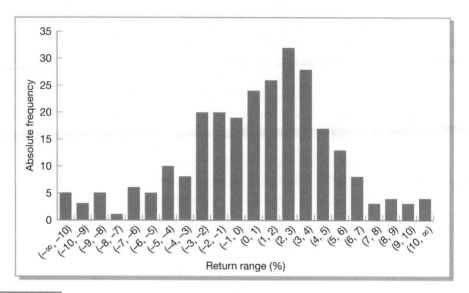

figure 28.1   Histogram: Monthly returns for the MSCI All Country World Index

Although histograms are not very widely used in finance, the reason for discussing them here is that the return of financial assets can occasionally be displayed in this form. They also provide a good visual introduction to continuous probability distributions, the most important of which we now turn to discuss.

The normal distribution

Statistical distributions are widely used in many financial applications. In fact, any time we want to forecast the probability of any target return, we must make an assumption about the underlying distribution.

You may remember from our previous chapter that random variables can be classified as discrete or continuous. Well, the same applies to probability distributions. We will not deal with the first kind here, but we will deal with a specific case of the second right away.

The **normal distribution** is a continuous distribution described by a horrifying expression. You may have seen it before, but if you haven't or don't quite remember it, sit down, take a deep breath, and take a look

$$f(x) = \frac{1}{\sqrt{2 \cdot \pi \cdot SD^2}} \cdot e^{-\frac{(x-AM)^2}{2 \cdot SD^2}}$$

(28.1)

In equation (28.1), x is a particular value of the continuous random variable X, e = 2.71828, π = 3.14159, and AM and SD denote the (arithmetic) mean and standard deviation of X, respectively. This expression yields the probability that the random variable X takes the value x, and now that we've seen it, for all practical purposes you may as well forget it. As we'll see in a minute, Excel calculates probabilities out of this distribution in the blink of an eye.

For many and varied reasons, this distribution plays a central role both in statistics in general and in finance in particular. We won't get into those reasons here; there are plenty of books that not only discuss this distribution in depth but also give you its history as well. We'll remain faithful to our goal and focus on the practical aspects of this distribution.

So, what can we stress from a practical point of view about the normal distribution? Several things. First, it is bell-shaped and symmetric around its mean. Figure 28.2 shows a normal distribution of returns with a mean of 12% and a standard deviation of 20%. Both the bell shape and the symmetry are clear from the picture.

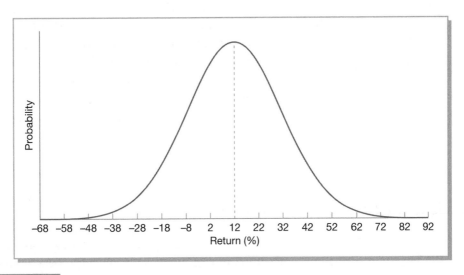

figure 28.2   **The normal distribution**

Second, the symmetry of the distribution implies that the mean is equal to both the median and the mode, so the normal distribution is in fact symmetric around these three parameters. The fact that the mean is equal to the median, in turn, implies that in the normal distribution half of the observations are below the mean and half above the mean. (This is not the case in asymmetric or skewed distributions, as we will see in the next chapter.)

Third, a normally distributed random variable is unbounded. In other words, the numbers on the horizontal axis are infinite. Note that this is a bit problematic when characterizing stock returns because stocks are subject to limited liability; that is, the most we can lose when we buy equity is the full amount of our investment, which implies that the minimum possible return is –100%. Having said that, this limitation is, from a practical point of view, largely irrelevant.

Fourth, the normal distribution is fully defined by only two parameters, its mean and standard deviation. This is just another way of saying that different combinations of *AM* and *SD* generate different normal distributions. Or, put differently, by knowing these two parameters, we know everything we need to know to make forecasts out of this distribution.

Finally, the probabilities one, two, and three standard deviations around the mean are well known. As you may know or remember, 68.3%, 95.4%, and 99.7% of the observations are clustered one, two, and three standard deviations around the mean. So, in the normal distribution of returns depicted in Figure 28.2 (which, remember, has a mean of 12% and a standard deviation of 20%), the probability of observing monthly returns in the intervals (–8%, 32%), (–28%, 52%), and (–48%, 72%) is 68.3%, 95.4%, and 99.7%.

Calculating probabilities

For what follows we're going to stay with a probability distribution like the one shown in Figure 28.2. To emphasize why the probabilities we'll estimate in a minute are interesting, note that the distribution of annual returns of the S&P 500 between 1926 and 2009 has a mean of 11.7% and a standard deviation of 20.4%, both very close to the mean (12%) and standard deviation (20%) of the distribution shown in Figure 28.2. Note, also, that a bit of statistical testing would establish that this distribution of annual (simple) returns is not statistically different from the normal.

Before we get to the numbers, note that all questions about probabilities for different values of the random variable of interest (the S&P 500, in our case), are actually questions about *areas* under the relevant normal distribution. These areas, in turn, are calculated by integrating expression (28.1) in the relevant intervals. (Stop! Don't close the book just yet! Excel calculates those integrals for us in the blink of an eye!)

Let's ask, for example, what is the probability that the S&P 500 returns, in any given year, 12% or less? That's easy. Because we know that the mean is equal to the median, and half of the area is below the median, then the probability is 50%. No sweat.

What about the probability that the S&P 500 returns, in any given year, 5% or less? That's only a bit more difficult. Take a look at Figure 28.3(a) overleaf. We need to calculate the area below 5%, and that can easily be done in Excel, as we will see at the end of this chapter. In any case, let's for now just say that the probability is 36.3%.

What about the probability that the S&P 500 returns, in any given year, at least 30%? This is again easy in Excel. We only need to take into account that Excel gives us areas *to the left* of the target return, and in this case we are inquiring about an area *to the right* of the target return, as Figure 28.3(b) shows. Again, for now let's just say that the probability is 18.4%.

Finally, what would be the probability that the S&P 500 returns, in any given year, between 5% and 20%? Again, it's easy in Excel. Take a look at Figure 28.4 on page 363. What we need now is the area between 5% and 20%, and for now let's just say that the probability is 29.2%.

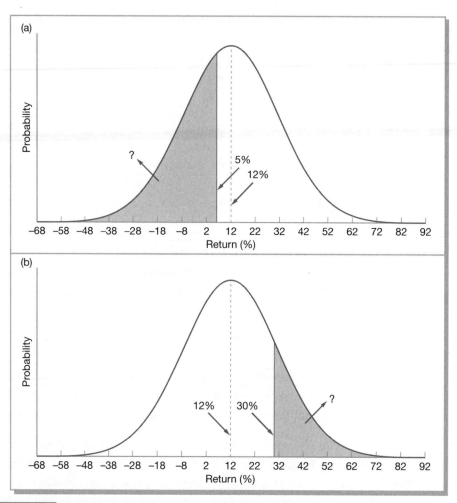

figure 28.3   Calculating probabilities of S&P returns

That should do it. We have considered probabilities less than a target return, more than a target return, and between two target returns. If after reading the Excel section at the end of this chapter you can reproduce the results we just discussed, then you will know just about all you need to know about calculating probabilities out of any normal distribution.

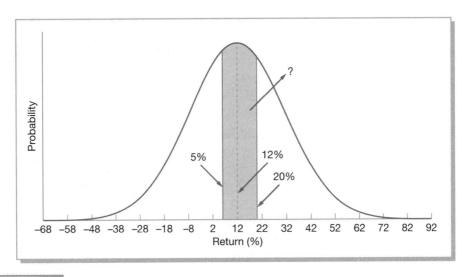

figure 28.4 Calculating more probabilities of S&P returns

The standard normal distribution

Actually, one more thing. Not incredibly important nowadays given the widespread use of computers, but you may find it useful at times anyway. Note that if we want to calculate a probability for any random variable of interest, we need to know the distribution's mean and standard deviation, and with these two parameters plus a target value for the random variable, we need to calculate an integral (ouch!) using expression (28.1).

That is very easy to do in spreadsheets, but tedious without them. And it gets even more tedious if we need to do this for different variables, with different normal distributions. Enter then the *standard* normal distribution.

This distribution arises from a simple transformation of *any* normal distribution, which consists of subtracting its mean from the random variable of interest, and then dividing by its standard deviation. More precisely, if a random variable X follows a normal distribution with mean AM and standard deviation SD, then the random variable $Z = (X–AM)/SD$ follows a standard normal distribution with mean 0 and standard deviation 1. If we go back to expression (28.1), and set $AM = 0$ and $SD = 1$, we will obtain the expression for the **standard normal distribution**, which is given by

$$f(z) = \frac{1}{\sqrt{2 \cdot \pi}} \cdot e^{-\frac{z^2}{2}} \qquad (28.2)$$

where z is a particular value of the continuous random variable Z.

So what's the big deal, you may ask, if expression (28.2) looks just a tiny bit less horrifying than expression (28.1)? (What's the difference between falling from the 68th or the 65th floor, right?!) Why is it that going from a normal distribution with mean *AM* and standard deviation *SD* to another with mean 0 and standard deviation 1 is such a leap forward? For a very simple reason: If we have no computer at hand, it makes a world of difference in terms of computing time and effort.

Suppose we wanted to find out the probability that 10 (normally distributed) assets, all of them with different means and standard deviations, return more than 15% in any given year. No Excel, no computer. Then we would have to calculate ten integrals using expression (28.1), after which we will be awarded a PhD and a two-week vacation in the Bahamas to make up for the effort.

But there's a shortcut. We can subtract from the target return (15%) the mean of each asset, and then divide by the standard deviation of each asset, which would give us 10 values of *Z*. And here comes the clincher: The standard normal distribution is tabulated, and having our 10 values of *Z* we can easily find the desired probabilities with the help of the table.

Tables for the standard normal distribution are widely available, and you can find one at the end of this chapter. You have probably used them before too. Just in case, let's use it once to find out the probability that the S&P 500 returns less than 25% in any given year.

Start by calculating the value of *Z* by subtracting the mean return of the S&P 500 (12%) from the target return (25%) and then dividing by its standard deviation (20%), that is, $Z = (0.25–0.12)/0.20 = 0.65$. (By the way, this number means that 25% is 0.65 standard deviations above the mean.) Then find on the table in the appendix the intersection between 0.6 (in the first column) and 0.05 (on the first row), and you should find the number 0.7422 or 74.22%, which is the probability that the S&P 500 returns less than 25% in any given year.

In short, the wide availability of tables for the cutoff points of the standard normal distribution makes it a convenient way to calculate probabilities when no computer is available. By the way, a spreadsheet also enables us to calculate probabilities by using the standard normal distribution, and we'll see how in the Excel section.

The big picture

The normal distribution plays a crucial role in both statistics and finance. It's widely used and easy to work with. Having said that, a word of caution. Remember that, often, the normality of returns is *an assumption*, not a fact. In other words, the returns of an asset may often be *assumed* to be normally distributed, but evidence may tell us otherwise. In those cases, using the normal distribution will be at best misleading and at worst dangerous.

Many assets do follow a normal distribution, but many others do not. The distribution of some assets may be skewed, or have fat tails, both of which imply departures from normality. There are many ways to test whether normality is an appropriate assumption, and we'll have a bit more to say about this issue in the next chapter. For the time being remember: Reality does not necessarily conform to convenient assumptions.

Excel section

Calculating probabilities out of a normal distribution is simple in Excel. Consider a series of normally distributed returns r, with mean AM and standard deviation SD. In what follows, you don't actually have to type r_0, r_1, AM, or SD; you have to enter *the actual values* for these magnitudes.

■ To calculate the probability that r takes a value lower than or equal to r_0, you need to use the 'normdist' command. More precisely, type

=normdist(r_0, AM, SD, true)

and hit Enter.

■ To calculate the probability that r takes a value larger than or equal to r_0, use the same command. In this case, type

=1–normdist(r_0, AM, SD, true)

and hit Enter.

■ To calculate the probability that r takes a value between two numbers r_0 and r_1, such that $r_0 < r_1$, use the same command. In this case, type

=normdist(r_1, AM, SD, true)–normdist(r_0, AM, SD, true)

and hit Enter.

We can also calculate all these probabilities using the *standard* normal distribution. Note, however, that we can do so only *after* properly standardizing the random variable that we're considering.

■ To calculate the probability that the variable r takes a value lower than or equal to r_0 by using the *standard* normal distribution, you first need to standardize r_0, which you can do in two ways. One is by simply calculating $z_0 = (r_0-AM)/SD$. The other is by using the 'standardize' command; in this case, type

=standardize(r_0, AM, SD)

and then hit Enter.

■ After calculating z_0 in one of the two ways suggested above, to calculate the probability that the variable r takes a value lower than or equal to r_0, you need to use the 'normsdist' command. Type

=normsdist(z_0)

and hit Enter.

Note that the 'normsdist' command does not require us to input the mean and standard deviation of the distribution because, by definition, these parameters in the standard normal distribution are 0 and 1. Furthermore, note that we can also use the 'normsdist' command to calculate the probability that the variable r takes a value larger than or equal to r_0, or the probability that r takes a value between any two numbers r_0 and r_1.

Appendix

Cumulative distribution function for the standard normal distribution

Each number in Table 28.2 represents an area between $-\infty$ and z^* or, similarly, the probability that $z \le z^*$; that is $P(z \le z^*)$. Each z^* should be read as the *sum* of a number in the first column and a number in the first row. For example, the probability that $z \le 0.22$ is 0.5871, and the probability that $z \le 2.48$ is 0.9934. Probabilities for z^* numbers lower than 0 are calculated as 1 minus the number in the table. For example, the probability that $z \le -0.75$ is $1-0.7734 = 0.2266$; and the probability that $z \le -2.31$ is $1-0.9896 = 0.0104$.

table 28.2

z^*	0.00	0.01	0.02	0.03	0.04	0.05	0.06	0.07	0.08	0.09
0.0	0.5000	0.5040	0.5080	0.5120	0.5160	0.5199	0.5239	0.5279	0.5319	0.5359
0.1	0.5398	0.5438	0.5478	0.5517	0.5557	0.5596	0.5636	0.5675	0.5714	0.5753
0.2	0.5793	0.5832	0.5871	0.5910	0.5948	0.5987	0.6026	0.6064	0.6103	0.6141
0.3	0.6179	0.6217	0.6255	0.6293	0.6331	0.6368	0.6406	0.6443	0.6480	0.6517
0.4	0.6554	0.6591	0.6628	0.6664	0.6700	0.6736	0.6772	0.6808	0.6844	0.6879
0.5	0.6915	0.6950	0.6985	0.7019	0.7054	0.7088	0.7123	0.7157	0.7190	0.7224
0.6	0.7257	0.7291	0.7324	0.7357	0.7389	0.7422	0.7454	0.7486	0.7517	0.7549
0.7	0.7580	0.7611	0.7642	0.7673	0.7704	0.7734	0.7764	0.7794	0.7823	0.7852
0.8	0.7881	0.7910	0.7939	0.7967	0.7995	0.8023	0.8051	0.8078	0.8106	0.8133
0.9	0.8159	0.8186	0.8212	0.8238	0.8264	0.8289	0.8315	0.8340	0.8365	0.8389
1.0	0.8413	0.8438	0.8461	0.8485	0.8508	0.8531	0.8554	0.8577	0.8599	0.8621
1.1	0.8643	0.8665	0.8686	0.8708	0.8729	0.8749	0.8770	0.8790	0.8810	0.8830
1.2	0.8849	0.8869	0.8888	0.8907	0.8925	0.8944	0.8962	0.8980	0.8997	0.9015
1.3	0.9032	0.9049	0.9066	0.9082	0.9099	0.9115	0.9131	0.9147	0.9162	0.9177
1.4	0.9192	0.9207	0.9222	0.9236	0.9251	0.9265	0.9279	0.9292	0.9306	0.9319
1.5	0.9332	0.9345	0.9357	0.9370	0.9382	0.9394	0.9406	0.9418	0.9429	0.9441
1.6	0.9452	0.9463	0.9474	0.9484	0.9495	0.9505	0.9515	0.9525	0.9535	0.9545
1.7	0.9554	0.9564	0.9573	0.9582	0.9591	0.9599	0.9608	0.9616	0.9625	0.9633
1.8	0.9641	0.9649	0.9656	0.9664	0.9671	0.9678	0.9686	0.9693	0.9699	0.9706
1.9	0.9713	0.9719	0.9726	0.9732	0.9738	0.9744	0.9750	0.9756	0.9761	0.9767
2.0	0.9772	0.9778	0.9783	0.9788	0.9793	0.9798	0.9803	0.9808	0.9812	0.9817
2.1	0.9821	0.9826	0.9830	0.9834	0.9838	0.9842	0.9846	0.9850	0.9854	0.9857
2.2	0.9861	0.9864	0.9868	0.9871	0.9875	0.9878	0.9881	0.9884	0.9887	0.9890
2.3	0.9893	0.9896	0.9898	0.9901	0.9904	0.9906	0.9909	0.9911	0.9913	0.9916
2.4	0.9918	0.9920	0.9922	0.9925	0.9927	0.9929	0.9931	0.9932	0.9934	0.9936
2.5	0.9938	0.9940	0.9941	0.9943	0.9945	0.9946	0.9948	0.9949	0.9951	0.9952
2.6	0.9953	0.9955	0.9956	0.9957	0.9959	0.9960	0.9961	0.9962	0.9963	0.9964
2.7	0.9965	0.9966	0.9967	0.9968	0.9969	0.9970	0.9971	0.9972	0.9973	0.9974
2.8	0.9974	0.9975	0.9976	0.9977	0.9977	0.9978	0.9979	0.9979	0.9980	0.9981
2.9	0.9981	0.9982	0.9982	0.9983	0.9984	0.9984	0.9985	0.9985	0.9986	0.9986
3.0	0.9987	0.9987	0.9987	0.9988	0.9988	0.9989	0.9989	0.9989	0.9990	0.9990

29

Stats III: Non-normality

We concluded the previous chapter with a word of caution, stressing that normality is a convenient assumption that may or may not describe properly the distribution of the variable we want to analyze. We now move on to discuss a few issues related to non-normal distributions, with a focus on the lognormal distribution.

Moments

All distributions, normal and non-normal, are characterized by parameters called **moments**. The first two moments we already know: The mean and the variance. For a normal distribution, that is all that matters. Remember, once we know the mean and variance of a normal distribution we know everything we need to work with it.

Not all distributions, however, are that easy to characterize. In other words, if we want to calculate the probability of obtaining a target return for an asset with a non-normal distribution of returns, we usually need more information than just the mean and the variance; that is, we need to know more moments. Note, however, that the problem remains essentially the same: We still need to calculate areas (mathematically, integrals) under the relevant distribution.

We'll now briefly discuss the third and fourth moments of a distribution, called skewness and kurtosis. From a practical point of view, moments higher than the fourth are irrelevant. If you understand these first four moments (mean, variance, skewness, and kurtosis), you'll be more than just fine.

Skewness

Not all random variables are characterized by symmetric distributions. In fact, it's not unusual at all to find assets whose returns are skewed in one direction or another. If you go back to the previous chapter and take another look at the histogram of returns in Figure 28.1, for example, you'll notice the lack of symmetry, with the left tail being longer than the right tail.

Figure 29.1 shows two asymmetric or skewed distributions. Figure 29.1(a) shows a distribution with a long right tail and Figure 29.1(b) one with a long left tail. The former is said to exhibit positive (or right) skewness; the latter is said to exhibit negative (or left) skewness.

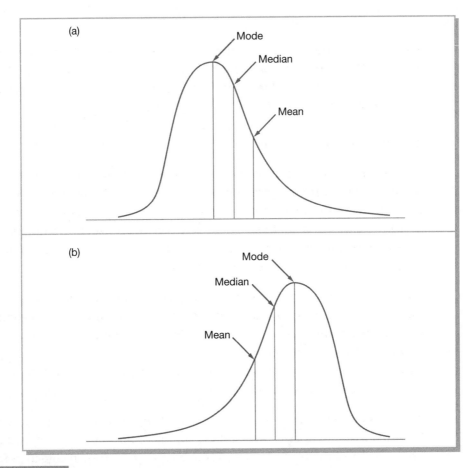

figure 29.1   **Skewed distribution curves**

An important characteristic of skewed distributions is that the mean, the median, and the mode are all different. (In symmetric distributions, remember, all three parameters coincide.) In fact, as Figure 29.1 shows, in distributions with positive skewness, the mean is larger than the median, which in turn is larger than the mode. In distributions with negative skewness, the opposite happens and therefore the mode is larger than the median, which is turn is larger than the mean. In both cases, the peak of the distribution is given by the mode.

To measure the asymmetry of a distribution we can calculate its third moment, the **coefficient of skewness (Skw)**, which is given by

$$Skw = \frac{(1/T) \cdot \sum_{t=1}^{T} (R_t - AM)^3}{SD^3}$$

(29.1)

where R_t represents returns in period t, T is the number of observations, and AM and SD represent the (arithmetic) mean and standard deviation of the distribution. A positive value of this coefficient indicates that the underlying distribution is positively skewed (a long right tail), and a negative value indicates that the underlying distribution is negatively skewed (a long left tail). In all symmetric distributions, this coefficient takes a value of 0.

In case you're panicking at the look of expression (29.1), fear not. As we will see at the end of the chapter, Excel sorts it all out. (Actually, Excel uses a slightly different formula that incorporates a small-sample adjustment; that is, a little correction that gives us a better estimate when the number of observations is small. However, because in finance we usually deal with large samples, you don't have to worry about this correction.)

Where does skewness stem from? In a nutshell, positive skewness arises when the mean is pulled up by some very high values (outliers), and negative skewness when the mean is pulled down by very low values. The negatively skewed distribution of monthly returns displayed in Figure 28.1, in the previous chapter, arises largely from a few large negative returns, such as the –19.8% in October 2008 and the –14.0% in August 1998.

Positive skewness may also arise naturally from compounding. Consider investing $100 in an asset with a mean annual return of 30%, and assume, first, two consecutive years of 50% returns (that is, 20 percentage points above the mean). At the end of these two years we'll have $225, for a cumulative (two-year) return of 125%. Now, beginning again from $100 assume two consecutive years of 10% returns (that is, 20 percentage points below the mean). After two years we'll end up with $121, for a cumulative (two-year) return of 21%. Finally, note that 125% is 56 percentage points above the expected two-year return (69%), whereas 21% is only 48 percentage points below the expected two-year return. Therefore, the distribution of compounded (or cumulative) returns is positively skewed.

Kurtosis

The fourth moment of a distribution, kurtosis, measures its peak and tails, usually relative to those of a normal distribution. A distribution with a higher peak and fatter tails than the normal distribution is called *leptokurtic*; one with a lower peak and thinner tails is called *platykurtic*.

Formally, the **coefficient of kurtosis (Krt)** is given by

$$Krt = \frac{(1/T) \cdot \sum_{t=1}^{T} (R_t - AM)^4}{SD^4} \tag{29.2}$$

and takes a value of 3 for the normal distribution. For this reason, instead of this coefficient, you may often find reported the coefficient of *excess* kurtosis (*EKrt*), which is simply given by $EKrt = Krt-3$. Thus, a positive value of *EKrt* indicates a high peak and fat tails, and a negative value indicates a low peak and thin tails, in both cases relative to the normal distribution. (What Excel calls kurtosis is, in fact, the coefficient of excess kurtosis. Also, as in the case of skewness, Excel introduces in the calculation a small-sample adjustment that you don't have to worry about.)

Many financial assets exhibit leptokurtosis. Most distributions of daily stock returns, for example, are characterized by fat tails. This indicates that large returns, both positive and negative, are more likely (often far more likely) than what a normal distribution would lead us to expect. As we stressed before, normality may be a convenient assumption though not always an appropriate characterization of the way the world behaves.

An example

To make sure you're on top of the first four statistical moments, let's consider the total returns of 10-year US government bonds. Table 29.1 reports the first four moments of the distribution of (simple) annual returns for the 50 years between 1960 and 2009.

table 29.1

Mean	7.6%
Standard deviation	9.7%
Skewness	0.90
(Excess) Kurtosis	1.23

The first moment indicates that the mean annual return of 10-year US government bonds has been 7.6%. The standard deviation of these returns (the square root of the second moment, the variance) has been 9.7%, which means that *if* this distribution were normal, then 95.4% of the returns should be contained in the interval (–11.7%, 27.0%); that is, two standard deviations each side of the mean.

The coefficient of skewness is positive (0.90), which indicates that this distribution has a longer right tail than left tail. This, in turn, indicates that when US bonds exhibit very large returns (in absolute value), these are more likely to be positive than negative. Finally, the coefficient of excess kurtosis is positive (1.23), suggesting that US bonds have delivered more 'large' returns (both positive and negative) than would be expected under normality.

Note, however, that the values of the coefficients of skewness and excess kurtosis cannot really tell us whether the departures from normality are substantial (or, as statisticians would put it, statistically significant). In fact, to test for these departures reliably we need to calculate the *standardized* version of these coefficients. Although those calculations are a little messy and we won't get into them here, the coefficients of standardized skewness and excess kurtosis reveal that although the skewness is statistically significant, the kurtosis is not. Hence, although the distribution of US bond returns has a longer right tail than left tail, the tails are not significantly fatter that those of a normal distribution.

The lognormal distribution

Consider a stock that starts a year trading at $100 and ends the year trading at $50, for a –50% return. To go back up to $100, this stock needs to return 100%. It's easy then to see the asymmetry in returns: A stock that goes down 50% needs to go up 100% to go back to its initial value. We could try any initial price and subsequent decline that you like, but we will always find the same: A stock that goes down by x% needs to go up by *more* than x% to go back to where it started.

If you recall the discussion in Chapter 1 about the difference between simple and continuously compounded returns, you may have realized that the percentages in the previous paragraph are all simple returns. But what if we wanted to calculate continuously compounded returns instead? Well, as you may remember, to calculate continuously compounded returns all we need to do is to take the log of 1 plus the simple returns. If we do that, our two simple returns of 100% and –50% would turn into $\ln(1+1.0) = 69.3\%$ and $\ln(1-0.5) = -69.3\%$ continuously compounded returns.

And what does this have to do with lognormality, you may ask? Note that if we express the changes from $100 to $50 and from $50 to $100 in terms of continuously compounded returns, the positive return and the negative return are symmetric; that is, the absolute value of both (69.3%) is the same. However, if we express the changes in terms of simple returns, the absolute value of the positive return (100%) is higher than the absolute value of the negative return (50%). In other words, continuously compounded returns are symmetric, but simple returns are positively skewed.

Now, here comes ... a theorem! I know, you don't even want to hear about it. But this one is simple and we won't prove it; we'll just state it. The theorem says the following: If any random variable $\ln(X)$ is normally distributed, then the random variable X is lognormally distributed.

That wasn't so bad, was it? Now let's see why this is relevant to our discussion. Recall that, if R and r denote simple and continuously compounded returns, we know that $(1+R) = e^r$ and $\ln(1+R) = r$. So, according to the theorem above, if $\ln(1+R) = r$ follows a normal distribution, then $(1+R)$ follows a lognormal distribution. In other words, if continuously compounded returns are normally distributed, then simple returns are lognormally distributed. Or, put differently, if the distribution of r looks like that in Figure 28.2 in the previous chapter, then the distribution of $(1+R)$ will look like the one in Figure 29.2.

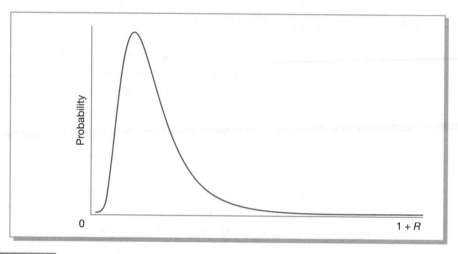

figure 29.2   **The lognormal distribution is positively skewed**

Note that the lognormal distribution is not symmetric but positively skewed. Note, also, that this distribution is defined only for positive values of the variable considered. As a consequence, in finance we often focus not on the distribution of R but on the distribution of $(1+R)$. This is due to the fact that, because R cannot be lower than -100%, then $(1+R)$ cannot be lower than 0.

Now, here's a little something that you should know. When academic financial economists deal with returns, they usually deal with continuously compounded returns. When they estimate correlations, or betas, or run econometric analyses, they usually do it with this type of returns. The reasons are many and varied, but an important one is that, as we've just seen, continuously compounded returns are more likely to be normally distributed (owing to their symmetry) than simple returns.

Investors, however, are largely interested in simple returns. This is because investors care about how much money they start with and how much money they end up with, and that can be straightforwardly measured by simple returns. And, as long as we believe (or find out through statistical testing) that continuously compounded returns are normally distributed, then simple returns *must* be lognormally distributed.

As is the case with the normal distribution, Excel can quickly calculate probabilities out of the lognormal distribution (as we will see at the end of the chapter), which means that the three expressions below are only for math freaks who hate loose ends! If a random variable $\ln(X)$ is normally distributed with (arithmetic) mean AM and standard deviation SD, then X follows a **lognormal distribution** with probability distribution, mean, and variance given by

$$f(x) = \frac{1}{x \cdot \sqrt{2 \cdot \pi \cdot SD^2}} \cdot e^{-\frac{[\ln(x)-AM]^2}{2 \cdot SD^2}} \tag{29.3}$$

$$E(X) = e^{(AM+SD^2/2)} \tag{29.4}$$

$$Var(X) = e^{(2 \cdot AM+SD^2)} \cdot \left(e^{SD^2} - 1\right) \tag{29.5}$$

where x is a particular value of the random variable X, $e = 2.71828$, and $\pi = 3.14159$. Expression (29.3) yields the probability that the random variable X takes the value x, and expressions (29.4) and (29.5) yield the mean and variance of X.

Calculating probabilities again

Table 29.1 summarized the first moments of the distribution of *simple* annual returns of 10-year US government bonds between 1960 and 2009. Table 29.2 summarizes the first four moments of the distribution of *continuously compounded* annual returns of the same bonds over the same period.

table 29.2

Mean	7.0%
Standard deviation	8.7%
Skewness	0.62
(Excess) Kurtosis	0.58

A bit of statistical testing (don't ask) indicates that the skewness and kurtosis of this distribution are not substantial (not statistically significant), which means that, for practical purposes, the distribution of continuously compounded annual returns of 10-year US government bonds between 1960 and 2009 can be considered normal. This, in turn, implies that the distribution of simple annual returns of these bonds over the same period can be considered lognormal.

As discussed above, investors are usually interested in simple returns, and the questions we'll pose refer to those returns. However, to get our answers, we need to use the parameters of the distribution of continuously compounded returns. This sounds messy, I know. If we care about one distribution, you may ask, why do we have to deal with the other? Simply because the parameters of a lognormal distribution are defined in terms of the parameters of the associated normal distribution.

If you take another look at expressions (29.4) and (29.5), you'll see that the mean and variance of the lognormal distribution are defined in terms of the mean (AM) and variance (SD^2) of the associated normal distribution. By the way, this is exactly the way Excel deals with the lognormal distribution. If we want to use Excel to calculate areas (probabilities) under a distribution of simple returns, we have to input the mean and standard deviation of the associated distribution of continuously compounded returns. Oh well, sometimes we just have to follow the crowd.

So, we could start by asking what is the probability that ten-year US government bonds return, next year, 10% or less. That is simply the area to the left of 10% under the lognormal distribution. As we will see at the end of the chapter, Excel can be used to give us this number, and if you calculate it correctly you should obtain 61.6%.

What about the probability that these bonds return at least 20% next year? That is the area to the right of 20% under the lognormal distribution. If you calculate it correctly, you should obtain 9.8%.

Finally, what about the probability that these bonds return between 5% and 25% next year? That is the area between 5% and 25% under the lognormal distribution, and if you calculate it correctly you should obtain 55.4%.

If after reading the Excel section at the end of this chapter you can reproduce the numbers we just discussed, then you will have learned just about all you need to know about calculating probabilities out of a lognormal distribution.

The big picture

However convenient the assumption of normality may be, many financial assets simply don't follow a normal distribution. Many distributions are skewed, have fat tails, or exhibit other departures from normality. The coefficients of skewness and kurtosis provide information about these departures, the former measuring the asymmetry and the latter the thickness of the tails of the distribution considered.

Of all the skewed distributions, the lognormal is the one that is most widely used in finance. Forecasting the probability of achieving a target return under lognormality is not difficult and, in many cases, is more accurate than forecasting based on the normal distribution.

Excel section

The coefficients of skewness and excess kurtosis are easy to calculate in Excel. Suppose you have 10 returns in cells A1 through A10. Then, choose any empty cell and do the following:

▪ To calculate the coefficient of skewness, type

   =skew(A1:A10)

   and press the Enter key.

▪ To calculate the coefficient of excess kurtosis, type

   =kurt(A1:A10)

   and hit Enter.

As mentioned above, Excel introduces some small-sample adjustments to these two coefficients; and, as also mentioned above, given that in finance we usually deal with large samples, you don't really have to worry about these adjustments.

In Chapter 27 we saw how to calculate some summary statistics one at a time. If you wanted to calculate some of those, plus the two above, all at once, this is what you do:

- Select the 'Data' tab.

- Select 'Data Analysis'.*

- From the options given, select 'Descriptive Statistics.' This opens a dialog box in which you have to do at least three things:
    - in 'Input Range' input the data range (A1:A10 in our case);
    - select 'Output Range' and input the cell in which you want the beginning of the output to be displayed;
    - tick the 'Summary Statistics' box.

- Click 'OK.'

To calculate probabilities out of a lognormal distribution, you need to keep in mind that Excel will ask you for the mean and standard deviation of the associated normal distribution. In other words, if you want to calculate probabilities out of a *lognormal* distribution of *simple* returns, Excel will ask you for the mean and standard deviation of the associated *normal* distribution of *continuously compounded* returns. This means you first have to calculate continuously compounded returns and then their mean and standard deviation.

Assume that the continuously compounded returns $r = \ln(1+R)$ of any asset of your interest are normally distributed with mean AM and standard deviation SD. This means that the simple returns $(1+R)$ of this asset are lognormally distributed. We are interested in calculating probabilities out of the distribution of $(1+R)$. Assume then that you have continuously

---

* If the Data Analysis option is not visible, it needs to be installed. You do this by clicking on the top left Office Button; then 'Excel Options'; then 'Add-ins'. In the 'Manage' drop-down menu, select 'Excel Add-in'. Click 'Go'. In the 'Add-Ins available' list, click on the 'Analysis ToolPak' box, and then click 'OK'. The software will then take you through the installation process.

compounded returns in cells A1–A10, and that you have calculated their mean and standard deviation in cells A11 and A12, respectively. In what follows, note that you don't have to type $1+R_0$, $1+R_1$, AM, or SD but *the actual values* for these magnitudes. Then:

■ To calculate the probability that R takes a value lower than or equal to R_0, use the 'lognormdist' command. Then, type

=lognormdist(1+R_0, AM, SD)

and hit Enter.

■ To calculate the probability that R takes a value larger than or equal to R_0, you use the same command. In this case, type

=1–lognormdist(1+R_0, AM, SD)

and hit Enter.

■ To calculate the probability that R takes a value between two numbers R_0 and R_1, such that $R_0 < R_1$, you still use the same command. In this case, type

=lognormdist(1+R_1, AM, SD)–lognormdist(1+R_0, AM, SD)

and hit Enter.

30

Stats IV: Regression analysis

W e've come to the end of our statistical review. Our last topic, regression analysis, has many and far-reaching applications in finance. It's also very broad and it can get rather technical, so we will only scratch its surface here. Our goal is to go over the very basics of running and interpreting regression models. And in finance, that is not only essential; it also goes a long way toward understanding, among many other issues, the relationship between risk and return.

Regression analysis: An overview

In a nutshell, regression analysis is a statistical technique that enables us to test a model (or theory, or idea) that seeks to explain the behavior of a variable. It works out this way:

- start with a variable whose behavior we want to explain;

- propose one or more variables to explain that behavior;

- link all the relevant variables in one expression or equation;

- collect data on all the relevant variables;

- estimate the proposed relationship;

- finally, run some tests on the validity of the model.

The variable we want to explain is called the *dependent variable* and the variables that we use to explain its behavior are called *independent* (or *explanatory*) *variables*. Therefore, there's one dependent variable (y) and k explanatory variables (x_1, x_2, ..., x_k), where k can be any number larger than or equal to 1.

A *cross-sectional* analysis attempts to explain the behaviour of the dependent variable at a given point in time across different units of observation, such as returns in 2009 across several industries, or income per capita in 2009 across several countries. A *time-series* analysis, on the other hand, attempts to explain the behaviour of the dependent variable over time, such as the returns of an industry over the past two decades, or the income per capita of a country over the last century.

Formally, the **multiple linear regression model** can be expressed as

$$y_i = \beta_0 + \beta_1 \cdot x_{1i} + \beta_2 \cdot x_{2i} + \dots + \beta_k \cdot x_{ki} + u_i \tag{30.1}$$

Let's think about this expression. The left-hand side shows the dependent variable (y) that the model attempts to explain. The right-hand side shows a constant or intercept (β_0); the k explanatory variables ($x_1, x_2, \dots, x_k$) that we believe can explain the behavior of the dependent variable, each multiplied by a constant ($\beta_1, \beta_2, \dots, \beta_k$); and an error term ($u$). The subscript i runs from 1 through n, where n is the number of observations in the sample. (As a convention, the subscript i, $i = 1, 2, \dots, n$, is typically used for cross-section analysis; and the subscript t, $t = 1, 2, \dots, T$, where T is the number of observations in the sample, is typically used for time-series analysis.)

Let's start with the interpretation of the coefficients. For any explanatory variable x_j, β_j measures the effect on y of a one-unit change in x_j, holding all the other explanatory variables constant. In other words, β_j isolates the impact of x_j on y. (Formally, β_j is the partial derivative of y with respect to x_j.) The intercept β_0, on the other hand, is the *expected* value of the dependent variable when all the explanatory variables take the value 0.

The error term can be thought of as comprising the influence on the dependent variable of all variables other than the ones included in the model. In other words, given that no model will be able to fully explain changes in the dependent variable, the error term collects all the unexplained behavior. The usual assumption is that the *expected* value (average) of the error term is 0, implying that the many influences on the dependent variable of the explanatory variables not included in the model cancel each other out.

The standard way of estimating a relationship such as (30.1) is by a procedure called ordinary least squares (OLS). We will not get into the details of this technique here, which is covered in most books on statistics or econometrics. We'll stick to our practical goal and just say that the OLS procedure yields the estimates of $\beta_0, \beta_1, \dots, \beta_k$, which we will call $b_0, b_1, \dots,$

b_k. These estimates, in turn, are the coefficients that we use to predict the expected value of the dependent variable, $E(y)$. More precisely, we predict $E(y)$ with the expression

$$E(y) = b_0 + b_1 \cdot x_1 + b_2 \cdot x_2 + \ldots + b_k \cdot x_k \qquad (30.2)$$

Note that, having estimated the coefficients b_0, b_1, ..., b_k by OLS, we then need specific values for x_1, x_2, ..., x_k to forecast the expected value of the dependent variable.

Finally, after estimating a model that attempts to explain the behavior of an explanatory variable, we are usually interested to know *how much* of that behavior the model actually explains. Enter then the R^2, sometimes called the coefficient of determination. This coefficient, which can take a minimum value of 0 and a maximum value of 1, measures the *proportion* of the variability in the dependent variable that is explained by the model. Hence, the larger this number, the better the explanatory power of the model.

Hypothesis testing

Most models yield some prediction about the coefficients β_0, β_1, ..., β_k. They may predict the sign of some coefficient (for example, that β_1 should be positive) or a precise value for some other (for example, that β_2 should be equal to 1). However, we cannot really test a model's predictions simply by comparing our estimates with their hypothesized values.

If this sounds confusing, it is important to keep in mind the difference between a sample and a population. Although we're always interested in the true value of the coefficients in the population, we almost always deal with samples. This means that our estimates are subject to sampling error, which is a way of saying that our estimates may or may not be equal to the true population coefficients.

And here is, precisely, where hypothesis testing comes in. You probably have heard expressions such as 'this coefficient is significantly different from 0,' or 'this coefficient is not significantly different from 1.' Well, what these expressions mean is that, having obtained our estimates and having run a statistical test on them, we are then able to draw a conclusion about the differences between our estimates and the true value of the parameters in the population.

To test a hypothesis about a coefficient we need both the estimate of the coefficient and its standard error, which is just a number that measures the precision of our estimate. The higher this number, the lower the precision, and the more uncertain we are about our estimate. Each coefficient b_j has its own standard error (SE_j).

An important hypothesis we often want to test is whether an individual beta coefficient is significantly different from 0. This is important because, if it's not, then the associated explanatory variable does not really help to explain the behavior of the dependent variable. This hypothesis can easily be tested with the so-called *t-statistic*, which is simply the ratio between our estimate of a beta coefficient and its standard error; that is, b_j/SE_j.

Formally, this test involves a *null hypothesis*, usually referred to as H_0, and an *alternative hypothesis*, usually referred to as H_1, such that:

■ $H_0: \beta_i = 0$

■ $H_1: \beta_i \neq 0$ or $H_1: \beta_i > 0$ or $H_1: \beta_i < 0$

Note that the null hypothesis is that the coefficient is *not* significant. Note, also, that the first alternative hypothesis ($\beta_i \neq 0$) is usually called a two-tailed test and the other two ($\beta_i > 0$ and $\beta_i < 0$) are usually called one-tailed tests. Note, finally, that running a one-tailed test or a two-tailed test is often determined by whether or not our theory implies a particular sign for β_i.

The simplest way to test this hypothesis is to compare the *p-value* (*p*) of the *t*-statistic with a chosen *level of significance* (α). The former is not trivial to calculate but is part of the output of any software that estimates regressions (including Excel). The latter is a chosen number that, strictly speaking, measures the probability of rejecting a null hypothesis when it's true. The most widely used levels of significance in finance and economics are 5% and 1%.

Having obtained the *p*-value of the *t*-statistic of a beta coefficient, and having chosen a level of significance, the rule to test the null hypothesis that beta is *not* significantly different from 0 against a *two*-tailed alternative is straightforward:

■ If $p < \alpha/2$ ⇒ Reject the hypothesis

■ If $p > \alpha/2$ ⇒ Do not reject the hypothesis

If the hypothesis is rejected, we say that beta is significant; that is, the variable associated with this coefficient plays an important role in explaining the behavior of the dependent variable. If, on the other hand, the hypothesis is not rejected, we say that beta is not significant and the opposite is the case. (If a *one*-tailed alternative is used instead, then the relevant comparison is not between p and $\alpha/2$ but between p and α.)

So much for 'theory.' If you were familiar with regression analysis but hadn't dealt with it in a while, hopefully the discussion refreshed your memory. If you were not familiar with regression analysis, then you *must* be confused! That's why we're going to move right now to discuss an example in which we'll deal in practice with all the issues we just discussed in theory.

Risk, return, and emerging markets

Table 30.1 shows the 22 emerging markets on the MSCI Emerging Markets Index, the most widely followed benchmark for emerging markets equity investing, as of December 2009. It also shows the mean annual return (*MR*), standard deviation of annual returns (*SD*), and beta (with respect to the world market) of all these markets in 1988–2009.

table 30.1

Country	MR (%)	SD (%)	Beta	Country	MR (%)	SD (%)	Beta
Brazil	37.7	53.4	1.58	Malaysia	16.5	29.9	0.87
Chile	25.3	24.8	0.72	Mexico	30.2	32.4	1.18
China	8.8	37.9	1.20	Morocco	16.4	19.7	0.21
Colombia	26.6	33.2	0.81	Peru	26.0	33.4	1.05
Czech Rep.	20.9	29.9	0.95	Philippines	17.2	32.4	0.92
Egypt	35.1	33.9	0.87	Poland	53.2	51.0	1.64
Hungary	26.2	38.0	1.54	Russia	47.4	58.8	1.94
India	20.8	31.6	1.02	S. Africa	17.6	28.0	1.19
Indonesia	33.0	52.1	1.15	Taiwan	15.7	37.8	0.99
Israel	12.7	24.7	0.89	Thailand	20.4	39.3	1.28
Korea	19.3	39.3	1.33	Turkey	52.6	59.5	1.42

Mean returns (*MR*) and standard deviations (*SD*) in %

The variable we want to study is mean returns in emerging markets. Let's say we believe that we can explain the differences in these mean returns by differences in risk, and let's quantify the latter with the standard deviation of returns (or, as is usually called, volatility). Let's also say that we expect these two variables to be positively related. So now we have ... a model! Our dependent variable is mean returns, our only explanatory variable is volatility, and we expect the β_1 coefficient to be positive.

Table 30.2 shows part of the output from an OLS estimation of our model. (At the end of the chapter we'll see how we can run regressions like this in Excel.) The model is estimated with 22 observations, one mean return and one standard deviation for each of the 22 emerging markets in our sample. The R^2 of the model (0.60) indicates that volatility explains 60% of the variability in mean returns across emerging markets. And don't rush to conclude that that is not much; it's actually pretty good for this type of model.

table 30.2

Observations	22		b	SE	t-stat	p-value
R^2	0.60	Intercept	−0.06	0.06	−0.95	0.35
Adjusted-R^2	0.58	SD	0.86	0.16	5.42	0.00

The estimate of the β_1 coefficient (b_1 = 0.86) indicates that, for every 1% increase in volatility, mean returns are expected to increase by 0.86%. The output also shows the standard error (0.16) and the t-statistic (5.42) of b_1, which we can use to test whether β_1 is (not) significantly different from 0. Given a 5% level of significance, a two-tailed alternative, the p-value of the t-statistic provided by the output (0.00), and the fact that $p=0.00 < \alpha/2=0.025$, we can decisively conclude that β_1 is significant. In other words, volatility does in fact explain the behavior of mean returns in emerging markets; and the higher it is, the higher that mean returns are expected to be.

Finally, a word about the constant which, remember, is the expected value of the dependent variable when the explanatory variables take a value of 0. Given that $p=0.35 > \alpha/2=0.025$, we cannot reject the hypothesis that this coefficient is not significantly different from 0. In other words, if an emerging market has no volatility, its expected return is 0.

Multiple explanatory variables

The risk variable we chose to explain the behavior of mean returns in emerging markets in our previous model was volatility, measured by the standard deviation of returns. But, obviously, we could have thought of another explanatory variable, such as beta. Table 30.3 reports the output of a regression in which we attempt to explain mean returns in emerging markets with beta as the only explanatory variable.

table 30.3

Observations	22		b	SE	t-stat	p-value
R^2	0.36	Intercept	0.04	0.07	0.51	0.61
Adjusted-R^2	0.33	Beta	0.20	0.06	3.37	0.00

You should have no problem interpreting this output by now. We ran the regression with 22 (cross-sectional) observations; we are able to explain 36% of the variability in mean returns; when beta increases by 1, mean returns are expected to increase by 20%; and we reject the hypothesis that beta does not explain mean returns ($p=0.00 < \alpha/2=0.025$), thus concluding that beta does have a positive impact on mean returns in emerging markets.

Now, given that we have found that both volatility and beta are important determinants of the variability in mean returns across emerging markets, you may be wondering whether we should include both of them in our regression. We could (and probably should), and the output of this model, now with two explanatory variables, is reported in Table 30.4.

table 30.4

			b	SE	t-stat	p-value
Observations	22	Intercept	−0.06	0.06	−0.88	0.39
R^2	0.60	SD	0.94	0.28	3.34	0.00
Adjusted-R^2	0.56	Beta	−0.03	0.08	−0.34	0.74

Surprised? A quick glance at the *p*-values of our two explanatory variables, volatility and beta, shows that volatility is significant ($p=0.00 < \alpha/2=0.025$) but beta is not ($p=0.74 > \alpha/2=0.025$). How can this be if we had concluded before that beta was significant?

This is due to a common problem in regression analysis called *multicollinearity*. This fancy name simply refers to a situation in which the explanatory variables are highly correlated among themselves. (In fact, in our case, the correlation between volatility and beta is a high 0.82.) This, in turn, usually translates into a situation in which each explanatory variable *appears* to be not significant, but the explanatory variables taken as a group do explain a substantial part of the variability in the dependent variable. Exactly our case.

Intuitively, what happens is the following. As we have seen, both volatility and beta, considered one at a time as explanatory variables, are important determinants of the variability in mean returns across emerging markets. But because volatility and beta are highly correlated between themselves, when we put them together in the same regression, they basically end up explaining pretty much the same variability in mean returns. In other words, each adds little explanatory power to the explanatory power already provided by the other.

The adjusted-R^2

Let's now focus for a moment on a coefficient reported in all the outputs above but that we have so far ignored, the *adjusted-R^2*, which is related to the issue we just discussed. Recall that the R^2 measures the proportion of the variability in the dependent variable that we explain with our model. Now, what do you think would happen to the R^2 if, whatever model we start with, we add one more explanatory variable?

Obviously, the added variable cannot 'un-explain' the variability of the dependent variable we were already explaining before its introduction. The worst that could happen is that the variable does not add any explanatory power at all, in which case the R^2 will not change. Hence, every time we add a variable to a model, the R^2 will either increase or stay the same. In fact, it should increase, however slightly.

The adjusted-R^2, however, penalizes the inclusion of another variable for making the model less parsimonious. In other words, every time we add a variable to a model, there are *two opposing* effects on the adjusted-R^2. On the one hand, it increases because the new variable adds some explanatory power (however small); on the other hand, it decreases because it penalizes us for making the model more complicated. Which of the effects dominates will depend on the explanatory variable we add.

If we add a 'good' variable, meaning one that will help us explain a substantial part of the variability in the dependent variable *that we were not already explaining with other variables included in the model*, then the adjusted-R^2 is likely to go up. If, on the other hand, we add an explanatory variable that either has little to do with the dependent variable or is highly correlated to other explanatory variables already included in the model, the adjusted-R^2 is likely to go down.

In short, then, the adjusted-R^2 provides a 'quick-and-dirty' test on whether it is convenient to add one or more variables to a model. As an example, note that if we start by explaining mean returns in emerging markets with volatility, the adjusted-R^2 is 0.58 (Table 30.2). If we then add beta as explanatory variable, the adjusted-R^2 *falls* to 0.56 (Table 30.4). This does not mean that beta is useless when we want to explain the behavior of mean returns in emerging markets. It means that, *if we're already explaining returns with volatility*, making the model more complicated by adding beta as explanatory variable does not really pay off. And this is simply because much of what beta can explain of the variability of mean returns is already explained by volatility.

Forecasting

One of the main goals of regression analysis is to forecast expected values of the dependent variable. Having estimated the coefficients of the model and chosen specific values of interest of the explanatory variables, it's all about adding and subtracting. Let's make a couple of forecasts from the model estimated in Table 30.4, whose expression we can write as

$$E(y) = -0.06 + 0.94{\cdot}x_1 - 0.03{\cdot}x_2 \qquad (30.3)$$

where x_1 and x_2 represent our two explanatory variables, volatility and beta.

So, what would be the expected annual return of an emerging market with average volatility (37.3%) and beta (1.13)? Simply input 0.373 (x_1) and 1.13 (x_2) into expression (30.3) and you should obtain 26.3%. What about the expected annual return of an emerging market with 'high' volatility (say, 50%) and beta (say, 1.5)? Again, input these two values into expression (30.3) and you should obtain 37.2%. Finally, what about the expected annual return of an emerging market with 'low' volatility (say, 25%) and beta (say, 0.75)? You know the drill by now, and you should have no trouble obtaining a 15.8% expected return.

A final comment

It is possible that you may have heard or read about a simple rule to test the significance of a coefficient which consists of comparing the absolute value of a t-statistic with the number 2. Under this rule, if the absolute value of the t-statistic is larger than 2, then we reject the *non*-significance of the coefficient in question; otherwise, the coefficient is in fact not significant. Is this rule different from the rule based on p-values we discussed above? Not at all.

Given a large sample, as we typically use in finance, both rules will almost always lead us to the same conclusion. The 'almost always' is due to the fact that 2 is an approximation to the correct number for large samples, which is 1.96 (for a two-tailed test and a 5% level of significance, both of which are implicit in the 'rule of 2'). However, in small samples, 2 may not be the right number against which to compare the absolute value of the t-statistic. As an example, consider that for the regression in Table 30.4, a 5% level of significance, and a two-tailed test, the correct number is not 2 but 2.09. (In case you're curious, this number comes from a Student's t distribution, for a regression with 22 observations and a model with two explanatory variables. Never mind ...)

In short, the rule we discussed based on p-values is easy to implement and very general. Sure, calculating a p-value is not trivial and you have to rely on a computer program to obtain it. But any program that estimates OLS regressions, including Excel, provides the p-value of the t-statistic of all the coefficients in the regression as part of the default output of the run.

The big picture

Regression analysis is an essential tool in finance. It provides a simple framework to test the hypotheses that follow from a model, and therefore to analyze whether or not the evidence supports it. And in the cases when it does, regression analysis can be used to assess the influence of one variable on another, as well as to forecast expected values of our target variable in different scenarios. In short, regression analysis is an essential tool in our financial toolkit.

Excel section

Running regressions in Excel is fairly simple, although it is fair to say that there are far more complete and sophisticated software packages for this purpose. Excel, however, does provide the elementary output that is sufficient in many cases. (It also has commands that provide you with partial information about a regression. You can, for example, calculate just the slope of a regression with only one explanatory variable with the 'linest' function.) We'll discuss here an option that gives you a fairly comprehensive output.

Let's assume you have three series of ten observations each in cells A1–A10, B1–B10, and C1–C10. Let's also assume that the first column displays the observations for the dependent variable, and the other two columns the observations for the two explanatory variables. To open the required dialog box you need to go to the 'Data' tab and select the 'Data Analysis' option. From the available options, search for 'Regression,' click it, and then click 'OK.'

Once in the dialog box, to run a regression with just *one* explanatory variable:

- Click in the box labeled 'Input Y Range' and then select the range for the dependent variable (A1:A10).

- Click in the box labeled 'Input X Range' and then select the range for the explanatory variable (B1:B10).

- Finally, from 'Output Options' select 'Output Range,' click the box next to it, and input a cell where you would like *the beginning* of the output to be displayed. (Note that the output is displayed over several cells. For a regression with just one explanatory variable, it should take 18 rows and nine columns.)

We will not go over the whole output here simply because it displays more information than we have covered in this chapter. Note, however, that you will find in the Excel output the number of observations in the regression, the R^2, the adjusted-R^2, the coefficients estimated, their standard errors, their t-statistics, and their p-values, all of which we have discussed.

To run a regression with more than one explanatory variable, the procedure has only one difference. In the second step above, after clicking the box labeled 'Input X Range,' instead of selecting the data for one explanatory variable, you select the data for *all* the explanatory variables. For example, if you had two explanatory variables in cells B1–B10 and C1–C10, you would click 'Input X Range' and then select the range B1 through C10.

Index